Changing Cities

Also by the editors

Ray Pahl, Rob Flynn and Nick Buck, *Processes and Structures of Urban Life*

Nick Buck, Ian Gordon and Ken Young, *The London Employment Problem*

Nick Buck, Ian Gordon, Peter Hall, Michael Harloe and Mark Kleinman, *Working Capital: Life and Labour in Contemporary London*

Ian Gordon (ed.), *Unemployment, Regions and London Markets: Reactions to Recession*

Ian Gordon and A.P. Thirlwall (eds), *European Factor Mobility*

Susan Fainstein, Ian Gordon and Michael Harloe (eds), *Divided Cities: New York and London in the Contemporary World*

Paul Cheshire and Ian Gordon (eds), *Territorial Competition in an Integrating Europe*

Alan Harding, Richard Evans, Michael Parkinson and Peter Garside, *Regional Government in Britain: An Economic Solution?*

Alan Harding, Jon Dawson, Richard Evans and Michael Parkinson (eds), *European Cities Towards 2000*

Ivan Turok, *Inclusive Cities: Building Local Capacity for Development*

Ivan Turok and Nicola Edge, *The Jobs Gap in Britain's Cities: Employment Loss and Labour Market Consequences*

John Bachtler and Ivan Turok (eds), *The Coherence of EU Regional Policy: Contrasting Perspectives on the Structural Funds*

Changing Cities

Rethinking Urban Competitiveness, Cohesion and Governance

Edited by

Nick Buck
Ian Gordon
Alan Harding
and
Ivan Turok

in association with the
ESRC Cities Programme

First published 2005 by
PALGRAVE MACMILLAN
Houndmills, Basingstoke, Hampshire RG21 6XS and
175 Fifth Avenue, New York, N.Y. 10010
Companies and representatives throughout the world

PALGRAVE MACMILLAN is the global academic imprint of the Palgrave Macmillan division of St. Martin's Press, LLC and of Palgrave Macmillan Ltd. Macmillan® is a registered trademark in the United States, United Kingdom and other countries. Palgrave is a registered trademark in the European Union and other countries.

ISBN-13: 978–1–4039–0679–3 hardback
ISBN 10: 1–4039–0679–3 hardback
ISBN-13: 978–1–4039–0680–9 paperback
ISBN 10: 1–4039–0680–7 paperback

This book is printed on paper suitable for recycling and made from fully managed and sustained forest sources.

A catalogue record for this book is available from the British Library.

A catalog record for this book is available from the Library of Congress

10   9   8   7   6   5   4   3   2   1
14   13   12   11   10   09   08   07   06   05

Printed in China

Contents

PART II   KEY SECTORS, PROCESSES AND INSTITUTIONS

List of Figures and Tables

Figures

Tables

Foreword

As the twentieth century drew to a close cities in many countries were emerging from a decade of decline and decay and finding new economic, political and cultural niches. This turnaround posed a series of critical intellectual questions which puzzled academics and policy-makers alike. Do cities matter more or less in a globalizing world – how and why? Can one define a successful city and if so one can one explain it? What kinds of theories do we have to explain the apparent renaissance of so many places but the continuing failure of others? What are the contributions of the related concepts of economic competitiveness, social cohesion and governance to success – however defined?

This book tackles these questions by looking at the varied experiences of a range of people and places. It has many important and new things to say about culture, finance, participation, property, neighbourhoods, gentrification and innovation in a wide span of urban settings. It attempts to identify what is new in relation to these topics and explores their intellectual and policy significance. What is more, while drawing its examples primarily from the UK for which the ESRC CITIES Programme and other research has provided a uniquely broad range of data on recent urban developments, it places those discussions on a wider comparative and intellectual canvas, locating them in the context of international theories, trends and policy developments. Its analysis and policy lessons will be valuable for researchers and policy-makers alike. In particular, its trenchant critique of the 'New Conventional Wisdom' which dominates academic and policy discussion of urban issues at the beginning of the twenty-first century, should be compulsory reading for anyone interested in cities – wherever they live or work.

This book draws substantially – though not exclusively – on the ESRC CITIES Programme in which all the authors and contributors were involved. This was the largest academic research programme on cities ever mounted in the UK and as Director of the Programme I am delighted to see the intellectual fruits of so much collaborative scholarship reflected in it.

This book will challenge and stimulate students new to the field. But it will also satisfy older heads looking to have their intellectual curiosity refreshed about one of the endlessly compelling and frustrating phenomenons of the modern world: changing cities.

MICHAEL PARKINSON
Director ESRC CITIES Programme

Acknowledgements

This book draws heavily on ideas and evidence developed during a programme of research on *Cities: Competitiveness and Cohesion*, commissioned and sponsored by the (UK) Economic and Social Research Council (ESRC), and directed successively by Duncan Maclennan, Ade Kearns and Michael Parkinson. We are indebted to the ESRC for their support of this major research effort, to a variety of co-funders in government and elsewhere, to a range of external supporters who offered advice and hosted relevant events, and to the programme directors for their leadership, including active promotion of dialogue among researchers working within the programme.

All the contributors to this volume worked on the programme, together with a large number of other scholars from whose work we draw extensively, in ways that can only partly be acknowledged through formal referencing of particular publications and presentations. Among those others whose collective contribution should be acknowledged are Ash Amin, Mark Andrew, Mark Banks, Iain Begg, Martin Boddy, Sophie Bowlby, Belinda Brown, Tony Champion, Paul Cheshire, Jon Coaffee, Fiona Devine, Iain Docherty, Keith Dowding, Richard Evans, Susan Fainstein, Tania Fisher, Jo Foord, Ken Gibb, Norman Ginsburg, Ron Griffiths, Peter Halfpenny, Peter Hall, Robin Hambleton, Michael Harloe, Doug Hart, Annette Hastings, Charles Husband, Chris Huxham, Peter John, Trevor Jones, Paul Joyce, Karryn Kirk, Mark Kleinman, Christine Lambert, Joe Leibovitz, Bill Lever, Sally Lloyd Evans, Andrew Lovatt, Andrew McCulloch, Neil McGarvey, Bill Maloney, Francesca Medda, Geoff Meen, Rosemary Mellor, Vassilis Monastiriotis, Barry Moore, Jimmy Morgan, Ronan Paddison, Gareth Potts, Karen O'Reilly, Monder Ram, Brian Robson, Gary Robson, Clare Roche, Stephen Rowley, Balihar Sanghera, James Sennett, Laura Smethurst, Graham Smith, Jo Sparkes, Rebecca Sterling, Murray Stewart, Gerry Stoker, David Sweeting, Stephen Thake, Nigel Thrift, Siv Vangen, Hugh Ward, Stuart Wilks-Heeg and Peter Wood.

The writing and editing of this book has largely been undertaken since completion of the programme, competing for time and attention with other projects. The editors are grateful for the generous encouragement of Michael Parkinson, and to Steven Kennedy of Palgrave Macmillan for helping to bring this collective enterprise to a successful conclusion. They are very grateful to the contributors for their enthusiasm, and for the

Robina Goodlad is Professor of Housing and Urban Studies in the University of Glasgow, and led the neighbourhood participation sub-project in the Central Scotland 'integrated city study'.

Ian Gordon is Professor of Human Geography at the London School of Economics; he led the London 'integrated city study' and co-directed the project 'Does Spatial Concentration of Disadvantage Contribute to Social Exclusion?'.

Simon Guy is Professor of Urban Development at the University of Newcastle upon Tyne, and co-directed the project on 'Economic Structures, Urban Responses: Framing and Negotiating Urban Property Development'.

Alan Harding is Professor of Urban and Regional Governance and co-director of the Centre for Sustainable Urban and Regional Futures at the University of Salford; he led the Liverpool/Manchester 'integrated city study'.

John Henneberry is Professor of Property at the University of Sheffield, and co-directed the project on 'Economic Structures, Urban Responses: Framing and Negotiating Urban Property Development'.

Keith Kintrea is Senior Lecturer in Urban Studies at the University of Glasgow, and co-directed the Central Scotland 'integrated city study'.

Richard Meegan is Reader in Urban Policy at Liverpool John Moores University, and directed the project on 'Pathways to Integration: Tackling Social Exclusion on Merseyside'.

Justin O'Connor is Reader in Sociology and Director of the Manchester Institute for Popular Culture in Manchester Metropolitan University, and directed the project on 'Cultural Industries and the City: Innovation, Creativity and Competitiveness'.

James Simmie is Professor of Innovation and Urban Competitiveness, Oxford Brookes University, and led the project on 'Innovative Clusters in the Uk and Europe'.

Ian Smith is Senior Research Fellow in the Cities Research Centre at the University of the West of England, and was a researcher on the Bristol 'integrated city study'.

Ivan Turok is Professor of Urban Economic Development at the University of Glasgow, and led the Central Scotland 'integrated city study'.

List of Abbreviations

ABI	area-based initiative
BAA	British and American Arts Association
BHPS	British Household Panel Survey
BRITE	Basic Research in Industrial Technologies for Europe
DETR	Department of the Environment, Transport and the Regions
DCMS	Department of Culture, Media and Sport
DTI	Department of Trade and Industry
ESRC	Economic and Social Research Council
FDI	foreign direct investment
FTSE	Financial Times Stock Exchange
FUR	functional urban region
GDP	gross domestic product
GLA	Greater London Authority
GLC	Greater London Council
IPO	initial public offering
MP	Member of Parliament
NCW	New Conventional Wisdom
NDC	New Deal for Communities
NHU	Natural History Unit
NSNR	National Strategy for Neighbourhood Renewal
OECD	Organisation for Economic Co-operation and Development
PAT	Policy Action Team
PIAP	Pathways for Integration Area Partnerships
R&D	research and development
RDA	Regional Development Agency
SFE	Scottish Financial Enterprises
SIC	Standard Industrial Classification
SIP	social inclusion partnership
SME	small and medium enterprises
SRB	Single Regeneration Budget

Chapter 1

Introduction: Cities in the New Conventional Wisdom

IAN GORDON and NICK BUCK

Introduction

This book has a double focus: on the evidence of substantial change in major cities of a mature economy within the past 20 years or so; *and* on how this relates to an influential set of ideas which envisage the emergence of a new urban era as a necessary response to a new international economy. We are at a point in time when the long decline in the fortunes of major cities in mature economies, widely noted during the latter part of the last century, appears to have reversed. And there is now a well developed view, across much of the academic and policy communities, as to the bases on which a resurgence of cities is to be expected, how cities are likely to change as a result, and what needs to be done to ensure that this is success-fully accomplished. This view draws together ideas about economic, social and political processes, and their inter-relationships, in a distinctively novel way. The evidence on which it draws is still fragmentary, however, and it is best seen as a set of hypotheses about the causes and effects of current developments, demanding critical empirical examination by social scientists, rather than a settled, reliable basis for interpreting and respond-ing to these developments. That at least is the orientation of this book which is presented as a first, substantial contribution to that analysis, draw-ing particularly on recent studies of change in British cities.

In historic perspective, current changes seem to represent, for some or possibly all major cities, another point of inflection in histories marked by repeated periods of ebb and flow. Over the long durée the outcome has clearly involved growth for these places, though others have faded and even disappeared along the way. Globally, as Soja (2000) and others have noted, cities are actually as old as civilization, and most of the major cities of the modern world have very long histories as centres of government, religion and (especially) trade. But the general urbanization of Western societies was a product of modern industrialization. Britain was a notable case, making a very rapid transition after the Industrial Revolution to

1

become the first nation with a majority urban population in the middle of the nineteenth century. And the form of modern cities was strongly shaped by the technologies of that era, when efficient energy production required large engines, and its transmission over any real distance was impossible. Steam-driven factories, trains and city-centre docks encouraged densely concentrated settlements, whose whole rationale might seem to have been undone since then by the combination of electricity, the internal combustion engine, containerization, and a shift away from heavy industry. Certainly all of these have contributed to a radical transformation of urban life and settlement patterns over the last half-century or so, involving some kind of 'de-centring' of the city in advanced societies.

Whether this meant that cities simply decentralized spatially or that cities as a form of organization were being marginalized – to be superseded by one or more 'post-urban' ways of structuring economic, social, political and cultural life – has been much less clear. In the Anglo-Saxon world at least, the dominant view was that what people wanted was *space* in which to conduct their personal and commercial lives with as much freedom as possible, *and* that new technologies of transport and communication were progressively freeing us from the 'tyranny of proximity' (Duranton, 1999) that underlay both modern and older cities. There were some notable deviations from this view, however: in continental Europe the middle classes still generally aspired to live in the heart of their cities; while the (predominantly Anglo-American) youth culture which emerged in this period was marked by a distinct antipathy towards the values of suburbia and exurbia.

Indeed, despite shrinking population in many of them, at a symbolic level cities have clearly staged a major comeback over the last quarter of a century. More than ever, films, television and novels are dominated by stories with recognizable big city settings – not simply of anonymous urban agglomerations, but identifiably of New York, San Francisco, London, Paris, Miami, Glasgow, Liverpool, New Orleans, Manchester, Amsterdam, Berlin and others, with some celebration of their distinct characters, cultures and vitality, as well as of the scenery which conjures these up. As in the great era of industrial urbanization, this celebration is admittedly double-edged, offering the viewer or reader the frisson of vicarious involvement in situations of risk, moral challenge and occasional horror, that most would be happiest to enjoy from the outside. Without doubt, most people would find modern (indeed post-modern) life radically poorer without access to the experience, sensibilities and cultural products of a variety of great cities and their occasionally overwhelming urbanity. But it is still a very different question as to how many would really prefer to live there, except as part of a youthful 'grand tour' or rite of passage, if both economic prosperity and opportunities to consume urban culture are now readily available in less stressful environments.

Similar issues arise in relation to economic activity: cities may have the 'buzz', flows of information and opportunities for cross-fertilization on which innovation and effective marketing depend, but how much of their activity (and employment) do firms actually need to base there to profit effectively from them, given modern techniques of communication and the division of labour? In this case, rising globalization suggests a further question: if large parts of activity do not actually require such access to specialized agglomeration economies, do they need really to be located in high-wage advanced economies at all?

Perhaps all that there is really agreement on is that these have become key questions as a consequence of a series of developments bringing radical changes in the parameters of personal and business choice over the past 25 years or so, including not only socio-economic and technological trends but also worries about environmental sustainability. These have been reflected in a very high level of *speculation* about the prospects of particular places or kinds of place (for instance, 'global cities') by journalists, academics *and* by those with financial stakes in various kinds of urban asset, notably in the form of property ownership. Such speculation thrives because the issues are potentially novel and of great strategic importance, but more fundamentally perhaps because the kinds of asset under discussion are so intangible – involving valuations of flexibility, variety, networking opportunities, rivalry and trust-engendering contexts – lacking either objective measurement or clearly identifiable markets. Hence much of the evidence on which people rely involves a combination of second-guessing how others will perceive situations with interpretations of short-run evidence about outcomes that may be heavily coloured by speculative behaviour. Whatever more fundamental changes may be under way, an effect has been to add substantially to the economic volatility of those cities figuring most prominently in this discourse, with boom and bust cycles associated with ideas of urban renascence, globalcityization and the role of cities in new 'dot.com' and media activities.

In this context, there is some risk of academic theorizations (and also of partial empirical findings) feeding this volatility, although they usually appear rather too late in the day to have much effect. Rather more directly and obviously they have fed into efforts by collective agencies to develop more concerted approaches to steering the development of urban societies in a new, more intensively competitive, post-Fordist, internationalized context. These have the merit of orientation to the long run, rather than immediate opportunism, and of elaborating an increasingly coherent framework of ideas linking economic, social, governmental and (increasingly) environmental issues. But, as we shall show in the next section, serious issues also arise in this case, not only about empirical foundations but (again) about the motives of those involved, particularly about the degree to which some political and institutional agendas shape the ideas that are adopted and disseminated.

The current challenge for urban research involves addressing both of these concerns, about facts and about ideology, while recognizing that urban change has to be addressed in an inter-disciplinary fashion, drawing together understanding of different kinds of process, and examining how these 'play out' in various combinations of local and global context. That was the central objective of the British *Cities: Competitiveness and Cohesion* research programme on which this book is very largely based. With over 20 separate projects, the majority looking at specific issues related to competitiveness, cohesion or governance, but also including four larger 'integrative studies' of major city-regions over a five-year period from 1997, this was the largest contemporary academic research programme on cities. It was also the first to directly address hypotheses about the emergence of a 'new urban era' and how a resurgence of cities might relate to societal agendas focused on competitiveness and social cohesion as fundamental to survival in a globalized economy.

Findings of the individual research projects have already been presented elsewhere (notably in Boddy and Parkinson, 2004). The aim of this book is to stand back and analyse their implications for the various hypotheses embodied in the New Conventional Wisdom (or NCW, as we label it) about the nature of change under way in major cities and its significance for wider societies. The new empirical materials are almost entirely based on the recent experience of British cities and the efforts of the UK's policy community in grasping and responding to this. But the conceptual issues to be addressed, and the theoretical literatures with which we engage, are international ones; indeed, conspicuously so, since they involve a combination of sets of ideas associated with different groups of European and/or North American scholars. On the economic side these include ideas about the significance of internationalization from both sides of the Atlantic (e.g. Sassen, 1991; Veltz, 1996); and of agglomeration, clusters and untraded interdependencies from a range of different US schools (e.g. Krugman, 1991; Porter, 1990; Storper, 1997) together with related European literatures on innovative milieux and industrial districts (e.g. Aydalot, 1986; Beccatini, 1987). On the social side these include predominantly North American ideas about social capital (Putnam, 1993, 2000; but also Bourdieu, 1985), European theories of social exclusion (e.g. Castel, 1998), and another American literature on neighbourhood effects (e.g. Jencks and Mayer, 1990; Wilson, 1987). On the political side there is a similar mix, with ideas coming from European regulationists (e.g. Aglietta, 1979), and North American political economists (e.g. Stone, 1989), among others. In fact, relatively little of the theoretical material is actually distinctively British, though we naturally draw on the large number of scholars from the

UK who have contributed to debates around each of these perspectives and/or engaged with contemporary policy issues around urban management, labour markets and regeneration. The point about the national context for studies drawn on here is *neither* to assert that British cities are necessarily typical of those across advanced economies (still less that they are harbingers) *nor* to ask the old question about whether 'foreign' theories apply here. Rather it is to recognize the ways in which history, specialization and the institutional context seem to matter for particular processes, since these are always variable, within as well as between national urban systems.

Our point of departure is, however, an essentially international one, the set of widely shared ideas about the emergence of a new urban era in advanced economies – the NCW – which relates this to a set of pervasive forces in a globalized economy. Since most of what follows is a critical examination of this NCW, we shall start in this introductory chapter by presenting a simple sketch of the NCW, and its relation to an earlier post-war perspective. In doing so, we shall temporarily ignore the various subtleties and contradictions within the literature that produced it, in favour of drawing out as coherent a version as possible of the 'story' and its logics. (For this reason also we do not attempt a scholarly referencing of the works which contributed ideas and/or stylized facts to the NCW, only acknowledging a few of the most widely known sources.) Although there are other contributory processes, with longer or shorter histories, here we emphasize the role of changes coming to the fore in the late 1970s/early 1980s, and the inter-connected aspects of those changes (over the impact of disconnected events). In these respects it might be seen as a sort of caricature of the sets of ideas underlying both current policy agendas and the genesis of the research programme from which this book emerged. But, aside from its value as a motivating focus for our book, there is reason to believe that it is at this sort of stylized level that conventional wisdoms (old and new) largely function in practice.

To provide some more concrete insights into the politics surrounding ideas about urban development, we then step down a level, so to speak, to review the succession of more specific themes and emphases which have marked waves of urban policy in the particular context of the UK since the late 1940s. The shifts in ideas here are more frequent, more narrowly focused on urban concerns, and rather unevenly paralleled elsewhere. In the latest version they do converge with the (broader and international) NCW, particularly in emphasizing the need for a much more 'joined-up' perspective. But the history of lurches between various quite one-dimensional views has its own light to cast on the relationship between ideas and the potential for real, progressive change in the cities of advanced economies (and not only in the UK).

The New Conventional Wisdom

The renewed optimism about cities at the start of the twenty-first century involves a shift from seeing them as essentially problematic residues of nineteenth- and early twentieth-century ways of organizing industrial economies towards the idea that they could again be exciting and creative places in which to live and work. As we see it, however, the *roots* of this new urban consciousness lie neither in a revaluation of urban ways of life nor in a spontaneous upturn in big city economies, but in much broader concerns with the social, economic and political changes required by a qualitatively different economic environment. These concerns are signalled by repeated reference to the imperatives of (economic) *competitiveness*, (social) *cohesion* and (responsive) *governance*, sometimes accompanied by concerns for (environmental) *sustainability*. None of these concerns are specifically 'urban', and neither are they necessarily linked to a renascence of cities. But in this particular context, and taken together as a set, they have been understood as implying a much increased importance for cities in securing societal success. Put crudely, cities were being seen as crucial to the achievement of competitiveness, cohesion and responsive governance (and perhaps environmental sustainability also) at a societal level. For cities in their turn, competitiveness, cohesion and governance come to be seen as key to their survival, individually and collectively. And finally, this set of economic, social and political concerns (again with the possible addition of the environment) is understood to be interdependent and mutually reinforcing, rather than as competing values to be traded off against each other.

A central purpose of this book, and of the research programme on which it draws, is to translate these very general ideas into more explicit social scientific terms and see how far the experience of major cities in an advanced society actually bears them out and points toward practicable ways in which the goals can be pursued. At a basic level this will involve looking for evidence that there have been some fundamental changes affecting urban processes, problems and potentials in the past 20 years or so, as compared to trends in the earlier post-war decades. Going much beyond that, however, invites the criticism that the each of the key 'concerns' or concepts we have referred to is much too fuzzy to be taken seriously either analytically or as the basis for serious policy initiatives – implying that it is a waste of time to take them any further. There is something in at least the first part of this argument, since the concepts are undeniably imprecise, ambiguous even, in ways that cannot be entirely accidental, and which help explain their widespread acceptance. But they *are* central to a way of talking about the strategic agenda for government which has been very widely adopted – indeed become hegemonic – since the 1980s, after the first flush of unbridled neo-liberalism. Perhaps significantly, invocation of these ideas has been most conspicuous at a transnational level, notably in publications of the European Union, and (especially) of the Organisation for Economic Co-operation and Development (OECD; see, e.g., OECD, 2001a, 2001b); adoption of this framework in national level discussion is well advanced across Europe, in Canada, Australasia and the Far East. This is less true in the USA where 'social cohesion' is less commonly linked with competitiveness, and as often used in the context of conservative cultural values or national security goals. Even here, however, significant examples of the NCW are emerging (e.g., American Assembly, 1993; Johnson, 1999). Even in Europe it is important to distinguish the new focus on cohesion across socially differentiated groups from the EU's long-standing usage of 'economic and social cohesion' to refer to the political cohesion of territories within the EU (especially the less competitive regions). OECD reports have argued that:

> there are close links between social and economic development, such that policies to support social cohesion may also increase investment attractiveness and business competitiveness. (2001b, p. 209)

> the governance structures of large cities need to be reformed in order to provide adequate frameworks for meeting the challenges of today such as sustainable urban development, increasing competitiveness in a global economy, strengthening social cohesion and nurturing local democracy. (2001a, summary)

In these arenas, a joint focus on competitiveness, cohesion and governance has been referred to as representing a 'new paradigm' (OECD, 2001b): in other words, a generally accepted framework for thinking about (in this case) policy issues, within which it is possible to conduct a rational and progressive debate about actual initiatives and policy measures appropriate to a new situation. Less positively, Harloe (2001) has characterized the application of this set of ideas to urban issues as representing the 'new liberal formulation'. This reference back to Harvey's (1973) initial, idealist interpretation of these issues in terms of equity and efficiency objectives implies particularly that the formulation conceals fundamental questions of power and vested interest. Our starting position is rather more ambivalent, and our borrowing of Galbraith's (1958) notion of 'the conventional wisdom' implies simply that – at various levels of sophistication – these ideas have become the *acceptable* basis of social thought and action, across business, academic and political communities. Galbraith's notion built on Keynes' famous observation that the actions of practical men depend crucially on ideas derived from past theorists. But he went on to highlight the continuing tensions between attachments to familiar, shared frameworks of thought and the 'onslaught of circumstances' which they found hard to accommodate. On the face of it, the new set of ideas with which we are concerned differs radically from the kind of conventional wisdom that he discussed because their bases lie in appropriating, rather than ignoring, the direction taken by 'circumstances' (or the 'march of events', as Galbraith also refers to them). But it is still relevant to ask – as we shall do throughout this book – some Galbraithian questions about:

(a)   the fit between a stylized and consensual conventional wisdom about 'change' and the more specific and uneven experience of it in particular places, population groups and institutions;
(b)   what is missed, hidden or exaggerated when these changes (and specifically those in cities) are approached through the lens of the conventional wisdom.

The NCW actually follows the model of earlier sets of social ideas in positing a sharp break between the forces shaping contemporary developments and those which prevailed in an earlier status quo, although the time horizons of the NCW are much shorter, with the crucial break being identified within the last quarter of a century. It is useful to start therefore by sketching its view of that status quo and of the key sources of change from it, before looking at the three key notions – competitiveness, cohesion and governance – in relation to which the role of cities has been highlighted.

The old status quo

In advanced economies, the post-war decades were characterized *sectorally* by the dominance of mass-production industries which emerged during the first half of the century and in terms of *market conditions* by fairly steady/sustained growth in product demand and relatively tight labour markets. Within this status quo, urban and regional economies were seen as principally subject to the rise and fall of particular activities in which they specialized and, in the long run, of the whole group of mass production industries. Beyond this, the combination of sectoral and market characteristics led to a continuing, strong emphasis on economies of scale, corporate planning in support of long-term investment projects, and internalization of economic relations (including supply of components, services and human capital requirements). One consequence was an increasing bias toward bureaucratic rather than market forms of economic co-ordination, with communications channelled through organizations (increasingly organized on a multiplant basis). Spatial proximity was accordingly devalued for many activities, and spatial divisions of labour on a functional basis were increasingly pursued (both regionally and internationally).

Within this context, the state's role was seen as threefold. First, it was responsible for minimizing economic uncertainties over the period during which investment commitments were being made. This included ensuring a steady expansion of the macro-economy, and securing other basic conditions for long-run investment (including planning the provision of major networks of infrastructure to meet expected needs). Second, the state was expected to provide basic services – which could not efficiently be supplied by the market – on a fairly standardized basis, with an emphasis on economies of scale and planning paralleling that in the private sector. And finally, the state was expected to provide a safety net for those exceptional cases/people whose basic needs were not successfully met through mainstream public and private provision.

Sources of change

From some time in the late 1970s this model was upset by a combination of factors. These included the working through of some long-established trends (e.g., industrial succession, international trade growth, communications improvements, growing prosperity and the rise of informational activities) to a point where they started to yield new kinds of effects. But a fundamental factor was the effective reversal of prevailing market conditions – as international product markets became more turbulent and excess supply of labour became the norm – leading to a reversal of the processes of internalization characterizing the previous period. If even major firms could no longer be sure of their likely production levels in a few years' time, the benefit–risk trade-off for self-provisioning in terms of services, component production and labour development would be less attractive. The general consequence was an increasingly competitive economy in terms *both* of economic co-ordination increasingly being conducted through markets (involving more interaction *between* organizations) *and* of more intense competitive pressures within these markets, requiring more actively competitive and adaptive behaviour to maintain acceptable profit levels and business viability.

Three particular features of the new order were increased internationalization (or 'globalization'), the growth of quality-based competition, and flexibilization. In terms of the first of these, *internationalization*, the established long-run trend of growth in goods trade as a share of GDP was assisted by further negotiated reductions in trade barriers. But more significant new developments included the opening-up of a wide range of 'urban' producer and cultural services to tradability, and rapid growth in the range and scope of multinational businesses. There was also a great increase in international capital mobility, partly achieved through monetary deregulation, with an increasing proportion channelled through (place-based) markets rather than directly through single organizations.

The rise of *quality-based competition* (highlighted by Porter, 1990) involved a number of mutually reinforcing factors on the supply and demand side, some of which – such as the impact of rising incomes – involved the working through of old trends, while others – such as the development of computer-based production control technologies – were more novel. For advanced economies at least, an increasing emphasis on quality-based competition and product differentiation might be seen as a response to severe difficulties in competing with producers who had access to radically cheaper labour supplies within the extended international economy. As a strategy it was seen to offer potential advantages to smaller-scale businesses (weakening the economies of scale argument), and to place a premium on quality inputs (including inputs of world-class market and technical intelligence).

The last of the hypothesized key aspects of economic change, *flexibilization*, involved both the minimization of longer-term commitments (through externalization and the scaling back of investment projects) and pursuit of skill-combinations, network linkages and so on which permitted more rapid recognition of (and response to) new market opportunities (Piore and Sabel, 1984). An implication was that the required social inputs into competitive economic performance could no longer be assumed to follow from a combination of organizations' internal management procedures and routine public service provision. In particular, competitive success was seen as now requiring the development of relations of trust and co-operation across organizational boundaries.

Competitiveness of cities

Central to the NCW is the vision of a world in which most kinds of protection from competition have been eroded, through technological change, communications improvements, and new instabilities in both tastes and the international economic order – as well as through neo-liberal enthusiasms for deregulation and economic integration. The effect has been to make competitive pressures a much more immediate and pervasive fact of life. The central economic imperative is then to compete and to build competitiveness, through a search for new opportunities and distinctive sources of advantage, and not 'simply' the pursuit of greater efficiency in serving established markets. And, if firms are becoming less self-reliant and more sensitive to external economies, forms of collective action are required which are more closely geared to this aim, and to shifting competitive circumstances.

More specifically, the NCW envisages a renewal of the importance of place-based external economies and the value of face-to-face relations, leading to a substantially enhanced evaluation of urban assets of all kinds (including their labour markets, pools of technical expertise, business clusters, and cultural/political capital). For a limited number of leading (global) cities with the capacity to meet the support needs of transnational command/control functions and/or competitive strength in very high order service activities, internationalization would provide a particular boost (Sassen, 1991). And, rather more generally, increasing city-level competition across national borders, both for foreign direct investment (FDI) and trade in city-based services, means that urban assets and urban economic performance matter more for national economic outcomes.

Taken as a group, major cities ought to benefit materially from these shifts and be recognized once again as key sites of economic opportunity, rather than as problem-beset residues of an era when poorer communications tied business to the city. But the emphasis on quality, high-level skills and diversity as sources of positive urban externalities suggest an uneven pattern of gains and losses. From the perspective of the NCW, it is not just that 'cities matter' but that the particular strengths and qualities of cities increasingly matter (Porter, 1990). There are greater incentives, then, for cities and city-regions to actively promote positive locational characteristics, including patterns of linkage and innovativeness which could assist locally-based firms in attaining competitive advantage and responding flexibly to changing market conditions.

Cohesion in cities

Social cohesion, like competitiveness, becomes a significant public issue in the NCW because the arrangements of the old status quo, with their clear divisions between public/private, and economic/social roles, can no longer be counted on to ensure the conditions for competitive success. This is partly a matter of whether the appropriate quality and flexibility of business inputs can be ensured to meet more demanding competitive requirements. Co-ordination functions which had been increasingly undertaken by (and often within) major firms would now more often take place outside them, largely through 'the market', though this would have to be underpinned by social capital in the form of networks, trust relations and shared conventions. The availability of these would be particularly critical in situations of uncertainty, especially where economic innovation was being pursued.

But it is also a matter of whether some of the old expectations about the social order (involving both security and some consensus on fairness and legitimacy) could continue to be met in the new circumstances. Among the reasons why this is foreseen as becoming more problematic are threats to individuals' security and ability to plan for their domestic lives/careers in a more 'flexible' economy. A second factor would be increasing individual-ization of relations in situations where outcomes seem to be more depen-dent on competitive activity than on solidarity or collective action. Finally, increased inequality could be expected as markets respond more strongly to perceived variations in individuals' contribution (or potential contribu-tion) to competitive success/failure.

These threats to cohesion might manifest themselves in various ways: in terms of a breakdown of residential 'community', family fragmentation, and the weakening of workplace-based organizations, including unions. But in any case, symptoms of a breakdown in cohesion would be expected to become particularly visible in an urban context. And if business compet-itiveness depended increasingly on place-based characteristics, local fail-ures of cohesion among the general population, as well as the business community itself, could have significant implications for competitiveness, especially in those places most heavily involved in the internationalized service economy. These changes went in parallel with a shift in focus on social problems away from one which emphasized economic disadvantage – poverty and unemployment – which the state might (or might not) seek to deal with on grounds of equity and social justice. Instead the focus moved towards issues of social integration. In the case of disadvantaged or less successful groups, this was reflected in a shift in the language towards more judgemental concepts such as the underclass or social exclusion.

However, just as social failure came to be seen as a possible contribution to economic failure for cities, certain forms of social success – and levels of integration among the successful – were now also seen as contributing to economic competitiveness. In particular the quality of social networks, the nature of formal and informal organizational life, and the degree of social trust were seen as potential resources for places and communities (aspects of their social capital, as Putnam, 1993, 2000, puts it). These were expected to contribute positively to economic competitiveness, either directly through the quality of business linkages, or indirectly through the quality of governance and the development of human capital.

Governance of cities

These developments have two major sorts of implication for systems of government and economic 'regulation', one relating to the boundary between public and private and the other to that between national/supra-national/sub-national control functions. In the first case, one side of the issue is that private actors (notably firms) have externalized more of their functions, some of which have to be taken up collectively (as a result of market failure): for instance, some forms of training/socialization for employability. The other side is that traditional forms of standardized public provision/regulation are insufficiently flexible for the new circumstances of change/instability, increased differentiation of products, and intensified international competition. Hence the public/private division of labour needs to be modified (both in relation to individuals and businesses), not only through deregulation but also through continuing involvement/interaction on a partnership basis.

In the second case, the issue is partly that the scaling of relevant economic arenas has moved both up and down from the nation-state, with great pressure on it both to release power upwards (in relation to monetary, trade and perhaps environmental regulation) and downwards (to cities in the frontline of competition for FDI and market shares in internationally traded services). But it is also a matter of finding the appropriate administrative scale at which to formulate and implement industrial, social and infrastructural policies (in collaboration with relevant private sector actors) to meet increasingly variable and changing requirements on a responsive basis. New forms of urban/regional governance are thus required in order to secure both competitiveness and cohesion, and to manage tensions between the immediate requirements of each in the interests of sustainability.

In important respects, then, governance – specifically, more responsive forms of governance – appears in the NCW as an answer to how the imperatives of competitiveness and cohesion are to be pursued and balanced, when neither state nor market can assure this. (Other recent usages of this language – as in the International Monetary Fund/World Bank's use of 'good governance' as a condition for aid and domestic efforts to reform 'corporate governance' – have in common a concern for regulation serving wider interests than those of the immediate power holders.) But we should also note that the new institutions of governance (including supra-national bodies such as the OECD and EU) have played a strong role in the propagation of NCW ideas, including the centrality of competiveness-cohesion as societal goals, as well as the vital role of cities in a changing world. The linkage between competitiveness and cohesion is a problem which is in part constructed by policy-makers, as well as a challenge for them to resolve.

At the heart of the NCW, as we see it, lies a belief that changed circumstances have brought new and/or stronger kinds of interaction between economic, social and political processes, which is one reason why cities are so important to it. Beyond that, it embodies also a notion of virtuous and vicious circles of development (or, perhaps more appropriately, 'triangles', since they involve these three specific dimensions of social organization). At local as well as national scales, achievement of competitive advantage,

social cohesion and effective governance are seen as being mutually reinforcing, while failure in any of these is supposed to make achievements of
the others less likely and more difficult.

Politics and shifting understandings of urban problems

From policy-makers the NCW calls for a highly integrated view of the
ways in which cities operate, and for sets of policies to enhance these,
cutting across conventional divides between economic, social, political
and spatial/environmental issues, as well as within these broad domains.
By contrast, the problem-oriented view of cities underlying policy
approaches since the Second World War tended to focus on one domain or
other as crucial at any time (although with a series of marked shifts in
understanding as to which was key). This seems to have been the case in a
number of countries, with various points of similarity in perspectives and
policy prescriptions adopted at different times, though with less consistency than in the subsequent switch towards the NCW. Here we confine
ourselves to a discussion of approaches pursued in a single country (the
UK) since the particular politics and sequence of events inevitably varies
between countries, in order to try to understand why policy perspectives
shift, and what light this might cast on the most recent switch to a 'joined-
up' NCW-based approach to urban policy.

From the 1940s to the late 1960s it is clear that the dominant factors in
shaping urban outcomes were seen by the British policy community very
much in spatial terms. In part this was because of a division of labour in
post-war reconstruction which was both institutional and intellectual, with
economic and social problems being handled – almost entirely – aspatially
(through national programmes of macro-economic management, to assure
full employment, and Welfare State construction, to meet all other social
needs), supplemented by a top-down regional policy. The third key dimension was more or less purely spatial, conceived of essentially in terms of
construction and environmental planning. In this context, such problems
within cities as were not going to be resolved by the national socio-
economic initiatives tended to be seen as a function of the spatial distribution of people, buildings and activities, whether at a local or a sub-regional
scale. A dominant metaphor was that of 'congestion', whether in access to
open space, transport, jobs or housing, alongside a concern with ordering
and re-ordering the spatial structure of cities and city-regions. A paradigm
was the Abercrombie plan for the London region in which planned decentralization was to be the major way of addressing these issues, and thereby
securing a whole range of socio-economic as well as environmental goals.
In practice, however, the (positive) effects of this approach were relatively

modest, most decentralization actually occurring through unplanned and un-ordered private initiatives, while there were other unintended impacts (including the social selectivity of decentralization) largely because of market forces which planners could neither reverse nor effectively manage.

When an alternative focus for urban policy emerged in the late 1960s, however, it was primarily as a response to perceived limitations in the success of full employment and welfare state policies, rather than those of spatial planning. A (re)discovery of persistent poverty and allied social problems, including delinquency, educational failure, homelessness and racial tensions (notably in inner-city communities), led to a sharp shift toward (micro-)social interpretations of the roots of a very wide range of urban problems. In this respect the UK followed quite closely a sequence of events occurring in the USA about 5 years earlier, as was also true of the ending of this phase. The core notions were effectively ones of implementation failure, either within state agencies or at a personal level within communities, in securing for some particular population groups the social and economic rights to which all were entitled under the post-war programmes. What was required were targeted local initiatives aimed both at raising expectations and securing more responsive policy interventions that recognized the holistic nature of the problems faced by particular individuals, households and communities. The approach was actually applied very selectively, with no impact on the very large numbers of people with similar problems outside the targeted areas. And, as time passed and economic crises made unemployment a much more central concern in these communities (as elsewhere), micro-social interventions came to seem less salient. But the key weakness which brought it to an end was that the changes in expectations, demands for expenditure and empowerment which were stimulated went well beyond the apparently uncontroversial ideas of securing effective implementation of established policies.

The second shift in the mid-1970s, with urban problems being redefined as economic in their basis, and more specifically as the product of systematic decline, disinvestments and depopulation in core cities, not only took over from the ebbing social approach but also completed the demise of the spatial/decentralization strategies. Both were now seen as fundamentally intellectually flawed in missing the key point about the primacy of economic forces and concerns, whether these were to actually be secured (as the right thought) by setting the market free, or (as the left thought) by pursuit of sectorally-focused intervention strategies. Actually this shift involved a dual switch of perspective, not only from a social (or physical) to an economic perspective on urban problems, but also from a regional to an urban (and even intra-urban) scale of concern with unevennesses in economic growth and decline. The evidential bases for these were (in the latter case) that disparities in rates of change were more marked on an urban–rural dimension than intra-regionally, and (in the former) a correlation between areas of economic/demographic contraction and of concentrated deprivation and disorder, notably in inner-city areas. Concern with these economic issues at an urban scale was undoubtedly heightened during the 1980s, when any general national initiatives to ameliorate the effects of deep recession were effectively outlawed. But, partly because of these circumstances, there was rather little to show for the benefits of urban economic policies, even in growth terms (except eventually in London Docklands) and hardly anything detectable in social terms (e.g., in relation to urban unemployment).

A further shift of perspective emerged during the 1980s, evolving (in central government, under Margaret Thatcher) alongside continuing practice of the economic approach, rather as the social approach emerged alongside continuing practice of spatial planning. The focus now came to be on political factors, particularly in the political character of urban local government, as the key underlying cause of persistent physical, social and economic problems in British cities. The diagnosis here had several facets, involving a systemic tendency to overspend (given external funding and weak local democracy), anti-business attitudes among the urban managerial class, a form of machine politics in Labour-controlled areas based on the provision of jobs and public housing, and a dependency culture also linked to the council's monopoly role in housing, education and social service provision. These facets were mutually reinforcing, and the (logical) policy response was to seek to reverse each of these: through a combination of privatization, promotion of competition, reform of local government finances, redistribution of executive responsibility away from local authority control, promotion of partnership-working, and (under Blair) a stronger focusing of political responsibility on visible elected leaders.

The research programme on which this book is based emerged just at the point when this roundabout of one-dimensional perspectives was coming to a halt. This development reflected:

(a)   a particular concern of the Blair government with 'joining-up', both of 'thinking' (i.e., understanding of causal connections across conventional divides) and of 'government' (i.e., integration of action at point of delivery as well as strategically);

(b)   a set of key policy concerns – competitiveness, work, crime, the family, education, the environment, etc. – each seen as having a strong urban dimension to them.

Nevertheless, the story of paradigm shifts in understanding of urban 'problems' over the previous half-century has a great deal of relevance to this programme, and what it can contribute to the joining-up process. One point to be made is that, although quite other (political) concerns were also involved, academics were party to each of the shifts in perspective which we have discussed and not only as individuals, since in almost all cases a majority of the research community was carried with them. But, while in every case there was a plausible intellectual argument to be made (with some evidential support) for the new position, in no case has a conclusive case been made that the previous approach was misguided or demonstrably inferior to what replaced it, either in general or in relation to changed circumstances. As Higgins *et al.* (1983) observed some years later about the (widely endorsed) shift from a social to an economic approach: 'What we have achieved . . . is a *different* analysis rather than necessarily a better one; our conceptions of the inner-city problem have changed rather than progressed, and perhaps we have simply exchanged one orthodoxy for another' (p. 194). The general case seems to be that paradigms get switched when successful implementation of the policies implied by the previous one proves more difficult than expected in the face of market forces and/or established political interests. For academics at least, a lesson could be that understanding of how these forces interact with policy initiatives should be more fully integrated into diagnoses of the problems.

One route to seeing this is to think of the set of urban problems recognized at various times since Engels' (1892) writing about the 'great cities' of the mid-nineteenth century as involving two intellectually (and politically) distinct elements. The first of these relates to the inability of unregulated market forces to deal with the *economic and social externalities* which flourish in the relatively dense environments of larger urban settlements. In Engels' analysis these are epitomized by the risks of epidemics spreading through and then beyond the insanitary, congested and badly maintained slums occupied by the poor. Extended into a general theory of environmental externalities, negative speculation and slum creation, this provides the intellectual basis for much of the spatial approach to urban problems. Similarly, the late Victorian theory about the risk of moral degeneration among the working classes in socially segregated cities (where those capable of providing a moral example had left: see Stedman Jones, 1971), updated to the context of Afro-American ghettos by Wilson (1987), anticipates the core ideas of a recently burgeoning US literature on peer effects in school/neighbourhood environments on delinquency and educational failure – and underpins much of the social approach to urban problems.

The second element, however, is simply one of poverty as an extreme manifestation of economic, social and political *inequality*. For Engels at least, the poor are particularly implicated in the production of negative urban externalities, inasmuch as they would actually choose (our language, not his) to live in overcrowded, poorly maintained dwellings close to their workplaces, given the cost of alternatives and their limited resources. Of course, these resource constraints are 'not of their own making', and they give rise to a set of other outcomes (made statistically visible in one-class areas) which are not necessarily linked in any obvious way to spatial externalities but are of some social /moral concern in their own right: for example, infant mortality, wasted talents, misery and unfitness for military service (or other work). These effects, and those of criminal, feckless or seditious behaviour, may or may not be exacerbated by spatial concentration or environmental factors, but they clearly have their roots elsewhere: they are fundamentally problems *in the city* not *of the city*, which will not be eliminated without some form of redistribution of real income, power and opportunities. Without this, problems associated with poverty can at best be displaced, not solved, as is evident from attempts to upgrade housing conditions without attention to the affordability (in rent *and* running cost terms) of improved accommodation for those on limited incomes.

All this is rather obvious, but highly problematic in its implications, since significant redistribution of real incomes is likely to be even harder to achieve in political terms in the relatively transparent conditions of a locality than through national programmes. There is a strong temptation (for academics as well as policy-makers) therefore to recast issues associated with the concentration of poor people in urban areas as problems of concentration, the urban setting, or the ways in which these are experienced, rather than as problems of individual poverty or powerlessness. And when practical experience shows this view to be unsustainable within one approach, the next temptation is to offer a radically recast version of the problem which (plausibly) by-passes this difficulty, by suggesting a different set of key factors and focusing on a slightly different sub-set of the range of urban problems.

The NCW represents a new start for thinking about urban problems, and one which is generally supportive of the 'joined-up' approach. But the history of shifting approaches to identifying, explaining and dealing with these problems provides grounds for caution and scepticism in relation to both. One issue is temporal: the continuing temptation to emphasize new circumstances and new understandings in the face of a kind of problem which is old, familiar and politically difficult. The other issue is spatial, with another recurrent temptation to see the roots of problems in local circumstances, remediable through limited action in places displaying the most acute symptoms. To avoid falling again into such traps, the ideas of the NCW need to be translated into researchable terms and tested/developed against the evidence of actual processes underlying the performance of contemporary cities.

Problems and questions

The lines of argument woven together in the NCW seem to provide the basis for a new urbanism which treats urban forms and ways of life as potentially vital for economic, social and political success in contemporary circumstances (and possibly also for environmental sustainability, though that is not an issue taken up in this book), in contrast to the anti-urbanism which prevailed through the last century. They provide a basis for optimism about the future of many (if not all) kinds of city, and also highlight types of action which would be required to secure success, both for cities in general and for particular cities which have increasingly to compete with each other in terms of quality.

Taken as a framework for considering cities and regions, the NCW assigns much more significance to the social dimension in current circumstances than under the previous status quo. At its heart is an argument that 'social' factors of various kinds now exert a substantially stronger role within 'the economy' than in the immediately preceding era. Actually it remains, like most of its predecessors, very much an economically driven model of change but with a weakening of the traditional boundary between the 'economic' and the 'social'. Under the previous dispensation key social functions were assumed to be taken care of within particular organizational structures (including private corporations as well as parts of the state, and stable residential communities/families), but these can no longer can be taken for granted as fulfilling these roles. Social cohesion and responsive governance will have to bridge these gaps on a more collaborative basis, largely (it is assumed) at an urban scale.

Overall the NCW perspective is a pretty functionalist one. It starts from claims about a number of more or less exogenous changes in the economic context facing all developed societies, and then predicts and/or explains others as consequences of these, typically as rational responses for survival in the new circumstances. However, it does not imply that all works for the best, with the hidden hand of competition actually assuring the 'best of all possible worlds'; rather, its holistic vision involves the co-existence of both virtuous and vicious circles/triangles. And, in important respects, it presents a set of challenges to which (it suggests) communities and policymakers need to respond, if they are to survive and prosper. But the NCW does not presume that there are adequate existing mechanisms to ensure that they always will succeed in achieving this, especially if they start from situations of weak competitiveness, limited cohesion and disconnected governance.

Like any conventional wisdom, the NCW tends to exaggerate the coherence, closure and determinedness of the system with which it is dealing, while the emphasis on 'newness' underplays elements of long-term continuity that might still bear much of the responsibility for recent developments. Clearly each of the processes which it highlights have always played some role in urban development, just as those it associates with the 'old status quo' continue to play a role. The shifts are ones of relative importance, although – with the kinds of interaction among them that the NCW emphasizes – these could well produce qualitative shifts in urban performance. There are real dangers, however, in rationalizing all important recent developments in terms of the new order that the NCW proclaims, when they may well have more to do with transition and the breakdown of an old order (as with the recessions of the 1980s), or with factors of continuing importance which the NCW plays down (notably that of power).

The NCW has an ideological as well as functionalist character, with dissemination and acceptance of the model being a necessary (if not sufficient) condition for its translation into reality. For example, the emphasis on competitiveness and cohesion might be seen as a consequence of new forms of governance in which the interests of private sector business are more directly incorporated in the formulation of public agendas, rather than as objective factors now requiring these changes in the policy system. In relation to The World Report on the Urban Future the NCW has been characterized as neo-liberalism re-launched 'with a human face' (Jessop, 2001, p. 1). Even so, in some key areas there actually seem to be inadequate motives/causes to produce the required outcomes (e.g. in terms of the 'hollowing out of the state' from below). And factors which have continually frustrated efforts to resolve 'urban problems', particularly the political obstacles to tackling social inequality, remain in the background, partially concealed under the fuzzier rubric of 'social cohesion'.

In this book we seek to cut through some of this fuzziness, asking what 'competitiveness', 'cohesion' and 'governance' actually mean in contemporary cities, how they are shaped, and what evidence there is of radical change in urban processes or outcomes over the timeframe of the NCW. The major findings and their broader implications are drawn out here through two sets of chapters. The first of these, in Part I, focuses on the concepts, examining what is encompassed in each, how they can be operationalized in an urban context, how far they (rather than other factors) can account for key patterns of outcome and new developments in cities over the last two decades, and what evidence there is for claims about virtuous/vicious circles. These deal in turn with economic competitiveness, social cohesion, governance and interactions between these. The second set, in Part II, look more closely at each of these issues in the context of particular key sectors, institutions and processes, as the basis for conclusions about the applicability, potential and limits of the NCW as a framework for understanding and steering change in cities. Following the ordering of Part I, these start with some key elements in the new *urban economy* (innovation, finance and culture), move on to a pair of processes relevant to levels of *social cohesion* (residential segregation of disadvantaged groups, and gentrification of inner urban areas), examine two facets of responsive *governance* (local social participation and city-wide economic boosterism), and finally explore two key institutions responsible for *interactions* among these: urban property and labour markets. A concluding chapter reviews the significance of the mixture of change and persistence emerging from these empirical studies, in relation to the task of moving both research and action beyond the less satisfactory features of the new conventional wisdom.

PART I

Concepts

Chapter 2

Cities, Competition and Competitiveness: Identifying New Connections

IVAN TUROK

Introduction

Within the NCW 'competitiveness' is supposed to represent the fundamental source of prosperity in an increasingly market-driven economy. It is a difficult notion to define and measure because it is multifaceted and not directly observable. Consequently it has been used in a variety of ways and contexts. The very idea of a city, region or nation as a competitive entity is contested. It has been criticized as meaningless and dangerous as a guide to economic policy by disguising special pleading on behalf of particular sectional interests seeking protection (Krugman, 1996a, 1996b). Others argue that it is important for understanding and policy because increasing international competition forces greater emphasis on quality and knowledge rather than resource availability and cost (Castells, 1996; Porter, 1990). The purpose of this chapter is to examine the usefulness of this perspective for understanding and responding to patterns of economic success and failure at the urban level, and to assess how far these patterns bear out the NCW's view of a fundamental change in the economic position of cities.

The competitiveness of firms is normally defined by their ability to sell their products in contested markets. As such it represents a latent variable that is not directly measurable, though with causes and consequences that may be measured. Consequently, a natural but confusing tendency is to equate the concept with some of these causes or consequences. Translating the idea to spatial units such as cities or nations, which are sites for all or part of the activities of a shifting set of firms, adds considerable complexity to the situation, both because of aggregation and because in some sense these places 'compete' for such activities (as well as 'their' local firms competing in the ordinary sense). Despite such subtleties, in practice when applied to cities the term is often simply equated with their economic position in relation to other cities. Hence a competitive city is identified as one with relatively high per capita incomes or employment. However, such indicators tend to reflect historical performance and inherited positions more strongly than current performance or economic potential. Competitiveness also features as a prominent goal of development agencies, although too often as purposive-sounding rhetoric rather than as a specific strategy for how to increase economic development. All this adds little to our understanding of how and why places prosper. Competitiveness can become a tautology conveying an impression of rigour and relevance, but superfluous to our existing economic lexicon.

Used with care, however, the concept does have more insights to offer for cities. This chapter argues that in this context competitiveness should be seen as covering three key determinants of growth and prosperity, namely:

(a)   the ability of a city's firms to sell their products in contested external markets ('trade');
(b)   the value of these products and the efficiency with which they are produced ('productivity');
(c)   the extent to which local human, capital and natural resources are utilized (e.g., the 'employment rate').

Competitiveness is a function of complex inter-relationships between these variables and should not be reduced to any single one of them. There remain unresolved questions about the factors and forces underlying these features and how the concept should be measured. The term risks representing the determinants of city prosperity too narrowly and concealing important variations between the competitive positions of different branches of a city economy (diversity). It may also obscure variable economic performance over time (volatility) and the uneven consequences of competitive success for different social groups and areas (inequality).

The structure of the chapter is as follows. The next two sections outline why the concern for competitiveness has gained such prominence in economic policy-making. The following two sections consider some of the ambiguities surrounding the nature and value of competition between places. Subsequent sections explore the changing sources of and obstacles to urban competitiveness, followed by a short conclusion.

Roots and responses to competitiveness concerns

The competitiveness notion has snowballed partly because of the increasing international mobility of capital and more open national markets: in short, *globalization*. Economies are connected more closely through rising exports and imports and increasing foreign direct investment. This has resulted from declining trade barriers, falling transport costs, improved telecommunications and the growth of transnational corporations (TNCs). The emergence of new economic powers in Asia and more competitive product markets has intensified cost pressures and increased insecurity. More integrated financial markets and international agreements between governments have made it more difficult for them to stimulate their economies by pursuing traditional macro-economic policies independently.

Various micro-economic, supply-side measures have been developed instead to improve the internal efficiency of firms and the value of their products, and thereby secure their share of world markets and jobs. Productivity in this broad sense of creating or enhancing competitive advantage has been portrayed as central to long-term economic progress. It is important for regions and nations to pay their way in the world, in terms of exporting sufficient goods and services to pay for imports. Consequently, productivity and trade performance are closely related to competitiveness.

A laissez-faire approach has been pursued in some countries, including liberalization of domestic markets, privatization of utilities, relaxation of environmental standards and withdrawal of other 'burdens on business'. By reducing the levels of regulation and taxation, governments have tried to lower the costs of production and create flexible labour markets to establish a business climate conducive to greater price competitiveness and higher profitability. This is intended to generate growth by stimulating private investment and attracting foreign capital.

Others have recognized the diminishing returns from cost-cutting in commodity production, the ease of imitation and the fact that the burden may have to be borne by the resident population in lower earnings, more precarious jobs and inferior public services. In order to protect people and places from a 'race to the bottom', they have actively assisted firms to compete abroad through non-price or quality-based competitive advantages that should be more enduring, including more sophisticated, reliable and branded products or greater customer responsiveness. They have supported new technologies, better work force and management skills, or singled out key industries for special help to move up the value chain.

These responses are echoed at sub-national levels. Rising competition, capital mobility and joblessness have heightened perceptions of external threats. Some policies have been overtly competitive in a defensive sense, including attempts to protect vulnerable industries or to discourage business relocation through subsidies (Cheshire and Gordon, 1996). Others have been proactive, including place marketing and financial incentives to attract investment. Civic leaders have competed more aggressively to capture flagship projects, tourism and jobs, using both the cost of local factors and the quality of amenities. Traditional policies were less explicitly competitive, including increasing the business formation rate and strengthening the growth capacities of local firms.

The latest trend is to exploit urban assets such as specialized labour pools, institutional networks and the lifestyle and cultural facilities of cities. Distinctive strengths are supposed to help places avoid vulnerability to mobile capital and a race to the bottom. They aim to attract talent and to develop special capabilities in order to export innovative products sold at premium prices (Chapter 8 provides examples of the commercialization of culture in cities). The NCW suggests that cities contain unique intellectual and other resources to make knowledge-intensive firms more internationally competitive. However, distinctiveness does not have to refer to a city's position in global markets: Porter (1995) points out that US inner cities could compete effectively in underserved local and regional markets, including products for minority consumers, because of their strategic location and access to a motivated unemployed work force. We return to these arguments later.

Government attitudes towards place-based competition

Sub-national policies of these kinds have traditionally been treated with ambivalence by European governments because of their uncertain net contribution to the national economy. Some governments have become more supportive, hoping to shape them to serve national political and economic purposes. Indeed, local development has increasingly replaced traditional equity-based regional policies (Anyadike-Danes *et al.*, 2001; OECD, 2001b). These sought to reduce spatial disparities by guiding investment away from congested areas to lagging regions with underused resources. Such carrot and stick policies have been cut, partly through fears that growth restrictions in buoyant areas might divert firms out of the country.

Instead, spatial policy has switched to promoting development from within by exploiting indigenous strengths. There is less emphasis on inward investment and more on creating environments where high-quality businesses can start up and succeed. This draws on endogenous growth theory where growth is seen to arise from enhanced local productivity and innovation through investment in human capital and research in leading areas of the economy (Crafts, 1996; Martin and Sunley, 1998). It is supported by arguments that innovation, institutional learning and the exchange of creative ideas ('knowledge spillovers') occur most effectively in industrial clusters organized at the city-region level (Cooke and Morgan, 1998; Kanter, 1995; see also Chapter 6 and the penultimate section below).

The change in approach occurred initially within the framework of 'top-down' regional and national policies. The main business development and training programmes were delivered locally but controlled centrally in order to prioritize national objectives. Over time economic responsibilities have been decentralized to regional or local organizations in order to permit greater responsiveness to variable conditions on the ground, rather than a centralized 'one-size-fits-all' approach. Development agencies now cover whole countries rather than selected 'assisted areas', in order to maximize growth potential wherever it exists. This bottom-up approach encourages more explicit territorial competition, prompting a concern that localities in a weak position at the outset will lose out to areas with greater competitive strengths and resources. It is another sign of a shift in emphasis in spatial policy from equity considerations to national efficiency.

Wider national reforms driven by a belief in competitive markets have also affected local authorities. Some reforms have sought to alter the culture of the public sector through greater emphasis on enterprise and opportunity at the expense of need and entitlement (Kearns and Turok, 2000). Competition has been used to allocate resources for area-based initiatives in sectors such as education, health, housing and employment (Oatley, 1998). Competitive bidding is intended to provide pressure and rewards for greater imagination and efficiency in service provision. Privatization has also opened up new areas of the urban economy to market forces, including transport, water and environmental services. Competition has increased between organizations *within* cities as well as between places, making strategic planning and co-ordination of delivery more difficult. Fragmentation and duplication of effort sometimes give the impression that insufficient consideration has been paid to the circumstances in which competition may or may not be appropriate.

The nature of competition between cities

Competition *between firms* is supposed to have two main benefits for economic development (Beath, 2002; Carlin *et al.*, 2001). First, it provides a *selection* mechanism; firms with out-dated products or inefficient processes do not survive, while new entrants introduce better products and techniques. Selection by exit and entry reallocates resources from inefficient producers and declining sectors to more efficient and growing ones (HM Treasury, 2001b). Second, it provides strong *incentives* to existing firms to improve their technology and organization. The threat posed by rivals encourages them to become more innovative and efficient, which increases their market share, lowers the average cost of production in the industry and reduces the price to consumers.

Both mechanisms are thought to improve productivity and growth across the economy. Firms often try to limit competition by securing a dominant position in their markets or by colluding to agree prices or market share. Government regulation is required to prevent this. Competition may also have important costs arising from market failure (neglect of research and development, training, derelict land and other externalities), which also calls for government action. In practice, competition often co-exists with forms of co-operation. Firms under pressure may collaborate with suppliers and customers in order to expand their expertise, develop specialist products and improve their access to markets. Beyond a certain point some forms of collaboration become collusion, which is why business associations have sometimes aroused suspicion.

Competition between places cannot operate in the same way. The agents and their powers are different and competition is moderated by other resource allocation mechanisms. Considering *selection* first, it is sometimes observed that 'cities cannot go bankrupt' if uncompetitive, unlike firms. New entrants also emerge infrequently and are usually insignificant compared with most markets in which firms operate, since building new urban economies is costly and slow. Most countries have public finance systems that cushion the impact of economic crises, and hence governments effectively keep declining cities 'in business' through transfer payments. In addition, there is a gap between civic leaders and actors whose assets are at risk from urban decline. Local authorities in many parts of Europe are insulated because most of their funds originate from central government on the basis of their resident population, which adjusts only slowly to economic decline. There is an element of need in their funding allocation, which partially compensates deprived areas. Areas of job loss also gain from social welfare expenditure for workless groups, which is another economic stabilizer. Centralized financial systems protect European cities from the spiral of decline that can face distressed US cities within a more decentralized regime (Hill and Nowak, 2002).

Yet places do still stagnate and decline, even if they do not 'close down'. There may be local reasons, such as exhausted natural resources, or wider shifts in the economy (Begg *et al.*, 2002). National transfers may slow or delay the process, but they will not reverse it without productive investment. New urban areas also emerge over time, showing a dynamic process of change at work that must affect the functioning of the overall economy in the long run. Edge cities and new towns grow on the back of the services and markets of their neighbouring cities, without their high costs or legacy of industrial decline. Some fiscal stabilizers have also been pared back. New methods of private finance and competitive bidding are bound to have more uneven spatial outcomes than previous procedures. Labour and property shortages in growth regions mean that local authorities are often encouraged to respond to market demand and accommodate new development, not try to steer it through planning restrictions or strategic use of infrastructure (Turok and Bailey, 2005). Thus, the possibility of a selection mechanism in place-based competition may be becoming more relevant. Some of the consequences are discussed below.

Similar observations apply to *incentives*. At issue are the benefits to the area from engaging in competition compared with the costs. This is a more complex calculation for cities than for firms since they are not single entities driven by the profit objective (though it may be much simpler in the case of formal competitions for special public resources or to host one-off events, since the organizational bidding costs may be marginal and the direct rewards much more substantial.) Even productivity is an insufficient overarching aim because it can be raised by deploying fewer resources for the same output (e.g., by labour shedding), which does not increase prosperity. Some places would find it easier to enhance their prosperity (and their contribution to national output and wealth) by activating underemployed resources (such as increasing the employment rate) than by raising productivity (Bailey *et al.*, 2002; Begg *et al.*, 2002). In addition, city authorities have less control over many of their assets than firms, so the links between what they do and the outcome is more uncertain. The calculation is bound to vary between the markets in which cities compete, depending on the nature of the competitive process and who experiences the benefit and burden. It is also likely to vary between countries depending on the link between local economic performance and local tax revenues. In general one might expect cities with inherent advantages at the outset to be more inclined to participate in competitive activities than those in weaker positions, because they stand more chance of success. Against this, cities with greater economic problems are likely to be under more pressure to engage in competition.

There is little or no direct incentive for city authorities in countries such as the UK to promote economic growth because the revenue from business rates is pooled nationally and distributed as part of local authorities' overall funding allocation, which is driven by a formula. (In recognition of this, the UK government recently proposed a scheme to reward local authorities for encouraging business in their area by allowing them to retain some of the revenues that arise from growing the business tax base. It is currently consulting on the scale of the incentive to offer and how to ensure that the distributional impact is fair.) This grant system generally cancels out the effects of changing property values on local authority revenues and household deprivation on their expenditure. Only population growth has any real fiscal effect and this is not necessarily positive. Growth imposes costs through transport congestion and environmental damage, and requires investment in physical and social infrastructure. Lack of public funds to tackle congestion and shortages of housing and schools may limit the capacity of places to grow. In addition, administrative boundaries separating residential suburbs from commercial cores complicate assessment of the effects of growth since the costs fall unevenly and the benefits leak out. Public authorities often encounter political opposition to new development, particularly towards new roads and housing around existing suburbs, and especially in pressurized regions. Such considerations can more than offset the gains from growth.

Nevertheless, a competitive political system, electoral pressures to create and safeguard jobs, and lobbying by selected business interests to help them grow mean that all except the wealthiest dormitory suburbs and towns normally make some effort to maintain or enhance their economic position. The intensity of their effort is bound to be sensitive to the economic cycle. The form it takes may also be symbolic as much as substantial. There are opportunities for most areas to access special resources for this purpose, such as regeneration budgets from central government, European funds or Lottery money, although the scale may be limited for places without assisted area status.

One of the difficulties facing local decision-makers is uncertainty about *what* policies to pursue. Their choice may be influenced by central government controls, the rules of other external funders, the pressure for visible actions, fashionable ideas or advice from consultants. They may also be swayed by special interests for whom the pay-offs from growth and development are more direct, such as major property owners. Other economic interests with larger numbers, smaller individual stakes and more diverse concerns find it harder to organize for collective action. This raises the obvious danger that the selected policies favour narrow interests. Overall there is little doubt that there has been a steady growth in local policies in Europe that are explicitly or implicitly competitive, even if the rationale is sometimes open to question and the incentives are not clear-cut, as they are in North America.

Virtues and vices of place-based competition

Place-based competition has not traditionally been considered important for the economic growth process. Common descriptions such as 'displacement' and 'zero-sum' imply it is unproductive and to be discouraged, since one area's success may only come at the expense of others (Cheshire and Gordon, 1998). It may be wasteful if subsidies are given to encourage business relocation, especially if this prompts retaliation and inflated subsidies or concessions on environmental or employment standards (a negative-sum game). There is a history of predatory poaching or beggar-my-neighbour behaviour in the USA through big inducements for firms to move between areas (OECD, 2001b). The EU have become concerned about member states offering such subsidies, or being blackmailed by firms threatening to move. Limits have been imposed on state aid in recognition that governments may turn a blind eye to such behaviour by local authorities if their competitor locations are abroad. Yet European integration and business mobility mean that competition occurs increasingly on an international basis. TNCs are more proficient than local firms at extracting subsidies by playing places off against each other (Win, 1995).

There are other instances where place-based competition may lead to a misallocation of resources from a national or even a local perspective. Civic pride and rivalry can cause unnecessary imitation and wasteful duplication of public facilities, especially between adjacent areas. They can lead to expensive promotional efforts for symbolic purposes and unwarranted incentives to host major sporting and cultural events. Meanwhile, support for sectors that are much bigger generators of sustainable economic activity may be neglected because they have a lower profile or the competition is less visible. Rivalry between neighbouring cities and towns can also undermine the reputation of both, and result in failure to develop complementary assets that would be beneficial all round. By sharing their knowledge and resources in collaborative ventures they might benefit from economies of scale and scope, and thereby gain a collective competitive advantage over other places (Cooke *et al.*, 2002b; Turok and Bailey, 2004).

Finally, competition between cities can widen social inequalities and generate human costs if there are consistent losers. Places may be disadvantaged to begin with, perhaps through their peripheral location, burden of dereliction, out-dated skills or outmoded educational or research institutions. Market forces may exacerbate disparities by skewing resources towards areas with more immediate commercial prospects or confidence among investors. Decline may be self-reinforcing, with weakened corrective mechanisms. Privileged cities may become even wealthier by attracting away investment, talent and entrepreneurial skills. This will fuel their development process, albeit at some wider cost in imbalanced labour and housing markets, inflation and slower national economic growth. The distributional consequences arising from an unequal spread of competitive assets are usually ignored in policies promoting a decentralized approach to economic development.

Of course, there may be positive consequences of competition as well. Pressure on local bodies may prevent complacency and encourage timely delivery of suitable infrastructure and services. It is vital for cities to maintain their economic base, especially with territorial transfers under greater scrutiny. Cities may seek to develop special areas of technological expertise to help firms access new markets. Provision of serviced land and property can facilitate business growth and avoid disruptive relocation of expanding firms to surrounding areas. Similar points apply to the retention and attraction of a mobile population. City authorities may build on their distinctive features, physical heritage and cultural traditions to develop new and original ways of attracting external visitors and investors. This can extend the range of investment opportunities, widen the choice of tourist destinations and enrich the quality of life for residents. An emphasis on quality, diversity and differentiation (dynamic advantages) is much more likely than imitation and cost-cutting (static advantages) to produce a positive developmental effect overall. The possibility remains that weaker cities will be less well equipped to compete on aspects of quality and better positioned to compete on cost for lower value projects, because of their cheaper property and lower wages.

Commentators tend to be ambivalent about deliberate encouragement of place-based competition (e.g. Oatley, 1998; Turok and Hopkins, 1998). It is unlikely to be inevitably beneficial or harmful. Much depends on the form it takes and the context in which it is pursued, including regulation of counter-productive and underhand practices by national authorities and the existence of compensating policies where appropriate. Governments have a role to play in creating an environment that encourages desirable practices, such as enhancing productive capacity, maximizing use of underemployed resources and stimulating innovation. Simple diversionary activities may be discouraged, unless there is a wider economic and social justification such as ensuring a better-balanced economy in terms of its regional distribution or the range of employment opportunities.

Competition between places is a reality, especially in an unorganized form through firms trading in wider markets. The ongoing performance of firms is influenced by various attributes of their areas – as we discuss in the following sections – in ways that vary from sector to sector. This is a more important feature of territorial competition with more significant consequences than the visible battles between public agencies to host prominent events or to win challenge funds. The concept of competitiveness can help to explore these dynamics by prompting questions about the local conditions that help firms to sell their products in wider markets. It has become popular to suggest that specifically *urban* conditions have become increasingly important in an era of more integrated markets and higher quality products and services. According to Porter, for example: 'The enduring competitive advantages in a global economy are often heavily localised, arising from concentrations of highly specialised skills and knowledge, institutions, rivalry, related businesses, and sophisticated customers' (1998, p. 90).

The competitive advantages of urban size

The geographic concentration of economic activity is very noticeable in modern society. The tendency for firms to cluster in a limited number of places suggests that cities have economic advantages, although the influence of planning controls and inertia need to be borne in mind as well. At the risk of oversimplification, one can distinguish two contrasting interpretations of concentration that underlie current debates about the development of cities. They share a common view that location influences economic processes and cities contribute positively to the national economy. However, they emphasize different ways in which geography matters to economic performance. They also have different implications for policy, including whether to promote industrial diversity or specialization, to devote priority to enhancing hard assets (e.g. infrastructure or labour availability) or soft assets (e.g. institutional networks or specialized knowledge), and whether to foster co-operation between firms.

The first perspective (discussed in this section) stresses the benefits of size and diversity that flow from having a concentration of economic activity and population within easy reach. The second perspective (discussed in the penultimate section) stresses the quality of the relationships between firms. The classic concept of *agglomeration economies* emphasizes the 'positive externalities', or external economies of scale, scope and complexity, that follow from co-location of many businesses. Geographical proximity and size increase the opportunities available to firms and reduce the risks to which they are exposed (Gordon and McCann, 2000; Parr, 2002; Storper, 1997). Size and proximity reduce the cost of labour and business services, and help to improve the efficiency with which inputs are used via better management, improved work force skills or better production techniques. Agglomeration also increases the opportunities available to workers and to providers of business and personal services, and hence the gains extend beyond individual firms and increase the overall productivity and growth rate of city economies.

One can identify three main kinds of economic benefits. First, firms gain access to a larger labour pool, which makes it easier to find specialist skills. Workers also benefit from a bigger choice of employers and better career prospects. Second, firms gain access to a greater range of shared inputs and supporting industries, such as equipment maintenance, marketing or design services, transport and communications facilities and venture capital. Cities are good locations for suppliers and distributors of business and commercial services because of the market size. Third, firms gain from a greater flow of information and ideas. There is efficient transfer of trade knowledge and intelligence through informal contacts, chance meetings or movement of skilled labour and management. These knowledge spillovers help to spread good practice and to develop new products and improved processes. A further distinction can be drawn between 'localization' economies, which are associated with specialized infrastructure, services and skills geared to particular branches of economic activity, and 'urbanization' economies, which relate to generalized urban assets (such as airports, educational institutions and municipal services) that serve a diverse industrial structure.

A city requires no particular organization acting on its behalf to gain most of these benefits, and neither does it require any special loyalty or shared values between firms, apart from the provision of public goods or non-traded infrastructure and services. Companies are independent units operating with flexibility in a market environment. Competition is the driving force and firms do not tend to co-operate on matters beyond their short-term interests (Gordon and McCann, 2000). Proximity increases the opportunities for them to trade, to recruit suitable labour, to access specialized know-how and to reduce market uncertainties, all of which help to improve their performance. The scale of activity determines the significance of these benefits: basically, the larger the better. The density and heterogeneity of firms are also sources of dynamism and creativity in strengthening the critical mass. Cities may acquire cumulative advantages over other places as a result of these externalities, leading to self-reinforcing growth.

The London case study supported this argument: 'The real strength of the London agglomeration effect . . . seems to consist in the random possibilities for connections and stimuli made possible by its sheer scale and diversity' (Buck *et al.*, 2002, p. 136). Simmie's study of innovation in London, Paris and Amsterdam also reaffirmed the importance of urban size and diversity in allowing firms to 'pick and mix' their inputs and connections with suppliers, research establishments, technology transfer institutions and technical training centres (Simmie, 2001). Firms also benefited from access to international airports, enabling them to gain 'time proximity' for face-to-face contact and effective knowledge transfer with international suppliers and customers.

Urban growth was the dominant trend throughout the world until fairly recently. Few doubted the advantages of cities and the connection between industrialization and urbanization. The prevailing view was that cities enhanced national economic performance through their scale and diversity. Writers such as Jacobs (1969, 1984) explored in detail the historic role of cities in economic development because of their versatility and dynamism. The variety of skills and productive capacities enabled cities to improvise, adapt and innovate across many products and processes. This led to the successful replacement of imports by local production, boosted exports and caused rapid growth, including manufacturing and services. Moreover, economic development was not a smooth, consensual process: the practical problems and inefficiencies of large cities induced creative responses and generated new goods and services for export that fuelled further growth. Jacobs also studied cities that became more specialized over time. Although this enabled efficiency gains, she argued that it induced stagnation in the long run because of the loss of adaptive capacity. The message was that the city had enormous strengths as a diverse, but inter-connected system.

Emerging disadvantages of city locations

From around the 1960s and 1970s two important processes challenged this thinking and raised doubts about the value of cities to the national economy. First, *deconcentration* caused a shift in population and firms out of many city cores towards suburbs and surrounding towns. Dispersal was partly a reflection of urban land constraints hampering the needs of modern production for extensive plant layouts, coupled with a shift from transporting freight by rail to motorway. There was also a search for cheaper premises and compliant labour for routine assembly work and back-office functions. Relocation of jobs was accompanied by residential decentralization, which had its own momentum with rising incomes, car ownership and people's preferences for more space, gardens and their own homes. Dispersal suggested that economic success did not require proximity and urban density.

However, deconcentration was more pervasive in some countries than others, depending on car and home ownership levels, public transport and attitudes to sprawl. It did not necessarily contradict the advantages of agglomeration, bearing in mind changes in the organization of industry and falling transport costs. There were also costs, or *diseconomies of agglomeration*, which offset the advantages. Two diseconomies operate as the scale of a city increases. First, dense concentrations of activity increase the demand for local land, which forces up property prices and rents for all land uses. Competition for land also causes displacement of lower-value industrial uses and routine office-based services by commercial and residential uses. Second, concentration causes congestion, which adds to business costs and worsens the quality of life for residents. It is often difficult for established cities to radically improve their basic infrastructure to cope with congestion because of the disruption caused.

The relative importance of the centralizing and decentralizing forces varies over time and between different industries and functions, depending on prevailing communication technologies and industrial organization. Governments can influence the outcome, as many compact European cities demonstrate. Investment in a good public transport system can alleviate congestion, improve commuting and facilitate internal information and trade flows. Maintenance of quality public spaces, vibrant central squares, landscaped parks and good neighbourhood environments may help to retain residents and attract private investment. A pragmatic approach to building controls, land-use zoning and development on the urban edge or in redundant urban spaces can relieve inflated property prices and help to accommodate urban growth through incremental expansion along transport corridors.

Cities in countries such as Britain have been disadvantaged in at least two respects. First, tight green-belt controls and the new towns have encouraged development to leapfrog to less accessible locations beyond the urban fringe (Begg *et al.*, 2002; Breheny, 1999). In addition, investment in urban economic infrastructure has been neglected over the years because of an anti-urban ethos coupled with a perception that urban problems are essentially social and related to poor living conditions. Thus, priority in capital investment has been given to housing and neighbourhood improvement rather than job creation. There has also been resistance from deprived communities to major infrastructure works on the grounds of dislocation, and a legacy of negative experiences following comprehensive redevelopment programmes in the 1960s and 1970s.

The economy of many cities was hit from around the same time by a second, more traumatic process of *deindustrialization*. Facing increasingly difficult trading circumstances, manufacturers closed many older inner-city plants to cut costs. This caused large-scale loss of manual jobs, curtailed the markets of local supporting industries and degraded the environment. The scale and speed of the contraction hit old industrial areas particularly hard, making it difficult to replace lost opportunities or to retrain the work force (Turok and Edge, 1999). Many cities were badly positioned in relation to surrounding towns, with a legacy of derelict land, out-dated infrastructure and obsolete skills. Extensive manual job loss also contributed to a range of wider social problems, the extent of which has only recently become apparent, including worklessness, ill-health, premature mortality, personal and community stress, debt, racial tension, family break-up and neighbourhood abandonment (SEU, 2001; DETR, 2000c; Wilson, 1997).

Some interpreted urban deindustrialization as the outcome of a new spatial division of labour among large corporations in which production was dispersed to lower cost locations while cities retained higher-level functions (Massey, 1984). These had a comparative advantage in remaining in the city cores for face-to-face contact. Metropolitan cities benefited particularly from a centralization of strategic control and R&D functions, while regional cities lost many of their corporate headquarters through mergers and take-overs. Others saw deindustrialization as the outcome of a similar process but on an international scale. It was the logical consequence of a new international division of labour in which production went offshore to emerging economies while selected global cities developed a new strategic role. This was to control, finance and support the international network of factories, service operations and markets: 'Alongside the well-documented spatial dispersal of economic activities, new forms of territorial centralisation of top-level management and control operations have appeared' (Sassen, 1994, p. 1).

Others devoted more emphasis to radical shifts in technology in conjunction with internationalization. They portrayed deindustrialization as part of a necessary transition towards a new 'informational' phase of capitalism whereby European and US cities become centres of advanced services dealing predominantly in information processing and control, and serving as nodes within new global networks. 'The new economy is organised around global networks of capital, management, and information, whose access to technological know-how is at the roots of productivity and competitiveness' (Castells, 1996, p. 471). These authors shared the basic premise that economic relationships within cities had become less important than the position of cities within wider international networks. Cities had become more open systems while remaining the foci of extensive networks of power and information (Massey *et al.*, 1999). 'Presence or absence in the network and the dynamics of each network vis-à-vis others are critical sources of domination and change in our society' (Castells, 1996, p. 469).

Urban networks and quality-based competitive advantages

In parallel with these arguments another set of ideas has emerged that has been highly influential in the NCW. It shifts the emphasis back towards the benefits of business relationships *within* cities, set within the context of global economic changes and the role of cities in the wider national and international system. Three new features have attracted particular attention: the importance of local collaboration between firms as much as competition, sectoral specialization over urban size and diversity, and soft or intangible locational assets rather than hard or physical assets.

Several writers argued during the 1980s that the economy was moving from an era of mass production to one of *flexible specialization* or *post-Fordism* (Amin, 1994; Hall and Jacques, 1989; Piore and Sabel, 1984). A growth in demand for less standardized consumer products was said to coincide with changes in industrial technology and the labour process, including the application of computers to various stages of design, production and distribution. A key feature of the argument was that these shifts supported the establishment of local networks of specialized and interdependent firms. According to Piore and Sabel (1984, p. 265), 'small enterprises bound in a complex web of competition and co-operation' had the flexibility to adapt more readily to changing market conditions, especially in high technology and design-intensive sectors.

Scott (1988, 2002) pursued a similar argument about the horizontal and vertical disintegration of functions in industries facing unstable and competitive markets as a result of the breakdown of Fordism. One of his key propositions was that the shift from large integrated corporations (which had relied on internal scale economies to supply secure markets) towards smaller fragmented firms favoured re-agglomeration. Specialization increased their focus and flexibility, and agglomeration reduced their costs. The outcome was a dense local network of producers engaged in sub-contracting and service relationships and benefiting from a specialized labour pool, typically located in cities. Scott has argued that industries such as clothing in cities like Los Angeles and New York can only survive increasing competition from low cost producers offshore by upgrading their technological capabilities and becoming more fashion oriented, which requires closer collaboration between firms.

Saxenian (1994) also emphasized the importance of local social relationships and the institutional context for business. Industrial performance was greatly enhanced where there was a culture of 'co-operative competition'. In a study of the US electronics industry she concluded that Silicon Valley's greater success over Boston's Route 128 was due to its decentralized, network-based system that encouraged informal communication, collaboration and learning between firms. This culture fostered greater innovation and adaptation to changing markets and technologies than the hierarchical, vertically integrated and excessively rigid institutional structure of Route 128. 'Paradoxically, regions offer an important source of competitive advantage even as production and markets become increasingly global. Geographic proximity promotes the repeated interaction and mutual trust needed to sustain collaboration and to speed the continual recombination of technology and skill' (Saxenian, 1994, p. 161). For a contrary interpretation of Silicon Valley's success, emphasizing federal defence contracts, large corporations and external ties, see Gray *et al.* (1998) and Markusen (1999).

Storper (1995, 1997) extended this to include a wider range of interactions between firms ('untraded interdependencies'). These were essential for mutual learning and adaptation in a context of economic uncertainty and rapid technological change. They included underlying conventions or common rules and routines for developing, communicating and interpreting knowledge about all aspects of production. These interactions were distinctive to each locality and gave it a particular competitive advantage that got stronger and became more specialized over time. These intangible assets discouraged business dispersal, despite many industrial inputs becoming more standardized and processes more routine. Consequently: 'the region is a key source of development in capitalism . . . the region has a central theoretical status in the process of capitalist development which must be located in its untraded interdependencies' (Storper, 1995, pp. 191, 221).

Similar arguments were developed about a range of closely related phenomena variously termed innovative milieu, new industrial spaces, learning regions, regional innovation systems, and the concept with the biggest impact on public policy, *industrial clusters* (Cooke and Morgan, 1998; Porter, 1990, 1998). Porter has been the most prominent advocate of the idea that place matters to international competitiveness because firms benefit from their surrounding environment through competitive and collaborative relationships with other firms and associated institutions: 'the drivers of prosperity are increasingly sub-national, based in cities and regions . . . Many of the most important levers for competitiveness arise at the regional level, and reside in clusters that are geographically concentrated' (Porter, 2001, pp. 141, 156).

The central proposition behind these arguments is that active co-operation between firms in business networks promotes trust and longer-term decision-making. This enables them to overcome some of the limitations of pure market relationships and to undertake risky ventures without fear of opportunism (Gordon and McCann, 2000). Firms are willing to act together for mutual benefit, including creating institutions to lobby on their behalf or to provide common support services. Proximity fosters some of the conditions for social interaction and collaboration, or 'social capital'. It can help interpersonal relationships and trust to develop, and promote a sense of belonging and shared interest. It can also help networks to build upon the distinctive cultural traditions and identity of places, and facilitate practical organization around collective action. The result may be strong urban or regional industrial clusters represented by their own business associations.

The latest twist is to shift the focus on to occupations rather than industries and people rather than firms. Cities are said to contain unique resources that attract highly skilled and talented people, who in turn make knowledge-intensive firms more internationally competitive. These novel urban assets include a distinctive lifestyle associated with cultural pursuits, entertainment and artistic occupations, and a social milieu that tolerates diversity and individuality (Florida, 2002b; Leadbeater and Oakley, 1999).

Conclusion

Running through this literature and the NCW more generally is a belief that fundamental shifts in the economy have occurred over the last two decades. These changes are thought to be inter-related and to have reinforced each other. They are said to have created the conditions for a revival of urban economies through clustering or agglomeration effects arising from the externalities, spillovers or synergies only available in cities.

First, in response to increasing international price pressures there has been greater emphasis in developed economies on quality-based competition (i.e., higher value, differentiated products with enhanced features and strong brand identities that can be sold at premium prices). This makes firms more reliant on proximity to market intelligence, technical knowledge and highly skilled labour than cheap routine inputs.

Second, in response to more unstable markets there has been a trend towards vertical disintegration (i.e., externalization and out-sourcing of non-strategic functions). This has given firms greater focus and flexibility to adjust their spending on labour and services more closely to their current needs. To perform well requires closer communication and co-operation between separate small and medium enterprises to develop effective service and supply linkages.

Third, falling trade barriers, improved transport links, enhanced telecommunications and more mobile capital have made globalization more pervasive. As well as increasing competitive pressures from abroad, it has extended firms' access to new international markets and financial resources, thereby creating greater opportunities for growth.

Finally, breakthroughs in technology have given rise to a whole new set of innovative industries, such as biotechnology, information and communication technology and the so-called creative industries. Their innovative character requires proximity to research facilities and technical expertise, and frequent exchange of knowledge and ideas through close personal communication. It also requires access to specialized labour and business services such as patent offices and lawyers.

These new developments are said to be particularly significant for the relative performance of cities because they offer them new competitive advantages. For instance, by re-establishing the importance of face-to-face contact across business and other organizational boundaries, they reinforce the significance of proximity. They also make it advantageous for firms to have good access to suppliers and collaborators, specialized services, sophisticated or 'thick' labour markets, international airports and advanced telecommunications. It is beneficial, too, for highly skilled labour and organizations providing specialized services to have access to a bigger choice of potential employers and customers. Skilled, mobile talent is also likely to be attracted by the wider range of recreational amenities, cultural and retail facilities in leading metropolitan areas. There may be a more tolerant social environment and greater choice of high quality residential environments available.

These shifts are supposed to have had additional significance for cities by providing renewed scope for a variety of policy actions that can make a genuine difference to local economic performance. For instance, they suggest that important benefits may be derived from relatively straightforward enhancement and upgrading of their 'quality' assets, including advanced skill-sets, research facilities, specialized services, international connections, cultural amenities, artistic communities and vibrant public spaces. They also suggest a more creative role for public policy in bringing together different firms and other actors in industry networks, sponsoring trade associations, stimulating business collaboration and supporting cross-fertilization of knowledge and expertise across organizational boundaries for learning and innovation.

Chapter 3

Social Cohesion in Cities

NICK BUCK

Introduction

In this chapter we introduce the issue of social change in cities, and how it is approached in current urban research and policy. Social cohesion is the broad term used in the NCW, as outlined in Chapter 1. It might appear to be the complement to competitiveness in understanding the success or failure of cities. However, there is an asymmetry between competitiveness and cohesion. The former has at least a potential status as explanation for the economic prosperity of cities although, as the last chapter has indicated, it is often identified with that prosperity. On the other hand, social cohesion has no explanatory status in relation to the social success of cities, though it is sometimes hypothesized to influence competitiveness. Instead it is used as a label for social success, often without much thought about its exact meaning. It is popular shorthand in policy discussion, but cannot be regarded as a useful single concept for exploring the complex issues involved in urban social structures and processes. Thus, if our purpose is understanding the social development of cities, then the idea of social cohesion will not take us very far. This gives two tasks in this chapter. The first is to probe more deeply what social cohesion means or, to put it another way, what is the 'good city' from a social point of view, while the second is to try to suggest how we might understand social processes and social change in cities, taking into account the sort of wider changes assumed by the NCW.

If the conceptual framework provided by the NCW is deficient, this is not to suggest that it replaced something demonstrably better. Urban research has struggled to find an approach which at once provides an account of social processes in cities which embodies a convincing account of social change but where that social change is not largely determined by economic processes. The earlier traditions of community studies contained an often vivid account of social life in cities, but one with significant limitations. They gave no clear or satisfactory account of the processes which led to change in cities, had no very clear model of the relationship between the social structure of cities and the processes which drove their economies, and saw individual places as abstracted from the wider society. While they often saw social processes motivated by competition, usually defined on the analogy of biological processes, there was no clear place for social conflict.

The transformation of urban sociology in the 1970s, including work influenced both by a Marxist framework (e.g. Castells, 1977; Harvey, 1973) and within a Weberian framework (Pahl, 1975; Rex and Moore, 1967), was based on a recognition of these limitations. In the sense that this turn was based on the need to focus on linkages between social and economic processes, and state structures, the tripartite model of competitiveness, cohesion and governance is a recognizable descendant of this turn, though one which its progenitors might now want to disavow.

One of the strengths of the new urban sociology has been that it at least tried to understand the inter-relationship between economic and social processes. However, capitalist economic relations in the end provided the central driving force of change for much of this work. Indeed, understanding the space remaining for effective social and political action, given the critical role of economic processes in shaping cities, has been a problem with which urban sociology has struggled since the 1970s, especially, for example, with the work on urban social movements (Castells, 1983).

The NCW, with its focus on both competitiveness and cohesion, appears at first sight to be a potential solution to this; but we are still left with a problem. To the extent that we can adequately make a distinction between the social and the economic, the social is defined in a rather one-sided way. While it accepts the embeddedness of economic processes in social structures, it is still an economically-driven theory. The model of the social structure of cities in this current paradigm tends to privilege elements which have the clearest demonstrable relationship (in either direction) with economic performance. It is thus close to a tautological system in which social cohesion is that which promotes competitiveness. If we want an adequate model of how the social structure of cities is now changing, it may involve shaking free from this paradigm.

The NCW also carries implications of changing roles for cities. Chapter 1 referred to a shift from seeing cities as the problematic residue of nineteenth- and early twentieth-century ways of organizing industrial economies, to a much more positive role. The reasonably clear economic specialization in this earlier era, with cities as central to physical goods production, to trade and to management and organization, had social structural consequences. These could be seen in the social composition of cities, their political organization, their capacity to sustain their current economic specialization, and their capacity or otherwise to adapt in the face of external threats to that specialization. In the old model it was always clear that different cities were structurally different from one another in terms of economic success, but also in terms of scale and specialization, and this could have consequences for different patterns of social class relations in cities. Structural features could equally have consequences for gender relations or ethnic relations in cities.

Part of the current urban social research agenda is still concerned with the residue of this era, if indeed it is fully past. In spite of the travails of UK manufacturing in the last quarter of the twentieth century, there are still recognizable continuities in the patterns of economic specialization. Aside from this, there are also urban social problems which can be linked to the failure of cities to adapt to the disappearance of earlier economic roles.

However, there is another key question: what are the drivers of social structure and social processes in the 'new urban era'? We will need to address this question throughout this chapter, but some introductory points are required here. Some of the changes implied by the NCW, such as increased turbulence in individual lives, and the decline of institutions underpinning security which force individuals to rely more on their own resources, are not necessarily specifically urban in origin, but may have specific urban impacts.

We can also identify some drivers which are likely to differentiate cities. One sort of functional specialization still has considerable currency: the idea of the global city. These cities are argued to have distinctive patterns of social inequality, and also distinctive migration patterns. More generally, the spatial division of labour within firms' production processes (e.g. Massey, 1984) will tend to reinforce distinct occupational structures in different cities. The focus on quality-based competition may also imply differentiation in terms of various sorts of labour quality, including entrepreneurship, flexibility and 'skill' in a more general sense. Differentiation of patterns of private consumption may also become a more important driver, and one that serves to increase the differentiation between cities, or at least parts of cities, by life cycle stage.

Social cohesion and the 'good city'

There is no very consistent understanding of the meaning of social cohesion. It might be considered in two ways: as a single concept, or as a label for a bundle of concepts. There is not much of a serious social science literature on social cohesion in the former sense. It does, though, seem to reflect certain values and assumptions which are distinct from other views of social relations: for example, those which see social conflict as central and creative, or by contrast those which see society in more settled terms and organized by institutions promoting social solidarity. Social cohesion becomes more important as an idea in the face of individualization. For some the idea that 'there is no such thing as society' is not a problem, but the idea of social cohesion becomes important to those who see the dominance of market relations in individual lives as threatening a descent into chaos.

There is another basis on which cohesion has come to seem more important, as a response to growing heterogeneity and diversity, especially in relation to ethnicity. In this case community cohesion is presented as an alternative to more specific forms of social conflict. In the context of ethnicity, Amin (2002) does, however, suggest that this risks covering over issues and conflicts within ethnic groups.

While social cohesion has this rather negative fearful sense, it does also appeal to ideas of what makes a good society or a good city, without really specifying or prioritizing them. However, as soon as we pose the question in these terms it is clear that there are a large number of possible values to which we might appeal, including (for example) openness, tolerance, prosperity, equality, creativity, security and solidarity. Some of these values may be in conflict with one another; and assuming some social choice amongst them, perhaps reinforced by selective migration processes, the result would be different combinations of these in different cities. Of course in some cities the outcomes might be sub-optimal in terms of all of these values.

If social cohesion is as vague as this, then it may be helpful to try to deconstruct the underlying dimensions. There are two sorts of approach to doing this. One approach, adopted by Forrest and Kearns (2001), and also used by the Cantle report on community cohesion (Home Office, 2001) stays reasonably close to the idea of cohesion, and aims to organize systematically the underlying ideas which are being appealed to. They identify five dimensions:

(a)   common values and a civic culture;
(b)   social order and social control;
(c)   social solidarity and reductions in wealth disparities;
(d)   social networks and social capital;
(e)   place attachment and identity.

Turok *et al.* (2003) adopt a similar structure of dimensions.

An alternative approach, adopted by Buck *et al.* (2002), abstracts rather further from the concept of cohesion. It suggests that cohesion, and also some of the other concepts and terms which are used in current debate (including social exclusion and social capital), refer variously to one or more of three dimensions which define the structure of a society. These are social inequality, social connectedness and social order. Of course, these dimensions themselves are complex, and subject to different interpretation.

Each has both negative and positive aspects. Social inequality may refer to inequalities in immediate material circumstances, perhaps in wealth or power or in longer-term opportunities or life chances, including inequalities which may be transferred across generations. Connectedness may refer to social contacts, and access to knowledge. It may also refer to the openness or closure of societies in relation to outsiders and new entrants, and their tolerance of difference. Social order may refer to issues around security, trust and uncertainty, as well as the nature and prevalence of social conflict, since different groups have stakes in the current order, and the preservation of order involves the protection of those stakes.

Indeed, our three dimensions will themselves be generated by a number of distinct processes affecting cities. Inequality in cities will be generated by industrial structure, and by the competitive processes which lead to changes in earnings inequality. It will also be generated by processes of residential selection. Connectedness will itself be influenced by the degree of inequality, but also by other factors which may generate social distance and population heterogeneity – race, class, family type – and also by the dynamics of the population (the degree of residential stability). Order may be influenced by the other two factors but may also relate to mechanisms of social control, or to the salience of shared norms. It also reflects the strength of group identities and their subjective interpretations of the proper functioning of cities.

Between these dimensions there *may* be all sorts of linkages – for example, strong networks connecting all social groups and lower levels of inequality may each serve to promote social order – although an ideology of social connectedness and/or equality of opportunity, or simpler forms of social control might be adequate alternatives. The language of 'social cohesion' tends to obscure such issues, conflating moral concerns over levels of inequality (or poverty) with functional questions of social order, which (depending on interpretation) might be almost definitionally related to competitiveness. This is a very important point given that actual levels of inequality have greatly increased over the past two decades for reasons which seem directly connected to increased competitive pressures and the pursuit of competitive advantage. It is also important to recognize that attitudes to all three of the dimensions are divided: not only may some individuals prefer greater inequality (or less) on general principle as well out of self-interest, but some individuals (or groups) may prefer disconnection from mainstream 'society', while attitudes to any given social order depend on what the alternatives are imagined to be, and attitudes towards change or uncertainty. Whether consensus on these issues can emerge will depend heavily on the heterogeneity of the city's population, and pursuit of any of the dimensions of cohesion has to engage with issues of 'difference'.

The idea of social cohesion, and also these attempts to deconstruct it, rather implies that there is a coherent urban social research agenda. In practice the topics which have recently been the focus of research are rather disparate, and mainly reflect certain long-standing concerns about the social processes and structures of cities; in particular, urban poverty, the impacts on everyday lives of urban change, and the changing social structure of cities and neighbourhoods (e.g. through gentrification, social and political movements, sources of social divisions and social conflict). The key question is how far the NCW has led to advances in relation to these core issues, and also how far the progress in these areas is really related and coherent.

Some of this research has more recently been informed by new literatures, especially around social exclusion and social capital, which have also been taken up by policy-makers. These bear some loose relation respectively to concerns with equality and connectedness and order, although exclusion implies disconnectedness (as well as inequality), and social capital commonly subsumes values promoting social order (as well as connectedness). The term 'cohesion' itself – and many of the concerns of policy-makers worried about its absence or vulnerability – frequently implies a privileging of issues of the moral, social (and economic) order.

However, the capacity to link these research agendas to ideas associated with social cohesion emphatically does not mean that social cohesion provides any coherence to the research agenda. Such coherence may in any case be unrealistic, or even undesirable, so the remainder of this chapter cannot in effect assess a social cohesion research agenda since such a thing does not exist. Instead it needs to provide an overview of how effectively and constructively the NCW has contributed to the understanding of social structure and social processes in cities, often in terms of relatively old research issues. It also needs to assess how far it leads to important gaps in the understanding of cities.

Social change and changing views of the social structure

Many of the key social changes which are hypothesized to have impacts on cities are national or international in scope. In the introduction we referred to a number of propositions about social change which underlay the NCW. These questioned whether some of the old expectations about the social order (involving both security and some consensus on fairness and legitimacy) can continue to be met in the new circumstances. Reasons why this might be more problematic include:

(a)   threats to individuals' security and ability to plan for their domestic lives/careers;

(b)   an increasing individualization of relations in situations where outcomes seem to be more dependent on competitive activity than on solidarity or collective action;

(c)   increasing inequality as markets respond more strongly to perceived variations in individuals' contribution (or potential contribution) to competitive success/failure.

This relates both to increased turbulence in families and the labour market, but also to changes in state roles, away from a welfare-focused nation state. For all these changes it is open to question how far they are changes in kind or changes in degree, and indeed how far they have actually gone. International comparison would often suggest that current between-country differences are rather greater than differences within countries at different points in time.

However, these suggestions about social change do raise issues about whether they imply a changed view of the social structure, by which we mean the structural bases for divisions in life chances and trajectories, and in interests which may be articulated through market choice or through the political process. Indeed, from some perspectives it raises the question of whether it makes sense to talk any more about structured social differences. There have been other changes which have called into question some of the more conventional views of the social structure, which underlie some older work on cities.

Taken from a long-term perspective, changes in occupational and industrial structures of advanced industrial societies, along with changes in families and working lives, have made it more difficult to see these societies in terms of conventional class structures. Such structures normally involved a substantial working class, a rather small upper class of employers and managers in larger organizations as well as professional workers, and an intermediate middle class, socially distinct from the working class. While there were significant divisions of material circumstances and life chances within the working classes, unemployment and poverty were largely working class phenomena. This had another side: the unemployed and the poor were still on the whole seen as part of the working class, and not as marginal to it.

This conventional structure has been undermined by the shrinkage of traditional manual worker occupations, and the growth and increasing diversity of the occupational groups that were originally in the middle classes, some of whom came to experience economic circumstances and risks which were similar to those of the traditional working classes. However, these changes were highly differentiated spatially. The conventional structure was also undermined by the increasing recognition of forms of poverty and disadvantage that were only indirectly associated with labour market circumstances, and in particular inequalities associated with gender, life-cycle stage, ethnicity and citizenship status. This has led to a set of debates, both political and academic, around the question of how the new social structure should be conceptualized.

Some approaches assert that increasing social fluidity and the diversity of identities on which an individual's social position is based mean that it is no longer constructive to think of social structure in terms of segmented groups. This line of work, developed by sociologists such as Beck and Giddens, rejects the continued salience of class and focuses instead on indi-vidualization. Individuals, freed from the traditional identities of class, respond more flexibly and reflexively to their social world. Beck (1992), in discussing risk society, places more emphasis on the darker aspects of this new world, and both writers see individuals as responding to system processes which are largely beyond their control. But neither author gives a central place to the structural regularities that can lead to inequalities in life chances.

This view is, however, still strongly contested by traditional proponents of class analysis, particularly Goldthorpe and his colleagues. They assert that although the size, material circumstances and life chances of different classes may have changed, society is still best seen as segmented by factors associated with labour market position, and particularly relations of employment, which generate structural regularities (Erikson and Goldthorpe, 1993).

Historically, British analysis of social class, social mobility and related issues has been notably aspatial, or even anti-spatial: it denied that there was any major basis for spatial variation in class processes, or that spatially differentiated resources had any role in class formation. This has contributed to a rather low salience of class analysis in urban sociology, but recent developments provide more basis for linkage to the study of cities. One approach focuses on the range of assets which underlie social divi-sions. Savage *et al.* (1992) distinguished between property assets, organi-zational assets and cultural assets. In their original formulation they suggested an emergent division between professional and managerial groups, which the authors noted had some particular spatial manifesta-tions. But in a more recent contribution Savage (2000) has sought a broader reformulation of class analysis which rejects the centrality of class consciousness (no longer tenable given the profound change which has occurred in the manual working class), but does see class cultural values as central to class definition. He draws on Bourdieu (1984) to point to the way in which culture is used as a resource in the formation of class, by estab-lishing distinctions and boundaries with other classes. He also points to a

change in the role of organizational assets, as the middle classes, in particular, are expected to behave in an entrepreneurial fashion in building their
career. He distances himself from the sharp differentiation between
managers and professionals in the earlier work, and aims for a broader view
of the sources of social divisions. He also argues for the centrality of class
in the analysis of social change, in contrast to Beck and Giddens:

> Their main problem is that they locate the springs of change away from
> the proximate worlds of everyday life and over-stress the systemic logic
> of social change. A reformulated class analysis, I argue, offers a means
> of understanding social change in a more mediated fashion, as a partic-
> ular articulation of local and global, individual and social dynamics, as
> a phenomenon that is attuned to continuity and change and recognizes
> our complicity in the social world we inhabit. (Savage, 2000, p. 151)

There are other approaches which still stress the centrality of structured
inequality, or more strongly structured segmentation, but question the dominance of labour market circumstances in generating inequality. In the first
place, the fact that people live together in households means that their life
chances and interests are shaped by the combination of labour market and
domestic roles they play. Gender inequalities in both domains mean that
gender has a potential independent role in structured inequality. The division
into households of different types also has consequences for inequality,
related in part to gender inequalities, and also perhaps to age inequalities. It
also has consequences for the pattern of social relations. Moreover, household formation processes in cities are rather distinctive (with, for example,
large proportions of households containing lone parents and single people),
and migration decisions are strongly related to major life-cycle changes. As
a result these household formation processes are also critical to change in
urban social structures, as a range of recent work shows (e.g. Meen and
Andrew, 2004). There are also major variations in the ethnic composition of
areas and, to the extent that different ethnic groups face very different social
and economic opportunities, this also contributes to the overall pattern of
inequality. Bowlby *et al.* (2004) show that these ethnic inequalities are found
independently of the economic success of cities, and in some of the most
prosperous cities with the lowest unemployment rates. There may be further
bases for social divisions, including, for example, health and disability.

There is an alternative view of the social structure which sees society in
terms of a new segmentation which has within it a distinction between insid-
ers and outsiders. Examples include the notion of the underclass, Hutton's
(1996) notion of the 40:30:30 society, and also much of the debate around
social exclusion. This is a structured view of society, and in principle runs
counter to the ideas of individualization which are part of the NCW.

However, it does tend to de-emphasize divisions within the 'insider' part of the population. This sort of model has been of considerable importance, positively and negatively, to work on urban poverty and social exclusion.

The discussion so far has hardly considered the spatial structure of cities at all. However, three points are most important here. First, there will be considerable variation in social structure in different parts of a single city, perhaps at the broad level (e.g., inner and outer areas), and even more at the neighbourhood level. Moreover, these socio-spatial patterns are not static over time. London has experienced a radical change over the last 20 years in the relative social positions of Inner and Outer London (Buck *et al.*, 2002). Second, the spatial structure of cities will reflect the social structure of the wider society. In a more class-divided society spatial segregation is likely to be more intense, and housing market institutions will intensify segregation. Third, the pattern of residential segregation will itself be a contributory factor in explaining the nature of social relations.

Social exclusion

We suggested earlier that alongside social cohesion two other concepts had been central to recent work on social change in cities: social exclusion and social capital.

The UK discussion of social exclusion arose out of European social policy. One specific context in which the idea has been deployed is that of the French republican notions of citizenship as involving 'solidarity' and 'inclusion', which in recent times has led to policies to '[re]insert' those who are deemed to be marginalized from the mainstream of the economy and society (Castel and Laé, 1992). More influential, however, has been the looser European Union use of the language of 'solidarity', 'inclusion' and (by extension) 'exclusion' as part of an attempt to find a common basis for discussion of European social policy issues across countries with very different traditions in this field, with one of the aims being to achieve a wider sense of belonging to the EU. In a British context too, as Atkinson (1998) has noted, 'it seems to have gained currency in part *because* it has no precise definition and means all things to all people'. However, as commonly used, the term social exclusion does seem to go beyond traditional concepts of poverty and deprivation in three respects:

(a) it suggests a multidimensional approach to both the causes and social consequencers of disadvantage;
(b) through an emphasis on persistent disadvantage it directs attention to processes causing persistence as well as those which generate disadvantage;

(c)   it implies agency, since exclusion is something that is done to people, allowing us in principle at least to move away from 'blaming the victim' and examine processes of closure and discrimination.

There are, however, two dangers in the use of the concept. One is in the possible implication that the 'excluded' are disconnected from the wider society, and hence the adoption of the insider–outsider model identified above. The excluded are still connected in at least three senses. In the first place, exclusion is generated by overall processes of social and economic change, and policy development needs to be aware of these linkages. Second, there remains significant mobility in individual circumstances, and exclusion is not (in general) a lifetime phenomenon, though it may have severe long-term consequences on life chances. Third, the 'excluded' are not necessarily shut out of social networks which include the non-excluded, and the existence of these networks, which may be an important basis for future inclusion (e.g., for getting jobs) remains an empirical question.

The second danger, evident in policy developments, especially in the UK but to some degree right across Europe, is to focus exclusively on one dimension of exclusion, involving the labour market. Levitas (1998) argues that concentration on re-integration through the labour market, without addressing other sources of exclusion, in periods when employment has become a less secure basis for social inclusion, misses a large part of the problem and simply replicates liberal views of 'society as market'. In fact, there are a wide variety of (other) different forms of social exclusion, operating at the individual, household or community level. Individuals may be excluded from households (young vagrants) or be excluded as households (lone mothers). The form of exclusion may be in terms of employment, housing, access to welfare services and benefits, social attachments and communal solidarities. Social exclusion may be transient (lone parents with pre-school children), endemic (low skilled workers moving in and out of an insecure sector of the labour market) or, perhaps, permanent (isolated old people).

Clearly, then, studies of cities need to operate with a concept of social exclusion that can encompass the elements of multidimensionality, process and agency mentioned earlier and that goes beyond the non-definition embodied in official discourses (which, in effect, defines cause in terms of empirically observable consequences). The need is to provide an adequate theorization of exclusion which links the concept to those social, economic and political changes that cause it to occur. Some progress has been made here in work by Mingione (1996), and others drawing on Polanyi's influential notions of modes of integration in modern societies, and also by Castel (1998).

Kesteloot (1998) has provided a more organized way of approaching this multidimensionality. This applies Polanyi's (1944) concepts of modes of social integration – the market, redistribution and reciprocity – to the understanding of deprivation and social exclusion. He argues that all three modes of integration shape individual life chances (though their impact varies cross-nationally), and corresponding to each mode of integration is a form of social exclusion. So there are three modes of exclusion based on:

(a)   the market, where economic restructuring leads to certain groups suffering a loss of market integration, with limited access to the labour market;

(b)   citizenship, or access to state redistribution, where declining quality and levels of services and benefits and increasing difficulties of access and/or access on stigmatized terms act as exclusionary processes for those who are reliant on the state;

(c)   community or reciprocity, where changes in households and in social networks, as well as processes affecting groups defined by race, gender or disability, increase exclusion through social isolation.

Of course, not all these modes of social exclusion affect the same people. Kesteloot depicts them by means of a Venn diagram in which three intersecting circles overlap. There are thus three distinct situations. First, where all three circles overlap, are those groups that are jointly affected by all three forms of exclusion. Second, where two circles overlap, groups suffer from two of the three forms. Third is the area where groups experience only one form of exclusion and for them especially other forms of integration may provide some compensation.

The processes that create these modes of exclusion work in complex and contradictory ways. Thus, for some, labour market exclusion is experienced as long-term unemployment, while for others it involves a series of temporary insecure jobs. For some, exclusion from citizenship takes the form of welfare benefits which constitute a poverty trap, while for others it takes the form of exclusion from all benefits (e.g., the homeless or asylum seekers). For some, community exclusion takes the form of weak individual ties (the disabled, many single person/single parent households), while for others, especially some of the ethnic minorities, it takes the form of poor links between the minority community and the wider society.

This framework can be seen in two ways. First, it suggests that the intensity of disadvantage will be greatest where more than one mode of exclusion is operating: for example, suggesting that it is where a benefits poverty trap exists, exacerbated perhaps by child-care needs or high housing costs, that labour market exclusion is likely to be most extreme. Such effects will be strongest where individual or community networks are weakest.

Conversely, the experience of prolonged labour market exclusion will deplete a community's resources with effects seen in lack of motivation and self-esteem. Second, it also emphasizes the diversity of experiences of exclusion, and suggests that we should not treat all forms of exclusion as if they were the same.

We would therefore argue that while there are considerable ambiguities in the idea of social exclusion, and at least some of its usages are dangerously close to ideas of the underclass, some work within this framework provides valuable new ways of looking at urban poverty.

This discussion of exclusion rather abstracts from spatial issues, but it is clear that the spatial dimension has been critical to the development of both research and policy. Kesteloot's framework above was, for example, developed in the context of understanding exclusion in neighbourhoods of Belgian cities. There are three issues here. First, migration processes will lead to residential segregation, intensifying the spatial concentration of social exclusion, as both Cheshire *et al.* (2001) and Meen and Andrew (2004) suggest. Second, it is possible that spatial concentration may of itself intensify individual experience of social exclusion, as Buck (2001) suggests. Finally, the intensity of disadvantage and exclusion varies significantly with the wider economic circumstances of different cities. Chapter 9 discusses these issues in more detail.

Social capital

While the current political and policy discourse concerning exclusion exists at some distance from the developing social science literature on this topic, the link between one highly publicized academic interpretation of 'social capital' (Putnam, 2000) and this discourse is much closer. In general terms, social capital refers to the resources which are obtained through membership of social networks, representing an economistic formalization of the old sociological observation that 'involvement and participation in groups can have positive consequences for the individual and the community' (Portes, 1998, p. 2). However, as Portes also notes, the contemporary political (selective) take-up of social scientific definitions and analyses of social capital have been marked by a focus of attention 'on the positive consequences of sociability while putting aside its less attractive features'. Also, by focusing on social capital as a non-monetary source of resources, something which is presumed to be generated by individuals and 'communities', to quote Portes again, it 'engages the attention of policy-makers seeking less costly, non-economic solutions to social problems'.

Even within the academic literature there are, however, substantial ambiguities about the meaning of the concept, with a great potential for slippage between differential versions, applicable in rather different contexts, and requiring distinct kinds of evidential support. One of these areas of uncertainty relates to the question of whether social capital is essentially an individual asset – developed and used by people to 'get on' or 'get by' on their own account, with unintended social spillovers which may be positive and/or negative – *or* whether it is an intrinsically social good. The most theoretically coherent approach follows from that of Bourdieu (1984), treating social capital as basically an individual resource, with any societal implications from its aggregate level, patterning and distribution being viewed as entirely contingent, and requiring investigation in particular circumstances. From this perspective, what is 'social' about the asset is simply that it is based in 'possession of a durable network of . . . relationships of mutual acquaintance and recognition' providing entitlement to 'credit, in the various sense of the word' (Bourdieu, 1985, pp. 248–9). This distinguishes it from both alienable forms of economic capital (money, goods and saleable claims) and embodied human capital (Coleman, 1988, 1990). To the extent that relationships are still facilitated by propinquity, social capital could then have a more explicitly spatial dimension than the more mobile forms of economic and human capital, but the extent to which this applies, with social capital being tied to particular spatial settings, is also a contingent, empirical question.

The second source of confusion, in parts of the academic literature but more pervasively in the policy discourse, involves a tendency to equate social capital with the resources obtained through it, the values which some forms of social capital may promote, and/or the social preconditions for sustaining certain kinds of social capital, conflating cause and (hypothesized) social consequences (Foley and Edwards, 1999; Portes 1998). An important instance is Putnam's approach to social capital (treated as a societal asset), in his influential book *Bowling Alone* (2000), which sees networks, norms and trust as contributing to the effective functioning of social and political institutions and to economic success. This approach raises questions about the causal mechanisms operating, and the strength of the hypothesized relationships. However, it provides the basis for a diagnosis of current American social ills (including many of the worrying features of contemporary urban life), back through declining levels of trust and civic political engagement, to presumed effects of political and social change on levels of social integration.

This argument has echoes of older academic and political critiques of anomie and the individualizing effects of urbanization (notably in the case of commercial metropoles such as London, New York and Paris), and fears about threats to social order, but it also links into contemporary hypotheses about the enabling role of urban agglomerations in relation to the trust-based business networks, widely seen as required for competitive success in more fragmented and rapidly changing economic conditions. In both cases, there is an acute need for greater theoretical clarification, as well as for empirical validation of the consequences which may or may not follow from stronger and more durable relations between individuals or businesses, and the relevance of proximity to these. Certainly we cannot presume that more social capital (i.e. stronger networks) is unambiguously positive in terms of its effects on either social order or social inclusion. Indeed, there are some obvious urban examples of tight networks within local communities which are 'anti-social' in terms of their effects both on 'order' (e.g. through organized crime) and on 'inclusion' (e.g. through closure of labour market opportunities against outsiders). The implication is that we need to be concerned not only with the degree of connectedness of city residents and businesses, but with the patterns of inter-connectedness, and with the (social) distribution of such social capital: that is, who is connected to, and cut off from, whom?

The discussion of social capital relates both to competitiveness and cohesion, and in relation to the former has been discussed briefly in the last chapter. It relates to both the connectedness and order dimensions outlined above. One set of hypotheses which has been addressed in recent work is whether cities in general display weak social capital (perhaps a consequence of urban anomie), or whether poor neighbourhoods in particular do. The findings of the London project would certainly lead us to reject a *strong* view of urban anomie, though evidence suggests neighbourhood affiliation measures are rather low (Buck *et al.*, 2002). Foord and Ginsburgh (2004) suggest that in deprived areas of inner north-east London, there is significant building of social capital, though not of the expected form: 'Nevertheless these undervalued, everyday and "hidden" networks, have emerged over many years through local association and economic activity and have provided important mechanisms for building particular forms of social capital and creative entrepreneurship. Furthermore they have engendered socially cohesive collective action in a tough urban environment' (p. 303). The stronger evidence for social capital as a community resource comes in gentrifying areas, discussed by Butler in Chapter 10 of this book.

From economic structure to social structure

One of our main concerns in this chapter is with a framework for discussing the independent effect of social structure and social processes on the future of cities. Neither exclusion nor social capital is particularly helpful here since the first is concerned with describing outcomes, while the second is concerned with causal factors, but it is very partial.

In the introduction to this chapter we suggested a number of ways in which the social structure and social composition of cities was liable to be influenced by their economic role and fortunes. Spatial divisions of economic roles will lead to spatial divisions of occupational structure. So, for example, London, with concentrations of higher-level control functions, will contain higher proportions of employers, managers and professional workers than other cities. In this view shifts in the industrial structure, or the pattern of labour demand, will lead via various adjustment processes to shifts in the social structure. Another view suggests that processes of globalization in the world economy are leading to increasing inequalities, even a polarization, in the social structures of cities. In particular, in cities at the top of the urban hierarchy, and with the most international orientation, it is suggested that there is growth at both the top and bottom of the occupational hierarchy at the expense of the middle.

However, it was also suggested above that a persistent issue for social analysis of cities was to provide an account of social structure or social change which was not predominantly driven by economic determinism. This is not to suggest that economic processes may not be dominant in explaining social change, as in the examples above, but that our account of social change must not exclude the possibility of independent influences. Chapter 5 focuses more directly on interactions between economic and social implied by the NCW. Here we shall briefly explore the reasons why social change may be more independent of economic change than in the accounts above.

In the first place, the adjustment processes between industrial change and social change may be subject to considerable variability which will weaken the link. The processes include migration, both domestic and international, changes in commuting patterns, occupational change and career mobility, movements in and out of unemployment and in and out of the labour market, and acquisition of human capital through education and training. If some of these processes work more efficiently than others, it is possible, for example, that industrial change might lead to increasing unemployment.

Moreover, these adjustment processes do not just happen in response to industrial change, but are the consequence of many individual decisions with quite other motivations. Most migration follows from households attempting to improve their housing, or because of changes in their family circumstances, rather than to find better jobs. Even for long-distance movement, which typically is more closely related to labour market signals, other factors such as education, consumption and lifestyle choice and refugee movements play a particularly significant role. Education and training is likely to be acquired with a view to long-standing opportunities in the current labour market, rather than in response to the shock of changes in the labour market, insofar as labour market opportunities are taken into account at all. Even most moves into unemployment will be a consequence of turbulence in individual firms, or difficulties in the match between workers and firms, rather than trend change in an industry. The cumulative impact of all these processes is rather indeterminate, and so the social structure of individual places will be shaped by these processes partly independent of labour market change, giving the social structure a degree of autonomy. Moreover, the considerations which lead to these choices may change over time. The revaluation of central areas as living environments, linked to changes in domestic consumption processes and family structures, as well as to economic changes, is an important example here and will be discussed further in Chapter 10.

Second, these choices are not a random pattern, but take place within a social structure within which places have meanings, and people will tend to seek to locate themselves alongside others with whom they identify, and separate themselves from other social groups. The connectedness of social groups within areas of cities will have a significant impact on how those areas change socially. Moreover, the inherited legacy of cities – occupational, cultural or political – is of enduring importance in shaping future social development. These will be embodied in different views of the social order of the city. There are also various more or less well-defined property rights within the city which residents seek to appropriate. Halfpenny *et al.* (2004) discuss the conflicting perspectives in suburban areas of Manchester as they undergo social change.

These processes take place in the context of an existing built form, and we must expect that features such as size and density will lead to adjustment processes operating in a different manner in cities of different sizes. They will also be shaped by a set of other institutions and markets, which are themselves rather independent of the economy (most notably the housing market and the education system). Some of these institutions will themselves be shaped by political struggles between interest groups within the city. More generally the structure of social organization of the city will also have implications for the political process and for urban governance. The ways in which urban governance may reflect local interests, and the degree to which it may shape the future of the city in response to those interests, are among the themes of the next chapter.

These factors give us clear grounds for expecting cities to evolve in ways which do not simply depend on their economic competitiveness. While it would be possible to discuss some of them in terms of social cohesion, exclusion or social capital, it is not particularly constructive to do so. Instead, the most useful research has addressed them as distinct substantive issues.

Conclusion

This chapter has suggested that the NCW provides a rather impoverished framework for discussing social processes in cities. Social cohesion lacks conceptual coherence, and we need to deconstruct it to identify research-able questions and to understand social change and social processes in cities. This is made clear by the absence of any significant research specif-ically on social cohesion, though the phrase 'community cohesion' is sometimes used as a label for research on relationships between ethnic groups. Urban social research within the NCW has been more likely to focus on social exclusion and social capital.

In summary, social exclusion can be helpful in moving beyond simple concepts of deprivation, to focus on processes of exclusion, and the expe-rience and wider consequences of exclusion. As a description of a divided society it is extremely inadequate in contrast to a structured view of inequality. It is important that urban social research does not treat the social structure in a piecemeal way, focusing only on the excluded (or indeed the affluent gentrifiers), but explores inter-relationships.

Social capital, provided it is adequately defined, is clearly of some importance in understanding how people get by, and perhaps how they get ahead. However, its role in creating social closure as much as its role in bridging communities must be understood. It has also been difficult to find clear evidence of independent positive effects of high levels of social capi-tal at the community level.

In this chapter we have thus mainly been concerned with the limitations of current research frameworks. There is another key question, however: what are the drivers of social structure and social processes in the 'new urban era'? How should we understand the ways in which equality and inequality, connectedness and disconnectedness, order and disorder are produced in cities today? We return to these issues in the concluding chap-ter.

Chapter 4

Governance and Socio-Economic Change in Cities

ALAN HARDING

Governance and cities

In the opening chapter it was argued that a concern with urban governance – and particularly the development of vertical linkages between the local, regional, national and supra-national tiers of the public sector and horizontal linkages between the public and private sectors at local level – is central to the New Conventional Wisdom about cities. More responsive and integrated urban governance, it was suggested, is increasingly seen as essential to the pursuit and balancing of urban competitiveness and social cohesion.

The 'governance strand' of this volume examines the extent to which there is evidence that the NCW is right to assert that reform of the structures and practices of urban governance is essential to the realization of urban competitiveness and social cohesion. In doing so, it takes seriously Gordon and Buck's argument that changing *ideas* about the significance of cities, and the way they are used to legitimize and shape policy decisions and institutional reforms, can be as important as real changes in the urban economic and social base. The challenge for this particular chapter is to pin down the concept of urban governance more clearly and to provide a conceptual framework for linking this notion to those of urban economic competitiveness and social cohesion.

This challenge is addressed in four stages. The next section looks briefly at the way the role of government as a whole in relation to economic and social change has been treated, conceptually, before considering the way the role of *local* government has been conceptualized within a broader understanding of the development of national welfare states. It then goes on to consider more recent conceptual accounts that deal with the changing forms and features of nation-states and how they might affect the way local authorities are positioned to deal with urban economic and social change. The following section considers some of the implications of those changes and argues the case for a new conception of urban governance characterized by a complex system of vertical and horizontal linkages and coalition-building and a shift in the balance between concerns with competitiveness and social cohesion. The final section relates the conceptual literatures to key recent changes in urban governance, focusing mainly on the UK, and summarizes some of the questions and dilemmas that researchers interested in the role of urban governance in enhancing competitiveness and building social cohesion face. This provides a context for the finer grained reviews of national and sub-national institutional and policy changes that follow in the governance-related chapters in Part II of the book.

Government, economic competitiveness and social cohesion

Our aim here, then, is to draw together those conceptual accounts that can best help us appreciate how understandings of *urban governance* in relation to economic competitiveness and social cohesion have changed and with what implications. Before we can shed any useful light on the notion of urban governance, however, we need to return to first principles and ask how the role of government, as a whole, in relation to economic competitiveness and social cohesion has traditionally been conceptualized. In one sense, this is a huge task that has exercised social scientists ever since the rise of political economy in the seventeenth century. Paradoxically, though, it is not something that economic theory – the body of literature that might be expected to have most to say on the subject – has concentrated upon. This is because mainstream economics, whether it draws upon neo-classical, welfare or Keynesian traditions, is overwhelmingly normative in its orientation. Whilst proponents of these three traditions often come to radically different conclusions about the causes and consequences of economic competitiveness and aggregate social welfare and the role of government in promoting them, each of them starts from assumptions about the way decision-making units, be they individuals, households or firms, *should* behave in principle and uses them as a basis for developing certain procedural schemas which, they argue, governmental choices should enshrine. They also concentrate overwhelmingly upon *national* economies and the levers that sovereign bodies at the national level can utilize. They rarely consider the economic and social 'steerage' that can be exercised by, or through, sub-national tiers of government. In other words, they tend to ignore urban governance.

Only in the case of Marxist political economy – whose adherents routinely reject what they see as an artificial separation of the economic, the political and the social – are some of these limitations, at least for present purposes, overcome. We therefore begin with one strand of neo-Marxist analysis which offers a particularly useful analytic-descriptive, as opposed to normative, account of the role(s) of 'the state' in economic and social change. O'Connor's central thesis in *The Fiscal Crisis of the State* (1973) was that, by the 1970s, advanced capitalist states were experiencing profound fiscal crises caused by the inability of national governments to respond adequately to the demands placed upon them for different but necessary forms of investment. The result, he argued, was a threat to the long-established co-existence of economic growth and social peace that had been a feature of the post-war 'developed' world. In a sense O'Connor's argument can be read as little more than an interesting period piece. Like many neo-Marxists writing at that time, he overplayed the 'crisis' tendencies he identified and underestimated the capacity of national governments to adjust public expenditure priorities significantly and in ways that, at least until now, have proved politically and economically sustainable. In another sense, however, his analysis prefigured a substantial literature on the way in which the forms and functions of nation-states have been modified: for example, as part of an alleged transition from Fordism to post-Fordism (Amin, 1994). We return to this more recent literature below. Whichever interpretation of O'Connor one prefers, however, what is important for present purposes is that, in order to be able to substantiate his thesis, he was forced to undertake a significant, concept-driven analysis of 'state' expenditures.

O'Connor argued, along typically neo-Marxist functionalist lines, that the twin imperatives of 'the state' were to secure *accumulation* and *legitimation*: that is to say, 'the state must try to maintain or create the conditions in which profitable capital accumulation is possible . . . [whilst also trying] . . . to maintain or create the conditions for social harmony' (O'Connor, 1973, p. 6) without appearing overly coercive in either respect. Adopting more recent terminology, the trick of effective government which he outlined is to provide a politically sustainable balance between economic competitiveness and social cohesion. Governments attempt this, according to O'Connor, through two alternative but indispensable forms of investment. Social capital – a term not to be confused with its more recent usage – is the totality of 'indirectly productive' investment devoted to securing profitability within the private sector. It comes in two forms. The least indirect form, *social investment*, comprises 'projects and services that increase the productivity of a given amount of laborpower' (O'Connor, 1973, p. 7), whilst the more indirect, *social consumption*, comprises expenditures 'that lower the reproduction costs of labor' (p. 7). The latter support individual life chances as well as enhancing profit-serving activities. The second major category, *social expenses*, is 'not even indirectly productive' but comprises 'projects and services which are required to maintain social harmony' (p. 7).

O'Connor accepted that his conceptual categories did not map perfectly on to individual public sector projects and services because few could unambiguously be said to serve only one of the functions he outlined. (Publicly financed transport infrastructures, for example, are investments that simultaneously serve multiple public and private, economic and social goals.) However, he did indicate the sorts of investment that broadly 'fitted' his categories. Social investment, for example, was taken to include all public sector investment in the physical environment, be it through infrastructure (road, rail, ports, airports, etc.) or contributions to the development of major utilities and the physical stock associated with public services, from schools, hospitals and research centres to sports stadia. It was also seen as comprising expenditure associated with the development of human capital through all levels of the education system and public R&D facilities. Social consumption was argued to comprise investments in publicly-provided but collectively consumed services (e.g., in housing, recreation, cultural facilities, child care), subsidies for the purchase of private services in such fields, and support for various forms of individual insurance against unemployment, disability, ill-health and so on. Social expenses, on the other hand, were said to include welfare payments that arguably limit social protest and anti-social behaviour but, in themselves, make no direct contribution to productive activities.

Whether or not one shares O'Connor's view of 'the state' as quintessentially manipulative, class-biased and crisis-prone, his rudimentary taxonomy of government expenditures is useful. It suggests the role of government as a whole in respect of competitiveness to be limited, on one hand, since its influence is largely indirect, but at the same time to range across the great majority of functions the public sector is involved in. At the same time he argued that the government role in respect of social cohesion is conceptually distinct and more direct but potentially vulnerable during periods of perceived crisis in respect of national competitiveness.

Local government, economic competitiveness and social cohesion

O'Connor's taxonomy is useful in identifying particular roles for government in respect of competitiveness and social cohesion, and the tensions between them. However, it is limited by its assumptions that 'the state' (a) can be analysed as a single, unified and coherent entity, (b) always performs its functions effectively and, by implication, uniformly across space, and (c) is trapped by certain 'structural necessities' into delivering a predictable mix of functions over time. In order to develop his account for present purposes, we need to explore how the division of public sector functions across different geographical scales affects the contribution of government to competitiveness and cohesion, spatially (and particularly, for present purposes at the 'urban' scale), and to understand the way the salience of scale and the balance of attention given to issues of competitiveness and cohesion can change over time. In attempting to achieve this we will first consider the main attempt to 'territorialize' O'Connor's analysis, Saunders' 'dual state thesis', before considering conceptual arguments that have questioned the durability of the 'scalar fix' that Saunders identified and begun to spell out the implications for the changing role of subnational government in respect of competitiveness and social cohesion.

Saunders' dual state thesis (1986, pp. 291–311) built upon functionalist neo-Marxist arguments about 'the role of the state' but provided a more sophisticated analysis of the spatial division of governmental labour. In essence, the dual state thesis argued that a distinction needed to be made between the 'productive' functions of the state – those that correlate most closely with O'Connor's notion of social investment – and those that concentrate more upon Saunders' understanding of social consumption (basically a combination of O'Connor's 'social consumption' and 'social expenses' categories, but omitting national transfer payments). In Saunders' view, historical evidence suggested the former were increasingly monopolized by government at the national and regional levels, the detail being decided upon by means of bargaining between national government and the peak associations of capital and labour. The latter, in contrast, were more and more the preserve of local government and were subject to more pluralistic bargaining processes, albeit within a framework determined at a higher level in light of perceived production needs.

The dual state thesis, then, offered a plausible 'ideal type' that appeared to capture long-run trends in the division of governmental functions along a vertical axis, particularly the rapid development of the role of local government in social consumption in the context of the expansion of national welfare states during the 30 years after the Second World War. Thus Saunders' main observation was that the local government role in respect of production – that is, relatively direct support for competitiveness – was extremely limited, whereas its role in social consumption (where the links with competitiveness were more tenuous) was dominant, increasing and focused more upon establishing the conditions for social cohesion. In setting out this distinction, Saunders was able to propose an answer to a conundrum that exercised many 'radical' theorists at the time, which was how government as a whole could simultaneously grant (social) concessions to non-economic interests whilst also continuing to prioritize economic competitiveness as a whole.

With the considerable benefit of hindsight it is clear that the dual state thesis, too, was a product of its time. As with O'Connor's arguments, what is of greatest interest here is not so much the purposes Saunders sought to serve through his analysis – concerns that he himself jettisoned in later writings – but the extent to which the allocation of functions between levels of government he described was a strongly-established historical trend. In fact conceptual arguments which have appeared since Saunders' contribution suggest that the roles of sub-national levels of government with respect to consumption and production issues are not eternally fixed but can change appreciably. The causes and consequences of a more recent shift have been analysed and represented in relatively abstract terms by a later generation of theorists who also took their cue from neo-Marxist analyses of 'the state', but argued that they were insufficiently sensitive to historical and geographical variation.

There has recently been considerable debate, within the context of strong globalizing processes and the challenges they set for national systems of economic and social management, about two inter-linked issues relevant to this chapter. One is the extent to which there has been a general, functional re-orientation within nation states characterized by a rise in salience of competitiveness issues at the expense of concerns with social cohesion. The other is whether we are witnessing a cross-national process of change in the way governmental functions are allocated at different spatial levels. Participants in these debates characterize them in different ways: for example, in terms of a perceived rise of neo-liberalism (Peck and Tickell, 2002), a shift towards a 'new regionalism' (MacLeod, 2001) and analyses of 'state rescaling' (Brenner, 1999), and the development of 'multi-level governance' (Bernard, 2002). Typically, though, they share an interest in developing insights originally provided by regulation theory.

Regulation theory in its various manifestations (Jessop, 1990) essentially argues that ongoing, inter-dependent processes of economic globalization and technological change not only create a new and much more problematic context for the pursuit of 'national competitiveness' but have simultaneously made that enterprise more urgent whilst rendering impracticable the nation-specific macro-economic management techniques that underpinned the post-war boom and its broadly benign social consequences. In the language most regulation theorists use (Lipietz, 1987), fundamental changes to the dominant 'regime of accumulation' have resulted in changing national 'modes of regulation'. As a result, new forms of multilevel governance – which vary in their detail but not in their basic orientation – are said to be emerging in which there is an understanding that improvements to 'national competitiveness' (a) actively need to be created and re-created, (b) generate pressure for social welfare provision to be more firmly linked, wherever possible, to changing labour market needs, and (c) depend less upon how a mythical 'national economy' is steered and more upon the way in which the competitiveness of firms is served by the particular contexts within which they operate. Part of that context, of course, is still provided by national, indeed increasingly international, macro-economic regulation; but much of it is also place-specific. Out of this growing sensitivity to place, it is argued, has evolved a growing commitment to 'supply-side' programmes delivered on a sub-national scale and often accompanied by the selective devolution of resources to sub-national institutions.

The implications of changes in modes of regulation at the sub-national, as opposed to national, level are not well explored within the regulation school. In the hands of some commentators, however, regulation theory has become a tool with which to analyse change at the sub-national/urban scale, too. Jessop's work, in particular, provides a framework for assessing the growing salience of sub-national competitiveness, the forms of institutional restructuring and policy change that might be expected to accompany it and the implications for the governance of social welfare (and hence the changing role of local government). With Peck, Jessop argues that all developed nation-states are going through some variation of an overall transition from a Keynesian Welfare National State (KWNS) to a Schumpeterian Workfare Post-national Regime (SWPR). As part of that transition, it is argued that:

(a)   macro-economic policy, necessarily, is increasingly co-ordinated at the supra-national scale;

(b)   national governments face pressure to refashion policy instruments and institutional structures in an attempt to promote sub-national supply-side improvements to economic competitiveness (whatever effects they have on the geography of economic activity within national boundaries), promote labour 'flexibility', and link benefit entitlements for the economically active to future participation in the labour force;

(c)   there is pressure for governmental functions, as well as being passed 'upwards' in some instances to supra-national governmental organizations, to be passed downwards, to the sub-national/urban level, and outwards, to non-statutory sectors, through partnership arrangements or the commodification of collective services that were once provided exclusively by public agencies.

Combining the insights from the dual state thesis with certain variants of regulation theory, then, we can begin to identify some important changes in the way the role of local government in respect of economic competitiveness and social cohesion has been understood and analysed. Around 20 years ago the conceptual literature on local government was dominated by explorations of its expanding role in the provision of social welfare services within a policy and resource framework largely determined at national government level, but interpreted and implemented locally. To the extent that production/competitiveness issues were part of that analysis, the local government role was characterized as broadly reactive, as consti- tuted, for example, by the function of the local planning system in allocat- ing land-uses between competing interests. In the interim period, however, two conceptual shifts are apparent. First, the salience of competitiveness issues (and an attendant 'local politics of production') has grown, and second, the more 'traditional' concern with analysing the role of local government in underpinning social cohesion has focused more upon the implications of expenditure constraints and policy shifts imposed at the national level and the way investment in social consumption activities can (or can be argued to) impact upon competitiveness.

Both of these analytical re-orientations are well represented in a rein- vigorated literature on local government (Stoker, 2000). We must be care- ful, however, not to overemphasize the importance of conceptual debate about the changing role of local authorities, important though it is. As Dunleavy (1980) long ago pointed out, there is a key analytical distinction to be made between local government and urban government. Whereas the former has a relatively simple, institutional focus, the latter must take into account the fact that formal sources of authority affecting life in urban areas, even in the most decentralized governmental systems, are highly fragmented and widely dispersed across levels of government and public agencies. Given the arguments made by regulation theorists, we must also go a stage further than Dunleavy and insist upon a distinction between urban government and the ultimate concern of this chapter: urban gover- nance.

A new urban governance?

We have noted how the dual state thesis argued that the functions of government in respect of competitiveness (production) and social cohesion (consumption) in the peak period of the development of national welfare states were broadly differentiated along a vertical axis, with national government assuming primary responsibility for the former while local government dominated the latter (albeit within a national policy frame- work). If we take the arguments advanced by regulation theorists seriously, however, two recent developments should have resulted in different patterns of functional differentiation between governmental tiers and a more complex system of urban governance in which local authorities and other decentralized agencies play an important but far from dominant role in the politics of production as well as consumption.

The first, triggered by a renewed emphasis on national competitiveness and a growing recognition of the role that sub-national production complexes play within it, will have resulted in governmental functions increasingly being differentiated along a horizontal, rather than vertical, axis as local authorities' production roles expanded and their functions in respect of social consumption have been redefined in order to underpin the search for competitiveness as well as social cohesion. As a result, 'urban government', as understood by Dunleavy, should increasingly be charac-terized by vertical linkages between key sub-national agencies (local authority departments and other decentralized public bodies) and national government departments in which, broadly speaking, (a) production issues have grown in importance, and (b) the provision of collective consumption services have undergone significant redefinition and retrenchment.

The second development, emphasized less in regulation theory but arguably just as important, would involve the intensification of *horizontal* links at the urban/sub-national level, triggered by a growing role for non-statutory organizations in the delivery of governmental goals. Three broad sets of factors arguably underlie this trend. First, in respect of production functions, the quest for competitiveness is clearly something that the public sector is incapable of achieving alone, given the indirect way in which it supports market developments, and therefore demands various forms of context-changing for, and accommodation, negotiation and joint work with, elements of the private sector. Second, in the social consumption sphere, a growing emphasis on efficiency and productivity in service deliv-ery should lead to a search for alternative forms of provision, sometimes resulting in the commodification of services that were once provided by local authorities (e.g., through privatization or contracting out to non-statu-tory service providers). Third, and strongly linked to the notion that the roots of economic 'success' and social peace are highly localized and place-dependent, government would need to build and/or take advantage of a variety of uncommodified economic and social bonds of trust, reci-procity and democratic engagement that can underpin social cohesion and economic competitiveness.

To the extent that they entail a move from a 'command and control' model of local service provision to one in which non-statutory sectors and diverse economic and social interests outside formal governmental organi-zations are involved in defining and delivering quasi-public goods, these horizontal linkages are about govern*ance* rather than govern*ment*. In other words, they refer to ways in which a variety of statutory and non-statutory organizations are collectively engaged in and mobilized behind attempts to deliver urban public goods that none could achieve alone. In this context, two further conceptual literatures that have been employed in the analysis of horizontal co-ordination in urban governance are worth noting. Neither is as functionalist as the accounts derived from neo-Marxist political economy.

Indeed, both stress the capacity for political choice and the way in which the actions and interactions of particular economic, social and political groups and forces can shape the development trajectories of places in cumulatively significant ways.

The first are urban coalition theories of one sort or another, and especially urban regime theory and the growth machine thesis (Elkin, 1987; Logan and Molotch, 1987; Stone, 1989). Both were developed initially within the USA and therefore analyse coalition-building activity in a national context in which the local government system is highly fragmented and decentralized and individual local authorities are heavily dependent upon locally raised resources and especially sensitive to local economic performance. Given this lineage, both concentrate predominantly on the development of local, public–private sector coalitions designed to improve competitiveness. Given that these forms of horizontal co-ordination form only a part of the urban governance agenda – especially in countries with more centralized governmental systems and/or in which local authorities have traditionally had stronger roles in the social consumption field – US urban coalition literatures have been substantially criticized by commentators in other national contexts for what is argued to be excessive localism and apparent voluntarism (Jessop, Peck and Tickell, 1996). Stripped of their ethnocentricity, however, both are useful in that they provide both a rationale and research strategy for the analysis of urban coalition-building.

There is already a substantial literature on the uses and abuses of US urban coalition theories in other national contexts (Harding, 1999). Briefly, though, both are concerned with the importance – and unpredictability – of interaction between politics and markets. Urban regime theorists, in particular, argue that in liberal democratic societies there are two, interdependent systems of authority: one based on popular control – that is, the various organs of representative government – and the other on the private ownership of productive assets, that is (largely) the business community. Business decisions are critical to public welfare, widely conceived, so public officials cannot be indifferent to them. Since productive assets lie substantially in private hands, officials cannot 'command' businesses to perform their socially useful functions; they can only provide inducements. It follows that, although there are some policy areas in which governments can achieve desired policy outputs through allocative means, there are many areas in which the control that public officials can exercise over outputs is less secure and predictable.

Wherever policy success relies upon the promotion of market activity, there needs to be bargaining and joint work between actors in the public and private sectors, and hence (at least in the US case) a process of horizontal coalition-building. In developing this argument, urban coalition theories effectively distinguish between local government and local governance. Stone, for example, argues that, 'successful electoral coalitions do not necessarily govern'. As a result, they need to promote relationships of mutual benefit between those organizations and interests that have access to, and can deliver, various resources, be they material (such as finance, personnel, and land and buildings) or intangible (such as political, regulatory, and informational resources). No single organization or group monopolizes these assets and there is no 'conjoining structure of command' to link asset-holders together. Urban coalitions are therefore 'informal arrangements by which public bodies and private interests function together in order to be able to make and carry out governing decisions'.

The growth machine thesis offers finer grained detail about the types of actor who play leading roles in local economic growth/competitiveness strategies. For Logan and Molotch, the key to the growth machine is the way 'parochial' (for which read 'local') capital can help create conditions in which non-local, 'metropolitan' capital is attracted to particular areas. The most active players within parochial capital, for Logan and Molotch, are rentiers (property-owners) who strive to maximize the rental value of their land and/or buildings by intensifying or changing the uses to which they are put. They are a particularly dynamic and self-serving sub-set of local private sector interests whose high level of commitment to local economic growth is explained by the fact that they are 'place-bound': that is, their material interests are geographically rooted. The focus of research based upon this understanding therefore involves an analysis of the way in which rentiers construct alliances with other business interests and public and quasi-public agencies with an interest in the promotion of competitiveness.

The second set of conceptual arguments – focusing upon the importance of 'social capital' – was substantially covered by Buck in Chapter 3. The social capital literature is less 'urban' and only partially about governance, but nonetheless poses some important questions about the localized characteristics that can both influence levels of social cohesion and economic competitiveness and be affected by behaviour within and/or by local institutions. It also covers a broad spectrum. At one end are accounts drawn from economic geography and 'socio-economics' that focus upon the importance of 'untraded interdependencies' in underpinning business innovation and growth (Amin, 1999; Cooke and Morgan, 1998; Storper, 1993). At the other is a political science-dominated literature that stresses the importance of civic culture and a strong civil society in creating social cohesion and providing the capacity for effective sub-national governance and, thereby, enabling innovative adaptation to economic change (Putnam, 1993). The importance of these accounts for current purposes are that they stress 'locality effects' and suggest that particular, locally embedded forms of economic and social linkages and networks can interact with local institutions in a way that promotes social cohesion and economic competitiveness.

On the basis of the conceptual literatures we have considered here, then, we can speculate that, irrespective of national context, we are witnessing the progressive breakdown of the old 'dual state' model and the evolution of new arrangements for urban governance in which inter-organizational linkages, bargaining and coalition-building – both vertically, between levels of government, and horizontally, between statutory and non-statutory agencies and interests – have come to play a more important role. Within this more complex system, concern with promoting urban economic competitiveness has grown, triggering the development of vertical linkages between those sections of sub-national and central government primarily concerned with economic development issues and horizontal linkages between particular urban local authorities, other public agencies concerned with production issues and elements of the private sector. The governance of urban competitiveness, however, remains substantially separate from the governance of urban social cohesion in the sense that the more established relationships and linkages between central and local government with respect to social consumption services remain in place but operate in a context in which there are pressures to outsource provision, to ensure that social provision links more directly to the promotion of competitiveness and to mobilize civic/non-statutory as well as governmental capacity. The questions that remain concern the implications of this conceptualization of 'the new urban governance' which has been, or could be, used for empirical purposes.

The 'new' UK urban governance and the Cities programme agenda

Given that 'governance' was not, initially, a central strand of the *Cities* programme that provides much of the material for this book, it would be unrealistic to expect that the projects represented in its pages will have been driven by the conceptual arguments outlined above. At the same time, though, none of the theoretical literatures examined here pretend to predict changes in any detail. Thus regulation theory, on one hand, indicates a number of generalized, cross-national tendencies but leaves open to empirical investigation the issue of how and to what extent these are translated, institutionally, into particular national contexts. Urban coalition theories and the literature on social capital, on the other, speculate about (but certainly do not anticipate) the nature of horizontal relationships between key institutions and interests at the local level and what makes them effective in producing particular outcomes in particular circumstances. In other words, a *post-hoc* rationalization of the conceptual importance of governance within the *Cities* programme is useful in identifying key themes and informing the interpretation of empirical work. By way of conclusion, then, it is worth linking the themes raised in this chapter with the particular UK context in which the *Cities* programme was undertaken as a way of introducing the more detailed 'governance' discussion of Chapters 11 and 12, in Part II.

It is clear that there has been a much more intense focus, in principle, on the issue of sub-national competitiveness on the part of both national and local governments in the last 20 years. This has led, irrespective of the party in government, to a constant succession of policy initiatives and institutional innovations designed to raise the profile and effectiveness of sub-national economic policy. During this period, local authorities were given specific powers and responsibilities for economic development for the first time (by a Conservative government), and a specific mission to pursue the economic as well as social and environmental well being of their areas and inhabitants (by a Labour one). Allied to an often bewildering range of short-term government area-based urban programmes – Burgess *et al.* (2001) recently identified 42 running concurrently – these changes have created a much enhanced 'local politics of competitiveness' that has many of the characteristics outlined in the last section.

These changes, however, have not been accompanied by the devolution or decentralization of powers to the urban level in any consistent or straightforward sense. Only in the case of London, with the recreation of a metropolitan authority and the creation of the country's first elected city mayor, have we seen the development of 'new' urban institutional capacity. And if one scratches the surface, it is far from obvious that government initiatives in the period in which the *Cities* programme was active represented a clear recognition of the importance of cities to national economic competitiveness. Under both Conservative and Labour national administrations there was a tendency to create new, non-elected agencies or partnership vehicles to deliver economic development and related programmes sub-nationally rather than put them wholly under the control of locally elected bodies. In many instances, programme resources were awarded through a process of overt inter-authority competition.

The recent, partial exceptions to this 'rule' are arrangements in the 'devolved territories' of Scotland and Wales and – to a lesser extent – in Northern Ireland and London where 'regional' development agencies, along with widely varying levels of control over mainstream expenditure decisions, have been put under the control of elected sub-UK institutions covering a minority of the total UK population. A similar process may see government-appointed regional development agencies 'democratized' if and when elected regional assemblies are created in at least some of the English regions. The process of devolution has been 'sold' as a response to economic disparities and the need to improve sub-national competitiveness but there is little evidence, as yet, that divergences between the nations and regions of the UK have narrowed or that greater regionalization has resulted in radically different approaches to policies or institutions in or for cities.

Elsewhere, whilst area-based programmes – especially since the Thatcher era – have acknowledged the important role played by local authorities, they remain tightly specified by national departments as well as heavily audited, usually through Government Offices for the Regions whose roles have expanded as the interface between the centre – and, indeed, the European Commission – and localities on economic development and related issues has grown. New programmes have also been relatively lightly financed, their collective 'value' continuing to be dwarfed by expenditure on 'mainline' services. The vast bulk of the latter, almost by definition in a highly urbanized country, are delivered disproportionately in towns and cities. However, there was little evidence in the *Cities* programme period, beyond the development of some relatively weak interdepartmental integration mechanisms, of national departments other than the constantly restructured one that oversees local government (at the time of writing the esoterically-titled Office of the Deputy Prime Minister) developing an 'urban mission' or looking seriously at the way their expenditures affect urban development trajectories. As a result, major government programmes (e.g., in housing, transport, health, education and science/R&D), continue to have differential impacts upon urban economic competitiveness whilst remaining – even in the devolved territories – relatively detached from urban policy debates. That is not to say that governments, when occasionally demonstrating their support for towns and cities, have not produced impressive lists of 'non-urban policy' investments (DoE 1988; DETR 2000c). The fact remains, though, that there is a world of difference between these rough spatial audits and something that was not seriously contemplated in the UK during the *Cities* programme period: a cross-departmental strategy designed to identify and build upon the competitive assets of key urban centres for the benefit of the national economy.

Even at the level of specific, targeted urban programmes, there was no clear attempt to build upon competitive potential. Instead, urban policy concentrated upon 'urban problems' and targeted resources on areas that were defined, statistically, as relatively deprived. The assumption, for much of the last 20 years, has been that 'the urban issue' is primarily about competitiveness (or, more specifically, its absence), but that attention should focus upon attempts to encourage markets to work more effectively in deprived urban areas. Of growing importance within that basic agenda was the idea that success is unlikely to be achieved unless 'local communities' are actively engaged in programme initiatives. In this sense, the value of 'social capital' was recognized in that 'community' development and engagement in regeneration policy processes in deprived areas has increasingly been seen as an essential corrective to professionally dominated, technocratic 'solutions'.

The one departure that became evident under post-1997 Labour governments was an acknowledgement that the effects of 'mainstream' local policies – that is, those largely concerned with social consumption – help determine competitiveness in its broadest sense. In other words, the attractiveness and effective functioning of urban areas was no longer seen as being determined only by the quality of business environments, narrowly conceived, but also by, for example, levels of local crime and educational attainment, the quality of housing, leisure and entertainments facilities and so on. Whilst this was a conceptual breakthrough that the *Cities* programme helped encourage, its effect, in practice, was to ignore the service-specific, inter-governmental policy communities that continue to determine the use of the bulk of mainline resources and to concentrate, instead, upon a further round of lightly resourced, experimental initiatives focused upon deprived areas. Hence the major reforms that occurred in local service delivery, including substantial moves towards the commodification of services (e.g. via 'Best Value') and the restructuring of local authority management regimes (via local government 'modernization'), were not linked effectively to the concern of urban policy to encourage selective, area-specific innovations in mainstream policy areas to support the search for competitiveness as well as social cohesion.

This brief sketch of the context within which the *Cities* programme developed suggests a very extensive potential 'governance agenda' and a huge variety of possible avenues for empirical research. Quite what an 'urban competitiveness strategy' might consist of, how a range of relatively incidental policy instruments could be mobilized to support it, what sorts of processes had proved most effective in achieving this and how they differed between places was one important set of concerns, particularly for the *Cities* programme's Integrated Case Studies. Understanding the mechanics of coalition-building – inter-governmental, inter-agency, inter-district, public–private and public–voluntary – was clearly another key theme, as were analyses of emerging mechanisms for linking the benefits of economic change to social need, recognizing and building social capital and enabling 'community involvement' in policy processes. Central to all these concerns was the degree to which urban politics and new forms of local leadership enabled – or discouraged – new approaches to the promotion of competitiveness and social cohesion and encouraged links between them, and whether changes in the broader institutional and policy environment facilitated, prevented or simply made no difference to local innovation.

Evidence of the findings of the *Cities* programme on these issues is presented in Part II of this volume. In particular, chapter 12 reviews the extent to which the governance of urban competitiveness changed and became more effective in the context of successive innovations in national urban policy, and Chapter 11, deriving from Goodlad and Meegan's research in Glasgow/Edinburgh and Liverpool, examines how far community involvement in neighbourhood regeneration enhanced social cohesion. In Chapter 15, we return to the New Conventional Wisdom' about the role of urban governance in promoting competitiveness and cohesion, and ask whether the shift from the dual state model to a more complex and negotiated system adequately describes recent change within the UK and, if so, with what consequences for the economic and social trajectories of UK cities.

Chapter 5

Integrating Cities

IAN GORDON

Joined-up thinking about cities

In the introductory chapter, we sketched a 'new conventional wisdom' (NCW) about the significance of cities within a changing international economic order. This set of ideas has evolved in various places within academic and policy communities since the later 1980s, and has since become central to the approaches of a range of public agencies, including the OECD, the European Union, and the UK government's Urban Task Force (DETR, 1999a) and Urban White Paper (DETR, 2000c). Its background lies in beliefs about the renewed importance of face-to-face contact and qualitative assets in a more flexible economy. The two central organizing ideas, as we see it, are that:

(a)   cities have a positive, creative role to play in this new context;
(b)   but achieving this requires an integrated approach, recognizing increasingly important interactions between economic, social, political, cultural and environmental processes, especially within cities.

These are powerful and attractive ideas, which together seem to form the basis for a genuinely 'new urbanism', reversing the pervasive anti-urbanism which underlay policy throughout the last century. This new urbanism extends current (American) usage of this term, which is mostly focused on advocacy of forms of modest scale, neo-traditional development as a means of recreating community values and minimizing environmental damage, through 'smart growth' and revival of the 'lost art of place-making' (Harvey, 1997; Leccese and McCormick, 2000; Talen, 2002), to incorporate related ideas from the international literature (e.g., DETR, 1999a) and a wider range of urban situations.

   That anti-urbanism had involved not a simple dislike of cities, but the view that there was something inherently problematic about the scale and form of modern capitalist cities – rather than modernity or capitalism (to put the issue crudely) – which made urban life troublesome, unnatural and dislikeable. Within the NCW, however, the quintessentially urban characteristics of *density, diversity* and *flexible social relations* are each perceived as substantial assets, needing nurture rather than cure. Moreover, past policies grounded in more negative views have themselves come to be seen as problematic in:

(a) undermining competitiveness by depleting these sources of strength;
(b) exacerbating social polarization by residential segregation, spatial mismatch in the labour market, and governmental fragmentation;
(c) worsening environmental problems by encouragement of overlong journeys by private motor vehicles.

As importantly, perhaps, established approaches to urban policy could be seen as overly constrained by professional divisions of labour, missing the point that cities are where 'it all comes together' (as Soja, 1989, put it). Strong local interactions between economic, social and environmental processes could produce dynamics of either urban success or failure. To secure success, and turn around those cities which were failing, the new message was that policies needed to be multifaceted and integrated, as well as sympathetic.

This is the aspect of the NCW on which we shall focus in this chapter. In approaching it, however, we have to be particularly conscious of two faces of the contemporary wisdom in general (as discussed in Chapter 1), since the distinction can too easily be elided in discussing interactions and the need for integrated approaches to policy. These involve, respectively:

(a) a set of potentially testable propositions about the impacts of change in the economic environment on particular trends and processes observable within cities, and on relations among these;
(b) more politically-oriented propositions, with a consensus-building fuzziness about key concepts, which tends both to obscure sources of conflict and to make it harder to apply an evidence-based approach to evaluation of their validity/applicability.

A central aim of this book is to concentrate attention on the first of these faces by framing clearer and more testable versions of the central hypotheses, and then seeking relevant evidence for and against these. This rather critical approach is not antagonistic to development of a new urbanism; far from it. Rather it is meant to assist development of one which is realistically based, and relevant to current urban problems and processes (including those which are not really new, though unsuccessfully handled with past approaches).

One aspect of the NCW to which these concerns apply is its emphasis on the potential of integrated approaches to urban development, policies and institutions: 'joined-up thinking' and 'joined-up government' in the jargon of the UK's New Labour administration. In the British context at least, as we noted in Chapter 1, this recent emphasis does represent a radical shift in governmental strategy, since it follows a very long period in which a series of more one-dimensional approaches to urban policy were pursued, each grounded in a particular diagnosis of the key factor underlying urban problems, and implemented through a particular departmental division of labour. The new approach embodies key ideas from the NCW about the inter-relation of economic competitiveness, social cohesion, responsive governance and environmental sustainability – including an optimism about the degree to which these can be mutually reinforcing – and about the significance of processes operating at an urban level for all of these. From our perspective these are all hypotheses requiring empirical evaluation, as with the other elements of the NCW. But the task is rather more difficult in this case since each of the elements which are supposed to be related are pretty fuzzily defined, even sometimes embodying quite distinct ideas, as we saw in Chapters 2 and 3. And with holistic arguments it is often hard to see which are supposed to be the crucial links.

To simplify the problem, we focus here primarily on possible connections between competitiveness and cohesion: those with governance are addressed by Deas in Chapter 12, while possible links with sustainability are discussed only in general terms, as they are really beyond the scope of this book. Even in relation to competitiveness–cohesion links, much of what we have to say is of a ground-clearing nature, identifying and clarifying particular paths of possible causal connection, with scope only for summary evaluations of what has been found in relation to specific paths. Before embarking on this task we should first consider some of the evidence that propositions about such linkages are actually important in relation to the new directions being taken by urban policy.

Urban triangles

In recent public debate about the future of cities, both in the UK and more widely in Europe, two sets of 'triangles' have been highlighted as requiring attention. The first of these involves concerns with the economy, equity and the environment (sometimes referred to as the 3Es), to each of which (for example) the recently established Greater London Authority (GLA) is formally required to have regard. In part this formulation seems to represent an effort to draw groups with quite different priorities into support for some broader-based governance or urban regime. But also it seems to reflect a view that all three concerns need attention in order to secure effective 'sustainability' of a city, and long-run achievement of any one of the goals. That this is not entirely clear presumably reflects the fact that it is at least partly a vehicle for consensus-building – as in the EU-funded *London Study* (ALG, 1997) prior to the GLA's start-up, which was largely directed at consensus building, as was the more recent *Liverpool–Manchester Study* (Sustainable Urban and Regional Futures Centre, 2002) – as well as a typically ambiguous usage of 'sustainability' to refer either to specifically environmental or generally long-term issues.

In the second version of the triangle the concerns are competitiveness, cohesion and effective or responsive governance. Here governance is inside the frame (and, by implication, part of the problem to be addressed), rather than standing outside, simply accepting responsibility for managing the other elements of the system. And in this case there is a rather stronger assumption that the elements are interdependent, leading either to a vicious circle, where some combination of poor competitiveness, lack of cohesion and unresponsive governance, drags the others down, or to a virtuous circle where success in one or two elements reinforces the others.

In both cases the issues are too broad and the propositions far too general to open them up to serious debate or evidence-generating research without deconstructing the elements somewhat and developing more specific causal hypotheses about the paths through which particular aspects of competitiveness, environmental sustainability, social cohesion and responsive governance may be connected. For three of the terms – competitiveness, cohesion and governance – this task has already been started in the preceding chapters, so here we will start from environmental sustainability.

In this case there are two related sources of ambiguity, or differentiation, in the concerns underlying the concept. One of these involves the spatial scale over which environmental effects are to be considered (i.e. the range over which spatial externalities are treated as relevant), between the contribution that local urban developments of different kinds may make to planetary outcomes (e.g. through global warming) and the most localized kinds of impact. The second involves the severity of the effects involved, and whether these are conceived of in purely physical/biological terms (with a range here between impacts on the survival of species, through the health of individuals, to aesthetic/life quality effects of unsympathetic development or loss of recreational opportunities).

In some cases the distinctions may matter rather little; for example, it is at least plausible that promotion of safer cycling scores in all terms, locally and globally. In other cases it matters very greatly, since what is a major benefit in one frame of reference may represent a major loss in some others. A focal case here is that of 'the compact city', advocated during the 1990s by British and other policy-makers as a means of simultaneously securing physical and quality of life gains both locally and globally, together with some positive social benefits (DETR, 1999a; Rogers and

Power, 2000). Some of the advertised gains are actually steps that are thought to be necessary to persuade mobile groups to live in higher density settlements, rather than genuine effects. But among the latter there are two significant elements, notably a reduction in traffic emissions of all kinds, as the need to travel falls and public transport options become more attractive; and a saving of greenfield sites outside the city from development. The first is a fairly unambiguous gain in physical terms at least, on almost all spatial scales, though the benefits may well be modest, both absolutely and relative to those achievable in other ways (i.e., by higher fuel prices: see Gordon, 1997). Gains from greenfield-saving will, however, be primarily in quality of life terms, and relatively localized, thus needing to be balanced against quality of life losses as urban open and personal spaces get taken for development.

This obviously creates difficulties in assessing what impacts more or less 'environmentally sustainable' cities are likely to have on economic competitiveness and social cohesion, since we cannot be at all sure what counts as a more environmentally sustainable city. Much more realistic is to consider whether more specific environmental outcomes (such as levels of traffic congestion and the perceived quality of people's residential and living environments) have a significant impact on economic growth, productivity or any of the dimensions of social cohesion discussed in Chapter 3; and, correspondingly, how any of these socio-economic factors might affect such local environmental outcomes or the more globally significant question of emission levels, particularly from personal travel. The sum of our knowledge about these relationships is rather limited. We may reasonably suspect that improvements in the quality of the local environment have a positive effect on absolute growth rates, while higher productivity and per capita incomes enable people to raise the quality of their residential environment, other things being equal. Even if empirically substantiated, however, these relationships tell us next to nothing about sustainability on a local, still less a global, scale. In the case of social cohesion (i.e., equality, connectedness, order and identity), there seem not even to be reasonably clear intuitions about how these might be connected to environmental outcomes, except insofar as a more cohesive local community (in all these senses) might be better able to manage *local* environmental externalities. Beyond such (apparently uncorroborated) hypotheses, the point seems to be that it is *possible* to devise externality-oriented policies which are at the same time economically efficient, good for the local/global qualities of life, and also for cohesion in all senses.

Turning to consider the relationship between economic competitiveness and social cohesion on an urban level, about which our research should have much more to say, there is again a difficulty about the multiple meanings of the two concepts. The main issues were discussed in Chapters 2 and 3, but should be summarized here. In the case of competitiveness, the ambiguities relate primarily to the number of distinct markets in which cities and regions effectively compete, particularly those for product sales by local firms, for inward investment, for attraction and retention of desirable residents, and for favours from higher levels of government in which particular places may do differentially well or badly. Variations in sectoral specialization and functional role may also make a difference to the ways in which competitiveness interacts with cohesion. So also may the spatial scale, between intra-urban locality and broad functional regions, at which the question is being posed, since spatial externalities (both positive and negative) can be very important. A distinction also needs to be made between the actual effects of higher or lower competitiveness on cohesion, and those of particular strategies taken to boost competitiveness, since these may have strong side-effects on cohesion irrespective of what actually happens to economic competitiveness. There is of course also a measurement problem, since competitiveness is not itself observable, i.e. it is a latent variable, indirectly reflected (with different kinds of bias) in measures of productivity, growth and exports (or, more broadly, of out of area sales).

In relation to social cohesion, the sources are more fundamental, since (as was noted in Chapter 3) conventional notions of cohesion tend to implicate issues of (in)equality, connectedness, social order and shared identity, which are conceptually quite independent, and which may or may not actually be empirically correlated. In this case we have then to think about the separate possible relations between each of these dimensions and some versions of competitiveness.

Despite the emphasis given to these links in the NCW, there is no clear-cut body of empirical evidence substantiating them, as Fainstein (2001a, 2001b) shows in her review of the literature on urban competitiveness, cohesion and governance. This counterposes arguments about the economic value of trust, social capital and deliberative decision-making (as in Potts, 2002), with findings on the increasingly divisive effects of competitive pressures and deregulation, both for 'losing' places (caught in a race to the bottom) and the 'winners' (where gentrification displaces the poor, and the rich withdraw from social responsibility). Overall, following Gough (1999), she concludes that: 'The relationship between competitiveness and cohesion appears indeterminate, dependent on economic potential, governance, social capacity, and history' (Fainstein, 2001a, p. 9).

Within the *Cities* programme, however, several 'integrative city studies' devoted particular efforts to trying to trying to pull together more systematic evidence about paths through which the relationship could operate on a city scale. Several of the thematic projects in the programme also have light to cast on specific links which might connect urban cohesion and competitiveness. In the remainder of this chapter we review the most relevant findings from these studies, looking first at the links from competitiveness to cohesion, and then at those operating in the reverse direction.

Effects of competitiveness on cohesion

The most obvious way in which competitiveness might be expected to affect cohesion would be through the impact of a stronger demand for labour on employment among marginal groups and hence on poverty, via reduced levels of unemployment and involuntary inactivity. How far this is realized in practice clearly depends both on the scale of the area involved and the type of employment affected. At the level of a locality within a city-region the impact may actually be very modest, since most of those eventually drawn into employment as the labour market adjusts are likely to be residing outside the area concerned. In the case of professional, managerial, and some other non-manual jobs where national recruitment plays an important role, this could also be true at the level of the city-region. At the level of broad economic regions, impacts should be much more substantial, especially if the employment boost were sufficient to take the region past the full employment threshold (of around 3 per cent unemployment) where structural barriers to employment for marginalized groups really start to dissolve (see Gordon, 2003b, and Chapter 14 below). Hence regional and national competitiveness are likely to have more impact on levels of social exclusion within a city than local or urban scale economic performance.

In terms of income inequalities – considering the top as well as the bottom end of the distribution – it is far from clear that improvements in competitive performance contribute to cohesion, especially when the gains take the form of higher productivity rather than growth. Cause and effect are very hard to disentangle here, but evidence from London and the South East in particular during the past couple of decades suggests that growth in GDP per head and in earnings inequality are positively correlated. This might be because these regions have benefited overall from increased inequality in the UK as a whole, resulting from a deregulated labour market (and the legitimation of individual acquisitiveness); or it may be because upper earnings groups have played a stronger role in pushing business competitiveness forward, in the context of deregulated and more flexible product markets (Buck *et al.*, 2002).

Turning to connectedness (as the second dimension of cohesion), the most obvious question is whether competitive success tends to promote residential segregation. The reason for expecting this is that households' demand for living close to higher status groups (and to good schools) is income elastic. Hence higher average levels of income, as well as wider income disparities, ought to generate more segregation (Cheshire and

Monastiriotis, 2003). The London integrative study found, however, that segregation of most kinds actually tended either to stay constant, or to contract between 1981 and 1991 when both average incomes and their dispersion grew particularly rapidly in the region (Buck *et al.*, 2002). The exceptions involved the segregation of couple-based from non-couple-based households *and* of the employed from the non-employed. In both cases, this was in the context of a clear shift in the balance of the two groups (within the region) towards the non-coupled and the non-employed. In the latter case, at least, where it is the expanding group which generates negative spatial externalities (as far as the housing market is concerned), it is predictable that this should lead to increased segregation.

The driving force for the growth of the non-employed actually stemmed from weak economic performance at the national level, rather than particularly within the region. But the implication is that if stronger regional economic performance reduced the level of unemployment, this should tend to reduce residential segregation, and hence encourage connectedness. So far as ward-level segregation of the non-white population is concerned, Buck and Gordon (2004) find no real evidence of higher levels of segregation in places (functional regions) with higher rates of unemployment, as distinct from bigger cities and areas with more industrial employment, for both of which this is the case (Gordon and Monastitriotis, 2003). On the other hand, in Amin's (2002) account of the emergence of strong ethnic segregation in three northern towns experiencing recent unrest, a significant part of the background (interacting with discriminatory housing policies) seems to have been the collapse of the industrial base on which both the white and Asian working class had depended.

A second aspect of connectedness which can be expected to be linked to competitiveness is that of family stability or fragmentation. More specifically, in the context of Afro-American ghetto areas, Wilson (1987) argued that high levels of male unemployment meant a lack of marriageable males – that is, of men economically and socially capable of sustaining a long-term relationship – and hence high rates of lone parenthood. Research in a British context has strongly confirmed this hypothesis, at least in terms of cross-sectional associations, showing that it is specifically male unemployment rates which are associated (in the presence of a number of control variables) with higher rates of lone parenthood, notably for non-employed lone parents (Buck and Gordon, 2004). Since higher rates of lone parenthood in an area appear to have knock effects on educational underachievement (see Gordon and Monastiriotis, 2003), this form of disconnection can feed back into higher local unemployment and weaker competitiveness. Indeed, this is one of five paths – others involving health effects of unemployment, fragmented work histories, attenuated job information networks, and prejudices in favour of family men as employees – through which processes of disconnection can serve to convert demand-deficient into structural unemployment (Gordon, 2003b).

For social order, the most obvious hypotheses are about the impacts of economic success, and inequality, on the incidence of crime and civil disturbances. For crime, three broad schools of thought all imply some connection between economic outcomes and crime rates (M. Kelly, 2000). First, the so-called economic theories – assuming a calculative mentality on the part of criminals – predict that property crimes in particular will rise where legal forms of economic activity provide less adequate incomes, and the opportunity costs of arrest and conviction are lower (i.e., in contexts of low incomes and high unemployment). Strain theory, on the other hand, implies a less rational determination of criminal behaviour – perhaps particularly in relation to violent crime – with this being triggered (consciously or sub-consciously) by a sense of frustration or grievance, for which one cause in particular contexts could be higher levels of unemployment, most notably where this is associated with (ethnic, social or educational) barriers to inclusion. Finally, social disorganization theory predicts that conventional moral and social standards will have less of a restraining effect on behaviour in situations where normal social control mechanisms in a community are weakened by mobility, heterogeneity *or* poverty. In the particularly sensitive case of breakdowns in local race relations, notably in the confrontations involving Asian Muslim youths in Yorkshire and Lancashire towns in summer 2001, as well as the particular triggers (in this case including racist political activity and media coverage), underlying factors have been argued to include social deprivation and generational divides, affecting *both* minority and majority local communities (Amin, 2002).

Two previous major waves of rioting in Britain, 10 and 20 years previously, underline the point that the issue is not simply 'race', and that there is no general relationship with local economic failure. In 1991/2 the disorders involved very largely British-born whites and were spread across a large number of housing estates, all with traditional housing in areas of about average economic success, but with concentrations of unemployed young men and weak social control (Power and Tunstall, 1997). In 1980/1 the focus was the inner areas of larger cities – Bristol, London and Liverpool, thus including both the least and the most successful among these – and the rioters were predominantly, but not exclusively black (Afro-Caribbeans), with a rather more concerted response to heavy-handed and prejudiced policing. Across these three waves of disorder, the only common factors appear to have been youth and unemployment, combined in different ways with other sources of strain and/or disorganization.

Impacts of cohesion on competitiveness

Links from one or more of the dimensions of social cohesion to economic competitiveness will typically be quite indirect. Hence they can only really be identified by exploring how particular factors of significance in relation to (urban) economic performance do or do not link up with the main sets of social consequences seen as following from varying levels of inequality, connectedness and order. From a review of the main candidate variables of both kinds (and of hypotheses in the academic and policy literatures), we have identified six plausible paths through which cohesion (or its absence) might plausibly be seen as impacting on competitiveness within a city or region:

(a)   aspects of connectedness or order affecting the willingness of mobile individuals with desirable characteristics (human capital and/or spending power) to live in the area;

(b)   aspects of inequality, disconnectedness and/or disorder affecting the supply of middle range skills (typically recruited within the city-region) via underachievement in the local school system;

(c)   aspects of order, in particular affecting the image of an area in the eyes of prospective inward investors – or tourists – and in extreme cases outward investors too;

(d)   aspects of inequality, connectedness and order affecting competitiveness through levels of crime to which businesses are subjected;

(e)   aspects of connectedness within a business (or business-related) community affecting levels of trust, and thereby willingness to participate in collaborative ventures with uncertain pay-offs, both in relation to innovation and to collective action in support of local economic development;

(f)   aspects of connectedness within a work force, and between work force and employers, affecting levels of productivity and the development of human capital.

In each case, the plausibility of the linkages postulated can be grounded in some sorts of empirical evidence, as well as a priori argument – and the intuitions of 'common sense'. But in every case there are also questions to be asked about the operational significance of some of the links, about the range of situations to which they apply, whether there are not countervailing forces, and whether necessary conditions are all met in the same situations. We turn to these now, considering each of these hypotheses in turn.

Cohesion and the attraction of valued residents

The basic hypothesis here is that crime, insecurity or other social tensions discourage mobile groups from living in an area – or tourists from coming – in ways which significantly weaken the area's economic competitiveness. At least in the case of key workers contributing human capital, this is an argument that needs to be sustained at the level of a functional urban region (FUR). It is not sufficient to show that there are neighbourhoods within a FUR where such people would rather not live, so long as there are other available sets of locations in the FUR where they would feel secure in conducting their and their families' lives. For major cities, where crime rates and other threats are more likely to cross the threshold of salience, this seems to mean either that key workplace areas for these groups have to present high levels of personal crime risk, or that there are no readily available residential areas (with schools, shopping and leisure facilities) in which such groups can feel safe. Given quite high levels of residential (and schooling) segregation over broad areas in larger cities, and the ability to contain the effects of burglary (as the most common actual threat) through a combination of security devices and insurance, this may not often be the case. The most obvious exceptions would seem to be where a major segment of the local population is seriously alienated (e.g., adolescents within some deprived ethnic group with a strong local presence). Another example could be that of young, qualified migrants whose attraction to a metropolitan area could be conditional on their being able to live, with some reasonable degree of perceived safety, not in the suburbs but in socially mixed urban neighbourhoods where isolation is not a relevant defensive strategy.

However, as the last example may suggest, security is not the only quality in social relations which can potentially affect the willingness of mobile groups to live in an area. Notably, Richard Florida (2002a, 2002b), whose work emphasizes the role that the attraction and retention of *talent* plays in competitiveness within the new economy, argues that *tolerance* is a crucial characteristic of the local social environment for this to be achieved. In his work this is indexed by the diversity of the local population, in particular the degree of representation of gay and foreign-born population groups. His argument focuses particularly on the attractive potential of a significant representation of 'bohemian groups' (represented empirically by the proportion of workers in creative occupations), both directly and indirectly as signalling 'a regional milieu that is attractive to and supportive of other types of human capital' (Florida, 2002a, p. 63). Across US cities he shows that the distribution of graduates is particularly strongly linked to his bohemian and gay indices, as well as to cultural and recreational amenities and city size. These characteristics seem to have a particular influence on concentrations of high technology activity, although one might expect the same to apply to concentrations of other knowledge-based activities, including advanced services.

The core of the argument, however, involves hypotheses about the influence of social openness on competitiveness via attraction of talent and promotion of innovative behaviour. This would reflect a particular form of social connectedness, but one which contrasts strongly with other versions of cohesion in which social and cultural capital are used to secure social closure and reproduction of a status quo. And places which score highly in terms of tolerance and creativity may well not be (or feel) particularly secure places – at least in their central areas – or be particularly attractive to other middle class groups (e.g. Savage *et al.*'s (1992) corporate middle class), whose tastes are more for domestic/rural recreations than more urban sophisticated activities. These groups may still manage to live quite well within dynamic city regions in the context of segregated outer areas, though it may require higher salaries to retain them in areas where overall house prices reflect the demands of those with stronger urban tastes.

Educational achievement and middle level skill shortages

The argument in this case is rather more straightforward. Whereas high level talent can be recruited in large part from national (and international) pools of 'talent', as McCann and Sheppard's (2001) analyses of UK graduate movements show, middle and lower range skills are very largely drawn from more local populations: for example, Gordon, Travers and Whitehead (2003) show that half the hard-to-fill vacancies in London were in occupations (below the level of professionals, managers and semi-professionals) where most employers were looking to recruit them from within the city. Hence their supply is dependent on the capacity of the local population and schooling system to produce an adequate supply of what is required, including (in major service centres) unusually strong demands for workers with basic office skills or potential. The output of schools is very heavily conditioned, however, by the social composition of their pupil intake, both directly and through peer group effects. In particular, analyses by Gordon and Monastiriotis (2003) point to strong negative effects on GCSE exam results from concentrations of lone parents, the unemployed, lower socio-economic groups and some ethnic minorities. In the first two cases at least, aspects of social cohesion – both inequality and disconnectedness – are clearly involved as causal influences in a process whose outcomes must affect the skill supply. And, at least in London, there is evidence of large-scale skill shortage (both in terms of hard-to-fill vacancies and employers' perceptions of skill deficiency among existing workers) in relation to middle range occupations in offices and service outlets, if not of a particular demand for qualifications (below degree level). But comparative evidence across areas (Green and Owen, 2001) does not currently point to any clear link with differences in outputs of local education systems: mostly what it shows is a general degree of supply inelasticity, since shortages are clearly strongest in successful areas with high and growing demands for labour.

Crime, disorder and urban image

Crime is among the 'soft' location factors which have increasingly been cited as relevant to location decisions, principally as an influence on the available quality of life for employees (e.g. Gottlieb, 1995). Despite growing concern expressed by businesses about risks to their workers, within the UK it never figures highly among factors affecting location on an inter-urban scale (see, for example, OMIS, 2003). Internationally, crime rates are perceived as an important influence on tourism, though generally only in relation to places with extremely high rates of street crime. Similarly, in the extreme circumstances of the Troubles, both investment and tourist flows to Northern Ireland clearly suffered. In mainland Britain, both Glasgow and Liverpool have suffered in the past variously from reputations for militant socialism, violent razor gangs or rioting, though there is a lack of hard evidence on the scale of effects. Within our research programme no direct evidence was gathered from potential inward investors, or discouraged tourists, but neither the Glasgow nor London city studies (which each considered this issue) found any indications that fear of crime or disorder in either city was holding back development: 'Any negative perceptions . . . [would] mainly affect where *within* the city investment occurs, not whether it comes to the city at all' (Turok *et al.*, 2003, pp. 52–3). And in London they did not figure at all among the reasons cited by the businesses potentially moving out (Buck *et al.*, 2002). These are issues, however, where thresholds are clearly important, and problems can be triggered by quite specific incidents. Hence we cannot know reliably how far social inequality and connectedness would need to deteriorate in order to have major negative impacts on the image of British cities as business centres, such as happened to New York in the late 1960s.

Business crime, investment and profitability

Firms which would not consider moving away could still be substantially affected in terms of profitability and growth potential through experience of repeated crimes such as burglary and vandalism. Indeed, recent survey data report 30 per cent of British businesses as experiencing some disruption to trading as a consequence of crime (BCC, 2004). A particularly high incidence of such crime in shopping centres suggests that more locally oriented businesses might be especially vulnerable, however. In that case there is likely to be more of an effect on local real incomes than on external competitiveness. The London study, which focused on firms that were likely to have wider markets, still found many that had experienced repeated crime. But surprisingly rarely among these was it seen as a major problem, since to a considerable extent it could be dealt with by effective and affordable security measures. Neither, though its form varied, was business crime a risk peculiar to areas of deprivation. As a motive for relocation it was clearly much less important than traditional concerns with premises, transport links and (sometimes) labour supply (Buck *et al.*, 2002).

Trust, clusters and business growth

As noted in Chapter 2, one element in the NCW with substantial support from the academic literature is the proposition that strong local social networks and 'institutional thickness' have become increasingly important for competitiveness. A particular reason is the need for greater collaboration between firms, and the level of trust required for these in a context of high risk and rapid change. A particular version of this argument is developed in relation to innovation and knowledge-intensive activities in Chapter 6.

Evidence from at least three of the projects in the programme, however, raised substantial doubts about the importance of the social capital available in particular places for firms' competitiveness capacity. One ground for this was that, while collaboration and external economies were both important, especially for the more innovative kinds of business, neither was necessarily very local. Key external economies for such businesses around London, including the pool of specialized labour, were found to operate at a broad regional scale, often across the Greater South East. And business collaborations with firms in other regions and countries were as likely to contribute to success as those with partners, clients and suppliers closer at hand (Gordon and McCann, 2005; Simmie, 2004; see also Chapter 6 in this volume). The second ground for doubt about the significance of cohesion was the limited value ascribed by businesses in our interviews and surveys to institutions or the opportunity to build relationships. The London integrative study found firms in the region to be very sceptical about the value of involvement in local institutions, and both this and the Glasgow/Edinburgh study found relatively few firms who recognized significant network-building advantages from spatial clustering. There were modest exceptions to this in all three cities, including an active network of 'business angels' in Edinburgh (Turok *et al.*, 2003), but there was much stronger evidence of the importance of straightforward agglomeration economies. The London study concluded that its value as a location: 'is predominantly in the array of possible business links that can be pursued to cope with shifting market circumstances, rather than in building more restricted and durable partnerships: agglomeration promotes weak rather than strong ties' (Buck *et al.*, 2002, p. 369). Simmie (2004) characterizes this as a 'pick and mix economy'.

Solidarity, motivation and productivity

In its simplest version, this hypothesis suggests that strong forms of identity, stability and social solidarity in particular communities should also facilitate co-operation in the workplace, offering some of the advantages which employers in primary labour markets have sought to create through their personnel strategies. Traditionally, such co-operation went with levels of unionization which are out of fashion under the NCW, the new, flexible economy apparently requiring a different culture of teamwork. Areas with a historically strong labour organization are supposed to have become unattractive to inward investment, although other (more open) forms of social cohesion may be positively valued in terms of the work habits and aspirations which they encourage. The *Cities* projects have little empirical evidence to offer on this, though the London study did conclude from its employer interviews that there was very little evidence of businesses feeling constrained either by local cultures of opposition/non-co-operation or by anomie. Particular dissatisfaction was expressed about the availability of 'soft skills' in teamwork and customer relations in some parts of the city (Buck *et al.*, 2002), which may be linked to their social structures, but not straightforwardly to any of the main dimensions of cohesion.

These empirical findings are (in varying degrees), fragmentary, tentative and place-specific and may well omit other plausible paths of connection between aspects of cohesion and competitiveness. But, taken together, they cast very substantial doubt on the notion in the NCW that there are generally significant and positive links from stronger social cohesion to greater competitive success at the urban scale.

Conclusions

Among the positive aspects of the NCW are: the recognition that economic, social, governmental (and environmental) factors interact with each other in the context of particular places; and acceptance that urban problems (and now potential too) require a mix of policies addressing all of these kinds of factor, rather than one identified as key.

There are also negative aspects linked to these, however, some of which we have already encountered in previous chapters. Among these are the fuzziness of the concepts used to represent these factors, and particularly the inadequacy of 'cohesion' as a way of characterizing the array of 'social' structures, characteristics and processes likely to affect competitive performance, governmental capacity and quality of life in particular cities. In the policy context this is dangerous because it can lead to both over-simplistic and over-optimistic assumptions as to how 'joined-up' action can pay-off, often by-passing those social factors which (still) make progress particularly difficult.

The problem is that the propositions of the new conventional wisdom fulfil not only intellectual but also ideological and political functions, for which ambiguity is an asset rather than a liability. Effective responses to the challenges of the new economy – as well as to more old-fashioned kinds of problem which are of continuing importance for city residents and businesses – depend on a strategy of clarification, disaggregation and empirical testing. A first effort has been made in this chapter, exploring one side of the 'urban triangle', the hypothesized link between urban cohesion and urban competitiveness. In one direction (from the economic to the social) this pointed to significant, but uneven connections for different situations and aspects of cohesion. In the other direction (from the social to the economic) only one connection was identified as potentially significant.

In Part II, a series of more focused examinations of some key sectors, processes and institutions will push this strategy rather further. From the present more broad-brush exploration, however, one particular lesson may be highlighted: this is the importance of being explicit about the spatial scales over which different kinds of process would be expected to operate, given both varying constraints on individuals' field of action, and the various kinds of spatial externality arising from interaction between them. Connections between economic competitiveness and social cohesion need to be seen in relation to a number of different spatial scales, and operate differently at each of these. Thus, if greater competitive success can be shown to substantially reduce social exclusion at the regional level, we certainly should not assume that local concentrations of socially excluded groups can be dissolved through initiatives to promote local competitiveness.

PART II

Key Sectors, Processes and Institutions

Chapter 6

Knowledge, Innovation and the Competitiveness of Cities

PHILIP COOKE and JAMES SIMMIE

Introduction

Within the NCW, the innovative capacities of major urban areas are a crucial element in the argument that a society's success in the 'new economy' depends on its cities, and that these are likely to be major beneficiaries from current economic changes. The general emphasis on innovativeness reflects beliefs *both* in the current/future importance of innovation-intensive sectors of the economy (including high technology industries and services) *and* in the enhanced significance of product innovation now as producers in the advanced economies are forced to engage in quality-based competition. The specific emphasis on cities' capacities relates to their continuing prowess as repositories and generators of knowledge, and especially of those entrepreneurial processes through which this is selectively transformed into marketable and commercially viable 'innovations' in goods and services. During the last century it was shown that substantial parts of this set of capacities could be institutionalized *within* a large corporation operating from multiple locations. In the 'new economy', however, it is believed that (once again) they are coming to depend very largely on:

(a) interactions across the boundaries of the firm;
(b) contributions acquired (through or outside the market) from other economic actors who are most reliably accessed on a local basis;
(c) the externalities of locating within particularly dynamic or supportive kinds of agglomeration.

There are differences of view as to how far the most favourable locations are actually those with closely related kinds of specialization, those with a more diverse array of strengths, or (conceivably) those that somehow combine specialization and diversity. Neither is it entirely clear how 'local' linkages need be in order to be effective, and thus whether innovativeness is a property of core cities (even perhaps of particular districts within them) or of more extended urban regions. But, at some level, agglomeration is seen as being a key to the innovativeness which the new economy specially values.

Empirical evidence certainly points to innovative activity being spread unevenly across space, and in many cases highly concentrated in particular urban regions. For example, if we consider the 'export' of patents to other countries as an indicator of globally significant innovative activity, we find (in three countries for which detailed locational analysis has been undertaken) that in the UK over 60 per cent of such activity occurred in the London region; in Italy over 67 per cent occurred in the Milan and Turin regions; while in the USA over 60 per cent of Japanese R&D laboratories were located in just four states (home to Boston, New York, Chicago and Los Angeles/San Francisco), where only 33 per cent of production plants were found.

Knowledge is defined here as covering the intellectual basis of technological products or processes, *and* the know-how/experience needed to develop them into marketable commodities. Both are required for innovation, as the process that turns new ideas and inventions into commercial products and processes. It is an iterative activity involving a series of interactions between different individuals, organizations and institutions during the development life cycle up to successful commercialization of new economic knowledge, whether in the form of a new product or a new process. Entrepreneurship is a key element in relation to risk taking and overcoming of the uncertainty that pervades the process of innovation.

Although individual innovating firms are the main actors in these processes, their high levels of concentration in a limited number of city regions suggests that there are also significant elements external to the firm, and characteristic of those cities rather than others. Within the USA, on an innovation index relating the density of innovations per thousand population to a national average (of 1), Audretsch (2001) shows San Francisco scoring 8.9, Boston 8.7 and New York 4.2, making them the top three, with Los Angeles seventh at 2.9 and Chicago tenth at 2.6. Some other cities do score below the US average (such as Miami at 0.5). An explanation for such 'city innovation advantages' (Cooke, Davies and Wilson, 2002a) lies in local knowledge 'spillovers', enabled by the 'social capital' that surrounds specific industry clusters in geographic proximity. Thus Boston and Los Angeles score high on innovative manufacturing 'spillovers' in varieties of computing and electronics, as does San José in California (within the San Francisco Standard Metropolitan Statistical Area). New York does so for office machinery and radio/television equipment, while for Chicago process control instrumentation is the leading example.

As Audretsch (2001) also argues, these 'spillovers' explain why the link between R&D activity and innovation, which was the focus of Griliches' (1979) 'knowledge production function', only holds for broad country or industry aggregates. At the micro-economic level, the strength of the relationship is halved in the case of the largest corporations, and fails completely for small and medium enterprises (SMEs), which are highly innovative in some sectors despite investing little or nothing in R&D. Entrepreneurial SMEs acquire economic knowledge largely through spillovers, including dynamic external economies, which can include 'local proactivity' to develop networks of social capital (Cooke and Wills, 1999).

In what follows, we shall first examine in rather more depth why innovation is crucial to competitiveness, whether in or outside cities, highlighting some weaknesses in the dominant 'innovation systems' paradigm (particularly in relation to the role of demand). Then we examine evidence on the spatial concentration of innovation within Europe, highlighting its links with international trade. This is followed by an analysis of clustering by firms and institutions in relation to a range of location factors. This leads to a final section that relates back to the role of cities in knowledge generation and 'knowledge economies'.

Our overall argument starts from the proposition that regional supply-side externalities involving knowledge spillovers and social capital are significant factors that distinguish the most innovative cities from the rest. These are a necessary but not sufficient cause of the high levels of innovation found in a minority of cities. In addition to these supply-side factors, demand also matters, but it is not simply or primarily a matter of local demand. In particular, exports and the circulation of international knowledge through trading relationships are significant in deciding which are the most innovative and competitive cities.

Why is innovation important to urban competitiveness?

A point of departure for explaining the degree of concentration of both R&D inputs and innovation outputs in major urban centres of innovation specialization and excellence is the traditional theory of comparative advantage. In the context of a world in which producers of comparable goods competed simply on price, this explained patterns of specialization in terms of differences in factor endowments, including inherent differences between places in their relative productivity in different functions. This might be simply a matter of industrial specialization, including that in knowledge-intensive sectors, or it may also include specialization *within* sectors in some particular functions, including those most allied to innovation. Adding a recognition of economies of scale, boosting productivity in those activities which are concentrated within a particular area, implies some intensification of this pattern of specialization, particularly for functions and types of firm where external economies are important (and positive). Within this framework, the role of innovation is implicit at most, as one of the factors contributing to 'productivity'.

The adaptation of this theory into a modern perspective on 'competitive advantage' (Porter, 1990) gives *appropriate* product innovation a much more central role, however, since competition is now supposed to be focused on the distinctive qualities which products offer (rather than simply a price:quality ratio). Within what have often become global value chains, Porter emphasizes the crucial role of firms' 'home bases', from which design and strategic marketing are controlled (and of *their* local environment), in determining competitive success. Particular qualitative strengths of specific city-regions – in relation to specialized skills, suppliers and information sources, rivalry among local competitors, and discriminating local consumers for some kinds of products – then emerge as both cause and consequence of localized clusters of successful firms in related kinds of activity. The clustering process is supposed to optimize productivity, innovation and entrepreneurship around specialized knowledge. Firms 'swarm', as Schumpeter (1975) put it, around these points of knowledge monopoly, trying to imitate or emulate the first mover firms.

Let us take software as an instance of this process of building urban competitiveness. Microsoft is a monopoly producer of operating systems software, securing its monopoly by litigation and acquisition of specialist firms that produce compatible products, such as Hotmail. Because Microsoft is less directly innovative than acquisitive, it depends on Silicon Valley firms (amongst others) to stay ahead technologically. This is why Seattle, home to Microsoft, is not among the leaders in the urban innovativeness ranking discussed above (although at 1.7 it is above the national average). Silicon Valley is home to numerous software firms – including Oracle, Siebel, and Adobe – and Microsoft has a presence there. Most of these firms are specialists in organizational software or (like Adobe) specialist access products. One of these specialities is enterprise resource planning (ERP) software that organizes activities such as a firm's logistics.

For the standardized production of solutions, where major man-hour commitments are required, such firms sub-contract to independents or allocate internally to branch software houses in Bangalore (India), where a major cluster of such producers has swarmed to access high quality, low cost labour (Fromhold-Eisebith, 1999). Thus one cluster has spawned another. For instance, where such software had high data security requirements, such skills were accessed from yet another software cluster where Internet 'firewalls' solutions were innovated, and where there are now some 3,000 start-up data security businesses in Herzliah, near Tel Aviv in Israel (see Teubal, 2001). In Dublin, Ireland, there is a major software cluster adapting the products of Microsoft, Oracle, Lotus and others for international use but to national specifications, including call-centre aftercare (O'Malley and O'Gorman, 2001). Four urban clusters (some global leaders in innovation, some less so), each specializing in distinctive parts of the software value chain, are the way this global industry organizes substantial segments of its products and markets. The key point is that each urban setting is globally competitive in its particular niche within the global value chain because it is competitive in some combination of capabilities that enhances the efficiency and productivity of the industry as a whole.

Continual innovation appears to be one of the most important characteristics of these nodes in international value chains, and innovation plays a significant role in the export base of such urban regions. Our evidence suggests that it is crucial to internationally competitive exports. Insofar as these contribute to the economic growth of cities, they form a key to their competitive success. Two self-reinforcing processes involved in innovation and exports also lead to the concentration of innovation in a minority of cities, namely trade and international knowledge spillovers. In order to trade competitively, innovators need to know what the leading world current best practice is in their particular specialization. Much of this will spill over from demanding international clients and customers via their trading relationships. The most open, trading cities with the strongest export bases will form nodes in the systems of international knowledge spillovers and circulation. Innovative firms in these cities should gain competitive advantage both from the quantity of trade and knowledge spillovers and from being the first to receive such new economic knowledge. These processes could establish a cumulative cycle of competitive advantage over cities with lower levels of trade and international best practice knowledge spillovers.

Within the research programme, an analysis was undertaken of the locations of customers and clients of samples of innovative firms in five city-regions, drawn from those who won awards under the Basic Research in Industrial Technologies for Europe (BRITE) programme (Simmie *et al.*, 2002). Results showed that in all cases national markets were important for sales of the award-winning innovations but, in three cases (the international trading cities of Amsterdam, Paris and London), more customers were located in the rest of Europe and the USA than in their own regional and local areas. In the other two cases, Stuttgart and Milan, this was less true, and for Stuttgart local customers were significantly more important than those in the US market. Taking over 60 per cent export sales as an indicator of internationalization, 100 per cent of the Amsterdam innovators fell into this category, compared with 86 per cent in Paris and 56 per cent in

London, but just 20 per cent in Stuttgart and 18 per cent in Milan (Simmie, 2001). This suggests both the importance of innovation as a basis of inter-national trading linkages, and also great variations between leading centres in the importance of these links for their innovative capacities, reflecting the extent to which historically these had functioned as international or regional centres

In the regional economic literature, export demand-based models have emphasized the role of cumulative causation and agglomeration in ampli-fying the effects of strong export performance. In particular, Kaldor (1970) and Dixon and Thirwall (1975) developed the idea that successful export-ing regions can exploit the benefits of economies of scale and specializa-tion, to raise their performance both in terms of exports and overall output growth. Later developments of these ideas in a neo-classical framework by Krugman (1991) explicitly incorporated the effects of external economies of scale, with geographical concentrations of economic activity improving productivity and thereby raising sales. Further, Krugman argues that much of the trade between nations (and regions) is based on such specialization to take advantage of increasing returns to scale, rather than differences in (initial) factor endowments. He does not discuss the particular processes through which external economies operate, but in relation to Porter's analysis the point is that much of the qualitative advantage offered by regions housing successful (innovative) clusters – including those associ-ated with specific supply-side qualities – can be seen as a consequence of their growth, not simply as an exogenous cause.

The argument that the degree of innovativeness of a city is likely to be a key factor in its competitiveness, and hence its growth performance, receives some support from micro-level research on factors causing firms to grow (Geroski, 1999). Beyond well-known generic tendencies – such as small firms growing faster than large (on average) and all doing better in booms – the one key feature to stand out amidst the complexities of the data was that growth depends on innovation. At the firm level the relationship can be erratic and uncertain, but an innovative (and growth-oriented) envi-ronment compensates considerably for micro-level market imperfections, meaning spillovers have a real economic value for entrepreneurship, innov-ativeness and competitiveness. One consequence, argued by Porter (1998b), is that clustering stimulates new firm creation through spin-offs as well as pure start-ups, since geographical proximity gives an advantage in access-ing new knowledge, new technologies, new funding opportunities, new skills and new markets. Barriers to entry under such circumstances are likely to be lower for an entrepreneur already in the knowledge pool, and those entrepreneurs are absolutely advantaged compared to those outside it.

This is underlined in a study of SME innovation and competitiveness by Cosh, Hughes and Wood (1999) where they conclude that the more innovative among small firms can act as a seed-bed for technological change and industry evolution, taking impetus for their innovativeness from the competitive environment in which they find themselves. The product innovators among such firms are likeliest to be taken over (cf. the Microsoft growth by acquisition approach already noted), while those that are process innovators are less prone to firm failure than other kinds of innovators. Accordingly, process innovators may be the best kind of entre-preneurially innovative firm to form the bedrock of a competitive urban setting, although to the extent product innovators retain product develop-ment authority they also help their location outperform others.

Evidence on spatial concentrations of innovation

Sub-national data on innovative activity and outcomes has awaited official recognition of their importance in driving trade and economic prosperity. In the case of the European Union this was early in the 1990s, although initially its data focused more on inputs than on outputs. The first available comparisons relating to 1995 recorded R&D expenditure as a percentage of regional GDP. For the UK these showed that by far the greatest concen-tration was across the Greater South East, a much extended version of the London region. In France there was a similar concentration in the Ile-de-France region around Paris, but also in the Midi-Pyrennees around Toulouse. A subsidiary concentration was found around Grenoble and Lyons. The fourth major European concentration was in southern Germany, in a broad region including both Munich and Stuttgart. Major urban areas were found within each of these concentrations, but both in Britain and Germany the regions also involved substantial hinterlands.

A more detailed analysis by Hilpert (1992) of the spatial distribution within Europe of publicly funded R&D found that up to three-quarters of this was concentrated in 10 'Islands of Innovation'. These were identified according to the following criteria:

(a) specialization in more than one of the three techno-scientific fields studied;
(b) more than 20 per cent of public R&D expenditures in the country concerned;
(c) strong presence of both research institutions and enterprises;
(d) roles as 'knots' in the web of European co-operation (Hilpert, 1992, p. iv).

The ten major European 'islands' identified in this way are Greater London, Rotterdam/Amsterdam, Ile-de-France, the Ruhr area, Frankfurt, Stuttgart, Munich, Lyons/Grenoble, Turin and Milan.

A weakness of this type of input data for measuring innovation is that there is no guarantee that expenditure on R&D always leads to commercial innovations that appear in the market place. Innovation outputs are clearly a better measure of real rates of innovation than inputs. In the USA, Audrestch and Feldman (1996) developed such a measure from a compilation of published product announcements. In the EU the Community Innovation Survey (CIS) now also provides an output measure of innovation, based on firms' responses to questions about new products or services they have introduced on to the market. Mapping of these at county level for manufacturing firms in England and Wales again shows that the Greater South East as a whole contains the highest concentrations of innovation, but at this spatial scale it is evident that the areas with high rates of innovation are actually outside London. In the case of manufacturing, innovation seems to be highly concentrated in a set of counties forming a western arc around outer London (the UK's manufacturing Sunbelt). In the case of knowledge-based services – which are actually much larger employers in this region – London's own performance looks stronger, but the highest rates of service innovation are found in a ring of counties right around London, and up to 100 kilometres or so out from the centre.

Whether the coincidence of high innovation rates for both manufacturing and services in the Greater South East reflects a common underlying influence or the effect of one on the other is an important unresearched issue. Do regions such as this benefit, for example, from traded or untraded knowledge exchanges between innovative services and manufacturing? It is conceivable that part of the relatively high performance of manufacturing firms in the South East is due to the easy exchange of management, financial, marketing and advertising expertise that is highly concentrated in the region. It may also be the case that the international consultancies in these fields based in London are key intermediaries in the transfer of knowledge of best practice from abroad. What is clear, however, is that within the advantaged area (in relation to both manufacturing and marketed services innovation) is an extended version of the London region.

The significance of clustering effects and other location factors for innovation

Explanations for the spatial clustering of innovations fall into a number of different camps. Some of these, adopting a life-cycle perspective, associate innovation with the early incubation phase of business development, and emphasize the supportive environment which larger cities or city-regions provide for new firm formation and development. This may take the form of local access to potential sub-contractors, service suppliers and skilled labour, to meet needs which the firm cannot yet provide for directly. This harks back in part to Schumpeter's (1939) view of exogenous inventions being sought out by entrepreneurs, brought into their (usually small) companies and turned into commercial innovations. A second line of argument focuses on the creative aspect of innovation, and highlights ways in which particular kinds of diverse, liberal and internationally connected agglomeration may stimulate and support novel combinations of ideas, with rapid feedback on both technological and demand trends. This 'buzz'-oriented perspective reflects some of Jane Jacobs' (1961) ideas about sources of urban vitality. In counterpoint to this, another more recent (and less anarchic) strand of argument has focused on the development of networks of trust among a local (or regional) community of firms as the basis for collaboration in otherwise very risky enterprises, and the development of shared bodies of tacit knowledge (Maillat, 1991). Part of the significance of this 'social network' view is that it suggests a particular role for local governance in catalysing the development of such networks (Gordon and McCann, 2005). This may be particularly helpful in assisting innovation among small and medium-sized firms which lack the internal resources that enable big firms to innovate more rapidly.

Though all of these ideas are widely canvassed within the NCW, evidence on the relative importance of the different kinds of explanation, their varying salience for particular sorts of activity, and the specific locational factors which determine where successful innovation is carried out is still generally lacking. Within the research programme, one major effort to explore these issues was pursued through a survey of innovating firms in the five-city BRITE study referred to earlier. In particular, firms were asked to rate the importance of a large number of potential reasons why they would choose to locate the development of a new innovation in their particular city region. Analysis of their sets of responses suggested five fairly distinct groups, relating to:

(a)   transport and communications (internally and externally);
(b)   traditional urbanization economies (skills and specialized services);
(c)   availability and costs of factors (premises, capital and labour);
(d)   production and consumption linkages (suppliers, customers, competitors, collaborators and informants);
(e)   social networks (friends, ex-colleagues, public business support services).

This ordering actually represents the average importance given to different types of reason, and seems to reflect a fairly traditional evaluation, giving priority to the harder location factors, and least importance to social networks. At a more disaggregated level, the highest rating was actually given to availability of professional labour, followed by access to international airports, and (then) to the national road network. Among the basic 'factors', premises were given most weight, and finance the least. Within the group of traditional urbanization economies, neither general nor specialized business services were rated as highly as availability of skilled labour pools. All of the aspects of transport availability (including rail and internal access to the central city) were accorded more importance than these services. Among the potential business linkages, proximity to collaborators was given the most importance, while very little weight was given to closeness of competitors. Each of the 'social network' connections received a rather weak rating, with the least so being availability of public business support services (Simmie *et al.*, 2002).

Overall, these figures suggest that factor costs are not the most important consideration in firms' decisions to locate their innovative activities, presumably because innovating firms are competing more on the basis of quality than of price. Thus, although they must have suitable labour, premises and capital, high costs can be borne because they are able to sell high priced innovative goods and services in international markets. In order to accomplish this, however, firms need access to pools of high quality labour, relevant services, and transport and information infrastructure. Professional and technical experts are essential to innovation. Without their knowledge and experience firms would find it very difficult to innovate at all. The interchange of ideas between them within their city region and with suppliers, customers and clients in other regions is facilitated by transport and communications infrastructure. Large pools of high quality labour and highly focused infrastructure systems are a key feature of the five cities studied. This is particularly true with respect to the international capital cities of Amsterdam, Paris and London.

Urbanization economies, such as those identified above, provide rich milieux in which firms may innovate. Nevertheless, innovating firms do not necessarily interact on a regular basis with other firms within the region, even those within their own sectors. Indeed, the ability to innovate without reliance on regular interactions or strong 'network' connections may be one of the advantages conferred by large metropolitan capitals such as Paris and London. The availability of large labour pools and thousands of other firms allows firms in these regions to 'pick and mix' their required inputs to innovation according to the stage of their development and their changing needs at these different stages. Firms located in the smaller urban regions (such as Milan and Stuttgart) that do not possess such extensive urbanization economies may need to collaborate more actively among themselves in order to reap similar economies of scale.

Differences between the more and less international of the centres were highlighted in relation to the importance accorded to proximities to suppliers and collaborators, with firms in Stuttgart (especially) and Milan giving significantly greater weight to local suppliers and customers. This rather parallels the differences in market areas that we noted earlier, and reflects the differing roles played by local supply networks in the innovation systems of the two regional cities as compared with the three international cities. Somewhat similarly, proximity to collaborators is more highly rated in Milan and Stuttgart than in London or Paris, though Amsterdam respondents also give a high score for the importance of proximity to collaborators. It may be inferred from this analysis that some of the local linkages associated with clustering behaviour of the Porter (2000) type are more common in the regional than in the national capital cities studied. The London 'integrative city' study found that innovating businesses in London were externally oriented, with no particular interest in local clustering, and that the positive effects of joint ventures and strong customer/supplier links were not at all dependent on where the other party was located (Buck *et al.*, 2002; Gordon and McCann, 2005). The comparative evidence suggests that this is not true of all successful centres of innovation, however, and that in Stuttgart and Milan at least firms value and use local networks and linkages more than firms do in the larger capital cities.

One implication is that there can be no single generally applicable model of the way in which cities contribute to the innovation process. But among the programme's studies of competitive developments in British cities, there was a notable lack of evidence associating local success with strong industrial clusters. In particular, from an econometric study of growth in 109 British cities during the last five decades, Begg and Moore found that: 'the degree of industry specialisation at the beginning of the period reduced employment growth in that industry in a city . . . This suggests that . . . any benefits from urban industrial clusters are weak or being offset by the benefits to be gained from dispersal' (Begg and Moore, 2001, p. 3).

Within the Greater South East, Hart and Simmie (1997) reported that local linkages were not a marked feature of innovative firms in Hertfordshire, while neither Gordon and McCann (2000) nor Oakey, Kipling and Wildgust (2001) found substantial evidence of active clustering inter-linkages among London and south-eastern firms. Simmie (2003) does find that face-to-face meetings involving project leaders were important for innovators in the region; but, with a typical frequency of once a month, and a time-frame of a day for the meetings, this did not require very close proximity. Within the IT cluster of the Thames Valley, where recorded levels of innovation are high, Buck *et al.* (2002) concluded that the main spatial externalities were in access to a shared pool of highly skilled labour. In line with the conclusion of Hendry *et al.*'s (2000) cross-national study, Simmie (2004a) concludes for the UK that:

> Contrary to the local clustering hypothesis, market-leading innovative firms seem to be part of an internationally distributed system of innovation . . . The knowledge and information they employ in innovation are concentrated within the firms themselves or gathered from non-spatial sources such as government and industry standards and regulations. Intermittent face-to-face meetings at trade fairs, exhibitions and professional gatherings are also important. Urbanisation economies are also significant because the size of an agglomeration influences the variety of inputs and contacts that may be made on a pick-and-mix basis during the development of an innovation. (p. 1,111)

Part of the reason for this is – contrary to some of the assumptions of the NCW – the continued and possibly growing importance of multinational corporations (p. 1,109).

Knowledge economies and the role of cities

We come now to a key implication regarding cities, innovation and competitiveness which arises from our earlier observations: that knowledge-based industry now accounts for 70 per cent of world trade, and rising; that an unknown quantity but not unreasonably the overwhelming majority of this production and trading activity occurs among cities; but that only a few cities in any given country are full beneficiaries of the status of 'knowledge economies'. We have noted the multiples by which US innovative cities exceed the average. This is more or less replicated for the same country when comparable analyses are performed for knowledge intensive services and manufacturing together. This was done by Norton (2000), who showed that when knowledge economy firms reach the stage where they are floated on stock exchanges by making an initial public offering (IPO) of company stock, what he calls 'Digital IPOs', the cities highest ranked by digital IPOs per million residents were the usual suspects plus a few. Easily top was San Francisco/San Jose with a score of 142 (against a norm of 1), second was New York (83), third was Boston (47) and fourth was Los Angeles (35) but Chicago was lower at eleventh (13), perhaps indicative of its rather more pronounced 'old economy' character than the others, as we hinted earlier.

Norton concluded that when we ask why this pattern reproduces itself so regularly, the answer begins to be evident. The financing of IPOs is done by venture capitalists. This mechanism interacts with the statistical indicators of number and density of a city's scientists, engineers and other technical human capital which either directly forms the entrepreneurial pool, or attracts entrepreneurs to the pool. The argument is that, geographically,

venture capital's need for ongoing management of its investments determines cluster logic. This is because of venture capitalists' need for rapid
'hands-on', face-to-face management interaction with their investments.
This can extend to 'private clusters' where management involves encouraging inter-trading within the portfolio (Cooke, 2002). Portfolio management is thus place-specific and conditions whether 'contact between the
VC [venture capital] partnership and the originating entrepreneurs
improves the chances that a fragile early-stage firm can traverse the slippery path to a successful IPO' (Norton, 2000).

If we home in even closer on that relationship in a particular industry
which is, despite its recent vicissitudes, something of an icon of the knowledge economy, the Internet, and specifically the location of high densities
of domain names, we see a comparable pattern with very high positive
correlations between concentrations of domain name locations and those of
venture capitalists (Zook, 2000). Zook shows that of the top ten venture
capital locations in the USA by number of investments in 1999, the highest
was San Francisco (1,120), the second Boston (439), third New York (305)
and fourth Los Angeles (225). He then shows that the highest density of a
variety of Internet production and consumption variables (including
domain names) is found in San Francisco, New York and Los Angeles, and
after regressing these variables he concludes, like Norton, that the spatial
correlation is no accident but rather that the location of venture capital
investing has played an important role in determining the location of the
Internet industry. What is interesting about this analysis is that, for the
Internet, the correlation between 'dot.com' businesses and venture capitalists is much higher than with scientists and technologists. In Norton's study
it is science and engineering talent that co-locates with venture capital to
explain the locations of the knowledge economy. But Internet talent is far
less circumscribed by scientific knowledge. Yet in both cases, at the heart
of the knowledge economies of the cities that display these characteristics
most prominently are, not universities or research laboratories but venture
capitalists. We can say with some confidence that cities with a good variety
of venture capitalists are likely to be the more competitive 'knowledge
economy' locations of innovative entepreneurship.

In the UK, we know the distribution of high densities of knowledge
economy business and it correlates with both high concentrations of
venture capital and the presence of highly-rated university research and
other kinds of scientific laboratories. These are largely in London and the
western side of the Greater South East, sometimes known as the 'golden
triangle' (ONS, 2001). A ranking of British cities in terms of knowledge
economy intensity – combining knowledge-based business density with
GDP and employment rates (Cooke *et al.*, 2001) – identifies just ten (out of
25) areas above the UK average, led by London and the area to its north

west, and including Cambridge, Oxford and two other areas within the Greater South East, plus Bristol, Cardiff, Edinburgh and Aberdeen (Scotland's oil capital). Venture capital overwhelmingly concentrates in London too, with small outliers in Cambridge and Oxford, and in Edinburgh. Much of the *regional* venture capital in the UK is public in origin or subsidized by public funding (R. Harding, 2000). Hence it is unsurprising, given what has been said already about the propinquity radius within which venture capitalists habitually work (Zook, 2000, quotes a one-hour car-ride as the limit in the USA), that in the UK the knowledge-based economy should be overwhelmingly found within around a one-hour journey of central London.

Summary and conclusions

In this chapter we have argued that knowledge, innovation and entrepreneurship are significant elements in the competitiveness of cities. They are also closely related to each other. We started with two basic observations. The first was that the advanced economies are becoming increasingly reliant on knowledge as the basis of production. The key inputs to more of an increasing number of economic sectors are based on scientific, technical or creative knowledge. Knowledge and experience are also significant in the development of innovation. This is widely regarded as the single most important driver of economic competitiveness and growth.

Our second starting observation was that knowledge and innovation are highly concentrated in a relatively small minority of urban regions. The reasons for this are not adequately explained by traditional production function analyses of firms. Thus some individually large firms seem to spend a lot of money on R&D for relatively small returns in terms of innovation. Conversely, many SMEs spend next to nothing on R&D and yet can be very successful at innovating.

Our explanation that links these two observations together is that some cities are more conducive to innovation among the firms located there, partly because of rich sources of knowledge. These either spill over from firms, organizations and institutions located in the region or circulate from other, similar, urban regions by way of international trade. This is both a supply and a demand side explanation of why knowledge and innovation are highly concentrated in some cities rather than others.

On the supply side we have shown that some cities have many times the knowledge resources of others. Prominent among these are San Francisco, Boston and New York in the USA, and London, Paris, Amsterdam, Milan and Stuttgart in Europe. It has proved difficult for firms in these areas to keep all their new economic knowledge to themselves. Consequently it spills over to other firms and actors via such mechanisms as local labour markets, supply chains and networks. Together these constitute what has come to be known as social capital, which is available in cities (as opposed to private capital which is confined to individual firms).

Rich local knowledge resources are critical to the development of innovations in cities. Nevertheles, these, on their own, are insufficient to ensure a continuous supply of intelligence about state of the art ideas and innovations in the international economy. As competitiveness is partly measured against success in gaining international market share and this is important in generating economies of scale, demand-side international knowledge circulation is also critical to innovation and urban economic growth.

The research findings summarized here suggest not only that innovation leads to exports, but also that knowledge circulates between urban nodes in the international economy partly as a result of trade. The most successful cities are therefore those that are able to establish a virtuous circle of local knowledge production and spillovers, combined with innovation, trade and the stimulation of demands from international clients and customers for leading edge products and processes. This much is consistent with propositions of the NCW. But the results lend much weaker support to some of its more specific hypotheses about the role of social networks in specialized local industrial clusters as the key to innovation. For some of the leading cities considered in the research (notably London), international as well as domestic relationships play a very strong role, although this is much less true of others (notably Stuttgart).

As far as clusters themselves are concerned, several other important qualifications to the popular model have been found. The first is that the relevant spatial scale often appears to be (at least that) of the functional region rather than something more local, and the second is that in broad structural terms a combination of *both* diversity and specialization now seems to be a key urban asset. Finally, at least within the most innovative of British regions (the Greater South East), it appears that key urbanization or agglomeration economies for innovators have rather more to do with facilitating opportunistic 'pick and mix' relationships than enduring social networks. All of these raise substantial doubts about the potential for policy to stimulate growth in failing cities through strategies to develop innovative local clusters.

Chapter 7

The Locational Dynamics of Financial Services in Regional Cities

NICK BAILEY and SHAUN FRENCH

Introduction

The chapter seeks to understand better the dependence of financial services firms on urban locations. The production of financial services has long been concentrated in cities, particularly the cores of the largest cities, and the sector has been one of the key drivers of the urban revival over the past decade. Within Britain, the eight largest core cities account for a quarter of all employment in Britain, but almost half of all jobs in financial services. These cities saw financial services employment rise by a total of 61,000 during the 1990s and this accounted for 8 per cent of their net growth. Excluding London, financial services accounted for 12 per cent of net growth. More precisely, the aim of the chapter is to understand how concentration and urban location benefit financial service firms in regional cities in Britain, and how these benefits vary for different activities or sub-sectors. Following the core themes of this book, one concern is to assess the relative importance of local factors as a whole in driving growth of the sector (compared with external factors), and hence the scope for local action to have a significant influence on the development of a centre. Another concern is to assess the importance for firm competitiveness of social cohesion, in the sense of shared understandings, conventions, norms of behaviour or trust between a network of local actors. The value of cohesive relationships is contrasted with the value of local competitive relationships arising from concentration or agglomeration.

Britain's secondary or regional financial centres have been little studied in recent years. Most research has focused on the impacts of restructuring on the 'global financial centres' or 'world cities', such as London. These have seen a growth in financial services activity as they play a crucial co-ordination role within an increasingly global financial system (Amin and Thrift, 1992; Sassen, 1994). One view is that the regional cities have benefited in

112

the same way, albeit to a lesser extent. Sassen (1994) argues that they function as centres of co-ordination within their regions, providing a home for the most advanced services and infrastructure. Leyshon *et al.* (1989) also argue that regional centres were undergoing a resurgence during the 1980s, in part by occupying national and regional roles which London had abandoned in favour of internationalization. The alternative view explored here is that regional financial centres are becoming increasingly 'thin'. They may gain in terms of the quantity of activities being carried out, but growth occurs predominantly in routine, lower order services while higher quality functions are increasingly lost to the global centres. This obviously has rather different implications for the development of these cities more broadly. Furthermore, as the mix of activities is very different, the factors underpinning the competitive position of these centres is likely to be different. While it may be possible to conclude about London that competitiveness is based upon a high degree of local cohesion between firms (Thrift, 1994), this may not apply equally to the regional centres.

The structure of the chapter is as follows. The next section describes spatial trends in financial services over the 1990s. This shows that the regional centres have performed well in terms of overall employment growth but suggests that there is a continuing drift of higher-order functions and higher quality employment to London. The following section outlines the range of factors which need to be examined as potential drivers of change. This incorporates local demand and supply factors as well as external forces. The section after that provides evidence for the relative contribution of these factors to trends in three regional cities with major strengths in financial services: Bristol, Edinburgh and Glasgow. This section draws mainly on interviews with a number of key actors in financial services firms and other organizations conducted as part of two of the 'integrated case studies' of the *Cities* programme. The final section concludes.

There are, of course, other aspects of the relationship between financial services and cities which would fall within the themes of this book, notably the impacts of change on cohesion in the sense of (in)equality or (dis)order. Following Sassen (1994), it would have been interesting to explore whether the restructuring of financial services within regional centres was driving processes of gentrification and displacement to the same extent as was evident in London or other global financial centres. Following Leyshon and Thrift (1995), the work could also have examined the impacts of restructuring on the withdrawal of financial services from lower income groups and areas within these cities. The concern in this chapter is a narrower one: to understand the drivers of growth in three regional centres. It is recognized, however, that this growth is not necessarily unproblematic or without negative consequences for significant sections of these cities (see, for instance, French and Leyshon, 2003).

Development of financial centres in the 1990s

Within Britain, employment in financial services is heavily concentrated into the main urban centres, particularly London (Table 7.1). The top ten centres contain half of all financial services jobs but only 27 per cent of all employment. London alone contains over 30 per cent of all jobs in financial services and more than the rest of the top 25 centres combined, reflecting its unique roles in national and international financial systems. During the 1990s, financial services employment became increasingly concentrated as the larger centres saw above average growth rates. One factor here is the improved performance of London. In the 1970s and 1980s, financial services growth in the capital was well below the national average as rising factor costs drove the decentralization of back-office functions to the rest of the South East (Gentle, 1993; Leyshon *et al.*, 1989). In the 1990s, however, financial services employment in London rose well ahead of the national average. London's strong performance might be partly attributed to cyclical factors rather than a re-concentration of employment in the capital; figures for the early 1990s were depressed by the recession which primarily affected London and the South East. The rest of the top ten centres are outside the South East, however, and they also saw financial

Table 7.1   *Concentration of financial services employment*

Size ranking	Share of employment		Change:	
	1991/3	*1998/2000*	*In employment*	*In share of employment*
1	30.3%	32.1%	13.8%	1.8%
2–5	10.4%	10.9%	12.2%	0.5%
6–10	7.4%	7.9%	14.3%	0.5%
11–25	11.0%	10.7%	4.9%	−0.3%
26–50	10.6%	10.5%	6.4%	−0.1%
51–100	11.3%	10.7%	2.3%	−0.6%
101–373	18.9%	17.0%	−3.2%	−1.9%
GB	918,700	988,200	7.6%	

Notes: Financial services are defined throughout this chapter as Divisions 65, 66 and 67 of the 1992 Standard Industrial Classification (SIC). Full-time equivalent (FTE) figures calculated assuming two part-time jobs equal one full-time job. Employment figures are for former local authority districts, averaged for successive time periods to reduce sampling errors. Greater London treated as a single centre, as are Birmingham/Solihull, Bristol/South Gloucestershire and Manchester/Salford.
Source: Census of Employment (CoE)/Annual Business Inquiry, via NOMIS.

services employment increase at well above average rates. Centres further down the size distribution tended to see much lower growth rates. At the bottom end of the distribution, employment in financial services actually declined slightly.

There are also some significant movements by individual centres within the rankings. A longer-term picture can be gained by making comparisons with the rankings for 1974 and 1984 produced by Leyshon *et al.* (1989: see Table 7.2). One interesting development is the rise of some of the smaller free-standing cities relative to the conurbation cores. Edinburgh, Bristol and Norwich have all seen significant increases in their rankings, with Edinburgh the most conspicuous success, rising from sixth in 1974 to second in 1998/2000. In part, this relative success might be explained by reference to more favourable local demand conditions which free-standing cities have enjoyed compared with the larger conurbations (Turok and Edge, 1999). Alternatively, success may have more to do with local supply-side factors or the current asset sets which these cities enjoy, although these are obviously related to the former. Having been less dependent on manu-facturing activities in the past, the freestanding cities have few of the phys-ical or social legacies of industrial decline that burden the major conurbations. This may give them advantages in competing for jobs serv-ing national markets. Other smaller cities have fared less well, notably Nottingham and Leicester.

A second feature of the table is the disparity in performance between the major conurbations. Birmingham, Glasgow, Leeds and Sheffield have held their position or risen slightly, but Manchester, Liverpool and Newcastle have seen significant declines in their rankings. Again, local demand may be part of the explanation, as Manchester, Liverpool and Newcastle have been amongst the worst performing cities in Britain over this period (Turok and Edge, 1999), but other factors are also at work. Glasgow, for example, has seen comparable declines in total employment but the financial services sector in the city has not suffered to the same extent. Table 7.2 also shows the progress made by a number of larger towns which have become significant centres of financial services employment, including Chester, Swindon, Milton Keynes and Peterborough. Of these, only Chester is outside the South East, suggesting that the overspill of activities from London may be an important factor.

Some insight into the types of activity carried out in different centres can be gathered from occupational data. A higher proportion of employment in professional or managerial occupations is taken to indicate that a centre has a greater concentration of higher order functions rather than routine processing or service functions. The dominant role of the City of London in national and international markets is evidenced by the high proportion of professional or managerial jobs in Inner London (58 per cent in 1994,

Table 7.2   *Ranking of individual centres by employment*

Ranking	1974 (1)	1984 (1)	1991/93 (2)	1998/2000 (2)
1	London	London	London	London
2	Manchester	Manchester	Birmingham	Edinburgh
3	Birmingham	Birmingham	Edinburgh	Birmingham
4	Liverpool	Edinburgh	Bristol	Bristol
5	Glasgow	Glasgow	Manchester	Glasgow
6	Edinburgh	Bristol	Glasgow	Manchester
7	Bristol	Leeds	Leeds	Leeds
8	Leeds	Liverpool	Liverpool	Norwich
9	Nottingham	Brighton	Norwich	Brighton & Hove
10	Newcastle	Norwich	Reading	Liverpool
11	Cardiff	Nottingham	Brighton & Hove	Cardiff
12	Norwich	Sheffield	Cardiff	Sheffield
13	Leicester	Newcastle	Bournemouth	Reading
14	Sheffield	Cardiff	Sheffield	Chester
15	Brighton	Reading	Northampton	Bradford
16	Bradford	Southend	Newcastle	Swindon
17	Reading	Bootle	Bradford	Peterborough
18	Southampton	Leicester	Southampton	Southampton
19	Northampton	Southampton	Southend-on-Sea	Bournemouth
20	Southend	Northampton	Sefton	Northampton
21	Bootle	Bradford	Leicester	Milton Keynes
22	Hull	Bournemouth	Calderdale	Newcastle
23	Guildford & Godalming	Ipswich	Swindon	Coventry
24	Bournemouth	Aberdeen	Nottingham	Reigate & Banstead
25	Ipswich	Coventry	Milton Keynes	Leicester

Sources:
(1) Leyshon *et al.* (1989, p. 174 – Table 10) based on Census of Employment data. Ranking based on total employment for individual years. Local authority district boundaries used except London which is Greater London.
(2) CoE/ABI, via NOMIS. Ranking based on FTE employment, with figures averaged for consecutive time periods to minimize sampling errors. Boundary definitions as in Table 7.1.

Table 7.3   *Professional/managerial employment in financial services*

	Percentage of all financial services jobs in professional/managerial occupations:		
	:---:	:---:	:---:
	1994	*2000*	*Change*
GB	44	50	6
London	54	66	12
Inner London	*58*	*70*	*13*
Outer London	*42*	*45*	*4*
Rest of South	42	47	5
Conurbations (excl. London)	40	42	2
Rest of North	38	41	4

Notes: 'Rest of South' comprises South West and East Anglia. 'Conurbations (excl. London)' comprises West Midlands county, South Yorkshire, West Yorkshire, Greater Manchester, Merseyside, Tyne and Wear and Strathclyde. 'Rest of North' comprises the remainder of Britain.
Source: Quarterly Labour Force Survey data for place of work (first and third quarter averaged for annual figure).

compared with a national average of 44 per cent: see Table 7.3). There is relatively little difference between the other areas. Between 1994 and 2000, the gap between Inner London and the rest widened significantly; it saw a rise of 13 per cent in higher-status occupations, over twice the average increase. Thus while the conurbations enjoyed strong growth in total employment, much of this appears to be of lower quality. Their share of professional and managerial jobs declined.

Cities and financial services

The distribution of financial service activities over space has three distinct features: concentration of activities in well-recognized centres, particularly in the cores of large cities; stability in patterns over time; and a hierarchy of centres which differ both in terms of their scale (breadth) but, more importantly, in terms of the range and types of functions present (depth). This section sets out a framework for understanding these spatial patterns and the types of factor which may be driving current trends described above.

Parr and Budd (2000) provide a useful starting point, arguing that the distribution of financial service activities conforms broadly to a central-place model when that model is revised to include the effect of external or agglomeration economies. In other words, the spatial distribution of each activity is determined by the trade-offs between three groups of factors: the need to be accessible to dispersed demand (a decentralizing force); the value of internal economies of scale or scope; and the value of external economies of scale, scope and complexity (centralizing forces). Although they limit their discussion to the distribution of financial services for intermediate uses (businesses), this framework is used more generally here.

The first factor, accessibility to demand, reminds us that the existing urban hierarchy is itself a factor behind the concentration of some financial service activities into urban centres. For banking services for smaller businesses, for example, the heterogeneous nature of demand makes face-to-face contact important for assessing credit risk (Porteus, 1995), and proximity to demand is therefore important. As demand from small businesses is distributed broadly in line with population, this sector has a strong orientation to existing urban patterns. Hence one asset of core cities is the access they provide to large local markets. The second factor, internal economies of scale and scope, helps to explain the extent of concentration of activities within a single firm, but not co-location. This would not necessarily benefit cities unless there were also external economies in terms of labour or property supply, for example. The third factor, external or agglomeration economies, explains the clustering of firms into recognizable financial centres and into cities more generally. A hierarchy of centres forms as different locational logics apply to different sub-sectors of the industry. Activities with strong external economies and little need to be oriented to a dispersed demand occur at few locations, or just one. One corollary of this is that the competitiveness of financial centres at different points in the hierarchy is likely to be based upon different sets of factors as they are attracting different sets of activities.

Some benefits of agglomeration arise from purely competitive behaviour between firms: 'the pure model of agglomeration presumes no form of co-operation between actors beyond what is in their individual interests in an atomised and competitive environment' (Gordon and McCann, 2000, p. 517). The sources of these competitive agglomeration economies include the existence of a large pool of specialized labour, the development of specialized services, or advantages in terms of access to localized flows of information. A distinction is made between localization economies which are a function of the scale of the sector in a given location, and urbanization economies which derive from the scale and diversity of the urban region as a whole (Hoover, 1937). Market-making activities enjoy strong localization economies as larger markets provide greater liquidity, reduce risk, enable larger transactions to be handled and increase efficiency by reducing spread (Parr and Budd, 2000). Internationally-oriented activities may derive more benefits from being located close to a international hub airport (an urban asset).

Cohesive agglomeration economies derive from the impact of strong interpersonal networks on economic interactions. These may produce common understandings or conventions among actors, a common 'culture', or even lead to the development of broader trust between them. This cohesion in turn may: reduce opportunism and thus risk in joint ventures; permit greater reliance on informal contracts, reducing transaction costs; encourage the sharing of information, promoting innovation; or enable groups to act in support of mutually beneficial goals without the problems of free-riders. Cohesion in the sense of social capital has to be developed and maintained by intense interactions, so new arrivals in a given location are not automatically able to access these benefits. Thrift (1994) discusses the importance of location within a financial centre for building trust with other market participants and for demonstrating that the firm will play by the rules and norms of behaviour of the market place. Porteus (1995, 1999) argues that social relationships are important for accessing and interpreting the information flowing into and around financial centres.

The existence of external economies, of course, leads to 'first-mover' advantages and path-dependent development, and helps to explain the stability of the hierarchy of centres. Others have pointed out that, despite the attention paid to 'clusters' in recent years, path-dependence need not rely on external economies (Coe and Townsend, 1998; Martin and Sunley, 2003). Historical or purely path-dependent processes may also work to sustain existing centres. One particular mechanism is the process of new firm formation; as entrepreneurs tend to establish new firms close to where they already live, this gives existing centres an advantage.

In spite of a high degree of stability in the spatial financial system, changes can and do occur in terms of both the breadth and depth of activity in a centre (Porteus, 1995, 1999), and this discussion suggests a number potential drivers. First, change may be driven by shifts in demand. Relative growth or decline of the regional economy will affect the demand for locally-oriented activities. This may help to explain the weak performance of the conurbations compared with free-standing cities, as noted above. More subtly, other sectors may adjust their location to the distribution of financial services if access to particular services becomes of increasing importance to them. The key example here is the gravitation of corporate headquarters to London over recent decades, driven in part by their increasing need to access capital markets directly rather than through bank intermediaries (Draper *et al.*, 1988; Gentle, 1993). As demand for these higher level services concentrates around the existing financial market places, so the centrality of these markets is reinforced in a cumulative process. London's dominance in these activities increases while regional centres lose higher-order functions.

Second, change may occur where there is increased pressure to achieve internal economies of scale or scope, or new opportunities to do so. There has been a significant increase in competitive pressure in financial services, driven by the growth in international trade in such services, regulatory responses from nation-states and developments in information and communications technologies (Gentle, 1993; Martin, 1999). Competitive pressure has driven further consolidation in the search for greater internal economies, while regulatory changes have facilitated the process through, for example, the reduction in restrictions on cross-sectoral operations. Each merger may have spatial consequences as duplicate operations are 'rationalized'. These pressures also drive spatial reorganization within firms, enabled by improved communications and by a more permissive land-use planning system since the 1980s. At the intra-regional scale, there has been a decentralization of functions away from corporate headquarters in London to secondary locations in the rest of the South East, as well as more localized moves within other city-regions, from central to suburban and ex-urban locations. At the inter-regional scale, the major trend has been the centralization of employment away from dispersed branch networks into 'call centres'. These have tended to see a movement of employment away from the South East and towards northern cities on grounds of cost and factor availability, driving employment growth in many secondary centres (Marshall and Richardson, 1996).

Third, the same forces are driving firms to reassess the value of agglomeration or external economies. Contrary to the 'end-of-space' arguments, the advantages of co-location appear to remain important, at least in the case of the major nodes such as London. Amin and Thrift (1992) argue that the persistence of the global financial centres can only be explained by reference to the continuing importance of social cohesion for these activities. These centres remain as crucial nodes for producing, accessing and interpreting information about the globalized industry, as well as sites for deal-making. Both sets of activities depend upon personal relationships. There are social barriers to gaining access to expert knowledge systems, and centres such as the City of London are important places where relationships are built, maintained and monitored.

Evidence from three regional financial centres

This section examines three of Britain's largest regional centres – Bristol, Edinburgh and Glasgow – and seeks to apply the framework outlined above. The aim is to understand the advantages which different activities gain from being located in these centres and hence the factors which underpin the success of these locations as regional financial centres. All three rank in the top five centres in Britain in employment terms with between 23,000 and 31,000 jobs in financial services. As detailed above, Edinburgh and Bristol have climbed steadily up the rankings since 1974, while Glasgow has remained stable: a strong performance for a northern conurbation. More recently, Glasgow has been the fastest growing of the large regional financial services centre (employment in this sector up by 35 per cent between 1991/3 and 1998/2000). Edinburgh has also performed strongly (up 24 per cent) while Bristol has seen employment static. Within these three centres, four groups of sub-sectors are examined in detail: fund management; retail banking and life assurance; regional corporate and commercial services; and teleservice operations. This section draws on interview and survey material collected as part of the two integrated case studies, covering Central Scotland and Bristol.

Before moving on to the detailed sectoral studies, it is worth examining some survey evidence which illustrates how different these regional centres are compared with the first-tier, internationally-oriented centre in London. Two separate business surveys were conducted, covering London and Central Scotland respectively. These sought the views of a representative cross-section of financial services firms and others on the advantages and disadvantages of being located close to similar or related firms (Table 7.4). As expected, financial services firms in the City of London stand out for the positive value they attach to agglomeration. Over a third of such firms valued their location for its access to shared intelligence or sources of information, and they were more likely to see advantages than disadvantages from the stimulus to competition and the access to a pool of skilled labour which flowed from agglomeration. In addition, financial services firms in London as a whole were more likely to cite advantages in terms of opportunities for making contacts, sub-contracting or collaborating (although only around 10 per cent of financial services firms did so). In Edinburgh and Glasgow, financial services firms were less likely to see advantages of agglomeration overall, and the advantages they did see were more likely to stem from demand-side factors. Just 13 per cent saw advantages from access to intelligence or information, but 18 per cent saw advantages in terms of increased demand. Quite different sets of assets or processes underpin the competitiveness of regional centres and, on this evidence, agglomerative effects appear relatively weak.

Fund management

Of the sectors examined here, fund management emerges as the one where firms in regional centres rely most significantly on agglomeration or localized clustering effects for their competitiveness. These advantages stem principally from competitive relationships between firms, although there

Table 7.4 *Advantages and disadvantages of agglomeration (%)*

	Advantages from:			Net advantage from:	
	Shared intelligence	*Interaction/ collaboration potential*	*Customer attraction*	*Competition*	*Labour pool/ poaching*
London					
Financial services firms:					
• City/fringe	37	10	3	8	6
• Rest of London	18	12	0	–9	0
All firms	11	5	4	–4	1
Edinburgh/Glasgow					
Financial services firms	13	4	18	–10	2
All firms	8	6	11	–16	0

Sources: London data from the 1996 London Employers Survey, as reported in Gordon and McCann (2000). Edinburgh/Glasgow data from the 2001 Central Scotland Business Survey.

are also examples of the importance of cohesion. London clearly dominates this sector with over 80 per cent of funds under management in the
UK, but Edinburgh has emerged as the second centre in Britain and
Glasgow has shown rapid growth in the past ten years. Together the
Scottish fund managers have seen their share of UK funds under management rise from 10 per cent in 1992 to 14 per cent in 1999 (British Invisibles,
2000). 'Scotland' is now ranked as the second largest fund management
centre in the UK, sixth in Europe and fifteenth in the world, but the great
bulk of this activity is accounted for by the two largest cities. Major operations have emerged from life assurance companies (Aegon Asset
Management, Scottish Widows Investment Management, Standard Life
Investments in Edinburgh; Abbey National Asset Management, Britannic
Asset Management in Glasgow) but there is also a range of more independent firms, predominantly in Edinburgh (Baillie Gifford, Edinburgh Fund
Managers or Martin Currie, for example).

While Bristol does not have the same scale of operation overall, it is
developing a reputation within the niche area of ethical or socially-responsible investment. Much of this activity does not involve the direct management of ethical funds, but Bristol does play an important role in shaping
industry practice. This is a rapidly growing market, driven primarily by
consumer demand but boosted by legislative changes (notably the requirement on pension funds to disclose the existence or otherwise of social,
environmental or ethical investment criteria since 2000) and the development of supporting institutions (symbolized by FTSE's decision to launch
a range of related indices in July 2001). Although funds are largely still
managed through City of London firms, Triodos (the largest dedicated
social bank in the country), established its UK head office in Bristol in
1995, and the bulk of the socially-responsible investment business of the
leading specialist Independent Financial Adviser, Holden Meehan, and the
stockbroker, Rathbone Neilson, is run through Bristol.

Fund management firms, particularly those in Central Scotland, recognized two sources of agglomeration advantage. First, the most important
asset for a fund management firm is high quality labour so there are external economies of scale for both firms and labour from labour pooling.
Recent expansion of the sector in Central Scotland had led to high demand
for qualified staff and consequently a spate of poaching. In the longer term,
firms recognized that expansion would deepen the labour pool to the benefit of all. Second, Scottish firms argued that there are important agglomeration effects in terms of the influence of the size of a centre on the flow of
market information locally. This was not about the circulation of information between local actors, however, but about the benefits of the 'pull' of a
large centre in terms of attracting visits by non-local actors. Companies in
which funds are invested (and those seeking investment) make periodic

visits to fund managers because of the importance of face-to-face communication to reinforce the highly codified information presented in annual
reports, business plans and other formal documents. General urbanization
economies are also of some importance to the sector, notably for access to
good communications services (especially the range of air passenger
services) and a high level of cultural amenities. More generally, quality of
life was considered crucial for attracting quality labour.

In general, local cohesion did not appear important for competitiveness,
although there were examples of cohesive behaviour helping the development of these centres. In the mid-1990s, when a succession of adverse
developments threatened to erode Central Scotland's critical mass, local
fund managers mobilized collectively in defence of their common interest.
They agreed to ensure that outside firms which did visit Scotland were
given a positive welcome, even where this might not have been 'economically justifiable'. The view was that this had been relatively successful,
although it was not tested for a prolonged period as external events (the
transfer of major funds to Scotland through consolidation) removed the
threat. More recently, fund managers have collaborated on an initiative to
improve recruitment into the investment support industry, an area in which
Scotland is gaining employment on the back of its fund management
success. Cohesion in Scotland was not only seen as an asset: the strength of
local social networks was recognized as a problem by some respondents
who argued that the industry needed to be seen as more open to in-comers
to attract the best talent.

Within the smaller and more specialized Bristol sector, cohesive relationships played a more important role. The concentration of providers and
allied institutions in Bristol has provided enhanced opportunities for
networking and the development and monitoring of specialist knowledge
and information. Links with local independent institutions with interests in
socially-responsible investment (such as the Schumacher Society and the
Soil Association) had proved valuable to firms. The development of the
sector was also seen to have been aided by particularly strong local demand
for socially-responsible investment products and services, which provided
a competitive benefit.

Even within fund management, the stress on local agglomeration
economies needs to be balanced by a recognition of the importance of
external links for shaping the performance of the sector. External connections provide access to market information as already noted, and firms saw
the main sources of process innovation as the major international centres in
the UK and elsewhere. One firm in Scotland explicitly recognized that its
location was peripheral in this sense and that it must therefore incur additional costs in networking externally. Even more importantly, within the
Scottish sector, there has been a marked increase in external ownership

over the past ten years. All but one of the major life assurance firms in Scotland de-mutualized during the 1990s and was acquired by a non-Scottish firm. On balance, this has had positive outcomes in terms of the level of funds. While two life companies (Scottish Amicable and Scottish Life) had fund management operations centralized to London, four others have seen a significant movement of funds to Scotland. Most spectacularly, Lloyds TSB chose to merge the much larger London-based fund management operations into its newly acquired Edinburgh-based operations (Scottish Widows Investment Partnership), bringing around £20 billion of funds to Scotland. Abbey National, Aegon and Britannic have also expanded their newly acquired fund management arms in Scotland. The margin between net gain and net loss is very narrow, however, and the success of these centres must be seen as relatively fragile at present.

In the longer term, consolidation and increasing size may reduce the importance of local agglomeration. Larger fund managers tended to argue that they were less dependent on the local labour pool or the critical mass of funds. A combination of falling stock markets, increased volatility and regulatory changes have also posed a substantial threat to the industry nationally, as they have encouraged pension funds to move from equities to bonds, reducing risks and management costs. These may ultimately drive further consolidation. On the other hand, a more cost-sensitive fund management industry may favour regional centres.

Retail banking and life assurance

The concern here is with the ability of the regional centres to attract or retain head office and central support functions. The growth of 'teleservices' is covered below, although it is recognized that the boundaries between these categories may be unclear at times. The main drivers of change in the regional centres in recent years have been external competitive pressures. In Edinburgh and Glasgow, the outcomes for the banking sector have been positive on balance but, for the life firms, the impacts are less clear and probably negative. The two Edinburgh clearing banks, Royal Bank of Scotland and Bank of Scotland, have moved from being relatively small, protected and uncompetitive at the end of the 1980s (Draper *et al.*, 1988) to being major players, in the top five in the UK and in the top 20 in the world (*The Banker*, 2002). They have taken over or merged with an English bank, as well as developing links internationally, but have retained Edinburgh as their headquarters. In Glasgow, the Clydesdale was sold by its former parent, Midland (which had prevented its expansion into English markets), to an Australian bank which has used the location as the headquarters for its expansion into the rest of the UK and Ireland. In all three cases, some high-level functions (notably corporate banking services) continue to move to London but both cities have benefited from the employment generated by the growth in service exports and the prestige attached to such high profile operations. By contrast, all of the Scottish life firms bar one have de-mutualized and been acquired by a non-Scottish institution, so control has shifted out of Scotland. In the short term, levels of activity have risen through a combination of overall economic growth and increased firm competitiveness, but the longer-term prospects are less certain. For one firm, Scottish Amicable, the brand has been extinguished by the new parent company, Prudential, leaving Scottish operations essentially carrying out processing for an English-based insurer.

The same processes of consolidation have also affected Bristol. In the short term, the effect has been positive on balance. The most notable gain occurred following the merger of Lloyds Bank with the Trustee Savings Bank to form Lloyds TSB in 1999. A decision was taken to locate the combined retail banking headquarters in Bristol, moving the TSB's operations from Birmingham. Senior managers in firms affected by merger and acquisition activity suggested that the numbers employed and the significance of the functions carried out in Bristol have either remained comparative, or have actually risen as a result of consolidation (French and Leyshon, 2003). Sunk costs, in terms of labour and capital, are important explanatory factors. As in Central Scotland, the medium to longer-term impact of such consolidation, particularly in terms of changes of ownership and control, is much more difficult to assess.

Location does not appear to be a primary factor determining firm success in banking and life assurance and such local ties as do exist owe more to competitive relationships than cohesive ones. As large employers, urban locations are valuable for the access they provide to a large labour pool, and urban transportation issues feature prominently in their concerns in all three centres. General urban assets feature more highly in firms' concerns than sector-specific issues. For example, Scottish Financial Enterprise (SFE), the industry body for financial services in Scotland, argued that the Scottish Executive should divert 'significant sums' away from its economic development body, Scottish Enterprise, into new transport projects (SFE, 2002). External connections are important as are local quality of life issues. There is little dependence on local suppliers for specialized services, as firms tend to buy from national and international suppliers. The banks in particular claim not to see significant inter-dependencies with other banks or with the rest of the financial services sector, and little in the way of common interest. Increasing competition was cited by senior bankers in Bristol as a limiting factor on information exchange in the context of local meetings organized by the Institute of Bankers or the Bank of England. In Scotland, there has long been a Committee of Scottish Clearing Bankers to look at non-competitive issues, but scope for joint action is seen as increasingly limited as relationships become more competitive. For most activities in which the banks are engaged, informational spillovers are relatively unimportant and the activities which might depend on these are already concentrated in London.

One partial exception has been documented by French (2000, 2002) in relation to life underwriting and life marketing. Concentration of the life assurance industry in the Bristol Triangle (Bristol, Cheltenham/Gloucester, Swindon) has engendered the growth of a local life assurance labour market as well as specialist professional institutions. As a consequence of such untraded inter-dependencies, actors in particular communities of practice have developed local ties which have played a role in the development and circulation of insurance practices. Although there is evidence that the life assurance industry in Bristol benefits from such agglomeration effects, it is much more difficult to assess the scale of their contribution to Bristol's competitiveness as a location for life assurance activity more generally, especially given the unevenness of such local ties vis-à-vis different communities-of-practice and life professions (French, 2002). Where such processes of local networking are most likely to have a direct impact upon locational decisions is through the labour market, in particular by contributing to the perception of Bristol as a place with depth and breadth of life assurance expertise.

Commercial and corporate financial services

One of the key functions of the centres examined here is to act as service centres for their regional markets, particularly for commercial and corporate financial services. The personal financial services market has been marked by commodification, centralization and distanciation. The commercial and corporate sector has been more resistant to these processes to date by virtue of greater complexity and heterogeneity of demand, and hence the more bespoke nature of the services provided, although increasing regulatory pressures may change this. Part of the success of a regional centre is therefore determined by the strength of the regional economy it serves. In respect of the commercial insurance market, all three centres benefit from the location of the regional and local offices of national insurance brokers and companies. The bespoke nature of commercial insurance business, particularly in the case of medium and large commercial risks, continues to place a premium on face-to-face interaction – between insurance companies, brokers and clients, and therefore on geographical proximity. Similarly, these centres benefit from local provision of a range corporate finance services. In the case of Bristol, for example, these include: stockbroking; venture capital and private equity finance (for example, Icon Corporate Finance and 3i); regional offices of the 'big four' accountants, and of corporate law firms (such as Osborne Clarke, with offices in London, Reading and Frankfurt as well as Bristol, or Burgess Salmon, which also has a London office).

An important driver of growth in regional centres in this sub-sector has been the increasingly international orientation of the City of London (Leyshon *et al.*, 1989). As City firms have focused on higher-value international business, this has created new opportunities for regional providers to compete for smaller domestic clients on both price and quality of service. Bristol, however, appears to have been slower than its competitors to take advantage of this opportunity and two factors may help to explain the lag. First, the local market for such services is smaller than in the case of other regional centres, such as Leeds, so it is difficult to achieve critical mass to sustain a viable local industry. Second, the quality of local business services, particularly accountancy and legal services, is an essential complement to this activity and these had been slow to develop in Bristol (although this is now changing).

Ongoing organizational restructuring presents a threat to Bristol's future role as a regional service hub. Respondents highlighted the process of 'regionalization', whereby companies are seeking to rationalize their operations by concentrating activity within a smaller number of regional capitals. Bristol was being forced to compete with the likes of Cardiff, Southampton and Reading for such activities. Similar re-organizations were occurring between Edinburgh and Glasgow. In the case of the commercial insurance market, Bristol's status as a local service hub is also likely to be increasingly threatened as information technology facilitates spatial reorganization. In the ensuing competition for high-end services, one respondent argued that Bristol will need to secure its position as *the* regional capital of the South West, with a modern urban infrastructure to match, if it is not to lose out.

Financial sector teleservices

The fourth and final sub-sector brings together teleservice operations in retail banking, personal finance and insurance. To some degree, the divide between these new activities and traditional banking or insurance operations is an artificial one since many of the latter have established their own teleservice operations. The justification for treating them as a distinct subsector lies in the basic similarity of their locational requirements and the fact that, as new activities, they have had the opportunity (at least in theory) to make original location decisions. Financial services have played a major role in the growth of 'teleservices', providing some of the earliest examples of this type of operation in the UK (Royal Bank of Scotland's Direct Line from 1985, and Midland Bank's First Direct operation from 1989), and accounting for around one-third of all teleservice activity. Scotland has had consistently above-average levels of 'call centre' activity, with the bulk of this concentrated into the cities of Edinburgh and Glasgow. Teleservices make up a very significant proportion of the growth in financial services employment in Edinburgh and Glasgow, especially the latter. Teleservices have also become an increasingly significant form of activity in Bristol. Gripaios *et al.* (1999) estimate that, of 32 major call centres located in Bristol, a quarter are in financial services.

Teleservices are generally portrayed as highly mobile operations where location is driven by factor cost and quality, notably labour and telecommunications infrastructure (Gillespie, Richardson and Cornford, 2001; Richardson and Marshall, 1999; Richardson *et al.*, 2000). The relatively plentiful supply of labour and property in many of the former industrial cities, combined with general urbanization economies, gives them an advantage for these activities. Evidence from Bristol, Edinburgh and Glasgow, however, suggests that local factors may be more important than previously recognized. Importantly, these derive not from external economies but from the path-dependent nature of processes of development in the sector. First, many existing financial services firms value having teleservice operations close to existing operations for reasons of communication costs and control. Proximity facilitates management of the risks and uncertainty associated with the adoption of new telephone-based forms of business (Bristow *et al.*, 2000). This brings advantages to locations with existing concentrations of financial services firms. Standard Life Bank and Scottish Widows Bank were both located in Edinburgh city centre for this reason, despite high costs and the relative scarcity of both labour and property there. Similarly, several of the insurance companies and brokers with headquarters or other significant operations in Bristol had opted to offer telephone-based services through the establishment of call centres located within the same building, or in very close proximity to their existing activities.

Second, historic or path-dependent processes operate both through the labour market for skilled and experienced personnel and sunk costs in building and office space. Intelligent Finance is in Edinburgh rather than Leeds (where its then parent, Halifax, was based) because it was started by acquiring the core staff team from an existing Edinburgh operation, Standard Life Bank. Relocating such a large group of staff *en masse* would have been very difficult. A similar story accounts for the location of Halifax's direct insurance operation, Esure, close to Direct Line's headquarters in Surrey. Spare office capacity, as well as an existing significant local presence, was cited as a key factor in the decision by Cornhill Direct to establish a new processing and teleservice operation in central Bristol, for example. In both Glasgow and Bristol, high-street banks took the decision to locate new teleservice centres locally so as to be able to relocate employees from branch and other operations in the city-region, rather than making them redundant.

Third, locational decisions may be influenced by previous experience of a particular area. These decisions may be highly cost sensitive but, at the margin, differences between competing locations are often small (Richardson *et al.*, 2000). This gives scope for more qualitative factors such as image, reputation and even personal experience to play an enhanced role, and it increases the probability of repeat business after successful investments. In turn, these factors give some scope for local policy initiatives (such as marketing campaigns) to influence location decisions. Glasgow was seen as having been particularly successful in this regard, as it was one of the first cities to market itself as a call centre location. There are several examples of early investors bringing repeat business to the city, with Direct Line the most prominent.

Conclusions

During the 1990s, the major cities in Britain have become increasingly important as sites for the production of financial services and, conversely, financial services activities have become increasingly important to the economic base of these cities. This is true for London and for most of the regional cities although, it should be stressed, not for all of them. The nature of this growth, however, appears quite different in the regional centres compared with the capital. While both have seen rising employment levels, the gap between them in terms of quality of employment has widened significantly.

This does not mean that financial services in these centres have become increasingly dependent on their particular city. A close examination shows that the majority of these activities are only weakly embedded in their localities. The competitiveness of regional financial centres owes little to local interactions or inter-dependencies between firms. Fund management is one exception, although this is only really a major activity in Edinburgh and Glasgow of all the regional centres in Britain. Even in this case, clustering effects stem principally from competitive rather than cohesive behaviour. Other exceptions include insurance underwriting and life marketing in Bristol where cohesive ties do appear important. In general, however, the financial service activities examined appear only weakly dependent on local external economies, and these are based on competitive rather than cohesive relationships. Some local factors do help explain the relative success of existing regional centres but these owe more to the influence of historical factors and pure path-dependent processes than to ongoing interactions between firms, as epitomized in the example of tele-services.

The most significant factors driving the growth of financial services in these regional centres have been external. Increasing competitive pressures in retail banking and life assurance, combined with opportunities created by changing regulatory frameworks and developments in information and communications technologies, have driven the search for greater internal economies of scale and scope and, in consequence, a spatial redistribution of activities which has favoured the regional centres examined here. As a result, the position of these regional centres appears increasingly precarious. They have become less oriented to regional demand and are competing more and more directly with other regional centres in national markets. The retail banks in all three centres examined here have moved into national and international markets, while direct banking and insurance operations export their products nationally. The restructuring of the financial services industry is one mechanism by which places have been brought more directly into competition with each other. One centre is increasingly substitutable for another, as spatial relocations following mergers or acquisitions show. As decisions to invest or disinvest in a particular location are often finely balanced, marginal decisions can have major consequences.

In such an environment, the scope for local action appears relatively small. On the one hand, there is a case for emphasizing efforts to retain key firms, rather than trying to attract inward investment. The largest firms are enormous assets which bring the city prestige, raise its profile and act as anchors for the sector locally. Once lost, they would be difficult to replace. On the other hand, there are obvious objections to the use of public money to support some of the largest and most profitable private companies around, as well as questions about how significant such interventions could hope to be. The vulnerability of individual firms to external forces of restructuring suggests that local policy-makers would be unwise to spend resources meeting the needs of individual firms, whether local or inward investors. The alternative approach is a more general focus on the quality of assets of each city: the general 'investability' of the city (Begg, 2002). Amongst the issues highlighted by this research are the importance of local transport connections and the general quality of life on offer.

Chapter 8

Urban Dilemmas of Competition and Cohesion in Cultural Policy

KEITH BASSETT, IAN SMITH, MARK BANKS and
JUSTIN O'CONNOR

Introduction: the turn to culture

One of the most striking aspects of urban research and policy development over the last few decades has been the increasing attention given to the role of culture and cultural development in the growth of cities and the quality of life of city dwellers. The role and contribution of the cultural in urban policy and research centres on two notions: the first suggests that urban research and policy is indeed more concerned with the values and re-presentations of those who produce and consume the urban; the second suggests that the value of the cultural arises out of being able to recast concepts that were formerly classified as social, economic or political as something new. Whether or not contemporary concerns about the cultural arise from an expansion of the field of interest or from a process of redrawing the subject of urban research (or indeed both), it is now widely accepted that ideas of 'culture' are in many ways central to city renaissance strategies (Evans, 2001; Hall, 2000; Verwijnen and Lehtovuori, 1999). Culture, it has been claimed, 'is more and more the business of cities' and the basis for their unique competitive edge (Zukin, 1995); capitalizing on cultural assets is now perceived as a key strategy in inter-urban competition (Hall, 2000; Scott, 2000). In parallel to arguments that link culture and economic development, large claims have also been made for culture's contribution to urban social cohesion and civic identity, and this widening array of claims has been reflected in a major expansion and proliferation of cultural policies at national, regional and city levels.

This chapter presents a critical overview of the varied claims that link notions of the cultural to city competitiveness and social cohesion, and the evidence to support those claims. We are asking two basic questions: to what degree have notions of culture expanded the field of understanding of cities and, second, to what degree have notions of the cultural been emancipatory in re-casting old conceptual frameworks for understanding cities?

Embedded within these questions is the idea that the contested notion of culture gives us purchase on a better understanding of urban competition, social cohesion and the relationship between these two qualities. In attempting to respond to these questions we will examine some of the problems and policy challenges evoked by the emergence of cultural policies.

Culture as an elastic concept

The first problem in understanding the role of the cultural in cities arises from the definition of what might be considered as cultural. Almost everyone who writes about culture begins by noting how notoriously difficult it is to define. This is partly because the concept has proved peculiarly elastic, taking different forms in different intellectual traditions and expanding or contracting according to the focus of debate (Swingewood, 1998). The definition problem is made more complex because some authors (e.g. Mitchell, 2000) deny the ontological reality of something called culture outside the discourses used to construct it. Culture is very much a contested concept, evoked in different ways by different groups for varied ends. In the recent past urban economic and political elites have used certain notions of culture to re-image cities in order to attract mobile capital, whilst subordinate groups have invoked other notions of culture in claims to territory, rights or resources. We are proposing to tackle the issue of defining the cultural sphere by reference to policy discourses. We accept the ontological ambiguity of the term but equally accept that substantive processes and outcomes exist within cities and that these processes and outcomes are labelled as cultural.

In approaching the definition of the cultural through policy discourses we are proposing that there are two basic categories of definition. The first concentrates on specifying activities within the urban lifeworlds that are specifically cultural (as opposed to other categories such as economic, social or political). Under this category of definition, a narrow definition of culture would simply confine it to certain forms of 'high art' or the recognized adornments of civilization. A slightly broader definition would include the whole of the 'subsidized cultural sector', covering film, literature, museums and the visual and performing arts. The 'related commercial sectors' would add the parallel commercial activities (West End theatres, etc.).

Broadening the definition further, we could include all of what have come to be called the 'cultural (or creative) industries'. These are the commercially driven sectors such as music production, film, broadcasting, advertising and fashion that are based on mass production and consumption of cultural products. These form the central core of Adorno's (1991) conceptualization of the culture industry. Through this definition and its expanding remit activities with economic value are labelled as cultural, such that Feist (2001) can claim the subsidized cultural sector as having a value of £570 million in turnover that expands by an additional £590 million when including the related commercial sectors. Debates centred on this argue that a bundle of 'cultural industries' are vital as drivers of a new urban economy.

Expanding this definition even further, we could include the cultural dimensions of production and consumption of products beyond those that are narrowly cultural. The argument here is that contemporary capitalism has been marked by both an 'economization of culture' (the turning of culture into commodities) and a 'culturalization of the economy', or the incorporation of aesthetic and symbolic dimensions into most aspects of commodity production and consumption. This also reflects an argument that cities are increasingly spaces of consumption rather than spaces of production. Scott in particular has argued that culture in this wider sense has become central to the whole functioning of the post-Fordist cultural economy (Scott, 1997, 2000). This has led some to argue that culture and economy have become so entwined as to be impossible to separate (du Gay and Pryke, 2002). Others have argued that there is a danger of overinflating the cultural economy in this way (Warde, 2002) and, although economy and culture are mutually inflected, distinctive economic and cultural 'logics' are still evident (Sayer, 1997). Thus this conceptual mapping of the cultural returns to the initial characteristic of this category: the cultural as a distinct and separate sphere of action.

The second approach to the definition of the cultural is based on the notion that the cultural is a transcendent entity. Finally, culture can refer, in a more holistic or anthropological way, to whole 'ways of life' of discrete social groups (Williams, 1958), or to the varied practical resources, processes or methods through which social and spatial life is reproduced and meaning created. Thus social, economic and political structures all become embedded within culture. This is a category of definition that is more likely to be employed through urban regeneration initiatives and policy related to changing the way that organizations and agencies (including local government) function. Thus promoting urban change, it is agued, becomes an issue of changing values and codes of meaning within disadvantaged neighbourhoods.

This discussion about definitional categories used in conjunction with the cultural reflects the observation that the substantive reality labelled as cultural is a contested arena. However, the employment of concepts of culture is related to issues concerning the restructuring of the urban economy both towards new processes of production and new spaces of consumption as well as how organizations and discourses associated with urban actors are changing. In order to explore further both the substantive changes in how cities are managed and function, and the processes by which the cultural is defined, we will move on to consider how cultural policy has emerged over the past 50 years.

Governmentality and cultural constructions

The discussion above has outlined the expanding definition of culture within urban and policy research. This suggests that culture is a socially constructed category, the substantive contents of which change over time. We have chosen to consider the role of the cultural as a substantive reality defined in relation to cultural policy discourses where both types of definition of the cultural are employed. This flows from an argument put forward by Bennett (1998) which suggests that the sphere of culture has been 'governmentalized' (p. 30) to the point where we can only sensibly think of the cultural in relation to government, although he indicates that culture is also the means of resisting government. Thus our expanding and increasingly elastic definitions of culture have reflected a widening policy discourse that has opened up new areas of social life to reformist government policies.

These processes are evident in the way culture in Britain has been articulated in changing policy discourses in the post-war period. Classifications of cultural policy development in the UK between 1945 and 1997 are offered by Bianchini (1999) who categorizes cultural policy in terms of its aims and outcomes (reconstruction, participation and marketing), and by McGuigan (2001) who classifies policy in relation to shifting discourses of cultural policy (state, market and civil), each of which defined culture in a different way and positioned cultural subjects within different discursive spaces. Broadly, cultural policy has moved from a position of being constructed around access to high culture subsidized by the state (a state discourse in the period of reconstruction), to a market discourse in the early 1980s in an 'age of city marketing'. Successive Thatcher governments encouraged a redirection of cultural policies away from social and welfare concerns towards economic development priorities. Culture was to be judged by its contribution to the national economy and urban economic growth through job creation, city centre regeneration, and city marketing to attract tourists and investors. More and more cities embarked on urban cultural strategies with varying emphases on cultural production and consumption. Glasgow demonstrated what could be achieved in transforming a city's image in its year as European Capital of Culture in 1990. Manchester widened its policy reach to include forms of popular musical culture and the concept of the '24 hour city' (Lovatt, 1996; Wynne, 1992), whilst Sheffield concentrated more on media development strategies (Oatley, 1996). Bristol pursued policies of culture-led regeneration through festivals and 'flagship' cultural infrastructures (Griffiths, Bassett and Smith, 1999). (Further examples from across Europe can be found in Bianchini and Parkinson, 1993.) However active local agencies might be in promoting the cultural image of places, the 'market discourse' justified art and culture as 'a first class investment' for the nation and repositioned audiences as passive, depoliticized consumers.

Under the McGuigan classification we are currently moving to a 'civil' discourse of cultural policy formulation where neither the state nor the private sector has exclusive control, but where the voluntary and community sectors take on a growing role in defining the nature of cultural intervention. The period 1993–7 looks in retrospect like a 'phase of transition', with a broadening of cultural policy aims and the introduction of the National Lottery as a major new source of arts and heritage funding through its provisions for 'good causes'. However, key questions for us are how far the New Labour governments elected from 1997 onwards have shifted policy discourses and cultural concepts in new directions, and the degree to which these changes have impacted on urban competitiveness, social cohesion and the ability to manage change.

New Labour cultural policies show evidence of both continuity and innovation. Some policies have been carried over in modified form from previous Conservative governments, but new foci of attention have also emerged reflecting New Labour's preoccupation with boosting the knowledge economy, building an image of 'Creative Britain' (Smith, 1998), and combating multiple forms of social exclusion.

At the national level, the formation of the Department of Culture, Media and Sport (DCMS) has been accompanied by a more strategic focus on the goals of 'access', 'excellence and innovation', 'education' and 'the creative industries'. The 1998 Lottery Act has attempted to spread the benefits of the Lottery more widely after criticisms that earlier rounds of 'good causes' expenditure had shown a concentration on London and elite art forms. The 'creative industries' have also become a major new focus of attention, on the basis of their alleged importance to economic growth, the knowledge economy and the information society (DCMS, 1998). Cultural policies have also been drawn more explicitly into programmes to combat social exclusion and community breakdown, and cultural projects have formed a growing, though still marginal, component of more recent Single Regeneration Budget programmes (Symon and Williams, 2001).

At the regional level, too, new institutional structures have emerged, such as regional cultural consortia, which work closely with the new Regional Development Agencies (RDAs) and local authorities. Local authorities themselves have been given more formal guidance on the construction of more integrated and comprehensive cultural strategies (DCMS, 2001b), aspects of which have been made subject to 'Best Value' comparisons. Thus not only are local and regional bodies becoming more involved in the promotion of cultural policies in a wide variety of policy areas (beyond traditional 'arts' concerns) but they are equally being asked to formalize their attitudes to cultural policy through formal written documents. For aid they often turn to a growing network of specialist consultancies (such as Comedia), organizations that have themselves become effective conduits for new ideas and cheerleaders for ever-expanding cultural strategies (e.g. Landry *et al.*, 1996).

In summary, the reach of cultural policy and the range of its institutional supports have expanded enormously, although (as we shall see) this policy expansion has not been without its critics and raises a number of major issues. Before pursuing these we first examine in more detail the claims and evidence for culture's role under the two broad headings of competitiveness and social cohesion.

Culture and the competitive city

Cities have been central to the development of activities and experiences that have acquired the label of cultural and, as we have indicated above, culture has become more and more the business of cities. Featherstone, Scott and others have argued that place, culture and economy have become highly symbiotic in the post-Fordist cultural economy, with culturally advantaged cities assuming greater and greater importance in a new symbolic, urban hierarchy (Featherstone, 1991; Molotch, 1996; Scott, 2001a). Thus the nature of activities within the urban economy has changed from production to consumption and from utilitarian manufacture to the production of aesthetic goods and services, and these new activities are located to a great degree in cities. In this transition from a Fordist to post-Fordist mode of production, attention has focused on two broad aspects of the relationship between culture and urban competitiveness. The first concerns the competitive advantages that can be obtained through the development and exploitation of a city's perceived cultural assets or infrastructures (Evans, 2001). These may comprise waterfront leisure developments, specialized shopping districts, museums, galleries and other artistic or learned institutions, many of which are increasingly linked to prestige physical regeneration projects or attempts to reposition cities as 'heritage' sites, 'cities of culture', 'sport cities' 'event cities' and so on (G. Evans, 2001; Hannigan, 1998). Culture has more and more become a major urban asset to be exploited in the competitive struggle between 'entrepreneurial cities' in a neo-liberal landscape. The second aspect concerns the economic value of a wider range of cultural or creative industries, often grouped in new 'creative quarters' (Banks *et al.*, 2000; Crewe and Beaverstock, 1998; Fleming, 1999; Montgomery, 1996). We consider each aspect in turn.

Culture-led regeneration and city marketing: the strategic use of urban cultural assets

Cultural assets combine to create opportunity structures for cities. The nature of the cultural assets can vary, and the purposes to which the assets are put also vary, but it is clear that urban policy-makers identify 'culture as a source of prosperity and cosmopolitanism in the process of international competitiveness' (Core Cities, 2002).

Cultural infrastructure as a source of employment and income generation

Ever since Myerscough's influential studies in the 1980s (Myerscough, 1988), policy-makers have been attracted to the argument that expanding cultural facilities in the subsidized and related sectors (such as museums, concert halls, galleries, etc.) not only generates jobs and income directly, but also has multiplier effects through the spending of workers, visitors and tourists on related activities in the catering and tourist industries. Many cultural strategies and development plans now routinely make such arguments, usually claiming substantial benefits for the local economy and urban growth.

In fact, although there are undoubted benefits, as Johnson and Thomas (2001) have shown, the kinds of studies used to justify these arguments vary widely in their rigour and compatibility. While employment multipliers typically range from 1.23 to 1.42, and spending multipliers from 1.11 to 1.76, such results are often difficult to compare with each other due to different definitions of the cultural sector. They are also difficult to compare with results from other sectors in the economy, and they typically ignore displacement and deadweight effects. More fundamentally, they also focus attention on narrowly economic goals, diverting attention from wider but more difficult to measure impacts on issues such as artistic quality, creativity and civic identity. Such approaches reflect an instrumental view of culture that we have already commented on.

Cultural projects as catalysts for urban regeneration

Accepting the importance of cultural institutions within cities, national and regional capitals intent on increasing their status and position in the urban hierarchy have also used investments in cultural infrastructures as catalysts for private investment and the property-led regeneration of derelict city centre areas. The original models were largely developed in the USA (Jones, 1998), typically involving private/public partnerships in the redevelopment of run-down areas with varying combinations of prestige cultural facilities (such as concert halls, art galleries and museums), new public spaces, exhibition spaces, hotels, conference centres, speciality shopping, and upmarket housing. This model, which proved particularly successful in waterfront locations (Marshall, 2001), was popularized by the British and American Arts Association (BAAA) in conferences and publications in the early 1980s (BAAA, 1999), and has been replicated in various forms in British cities.

Another source of influence has flowed from Europe, where public investment and planning has played a stronger role in regeneration (Jauhiainen, 1995). For example, the cultural *grands projets*, which were a prominent feature of the Mitterrand era in France, played a significant role in the regeneration of different *quartiers* in central Paris. Cities such as Barcelona have also transformed themselves through regeneration projects in which cultural infrastructures have played a crucial part, and Bilbão, with its famous Guggenheim museum, is only one of the more recent examples of such a strategy in practice.

In Britain, such ideas have been incorporated into more and more regeneration projects over the last few decades, particularly since the Lottery began providing funds for large-scale capital expenditures in the mid-1990s. For example, the Tate Modern development has consolidated the already extensive, South Bank cultural quarter in London (Newman and Smith, 2000); the Lowry centre has been a central feature of the redevelopment of Salford Quays; and in Bristol the @Bristol museum complex has had a critical, catalytic role in the redevelopment of the city's Harbourside redevelopment (Bassett, Griffiths and Smith, 2002b). Examples could be multiplied from Birmingham, Liverpool, Cardiff and many other British cities.

Many of these schemes have been highly successful in achieving the regeneration of targeted areas, bringing many benefits to the cities that have supported such schemes. However, such projects have also had their critics (Beazley, Loftman and Nevin, 1997; Loftman and Nevin, 1996). Not all such projects have been successful (the Royal Armouries at Leeds and the National Centre for Popular Music at Sheffield) and, as several analyses have shown, prestige city centre projects often generate few well-paid jobs for local residents in adjacent, high unemployment areas, and can exaggerate the gap between city centre cultural provision for middle-class consumption and the provision of more diverse forms of cultural infrastructure in more peripheral and poorer areas. Prestige cultural facilities, such as concert halls, may also provide little more than 'safe' forms of corporate-sponsored, cultural consumption, diverting resources from more innovative, and community-based programmes, where results are longer term and lower key. Prestige cultural projects thus have their place, but the challenge is to integrate them more fully into a broader array of cultural initiatives that bring benefits to a wider range of social groups in the city.

'Capitals of culture': raising the stakes in the cultural arms race?

Over and above the construction and supporting of cultural institutions within cities, festivals and similar cultural events have become another important facet of inter-city competition. The competition to become 'European Capital of Culture' has become a particularly coveted prize in what Richards (2000) has called 'the cultural arms race'. Since Athens became the first European cultural capital in 1985, the competition has become more intense and cultural programmes more varied and all-embracing (Sjoholt, 1999). In Britain, the designation of Glasgow as the capital of culture in 1990 was judged a turning point in generating British interest in the competition (Bianchini and Parkinson, 1993; Boyle and Hughes, 1991). Glasgow's cultural bid was part of its response to the collapse of local manufacturing, and represented an attempt to renew its inner areas and transform its international image. The year-long programme of events achieved a big increase in publicity, tourism, and employment.

However, Glasgow's experience also reveals some of the underlying problems with this strategic use of culture. The Glasgow programme was an uneasy amalgam of different approaches to place-marketing and the celebration of local culture, and ran into opposition from the 'Workers City' group of residents and local artists who criticized the programme for what they saw as the sanitizing and depoliticizing of local culture for marketing purposes (Boyle and Hughes, 1991). It was argued that the Year of Culture was a missed opportunity for building a grassroots, cultural revival drawing more on the city's more militant and socialist traditions.

Subsequent analyses have also put the short-term economic benefits into perspective. The new jobs created did not come anywhere near offsetting the decline in total employment of 10.2 per cent between 1989 and 1994, and the decline of manufacturing employment by 36 per cent. More wide-ranging studies of European Capitals of Culture (e.g. Richards, 2000) have also confirmed how quickly the economic and re-imaging impacts can dissipate. This is not necessarily an argument against the concept itself, but it is an indicator of the need to see a Capital of Culture programme as but the basis for a sustained, long-term cultural strategy that needs continual review and renewal. Such a sustainable programme means paying more attention to a wider range of popular cultural forms, engaging with a wider range of local cultural traditions, and pumping more investment into processes of cultural production rather than subsidizing mass consumption.

In 2002 15 British cities competed for selection as Capital of Culture in 2008. The criteria were demanding: a year-long programme of events which builds upon a shared vision of the city, involves the widest possible range of local people and visitors, connects with events in other European countries, and which has international impact. The bid documents suggested that cities were learning from earlier experiences and trying to make their programmes more inclusive and sustainable. Newcastle's bid document, for example, promised 1,000 projects and a £100 million programme of events, and referred to benefits such as the building of local confidence and pride, cultural innovation, re-shaping the image of the city, and improving the quality of local life. It is indicative of how far we have come from the narrow and often peripheral, local government arts policies of the 1970s.

The role of cultural infrastructure either as public or private institutions or as programmes of events reflects a conception of culture as a distinct and separate aspect of urban life and as a demonstration of the transition of cities from spaces of production to spaces of consumption (of cultural artefacts and experience). However, the development of cultural infrastructure is also identified with the construction of social cohesion through the construction of common identities (related to civic identity) around which different communities within the city can work (we return to this assertion in the next section). The main tension that emerges from these changes relate to the questions of whose culture is being consumed and promoted (see Zukin, 1995). This tension is illuminated best in the analysis of Glasgow's formulation and implementation of its Year of Culture programme. Equally, behind Barcelona's iconic status as a city that has regenerated itself through the promotion of urban culture, there are other stories of a displaced working-class population moved on to make way for the new urban identity constructed for a wider audience than the citizens of Barcelona alone.

The 'cultural' or 'creative' industries: producing culture

Policy-makers and academics have increasingly seen the cultural industries (as defined above) as a source of new employment possibilities, especially given the de-industrialization and economic restructuring experienced in British cities since the 1970s (Bianchini and Parkinson, 1993; Crewe and Beaverstock, 1998; Landry and Bianchini, 1995; Pratt, 1997; Scott, 2000; Smith, 1998; Wynne, 1992). More generally, cultural firms have been characterized as being on the leading edge of structural change associated with the shift from Fordist to post-Fordist economies, where design-led, information rich companies work within a new 'flexible' organization of production (Amin, 1994; Lash and Urry, 1994). The culture industries have thus come to be regarded both as a source of new employment and also as shining examples of how the new economy will be organized. Cities are now beginning to address the problems of promoting such knowledge intensive industrial growth in conjunction with cultural policies aimed at providing a 'creative milieu' conducive to the attraction and retention of knowledge or 'symbolic' specialists (Scott, 2000). Evaluating these kinds of claims requires some deeper understanding of the scale and dynamics of the cultural industries.

The cultural industries: scale and location

Measuring the size and importance of the cultural industries turns out to be fraught with difficulty. In the introduction we quoted Feist's estimates of a £57 billion turnover for the sector as a whole. The Cultural Industries Mapping Document (DCMS, 1998) also estimated that around 4 per cent of the total national work force was employed in the cultural industries. Employment associated with cultural *production* (television, film and radio, artistes and performers, and advertising) is strongly concentrated in Greater London, and employment levels diminish as we move down the urban hierarchy and from South to North. Employment within activities relating to cultural *consumption* (book-selling, restaurants and bars and running cultural venues, etc.) is fairly level outside London. Growth rates have generally been high (a 22 per cent increase in employment in cultural production and the media between 1995 and 2000).

Although the general patterns and trends are clear enough, it is important to note a number of limitations in using this kind of data. Statistics are often based on outmoded industrial and occupational categories that make collection and analysis difficult, with 'cultural' jobs being dispersed and buried across a range of SIC categories (Pratt, 1997). Matters are also complicated by the large numbers of part-time jobs, first and second jobs, unpaid jobs, and high levels of self-employment which are found within many cultural sectors. Different authors have adopted different ways of handling these problems, with different results. In the case of Manchester, for example, research has estimated that 3.6 per cent of total employment is contained within the cultural industries, whilst around 6 per cent of employment is in 'the cultural sector': that is, workers in cultural industries plus those who hold cultural occupations in non-cultural industries. In Bristol, 3,000, or 1 per cent of total jobs, are in the cultural industries according to a 'narrow' definition, but over 10,500 jobs can be identified using Pratt's broader definition of a 'cultural industries production system'. However, Pratt's definition, which includes such categories as employment in the production of electronic components, is a particularly generous one and difficult to defend (Pratt, 1997). Nevertheless, figures for larger cities outside London probably now vary between 3 and 6 per cent, in many cases comparable with more 'mainstream' and embedded sectors such as the construction industry or post and telecommunications (O'Connor, 1999a).

The organization and dynamics of the cultural industries

The cultural industries have emerged as part of the rapid growth of the service economy since the 1970s. Many of the processes at work are common across the service economy, but distinctive differences also emerge in the case of the cultural industries. Hesmondhalgh (2002) traces the linkages between their growth, the forces of globalization, corporate restructuring, the emergence of new technologies, and changes in government regulation. What stands out in many cultural industries is the simultaneous emergence of giant, vertically-integrated, media conglomerates alongside the multiplication of small, often innovative companies; the large-scale impacts of new technologies such as digitalization; the importance of successive waves of marketization and government deregulation: and an organizational structure which combines looser corporate control of creative inputs with much tighter controls of the processes of reproduction and circulation of the product. The job market is also characterized by high levels of temporary and part-time employment for most creative workers.

Scott's analysis is somewhat similar but he has placed more emphasis on the importance of place and spatial clustering (Scott, 1996, 1997, 2000). Thus *production* is almost always organized in dense networks of small and medium sized firms that are strongly interdependent, form 'multifaceted industrial complexes', and which rely for their successful functioning on a range of institutional infrastructures that promote trust and co-operation between producers. Agglomerative tendencies are strong, and cultural products industries are thus often found in localized, spatial clusters in favoured urban centres. *Distribution*, on the other hand, tends to be dominated by a handful of large cultural and media conglomerates operating across global markets. Although the sites of cultural clusters are typically world cities or nationally dominant cultural nodes such as Paris and Los Angeles, Scott suggests that certain favoured cities further down the urban hierarchy may be able to sustain smaller, though perhaps more dependent, clusters of activity.

The problems faced by most cities in the UK in developing and sustaining such clusters are well illustrated by the recent report for the Department of Trade and Industry (DTI) on business clusters in the UK (DTI, 2001).

The report identified 154 clusters in the UK using a particular set of measures, but in the cases of the creative industries, where 50–70 per cent of employment was concentrated in London, no clusters could be identified in other regions using these measures. For policy-oriented reasons a less demanding set of criteria had to be used to identify what were termed 'embryonic' cultural clusters.

As an example, one such embryonic, creative industries cluster was identified in the South West region, concentrated in Bristol, and mainly based on television and digital media. This included major regional production centres for BBC Bristol and HTV-West, and a range of smaller media companies. However, when examined in more detail (Bassett, Griffiths and Smith, 2002a) this broad cluster separates into several mini-clusters, the most notable centring around natural history film-making and three-dimensional animation. The largest and longest established is natural history film-making, where Bristol has cultivated its image as 'the green Hollywood', and 'the home to more wildlife TV specialists than any other city on Earth' (publicity material for 2000 'Wildscreen' film festival in Bristol). This cluster centres on the BBC's Natural History Unit (NHU), established in the early post-war period, but includes a cluster of smaller, mostly independent film production companies (many of which are spin-offs from the NHU) which specialize in natural history and science, supported by a wider network of small firms and freelance individuals providing specialist support services. These firms are for the most part spatially clustered in a small area within the city, close to the BBC. Analysis of the origins, growth and current dynamics of this cluster (Bassett, Griffiths and Smith, 2002a) shows not only the factors which have embedded it in the city, but also its vulnerability to national and global forces such as changes in the US television and cable markets, and the limitations of public policies attempting to spawn and multiply such clusters.

Manchester also emerges in the DTI report as a location for embryonic clusters, centred on television, radio and film production, and on leisure software (computer games). Other research has also pointed to fashion, music and new media design as important sub-sectors. Small firms dominate in most of these sectors and production chains. They are strongly networked and integrated, so that cross-sector alliances and co-operative projects are commonplace. A key area of spatial clustering is the Northern Quarter, a once thriving retail and commercial area that declined in the 1970s but was re-colonized in the 1980s by firms looking for cheap premises. Today, the Northern Quarter contains over 300 small cultural firms and increasingly is attracting larger firms and corporate investment.

In some ways cultural industry clustering is different from other forms of clustering in that there is a much closer link to the symbolic value of place (Scott, 2000). This symbolic value can have significant economic impacts, sometimes with counter-productive consequences. Such processes have been documented by Zukin (1988, 1991) in US cities where the clustering of cultural activities in once run-down areas has raised the status of those areas and sparked spirals of gentrification and displacement of the original cultural colonizers. In the UK, for example, the colonization of Manchester's Northern Quarter by larger, corporate investors and property developers has begun to displace the 'creative milieu' and may undermine its viability. Further incentives may be needed to ensure that 'seedbed' cultural industries are not displaced from such city centre sites. Chatterton and Holland (2001) have shown how similar processes are at work in the 'night-time entertainment economy' where the inroads made by corporate chains multiplying themed bars and restaurants have begun to undermine Newcastle's 'alternative nightlife infrastructure' (Chatterton and Holland, 2001, p. 133).

Cultural industries, image, atmosphere and the 'creative city'

The competitive value of cultural industries to cities cannot be satisfactorily measured using only employment records, revenues generated, or other economic indicators (O'Connor, 1999a). Thus cultural industries also provide the city with the more intangible forms of symbolic or cultural capital (Bourdieu, 1984). Because of their emphasis on generating cultural as well as economic value, cultural industries also play a wider role in creating an *image* of creativity and innovation, dynamism and change that is attractive to potential investors (Castells, 1996; Kearns and Philo, 1992). Cultural industries help cities become 'places to be seen', 'cool places' which are attractive to commercial, corporate and residential developers. This contribution that cultural industries make to the 'feel' of the city, though difficult to quantify, cannot be underestimated. For producers (of various kind), this 'feel' may be imagined as an intangible, non-discursive quality that acts as an impulse to creative action: a kind of Marshallian '(post) industrial atmosphere'. The pursuit of a cultural or creative lifestyles, in conjunction with like-minded others, is often a key incentive to locate in a city, and producers feed off the atmosphere and help reproduce it through their own patterns of cultural production and consumption (Banks, 2002). For the cultural consumer, too, cities may be described as having a positive 'atmosphere', as leisure activities and entertainment of varying kinds tempt the city user with diverse and rewarding ways to spend their money and free time (Hannigan, 1998).

Cultural industries have also been seen as representing the leading edge of the post-Fordist economy (Lash and Urry, 1994), demonstrating the kind of innovative entrepreneurship and flexible working patterns that need to be adopted more generally across industrial sectors. The skills involved (such as communication, co-operation, problem solving, risk-taking, flexibility and creativity) are those most in need in the creative, knowledge economy that figures so large in New Labour and some academic discourses (Buckingham and Jones, 2001; Smith, 1998).

These skills are also those needed to sustain the vision of 'the creative city' (Landry, 2000; Landry and Bianchini, 1995; see also Florida, 2002b). The argument here is that in the future the most successful cities will be those which have found ways of generalizing the cultural creativity that can be found in the cultural industries across all economic, social and administrative sectors. These ideas have been central to the European 'Creative Town Initiative', with towns such as Huddersfield trying to use a newly developed media quarter as the basis for a 'cycle of urban creativity' aimed at transforming the whole economic structure of the town away from declining traditional industries to a sustainable learning economy. Although there is some evidence to support some of the more modest claims made for these approaches (e.g., O'Connor's work on the 'new cultural intermediaries' and cultural entrepreneurs in Manchester), the larger claims have yet to be justified in any detail. Indeed, historical research on 'creative cities' by Hall (1999b) and others demonstrates just how elusive the determining factors can be, and how difficult to replicate through policy-making.

There is plainly a range of economic activities that takes place in cities and that relates to the creation of cultural or aesthetic goods and services. Some of these activities are highly commercialized with a strong relationship with economic capital. Firms and organizations that engage in the cultural economy employ a not insignificant number of people and offer important examples of how contemporary businesses organize themselves flexibly in relation to changing economic conditions. However, there are problems in that the labour markets of cultural industries tightly bound by social and cultural capital can be exclusionary to those who do not have access to specific forms of capital. The employment created can be poorly paid and highly uncertain in tenure. It equally raises the issue of how provincial cities can play a role in the cultural economy in the UK when so much of the economic, social and cultural capital of cultural industries in this country is embedded in the Greater London area.

Culture and social cohesion in cities and regions

Cultural policy claims that culture 'is a means of defining a rich, shared identity' engendering 'pride of place and inter-communal understanding' (Core Cities, 2002). However, we have also indicated the tensions inherent in the promotion of cultural regeneration and programmes of events in that not all cultures (as ways of life) are represented. Here we want to consider a sphere of cultural policy discourse that goes beyond the simplistic creation of problematic city-wide identities. We will consider the discourse that links cultural development more to issues of social inclusion and social cohesion. Concepts of social inclusion and social cohesion have become increasingly important in government discourse and policy-making over the past decade, displacing narrower and more traditional concepts of poverty (Levitas, 1998). Current claims made for the positive links between culture and social cohesion can be traced through a series of reports and documents.

Culture, cohesion and urban policy

Contemporary governmental thinking about the role of cultural policy in relation to social cohesion can be traced back to the work of the Social Exclusion Unit, established in 1997. One of the eighteen Policy Action Teams (PAT 10) set up to carry this work forward explored the way in which art, sport and other cultural activities could have a positive impact on health, crime and unemployment in deprived communities. The PAT 10 report argued that 'arts and sports, cultural and recreational activity, can contribute to neighbourhood renewal and make a real difference to health, crime, employment and education in deprived communities' (DCMS, 1999, p. 8). The underlying argument linked participation in cultural activities to the development of individual skills and self-confidence, to the building of community identity, to strengthening links between individuals and their wider communities, and to support for economic growth. Both DCMS and the Arts Council subsequently prioritized work in this area, commissioning research to establish the nature of the links, and attempting to develop appropriate performance indicators (Arts Council, 1999; DCMS, 2001a).

As a result cultural themes have become more prominent in broader regeneration and community development policies linked to social inclusion and cohesion. For example, in Bristol, more cultural projects have been included in recent SRB (Single Regeneration Budget) bids and allocations. Earlier rounds of SRB funding concentrated more on the 'traditional regeneration concerns of physical renewal, training and skills and on issues of health' (Griffiths, 2001), but SRB Round 4 signalled a significant change. It included funding for a major media project providing opportunities for young people in one of the city's most disadvantaged communities to participate in digital arts. Another thematic project, called YOUR (Youth Owning Urban Regeneration), focused on ways of involving young people in regeneration in different areas of the city through involvement in a variety of arts-oriented activities (Kimberlee, Hoggett and Stewart, 2000). Arts

and cultural projects linked to social inclusion and community development have also formed an important component in the New Deal for
Communities programme that covers a large area of the inner city.

However, such trends should not be exaggerated. In a recent survey of
65 SRB programmes in three English regions (London, the North West and
Eastern) over half (35 programmes) had no projects with a 'cultural
content' (Symon and Williams, 2001, p. 61), although the same survey
noted that 31 programmes had organized some 109 projects with a cultural
content. Similarly, a review of the delivery plans of the 39 New Deal for
Communities (NDC) programme has revealed that cultural activity has
only been included as a specific 'domain' in relatively few of the 39
programmes.

Additional funding for cultural projects linked to social inclusion also
flows into cities through the National Lottery funds for 'good causes' (such as
arts and sports projects). Lottery money has become more important for cities
over the past seven years, although not all this money is directly targeted at
tackling social exclusion. The average level of awards across all six of the
'good causes' in 24 large English cities was £226 per head for the period 1995
to February 2002 (or £32 per head per annum). The average local authority
annual budget for cultural and recreational activities (for 16 unitary authorities in large dominant English cities) in 2000/1 was £47 per head.

Evaluating the impacts: do cultural policies make a difference?

The PAT 10 report, whilst laying out arguments why cultural participation
should have positive benefits for social cohesion, also noted the lack of
'hard evidence' for the regenerative impact of arts and culture. In spite of
subsequent research efforts the relationships remain elusive.

Jermyn (2001) provides a general overview of a swathe of relevant studies, identifying at least 20 alleged benefits from greater cultural participation. Coalter (2001) concentrated on five outcomes associated with arts and
cultural projects: personal development, professional development (and
employment), community development, a changed sense of place and local
identity, and better health and well-being. Matarasso (1997) analysed the
social impact of a wide range of cultural projects along six dimensions,
including measures of personal development, social cohesion, community
empowerment, local image and identity, imagination and vision, and health
and well-being. With regard to social cohesion, his report claims that
participation in local arts projects almost without exception brought people
together in a way that reduced their isolation and social exclusion. The
projects provided neutral spaces where friendships could develop; they
encouraged partnership and co-operation; they often brought old and

young together; and some promoted inter-cultural understanding. Participation in the arts also helped to empower people economically by providing them with organizational and other transferable skills. In a more recent publication for the Joseph Rowntree Foundation, *Creative Regeneration*, Dwelly (2001) reviews in positive terms 10 community arts projects in poorer areas in Wales, including community festivals, estate recording studios, video projects, community theatre and creative dance. Amongst the achievements listed are improvements to community morale, bridge building between communities, increased self-esteem, development of new skills, engagement with people who are often hard to reach through other policies, and the development of creativity and talent.

Alongside such general studies there is also a range of more detailed research that has sought to evaluate the links between art, culture and educational improvements. In spite of quite sophisticated methodologies precise linkages are difficult to prove, though localized studies continue to suggest that some benefits are being generated in some areas. Research in Bristol, for example, has pointed to the benefits of arts-based projects based in schools in disadvantaged areas. A school in the heart of one of the poorest council estates has offered pupils the chance to take part in a range of arts-based projects involving dancers, musicians and other personnel from leading local companies. Research suggests that participation in such extra-curricular activities has not only improved pupils' expressive and artistic skills, but has also led to better exam performance and improved perceptions of the locality (Kelly and Kelly, 2000, p. 28).

The main weakness of many of these studies is the lack of systematic, long-term evaluation. The numbers of people involved in arts and sports projects in urban regeneration areas are still relatively small. The evaluation of such projects often relies on post-project attitudinal questionnaires, but without proper baseline studies to measure improvements from a known base. The evidence that does exist has often been carried out unsystematically over a relatively short time period in an environment where arts practitioners are sometimes hostile to the very notion of evaluation. There is also the problem of generalizing across sub-sectors, since different arts and cultural activities vary greatly in their ability to encourage participation. Interactive effects may also be important: cultural participation may be highly effective only in contexts where it reinforces the positive effects of other, non-cultural policy initiatives (such as skills development and job creation). Finally, it is not clear whether social cohesion is a distinctive category of benefit or an aggregate effect that encompasses a whole network of positively interacting benefits of inter-related policies.

Even more uncertainty surrounds the issue of the relationships between cultural development and social cohesion once we bring competitiveness back into the picture.

Culture, competition and cohesion: virtuous or vicious cycles?

The discourse linking social cohesion to notions of culture centres on the constructions of identities that offer both internal and external motivation to individuals and groups living and working in the city. In this sense it is culture used in the sense of a 'way of life' or as a set of values that underpin the use of the concept. Social inclusion and social cohesion have proved to be elusive, complex, and multidimensional outcomes that can interact with competitiveness in many different ways. But New Labour rhetoric has tended to emphasize the mutually supportive, synergistic relationships that can exist between social cohesion and competitiveness (Fainstein, 2001b). A virtuous circle is assumed in which competitive success supports greater social inclusion and cohesion, which in turn reinforces urban competitiveness. Increasingly, cultural activities have been drawn into this benign scenario in a supporting role. Culture supports city competitiveness in the various ways outlined above, and competitive success provides resources and opportunities for greater social inclusion. At the same time, skills and attitudes learnt in cultural activities have direct economic benefits for the individual and for the communities in which they live.

However, the relationships between competitiveness and social cohesion can work in other, more negative ways. Thus competitiveness can be linked to social segmentation and disintegration in vicious circles, in which competitive success may breed growing inequalities and social tensions, or competitive failure may lead to increasing poverty, marginalization and resentment (Fainstein, 2001b). Policies to support social cohesion may thus work in some situations but not in others, making the relationships between competition, cohesion and governance dependent on combinations of factors operating in particular local contexts. Thus cultural programmes which form part of virtuous circles may be much more beneficial in their impacts. As part of vicious circles, they may be little more than a means of managing social decline or defusing dissent. On the other hand, cultural participation that develops self-confidence (and a sense of common identity and purpose) may galvanize communities that have lost hope into co-ordinated demands and action that provides a platform for economic recovery. Again, more research is needed in a greater variety of local contexts and over a longer period of time to tease out which relationships actually hold.

Criticisms and debates

It is evident that enormous strides have been made in cultural policy and cultural debates over the past few decades. In policy terms, cultural policy for most cities for much of the post-war period was a largely minor and peripheral arts policy, palely echoing at the local level an elitist, national cultural strategy which was run by arms'-length quangos of the great and the good. Over the past few decades arts policy has grown into a wide range of increasingly comprehensive cultural strategies, supported by an array of national, regional and local institutions. Culture is now much more central to debates about urban competitiveness, social cohesion, civic identity and the local quality of life. City governments are more alive to the value of their cultural assets and the benefits of cultivating new and fast-growing cultural industries. Thus in responding to the two questions posed in the introduction, the increasing use of the cultural concept in urban research and policy-making reflects a broadening of the debate about urban change to include practices and experiences such as the informal arts economy and the increasing importance of creativity and consumption to the economy as a whole. These are substantive changes that have been incorporated into discourses of urban change through the use of cultural policy. This has also reflected the redrawing of the boundaries of the social, the economic and the political in cities. Thus the growth of the cultural economy in cities has also forced researchers and policy-makers to re-think the boundary and scope of the formal mainstream economy in relation to new economic entities such as the cultural economy.

There is much to applaud in all this. Concepts of culture have been widened through intellectual debate and policy discourses; rigid cultural hierarchies and unexamined elitist assumptions have been brought into question; cultural activities have been diversified and popularized; and many cities have been equipped with an impressive array of new cultural infrastructures which have acted as catalysts for urban regeneration (at least of their central areas). There is also more critical awareness of the deficiencies of past policies, with recognition of the need to achieve a better balance between economic development and community participation goals, between cultural production and consumption, between 'flagship' projects and local community development, and between investment in city centre and more peripheral locations within the city.

Some have seen the way forward as the further expansion of cultural objectives. Bianchini, in particular, has argued for what he calls 'cultural planning' as the next step forwards, taking the contribution of culture to another level. It rests on a broad, anthropological definition of culture as a 'way of life'. It expands the field of cultural action from the arts and cultural industries to sports, recreation, architecture and planning, heritage, tourism, eating and entertainment, the characteristics of a city's public realm, and its identity and external image. Cultural planning would involve a sea change in local policy in that it makes the exploitation of local cultural assets and resources central to urban development. As a result culture becomes a major focus and a dimension of all aspects of urban policy and administration. Cultural planning draws upon and generalizes the resources, and modes of thinking and working in cultural productions. It is holistic and inter-disciplinary in approach, innovation-oriented, critical and questioning, people-centred, and informed by critical knowledge of traditions of cultural expression.

There is much to be welcomed in such a perspective that tries to transcend the limitations and deficiencies of existing policies, but arguably the expansion of culture to include almost everything also risks the danger of making culture so broad it becomes meaningless. Such a perspective also fails to transcend a number of problems that run through cultural policies and discourses at a deeper level.

First, the very scale and reach of culture and cultural policy now raises problems. This is partly the result of the way cultural policies and discourses have grown. As Gray (2002) has noted, cultural strategies have grown through 'attachment' to the aims and goals of other, more traditional or higher priority policy areas. Thus cultural policies have been taken up because of their perceived relevance in generating jobs and growth, in tackling social exclusion and its attendant problems such as decline, and in shaping civic identities and marketing images. Thus culture has perhaps not been properly considered in its own right. It has become 'instrumentalized' as an arm of state policy, and stretched too far across a range of policy areas in an incoherent way.

Second, the perceived instrumentalization of culture has sparked a backlash in some quarters. Critics have been worried by what they see as the overextension of state influence on art and culture, making it yet another instrument of social policy. Brighton (2000), for example, has referred to New Labour policy as 'the tragedy of Soviet Socialist Realism re-played as a social democratic farce'. Other critics have objected to the deliberate rejection of value hierarchies that distinguish 'high' and 'low' cultures in terms of their intrinsic merit in official discourse. Whereas supporters of the idea have seen this as progressive, critics have seen such uncritical populism as contributing to a 'dumbing down' of culture. In the process art is in danger of losing its critical edge as an activity that is fundamentally hostile to power and the state. The lumping together of so many activities as cultural leads to a loss of critical edge and critical judgement. (For a lively range of views see the varied contributions in Wallinger and Warnock, 2000.)

Third, instrumentalism fosters a bland and overly benign view of culture. This is reflected in the implicit assumption in New Labour discourses that art and culture contribute to social harmony and multicultural understanding, and that a developing sense of cultural identity and the ability to express oneself with growing self-confidence must contribute to social cohesion. This seems to be a benign, instrumental way of viewing art and culture and its relation to social order. It ignores the way culture and creativity can accentuate difference, and provoke dissent and critique. There is after all a long tradition of community art going back to 1970s, inspired by a radical libertarianism which sees participation as a route to giving poor communities a voice and confidence to challenge institutions of power. It is a tradition that links cultural expression to forms of political protest and activism that challenge rather than reinforce local political order (Orton, 1996).

Fourth, it could be argued that in spite of recent developments, cultural policies are still driven to a great extent by neo-liberal ideologies that are forcing cities to become more entrepreneurial in the pursuit of competitive success (Peck, 2001). Such entrepreneurial competition drives the formation of private/public partnerships, growth coalitions and urban regimes which orchestrate investment in prestige projects and growth-oriented policies. In such a context, cultural policies are easily drawn into the competitive processes of place-marketing and urban re-imaging. Cities seek to accumulate collective symbolic capital to realize the monopoly rents that accrue to the exploitation of their unique, cultural qualities (Harvey, 2002).

However, these processes have their own internal contradictions. Competition results in the increasing commodification of culture and place, but this commodification often tends towards homogenization. As more and more cities compete with each other, driven by multinational development companies and serviced by specialist consultancies and teams of architects, there is a tendency towards homogenization that undermines uniqueness and the prospect of reaping monopoly advantage. Such homogenization is already evident in the serial reproduction of many waterfront developments, incorporating variations on the same basic thematic elements. But the attempt to commodify and market 'authentic' local cultures, histories and traditions also opens up space for multiple forms of localized resistance. The challenge, as Harvey suggests, is to build on local cultural uniqueness without descending into reactionary localisms and nationalisms.

This is not easy, and arguably existing policy discourses are inadequate for the task. It means transcending existing policies which merely re-cycle bland, conflict-free and one-dimensional images of localities for marketing purposes to involve local populations in the creation of distinctive places. Some ideas are evident in the attempts by so-called 'core cities' outside London to develop their distinctive, regional cultural differences and become centres of cultural excellence and regional leaders in their own right, developing in a symbiotic and interactive way with the metropolis rather than simply trying to compete with it and with each other using the same priorities and models (Comedia, 2003).

Chapter 9

Neighbourhoods and Poverty: Linking Place and Social Exclusion

ROWLAND ATKINSON, NICK BUCK and KEITH KINTREA

Introduction

The many areas of deprivation in towns and cities exist because of underlying social and economic inequality. This inequality is translated into spatial concentrations of affluence and deprivation by the legacy of past patterns of residential development and the dynamic operation of the current housing system. People who have choices often live where others who have a similar set of values and experiences live. At the other end of the spectrum, people with few resources are constrained to live in the least attractive areas that are generally occupied by other people like themselves. Many, but not all, of the poorest areas are dominated by social rented housing. However, the connections between individual poverty and disadvantage and area deprivation are complex, and in particular it is difficult to assess the degree to which people are disadvantaged by where they live; that is, how far living in places opens up or closes down opportunities for their residents. Moreover there are issues of scale. It is possible that people are disadvantaged by living in regions with weak labour markets, and that they are disadvantaged by living in more deprived neighbourhoods. It is likely that different processes generate these effects, but it is also possible that they are reinforcing. This chapter looks at these connections, drawing on the international literature, UK survey data sources and studies in Scotland and the South East of England.

Urban policy in Britain, like much of Western Europe, has concentrated its efforts on the poorest urban neighbourhoods. The earliest of these experiments go back 30 years and more to the time of the 'rediscovery' of poverty amid post-war prosperity. In the late 1990s a range of neighbourhood-based initiatives proliferated across the UK with various 'zones' and 'areas' being declared to deal with different aspects of social exclusion (such as education, young people, etc.). At the same time there was an

154

increased emphasis on 'bending' mainstream services through improved planning processes in order to better suit the needs of the poorest areas.

This policy fits within a wider framework, the New Conventional Wisdom, linking competitiveness, cohesion and governance, which was outlined in Chapter 1. Some commentators, from a social democratic perspective, have seen the emphasis on the link between social cohesion and competitiveness as providing an enduring justification for redistributive social policy in an era when its justification on the basis of equity and social need is more weakly supported. For others, this same link justifies policies for the reintegration of the socially excluded, in order to minimize long-term threats to social order. This means that the concern about urban poverty is not just focused on life chances for individuals, but also with its effects on the social and economic functioning of cities.

The chapter is also informed by international debates on urban poverty, working within different theoretical frameworks. A key theme concerns polarization in global cities (e.g. Sassen, 1991). Another strand concerns work, particularly in the USA on ghetto poverty (especially Wilson, 1987, 1996). Parallel European and British work has focused on the idea of social exclusion (e.g. Levitas, 1998; Madanipour *et al.*, 1998). From these literatures it can be observed that there are a set of hypothesized changes in large metropolitan areas:

(a)   increasing inequalities in occupational structure, labour market opportunities and household income distribution;

(b)   a larger group experiencing poverty and other kinds of social and economic disadvantage;

(c)   deepening residential segregation between income groups and ethnic groups;

(d)   a tendency for groups experiencing poverty and disadvantage to become more separate from 'mainstream society' and to form an outsider population, variously labelled the 'underclass', the 'socially excluded' or the 'marginal', who have distinctive patterns of social life or ways of living;

(e)   in the context of long-term deindustrialization, where traditional stable employment opportunities for residents have disappeared and residential segregation has increased, there is an increasing social disorganization of communities. This has consequences for a range of other outcomes, including family life, the socialization of children and young people, and crime and social disorder.

While there may be widespread agreement with the existence of these changes it is important to separate out the different components of change, because there is no necessary relationship between them. Certainly it seems probable that there will be some causal relationships between some of these outcomes, but these must be established empirically, not just assumed to exist. For example, there could be increasing inequality without any increase in the size of the group experiencing disadvantage. It is equally possible that inequality may widen or the number of people in poverty may increase, or both, without increasing residential segregation or social disconnection. One of the sources of confusion is that these different outcomes tend to be the concerns of different disciplines, each working in isolation.

In this chapter we are concerned with the causal relationships between these tendencies. In particular, how far are the links between overall inequality and the increase in the numbers of the poor (a and b) and residential segregation (c) mutually reinforcing? On the one hand, evidence from Cheshire *et al.*, (2004) suggests that increases in (c) may be caused by (a) and (b). On the other, the 'area effects' debate is essentially about whether (b), and also possibly (a), are in part a consequence of (c). There is also a question of how far the social distance of the poor from the rest of society (d), if it exists, is caused or extended by residential segregation (c), as well as by increasing inequality (a). Finally there is the question of the consequences of this increasing social distance for the social disorganization of communities (e) (i.e. the system-wide consequences of area effects for social order).

In exploring these questions we return to some of the key issues raised in Chapter 3. In particular, since current policy is often expressed in terms of social exclusion, we consider how this shift in vocabulary from the static language of poverty enhances understanding of deprived urban areas. As Chapter 3 suggested, social exclusion, while often diffuse, does have potential advantages as a concept, including multidimensionality, a focus on exclusion as an active process rather than just a state, and, in consequence, a concern with understanding changes in people's lives through time. Its potential danger is that it implies a false dualistic, insider–outsider model of society, rather as the underclass concept did, and underestimates social connectedness.

In this chapter we use exclusion critically, in the light of these broader meanings. We also pick up from Chapter 3 some issues concerning how cities vary. What implications do factors such as overall economic competitiveness, economic function within the national and global system, size, and urban structure have for the experience of urban poverty? At what spatial scale should we be examining and addressing issues of urban policy? To address these questions we draw on three main studies: one based on the British Household Panel Survey (BHPS), which is the first to explore neighbourhood effects at the national level; another of localities in Edinburgh and Glasgow; and one of neighbourhoods across the London region. The Glasgow/Edinburgh study specifically looked for evidence of neighbourhood effects at the local level while the London study was more generally aimed at identifying influences on success and disadvantage.

Area effects

One of the key ideas which links places with people is the idea of 'area effects' or 'neighbourhood effects'. This can be encapsulated in the question of whether living in one area rather than others might affect the life chances of residents. Research on area effects normally focuses on relatively small neighbourhoods, and this is the main focus of this chapter. However, it is also possible that there are differences at a broader spatial level. Neighbourhood effects may be defined as the independent, separable effects on social and economic opportunities which arise from living in a particular neighbourhood. The area effects approach suggests that deprived people who live in the most deprived areas may have their life chances reduced as compared to their counterparts in more socially-mixed neighbourhoods. Demonstrating neighbourhood effects therefore involves much more than showing that there are variations in area deprivation: these might simply follow from residential sorting. There is a wide range of possible reasons for these effects including increased pressures on services, inward-looking attitudes, stigmatization, weak social capital and the attitudes of service-providers to residents of such areas. In practice there may be a number of different types of intrinsic area effects, some of which do not necessarily follow from population deprivation, and which do not necessarily relate to social exclusion. These include, for example, environmental pollution, features of the built environment, or the quality of local services.

Area effects are often implicitly assumed by the government's urban policy which has seen increasing numbers of programmes directed at poor communities rather than using universal welfare entitlements to target poor individuals. While it is well known that the majority of poor people in Britain live outside areas defined as poor (e.g. Lee and Murie, 1997) it has also been argued that concentrating funding on deprived areas delivers greater levels of help to those in need and helps to break the link between poor places and people (G. Smith, 1999). Area effects are not the only possible justification for these policies: for example, there may be equity or welfare arguments for policies to mitigate aspects of an area which are the subject of dissatisfaction, or ensuring equal quality of public service delivery. There may be a view that some spatial inequalities give rise to threats to social order which have wider effects on social cohesion. However, where spatially targeted policy aims to improve individual social and economic outcomes, it does rest on the assumption that there are significant area effects. Figure 9.1 indicates the range of mechanisms by which area effects may be transmitted, thus making poverty more difficult to escape in deprived areas.

Evidence on area effects

Searching for evidence on area effects is not straightforward, partly because it is so difficult to separate out what is genuinely caused by living in an area, and what arises from the capacities and resources which people bring to situations from their past experience, independent of where they are currently living. Because of this it is important to have high quality data on both neighbourhoods and individuals in order to control for possible interactions, though even then there are some significant problems in identifying effects. As a result it is often argued that after ethnicity, class, gender and other individual background factors are taken into account, the contribution to a range of social problems by virtue of place of residence is either very small or non-existent. US studies that indicate that living in a poor area has a detrimental effect have been usefully summarized by Jencks and Mayer (1990), Ellen and Turner (1997) and by Brooks-Gunn *et al.* (1997). They generally conclude that area effects exist, but are relatively small. More recent studies based on housing mobility experiments (Duncan *et al.*, 2004) do find positive benefits from moving to better neighbourhoods. It should be noted that most of the US studies focus on outcomes for children and adolescents, and there are plausible reasons for believing that effects may be stronger at these ages than in adulthood.

Some authors are dubious whether area effects operate outside America because the USA is characterized by wide income disparities and a close connection between employment, income and housing quality, which are mitigated in much of Europe by welfare states and social housing. The USA also has more extreme racial segregation (Ostendorf *et al.*, 2001). Nevertheless, a growing number of authors are beginning to recognize that area effects are also potentially important in the British context – for example, Somerville (1998), Smith (1999) and Dabinett *et al.* (2001) – although they all agree that better evidence is required.

The investigation of area effects can take a number of forms. They can involve systematic comparison of personal outcomes in a large number of areas using national survey and census data. These can also include focused case studies of areas contrasting on the hypothesized inputs to area variation. Case study contrasts between different regions may also provide evidence about the extent to which the experience of living in deprived neighbourhoods is influenced by the wider neighbourhood context. The

Figure 9.1 *The different kinds of area effects*

Types of Area Effect	Mechanisms
Concentration	• Stress on services • Socially homogeneous households living together
Location	• Isolation from labour market and from other parts of the urban area • Housing market (private) • Housing allocations (public) • Lack of private finance (e.g., redlining)
Milieu	• Social networks within the same area • Contact and contexts for deviance • Patterns of daily life repeated in the same locality on a daily basis
Socialization	• Education • Child rearing • Friendship • Socialization
Physical	• Poor quality built environment • Low housing quality • Low quality or non-existent amenity, such as sports centres or parks
Service	• Talking down to local people by public service workers

different types of study have different strengths and weaknesses. The systematic national studies provide a wide variation in neighbourhood experience, and therefore make it easier to identify associations between neighbourhood socio-economic disadvantage and individual disadvantage; by contrast, case study approaches find it more difficult to exclude the effects of other idiosyncratic neighbourhood differences. Systematic statistical studies find much greater difficulty in identifying the particular causal pathways which may be producing the neighbourhood; richer qualitative data from case studies can provide such evidence, and also give a better sense of the experience of social exclusion in different sorts of area. Below we report evidence from three studies: a national study using longitudinal survey data (Buck, 2001; McCulloch, 2001), and local studies in the London region (Buck *et al.*, 2002) and in Scotland (Atkinson and Kintrea, 2001, 2002, 2004).

The national study was based on analysis of the BHPS data, matched to area deprivation data, and also analysis of small area census data exploring non-linearities in the relationship between personal characteristics and outcomes which would imply the existence of area effects. The analyses suggest very substantial variation in residents' perceptions of areas, their desire to move away and their attachment to area, and their fear of crime related directly to neighbourhood social and economic deprivation. However, when considering variations in life chances and social and economic outcomes, the effects were substantively more modest in scale, although still statistically significant.

There is evidence that in deprived areas both people's expectations of starting a job and their actual probability of starting one are lower, controlling for individual characteristics, and similarly, chances of leaving poverty are lower, and of re-entering poverty are higher than in non-deprived areas. All this is consistent with exclusionary processes placing barriers to exit from disadvantaged states, which are greater in deprived areas than in non-deprived areas. However none of these effects is very large. Thus, for the logistic regression models of probabilities of various outcomes, the effect of a one standard deviation increase in area deprivation is to reduce the probability of leaving poverty by around 12 per cent. By contrast, being a lone parent with no qualifications and no work experience reduces this probability by around 45 per cent. Similarly the probability of entering poverty is raised by around 10 per cent by a one standard deviation increase in area deprivation, but it is doubled for a lone parent without qualifications. These models exclude housing tenure, which is strongly related to the outcomes in question, but is associated with area choice. When tenure is included, the association with area deprivation is reduced, though it remains statistically significant.

Research on neighbourhood effects has been forced to use whatever spatial scale of data was available, and this has typically been at a larger scale than is implied by many of the hypothesized influences (i.e. a scale beyond which regular social interactions might be expected). The BHPS research investigated small-scale effects, down to the nearest 500 people, and how effects varied with increasing scale, up to a 10,000 population unit. This varies with the nature of the outcome. Non-monetary poverty has the sharpest difference, with the coefficient for the smallest scale being nearly 40 per cent greater than that for the largest scale used. Not having close friends in employment, poverty entry and poverty exit display smaller but appreciable differences in the same direction. For entry into work the scale differences are minor, and for expectations of employment, they work in the opposite direction (i.e. they are greater in the larger areas).

It is sometimes hypothesized that weak social capital (e.g., limited social networks) may contribute to social exclusion, and that this may be associated with living in a deprived neighbourhood. Buck (2001) suggests a very mixed pattern of association. In particular there is only weak evidence of greater social isolation in deprived neighbourhoods, and no evidence of fewer friend contacts in such areas, although the likelihood of friends being employed is lower. Indicators such as social trust tend to be much more strongly associated with social class than with neighbourhood deprivation.

Policy often relies (explicitly or implicitly) on the assumption that effects were non-linear, with an increasing association in more deprived areas; but analyses of the majority of outcomes in the individual level analyses suggests a continuous steady relationship across all levels of deprivation. In the case of neighbourhood social capital the greatest differences are between affluent areas and average areas. However, for one outcome, poverty exit, there is reasonably clear evidence of a non-linear association involving a markedly greater deterioration in the worst areas. This would support a view that in this respect concentrations of disadvantage do contribute to social exclusion.

Analyses using aggregate data on educational achievements, crime and lone parenthood suggested that in each case, except for property crime, there were some significant contextual/neighbourhood effects (Gordon and Monastiriotis, 2003, 2004). But these were linked to quite particular sets of population characteristics rather than generalized measures of deprivation, and were often stronger in relatively advantaged areas. Hence it could not be assumed that reducing disparities between areas in population mix or the incidence of unemployment would necessarily improve overall outcomes across broader areas. For example, in the case of education, there is evidence of an effect associated with the proportion of lone parents in the population, and this appears to operate through disciplinary issues such as absenteeism. However, the major differences are between areas with very low proportions of lone parents and areas with average proportions, rather than between areas with very high proportions and the average. There is also some evidence that higher levels of educational deprivation are associated with increased levels of some types of violent crime, and also of an influence from higher levels of male unemployment on increased lone parenthood. Thus, as with the individual level analyses, the emphasis is on diversity of potential effects rather than a single uniform process of area disadvantage generating social exclusion.

This national research thus suggests that there are significant associations between area deprivation and individual outcomes, but these are by no means as simple and uniform as policies may assume; neither is there any clear evidence that there is a sub-set of the poorest neighbourhoods for which the effects are very much stronger.

Evidence from Edinburgh and Glasgow

Research on area effects in Glasgow and Edinburgh (Atkinson and Kintrea, 2001, 2002, 2004) worked from two distinct angles. Taking pairs of deprived and socially mixed areas in Glasgow and Edinburgh, a survey of 200 households was carried out in each. In addition, in-depth interviews were carried out with 50 key actors working and sometimes living in the four areas. The research was designed to assess the comparative scale of exclusion in different contexts as well as looking at the perceptions of individuals well placed to give an overview of social life in each of the areas. By comparing people in similar social contexts yet in different locales the research opened up the possibility of observing key outcomes for people in similar situations. Most importantly it gives us some potential insight into the processes which might generate area effects.

The two deprived areas were similar to many others in Scotland and the north of England. Both were originally built as council estates in the postwar period to serve slum clearance and general needs. They were physically distinctive and separated from the surrounding urban fabric by other land uses and major roads, and were located at the edge of the urban area. Both areas were still dominated by social rented housing and, in spite of successive rounds of regeneration, they remained among the most deprived 5 per cent of residential areas. In both cities the population of the deprived areas was overwhelmingly white and unskilled working class. Levels of unemployment were much higher in the deprived areas than in the socially mixed areas, as was ill health and disability. The majority tenure in these mixed areas was owner-occupation. There were some differences in the character of the Glasgow and Edinburgh mixed areas, with the Glasgow area a peripheral working-class suburb, but with a higher share of skilled workers (group C2) than the equivalent deprived area. The Edinburgh mixed area was an inner-city neighbourhood, predominantly made up of flats, with small households and a more balanced social class structure.

There were important differences in the city contexts which had impacts on the neighbourhoods. Glasgow has some of the largest most intense spatial concentrations of poverty in Britain. The city as a whole also has some of the worst experience of labour market inactivity related to long-term sickness and disability, and more recent employment growth has tended to reintegrate the socially excluded into the labour market only very weakly. Changes within social housing and the limited extent of private housing in the poorest areas have tended to increase the segregation of the poorest. In Glasgow, the poor area was therefore in low demand and population was falling quite fast as houses were demolished, while the deprived Edinburgh neighbourhood was more stable in consequence of a more buoyant housing market. The labour market of Edinburgh was also relatively strong, with consistent growth in the 1990s.

The discussion here is mainly concerned with assessing the processes through which area effects may operate: social isolation, shared norms and values, and stigma. However, the area surveys did confirm the disparities in outcomes, especially employment outcomes, and suggested that they related in different ways to housing tenure and class. Housing tenure was strongly related to employment in all areas, with homeowners being more likely to be employed than social renters; but homeowners were much less likely to be employed in the poorer areas than their counterparts in socially mixed areas, while the area differences amongst social renters were narrower. The likelihood of employment of those in similar social classes also differed between deprived and mixed areas, and patterns were rather different in Edinburgh and Glasgow. In the former, employment rates by class were largely similar for the higher social class groups, though there was some divergence for social classes D and E. In Glasgow, on the other hand, there was much greater divergence in employment prospects for those around the middle of the class distribution. Together these results are suggestive of greater relative disadvantage being experienced in poorer areas by those whose individual characteristics do not imply the greatest disadvantage. However, before concluding this it would be important to control also for a wider range of background factors.

Social isolation is one of the intervening factors which may contribute to area effects. It is, however, relatively complex and multidimensional. Ties outside the neighbourhood may contribute to widening opportunities, and if residents only rarely leave the neighbourhood it may be a signal of circumscribed horizons, so the particular nature of the external ties and trips will be important. We rely here on survey evidence on the extent to which residents made trips outside the area and on the location of their family and friends, and also on key actors' perceptions.

Patterns of daily mobility more often extended beyond the neighbourhood boundary in the mixed areas. This was linked to greater levels of people in work and a greater spread of workplaces, since residents of deprived neighbourhoods more often held jobs based within the same neighbourhood. However, when broken down by tenure a counter-intuitive pattern emerged. Mobility rates for owners were slightly greater in the mixed areas, while local authority tenants' movement out of the neighbourhood was greater in the deprived areas. Rates of mobility were generally higher for the Edinburgh neighbourhoods. Overall the quantitative work did not appear to support the contention that residents of deprived areas are physically isolated. Indeed, using council renting and low social class as proxies for poverty, the results show these groups to be rather less isolated than their counterparts in the mixed areas in terms of their travel behaviour and, for tenants, their car ownership rates. We will see below that there is other evidence of isolation effects from qualitative interviews.

Information on social networks seems to offer some evidence on social isolation. The Edinburgh deprived area has much the highest proportion of residents who have predominantly locally-based friends and family, suggesting that residents there are much more inward-looking. However, in the case of the Glasgow deprived area the proportion of local friends and family is not especially high, in contrast to the Glasgow mixed area, reflecting perhaps the traditional working-class roots of this neighbourhood. The area that stands out most is the mixed Edinburgh area where very few households had either friends or family in the same locality, reflecting its role in the housing market of providing transitional accommodation. However, measures examining residents' links with acquaintances who have jobs and acquaintances who live in different housing tenures suggests relative isolation among the jobless and the council renters who predominate in the deprived neighbourhoods.

Our in-depth interviews suggested social and physical isolation could be observed but that the experience and nature of isolation was varied, and no overall pattern emerged. For example, it was possible to be well integrated locally but distant from the wider activities of other parts of the city. Some interviewees were of the opinion that such isolation was more tangible in deprived areas. One suggested: 'People in this area don't make a connection with the rest of Edinburgh, maybe they'll go to the [name of shopping area in adjoining part of city] but go up the town? Most people have no reason to go outside the area. They've no money to spend up the town' (Community Centre Administrator, Edinburgh deprived area). Adults were also isolated within their estates from the rest of the city around them, but: 'People aren't so isolated as they used to be. People do travel to the centre of town [i.e. Edinburgh city centre] for shopping and socializing' (Community worker, Edinburgh deprived area).

There were additional practical problems resulting from isolation. Some informants suggested that many people were reluctant to leave the estate for work because they lacked confidence. Territoriality (e.g. through gang membership) in the deprived areas was seen as both prevalent and effective in producing isolation. Spatial divisions, unseen to outsiders, were also reinforced by the competition for resources that has resulted from the availability of regeneration money. It was difficult to strike a balance between community ownership and avoiding territoriality. While isolation was viewed as something that occurred in both mixed and deprived areas, however, in deprived areas the experience was worse because of material deprivation and poor services.

The idea of area effects suggests a connection between place and shared values: that is to say, that normative frameworks may be, in part, restricted to a locale. Commentators, such as Murray (1996), have often argued that deprived areas contain normatively deviant populations wherein criminality is seen as a standard response to, and sustained by, deprivation. Our results, however, indicate that living in an area with crime does not lead to it being seen as normal. The desire to move to find a safer area was greatest among those living in the deprived neighbourhoods and is further supported by evidence from studies of the abandonment of neighbourhoods in England (e.g. Holmans and Simpson, 1999), which shows that crime is one of its key drivers.

Our in-depth interviews suggested that there was a perception that some values held in the deprived areas held people back. However, it was perhaps less clear that different values in the mixed areas enabled people to do well. The view of some interviewees was that in deprived areas:

> The attitude to work is different . . . they don't have a work ethos and they don't see the purpose of education and training and that happens more here than other similar schemes [i.e. housing estates] in Glasgow in my professional experience . . . It's long-term dependency on the state, it develops an ethos of dependency and an ethos of 'why should I do that?' People don't take responsibility. (Community care worker, Glasgow deprived area)

Inward-looking attitudes were often seen as stemming from extended family networks that enabled stronger mutual support but tended to focus on the immediate neighbourhood as the territory of everyday life. It was often argued that in the deprived areas what many outsiders perceived as an aversion to work was also a rational response to high rents and benefit traps which made getting a job problematic given the prevailing levels of skills and likely wage levels. Writers such as Bourgois (1995) have argued that such apparently harmful local value systems are responses to economic and social pressures that have concentrated poverty, leaving few economic opportunities.

It was possible to get a deeper idea of the differences between areas when some interviewees had worked in both deprived and non-deprived areas. One teacher had worked in both and highlighted some of the differences: 'There was not as much teaching, put it that way. You were more a social worker a lot of the time . . . things like homework were very difficult and we didn't pursue it to the same extent that we do here' (Teacher 1, Edinburgh mixed area). Elsewhere, an interviewee from the mixed Glasgow area maintained that young people coming from the neighbouring deprived area to his school were 'almost by definition from unambitious backgrounds; they are not socially mobile'. Within the deprived areas, limited social and geographical horizons among children were regularly identified. These patterns were sometimes explained in terms of poverty but more often were related, particularly for children, to staying in the same area for long periods of time and observing that not many other people left the area:

> I think part of it may be unemployment, because if you get an area where people are at work all day and they are all going off and doing their own things, whereas they are not here. People don't tend to move very far, their horizons are quite narrow – particularly the kids. Some of the kids brought up here move very small distances. Even from here into town [Edinburgh city centre] is a big thing for them. (Social Worker, Edinburgh deprived area)

In the deprived areas the cohesiveness and warmth of the 'community' was regularly alluded to. However, the patterns of social networks in the deprived areas more generally were also shaped by the relative isolation and social homogeneity of the areas which some believed led to an insularity that also affected aspirations. Among interviewees in the deprived areas there was a consensus that at least some groups in the population not only rarely went out of the estate but also viewed the world outside as forbidding. But isolation was exacerbated by certain social positions: for example, lone parents faced additional barriers.

Perhaps the clearest single outcome observed from the Scottish research involves the issue of reputation in structuring opportunities and experiences for the residents of the two deprived areas. This was evident in both the survey work and in interviews. Most significantly the question 'Is there anything about living in this area which makes getting a job more difficult?' elicited a response from more than a quarter of residents in both of the deprived neighbourhoods that the reputation of the area was problematic. Only one individual in the socially mixed areas cited this as an issue. This suggests that stigma plays virtually no part in the lives of residents in the two mixed neighbourhoods. This was also borne out in the interview work where mention of stigma or reputation was greeted with incomprehension, since it simply did not make sense to talk about life in the neighbourhood in those terms.

Overall, the distribution of those who cited stigma as a problem was very uneven. Those in jobs and owner occupiers were more likely to see it as a problem than the unemployed and social housing tenants. It may be that those with greater resources or assets with greater connections to the world outside the estate more sharply experience the shame or stigma attached to their address.

With respect to barriers to choice of neighbourhood location, there are signs that living in deprived areas is a matter of constraint rather then choice. Overall relatively few people said they had moved to the neighbourhood because there was no other choice, although in the Glasgow deprived area this reached 17 per cent. However much higher proportions in both deprived areas indicated that they wanted to move, but were constrained from doing so. Wanting to move is particularly linked with the desire to live in a better neighbourhood, and specifically with wanting to live somewhere safer.

Social isolation is clearly a factor in social exclusion. There is some evidence, especially from our in-depth interviews, of strong isolation of the form which limits ties leading to greater opportunities in the deprived areas, though the pattern is nuanced. The same sources provide some support for the view that shared values developed as an adjustment to poverty may narrow residents' horizons. The stark findings about the perception of stigma and reputation in the deprived areas, but not at all in the non-deprived ones, are important in showing how area effects operate. Stigma was felt more strongly in Edinburgh than Glasgow, and to a greater extent by people in work.

Evidence from London and the South East

Deprived neighbourhoods in the South East, which are concentrated in Greater London, especially in a horseshoe-shaped area to the north and east of the City, have very different characteristics from those in Edinburgh and Glasgow. Poverty is less closely associated with ill-health and long-term labour market exclusion, and there are not the same issues of peripheral and physically isolated social housing estates. All kinds of housing is in high demand and a buoyant housing market is increasing the social mix of traditionally poor areas as property prices escalate. Buck *et al.* (2002) observe that London is not a city divided sharply into rich and poor areas. There are also intense population pressures, not least from in-migrants, many from outside the UK, and most poor areas have diverse ethnic mix that is almost completely absent from Scottish housing schemes. This does mean that London poverty has other dimensions, asso-ciated with discrimination and citizenship issues. It does share with the Scottish cities problems of residualization in the social housing sector (i.e. a concentration of those unable to take advantage of opportunities to leave the city). Poverty in London also coincides with a job-rich labour market which has very different characteristics from most other British cities, albeit that for those with low skill levels low pay in comparison to the cost of living is a significant barrier to taking up employment.

In these circumstances what it means to live in a deprived neighbour-hood is very different from Glasgow or even Edinburgh. In Scotland some of the evidence points to a poor neighbourhood being a drag upon people's opportunities, but this is much less clearly so in London. In London, neither analyses of data relating to segregation nor the evidence of inter-views suggest a notable growth of high concentrations of highly excluded people living in large scale and highly segregated areas. There is, though, a concentration of deprived households, including a small proportion who could be regarded as 'truly excluded', on some social housing estates. The most difficult of these have poor housing, poor environments and high crime and incivility, and consequently heightened feelings of insecurity. However, in London, neither the housing nor the job markets are so divided as to extend this limited form of area-based deprivation and exclusion across large parts of the inner city.

A caricature of social life in London is one of big-city anomie. While this is true for some notably excluded groups, such as the long-term sick and some older people who experience isolation, it does not hold for most. The research found that, controlling for population composition, people in London were just as well connected socially as people elsewhere. Importantly, social networks tended to be widespread with little sense of isolation in inward-looking neighbourhoods, even for poorer residents.

The London study also examined employment and unemployment. Here there was some evidence that there were some factors originating in local neighbourhoods which made the problem of unemployment worse for less skilled workers. In areas where there were concentrations of unem-ployed people who were victims of a volatile labour market it was likely that informal networks of job information had deteriorated to their further disadvantage. Together with the knock-on effects of male unemployment on the stability of family life it was not unreasonable to expect there to be further negative effects on unemployment rates in areas of concentrated poverty, with workers more disconnected from the job market; however, such effects could not be easily quantified.

A little evidence of employer discrimination based on area of residence (relating to predominately white areas) was uncovered, echoing the theme of stigmatization which was such a strong finding of the Scottish study. A managing director of a printing firm located in a relatively poor area of south-east London, for example, maintained:

> If you employ people in walking distance of here you can bet your bottom dollar they are going to be unreliable. They are going to have high absenteeism records. It's a generalization but this is how you feel . . . This is a dumping ground for families with problems. It's a deprived area . . . it just perpetuates itself; you can see it going through the generations and it's sad . . . it's social deprivation and it's not easy to take on board when you are an employer.

Yet the evidence across the board for the separation of people in deprived areas from the rest of society from the London study is rather weak. Migration flows, and the demographic structure of London, mean that it has a large share of the sort of people who tend to experience disadvantage. This is compounded by high housing costs, which means that wages have to be higher to make it worthwhile for an unemployed person to take a job. This may also be compounded by employer discrimination. Local neighbourhood factors seem to be relatively weak.

Conclusions

Social exclusion, in both policy and academic debates, has been seen as a process exacerbated by the spatial concentration of poverty. There has been a lack of clear evidence that it is worse to be poor in a poor area in the UK in spite of widespread interest and the influence of US studies. This chapter has shown that evidence we have collected suggests that area effects vary in importance and intensity, and what it means to live in a poor area can be substantially different in different parts of Britain and for different population groups.

The more extreme claims in the literature on poverty in cities, which hold that there is an increasing group living in poor areas who are excluded from mainstream urban life do not seem to be justified in the British context, although the Britain-wide BHPS study does show significant associations between neighbourhood deprivation and individual outcomes and life chances even if they are ultimately less important than personal characteristics. The Scottish study provides some insights into how relative isolation within poor communities is a mechanism of social exclusion. For some people, their life in their neighbourhood is restrictive and this has an impact on values and behaviour that in turn acts as a barrier to wider contact with the labour market and the social life of the city. At least in some contexts, being poor in a poor area can be a source of intensified disadvantage.

Yet this kind of observation is more a product of understanding the perceptions of what it is to live in poor areas than a result of the concrete evidence of quantitative studies which seek generalizable knowledge. In any case, local quantitative studies have significant technical demand which our research design did not fully overcome. But it is important to understand that there are cultural factors as well as objective situations and that the cultural factors can influence outcomes. The Scottish study in particular revealed a self-defeating fatalistic logic about what individuals living in deprived areas could achieve in their lives (Atkinson and Kintrea, 2004).

However, the contrasts between the findings of the London and the Scottish studies and, to some extent, the contrasts between the two Scottish cities prove to be instructive about the sources of disadvantage. They suggest that the wider regional context contributes importantly to individual life chances and opportunities. While there are some superficial shared characteristics between deprived areas in Glasgow and London, notably the role of social housing in providing affordable housing, the contextual differences are very significant. There could hardly be a bigger contrast between other key factors at work in Glasgow and London. In the extensive, low-demand, partly demolished, stigmatized and still declining peripheral social housing estates of Glasgow, white residents of predominantly Scottish origin have to cope with a city economy struggling to achieve an adequate response to the collapse of manufacturing. In the overheated London housing system, with affluence and poverty often in close conjunction, recent migrants form a ready demand for any kind of affordable housing and residents have to pit their varied but often deficient skills within its dynamic and growing labour market. This does present a problem in identifying how far more intense problems found in neighbourhoods in cities and regions with weaker economies are a product of the different operation of city or region scale processes or of the neighbourhood scale processes.

Individual attributes, as the national BHPS study reveals, are also critical. As the research shows, these effects are differentially felt according to a range of ameliorating and exacerbating factors. Car owners in poor areas, for example, may be more able to escape poorer service quality in deprived areas. Lone parents, on the other hand, may find that the experience of isolation is intensified living in a flat on a peripheral housing estate. Low levels of human capital among individuals, both in terms of formal skills and softer personal attributes, is the key reason for the persistence of unemployment as a characteristic source of disadvantage in the London labour market.

All of this raises important questions about what policy should be towards deprived areas. Area-based initiatives have acted as a brake on some poor areas getting worse or have slowed down decline but have not made a fundamental difference to their role (Dabinett *et al.*, 2001). Current English policy goes along with the idea that living in a poor area is a source of disadvantage ('no-one shall be disadvantaged by where they live'). But it stops short of proposing routes to a more spatially integrated urban society as opposed to the thinning-out of poverty or its superficial amelioration in targeted areas. Atkinson and Kintrea (2002) have suggested the policy prescription which follows from neighbourhood effects is to more seriously desegregate deprived communities by using the planning system and paying attention to the social geography of social housing investment. They also suggest intensifying existing area-based initiatives with the aim of transforming the social base of existing deprived communities. However, Buck *et al.* (2002) maintain that it is not evident that disadvantaged people in inner London would find any gain in moving out to more socially mixed areas, not least because poor areas supply more of the kinds of services that poor people rely on, including many voluntary and cultural services aimed at excluded minority and recent migrant groups.

This, however, does not mean that concentrations of disadvantage in London are not important from the viewpoint of social justice but just that, in themselves, they are not clear sources of further disadvantage. The weakness of the evidence on quantifiable area effects should not be used to underestimate the personal impact of living in areas of degraded quality, high crime and poor basic services. However, in thinking about how social inclusion can be achieved it would pay also to concentrate on the collision between two endemic problems: low pay at the bottom end of the job market and high housing costs combined with deep benefit traps.

Chapter 10

Gentrification*

TIM BUTLER

Introduction

The last quarter of the twentieth century saw the emergence of gentrification (the up scaling of previously working class housing in inner city areas)
in many of the world's major cities, generally those with a developed
services economy. The gentrification of large metropolitan centres has
differed quite significantly from that in other cities. This chapter focuses
mainly on the gentrification of inner London over the past quarter of a
century but draws some contrasts with the emergence of gentrified areas in
other major cities in the UK. It is argued that London's gentrification, and
its distinctiveness, is largely driven by its cosmopolitanism as a global
centre for services, culture and knowledge. As such, it acts as a kind of
benchmark by which emerging middle-class neighbourhoods elsewhere in
the UK compare themselves. For example, in Mike Savage's (Savage *et al.*,
2004) work on the gentrification of Chorlton in Manchester, not only he but
also many of his respondents make comparisons between living in
Chorlton and gentrified areas of London.

Gentrification is an important analogue for the social changes that have
accompanied the urban restructuring of the late twentieth century in which
cities have become increasingly de-industrialized, in competition with one
another and in an uneasy relationship with both their national states and
their surrounding regions. The ones that have emerged as at least partially
successful in this competitive environment have seen themselves take on
new functions: as centres for the *production* of increasingly sophisticated
financial instruments, of business and other services, and of culture,
knowledge and media. Whereas previously the function of urban-based
services was to oil the workings of the industrial economy and/or to function as the cultural glue that held their class-based networks together, it is

* I would like to acknowledge the contribution of Garry Robson, who undertook
much of the fieldwork on which part of this chapter was based and who was
responsible for many of the ideas discussed here.

not too great an exaggeration to claim that it is these forces which now drive the urban economy. At a more general level, it might be argued that successful urban economies are *social* economies (Amin, 2000) whose work forces are no longer primarily the huddled industrial proletariat but the disparate middle classes.

Gentrification emerged at some time in the late 1960s as a bit of game in both the media and the academy as a way of making fun of wayward members of the middle-class who seemed to want to live in run-down areas of north London and bring back to life Victorian middle-class houses that had long descended into neglect and multiple occupation (Glass 1964). In contemporary urban terms they were a 'neither/nor' class (Jager 1986). The upper class with their hangers-on and the intelligentsia had both of course never left the city and continued to populate large swathes of it (Mayfair, Kensington, Chelsea, Hampstead and Blackheath, for example), whilst the working class were increasingly desperate to join the middle classes in the white suburbs. In a way, it is fair to characterize the incomers as a 'cultural new class' as they were often referred to in North America (Brint, 1984; Ehrenreich, 1989; Gouldner, 1979), as distinct from the social and business aristocracy, the culturally rich (but often cash poor) intelligentsia and the largely philistine and socially insecure managerial middle classes. This 'new class' crossed the boundaries between private and public, high and low culture, and not for the first time the media stereotypes ('The Stringalongs' from the *Trendy Ape* strip cartoon in *The Listener*, for example) got it about right. Looking back, we are able to see these people – journalists, broadcasters, advertising executives, plus media-savvy lawyers, bankers and academics – as the shock troops of what is now termed the 'new economy'. The gentrification of London has therefore represented the emergence of a new and social economy whose rise has powered, and been driven by, the development of a particular form of economic globalization over the last 25 years. So what started off perhaps as a source of media fun has now become central to the social and economic changes that have occurred across the UK economy. These changes have increasingly driven wedges between what has happened in London and Britain's other cities and, in both cases, in their relations with their respective suburbs and regions. Inner London's housing market has now been largely removed from the UK and is benchmarked against that of New York and Paris.

In the transformation of London from what was essentially a ruling and working-class city to what is increasingly a middle-class city, both the city and the middle class have changed. Both have become more variegated and the ecology of the city has emerged as a dappled mosaic of cultural and economic assets deployed in a complex variety of social backgrounds, lifestyles, aspirations and housing markets (Ann Power uses the apt description 'speckled' to describe the ecology of gentrification in Britain's cities). In almost all cases, the middle classes are in a minority but, every-where they have settled, their influence on the local ambience has been out of all proportion to their numbers. Of course, there are still large swathes of London which are largely unaffected by this, either because they are beyond the means of all but the best paid banker or pop star or because of the still dominant social housing projects of an earlier age. For others (and this increasingly includes middle-class people), the workings of the inner London housing market mean that without a household income of – say – £70,000 you cannot afford even a small flat in inner London (for example, I estimate that two university professors with no appreciable savings would be hard put to it to buy a small flat together in Islington). Thus gentrifica-tion, in London and elsewhere, is a way of describing and explaining how the social structure of cities has changed over the last 25 years and how this is now affected on the one hand by lifestyle, choice and aspiration and, on the other, is constrained by issues of social exclusion, globalization and economic restructuring.

It is not just the city that has changed; so also has our conception of social class, having for decades been one of the most trustworthy social measurement devices in sociology. At one time, most sociologists would disagree about the nature of class but concur that it was the central concept in ordering social relations: a claim that has now become hotly debated. According to Savage *et al*. (2001), what unites the various critiques of the 'class societies of capitalist-industrial society' is 'the idea of the end of class' (p. 877), from which he develops a third way position which argues that 'class identities are ambivalent and weak, but that this is compatible with a form of class analysis' (p. 877). Whilst Goldthorpe gets around the problem of class identity by using rational action theory, Savage draws on Bourdieu's work, which essentially holds that the power of class is such that people find it difficult to articulate it in class terms. Savage and his co-authors (2001) investigate this in a study of four areas in and around Manchester. Their conclusion is that people use class to describe the soci-ety around them but are very shy or at best ambivalent about locating them-selves in that class structure; class is not a way in which they choose to explore their identity. This is particularly the case with those who could now be located within the middle class, who stress 'ordinariness' as the defining characteristic of their middle classness or their normalcy in the sense that they are of neither of the extremes of working or upper class. 'Whereas Bourdieu would direct attention to the multiple strategies used to display and construct cultural distinction of one type or another, nearly our entire sample chose to play down any cultural distinction they may be able to lay claim to in order to play up their ordinariness' (Savage *et al*., 2001, p. 889). In other words, they are resisting any form of social fixing or typing in order to be 'themselves'. However, as Savage notes, they in fact understand their position in terms of a complex juxtaposition between themselves as individuals and social class as a kind of social benchmark.

This insight has a lot to recommend itself in understanding the gentrification process in general and that of London in particular over recent years. Partly, this is because there is a complex relationship between the wish for 'ordinariness' and 'distinctiveness' in the gentrification process where, I argue, people are seeking out different ways of living distinctively in ordinary settings. It is also relevant because the other aspect that has become lost is the triangulation between social class, social networks and spatial location (Blokland and Savage, 2001). The study of working-class neighbourhoods, such as coal mining villages or London's East End, tended to focus on the class aspect and the spatial arrangements received relatively little attention. It was assumed that they were 'relatively class-homogeneous, small uncontested places that hosted cohesive communities' and that the identities that could be drawn from living in a certain place were 'quite straightforward' (Blokland and Savage, 2001, p. 223). The same point might be made about single class suburbs in which many middle-class people were brought up. However, the creation of mixed class communities in which people are choosing to live in close spatial (if not social) proximity to other groups gives rise to the need to understand what the ties of space are and how identities are constructed. These identities are likely to be multiple and contested and to vary from place to place. The extent to which they are driven by space and class needs to be investigated.

The chapter draws on recent work, undertaken in London as part of the ESRC *Cities Programme*, to explore the ways in which the urban middle classes have responded to the externalities of restructuring and globalization. It is suggested that they have done so in ways which draw upon their own cultural values and aspirations as resources with which to adapt to the new social and economic realities. Neither can all middle-class gentrifiers simplistically be seen as 'winners'; for many of them, the neo-liberalism that has been associated with globalization has posed a major threat to their way of life. Following some general comments about urban change over the last two decades, the chapter examines the gentrification process in London over this period. It is argued that, on the one hand, the gentrification process in London has been driven by its development as a global city and, on the other, by the personal biographies of its middle-class inhabitants. It is suggested that the variation noted in the gentrification process can be ascribed, in part at least, to the ways in which different groups engage in the process of 'narrative construction' which is associated with different areas. What they share is some form of idealized notion of community and association which provides a counterpoint to the lived reality of respondents' increasingly unstable everyday lives.

The social and urban context of gentrification

For much of the last half of the twentieth century, large cities lost population and this remains true of southern European cities. Elsewhere in Europe, most particularly in Germany, they are growing once again. 'Liveability' appears to be one of the main criteria for success, which often translates into having clearly identifiable pre-industrial 'heritage' features (for instance, a university quarter: Cheshire, 1995). In Britain this may work as far as small cities are concerned (Norwich and York might be examples, despite the fact that both only acquired universities outside the city in the 1960s). Of the large metropolitan conurbations, only London has staunched the population flow. London suffered a massive haemorrhaging of its population in the decades following the Second World War, particularly between 1971 and 1981 when many of its inner boroughs suffered a *net* out-migration of 40 per cent. This slowed in the 1980s and the 2001 census shows an overall gain of population compared to 1991; this growth is particularly marked in the inner London boroughs. This contrasts in several ways to the trends in the other conurbations where the loss of population continues, and where it is those with most economic and social assets who are repopulating the inner areas, which is the opposite of elsewhere (Champion and Fisher, 2004; Ford and Champion, 2000). It is a complex picture but it seems that in London, as people acquire middle-range skills they tend to leave, whereas those with no skills and assets stay as do those with high stocks of human and cultural capital. In particular, it is professional workers and their households who are contributing to the rebuilding of inner London's population. Elsewhere in the UK, these are the people who are leading the exodus from the city and going mainly to surrounding suburbs and small towns. In this sense, at least, London is different from other cities.

The reasons for this are complex but in essence, as I have already argued, have to do with London's status as a globalized and highly cosmopolitan capital city, whose labour and housing markets are qualitatively different from those elsewhere in the UK. The nearest exception is Edinburgh which is the seat of Scottish governance and the UK's second finance centre, with a housing market to match (Bondi, 1999). London works a 20-hour day and its key workers include the intermediaries who enable it to function as a financial and services node in the global economy. Its service industries act as a powerful magnet to the brightest and most ambitious graduates from the UK higher education system and from abroad (the birthplace of nearly a quarter of its population). Its professional labour market is probably more feminized than elsewhere. These labour market factors have become more exaggerated in the last 20 years or so. Functions which were undertaken in-house during the industrial age are now contracted and brokered through a series of specialized functionaries which has given rise to whole new industries of regulators, lobbyists, consultants and lawyers. These are concentrated in London and work on a national and international stage. The pressure on such people to minimize travelling time rather than tackling long commuter journeys has given a huge boost to living in the inner city. This is particularly the case where both partners in a household work in central London or the City and where there are issues of child care.

However, this functional and rational explanation does not satisfactorily explain why inner London has become a place that people do not rush to escape at the end of the working day. For many middle-class professionals, the suburbs were their childhood homes and it was 'death out there': a cultural desert based around bland sameness. The inner city offers a direct contrast; not only are there opportunities for entertainment but also for difference and excitement. For those for whom the cultural capital rich environment of higher education was a defining moment, there is no going back. On the other hand, for many inner London working-class families, even if their children graduate into the ranks of the middle class it is simply not possible for them to stay in the inner city, and the pull of the suburbs and beyond is irresistible. Whilst the employed population may have experienced an upgrading of occupation skills (Hamnett, 1994a, 1994b, but see also Breughel, 1996), the overall effect is that housing constraints are leading to a polarization in many parts of inner London. The defining distinction amongst those living in inner London is between those who are relatively advantaged in cultural and economic terms and able to access the private housing market, and those who are excluded from this marker of social inclusion. Such has been the dynamic of the gentrification of inner London.

As with class, gentrification is a process about which we feel ambivalent. The social, cultural and housing map of Britain has become far more complex, diverse and apparently contradictory over recent decades. Relations between the social, spatial and economic have been re-ordered in often quite fundamental ways. Gentrification has been a close and faithful handmaiden to this process. It has reflected in its different ways the upscaling, downsizing and conflicting nature of what has been happening in cities in the UK and elsewhere. However, gentrification is only one of the ways in which the middle classes have been manifesting their changed existence. As the middle classes have become more diverse, so have their housing choices. Some traditional suburbs have become relatively marginalized and have experienced stress and threat as a consequence of demographic transitions and economic restructuring (*The Economist*, 19 January 2002). Shops have closed down with the growth of car ownership and dependency and these suburbs no longer meet emerging middle-class household needs.

Congestion, poor road links and unreliable public transport mean that such places no longer adequately serve either the inner city or outer fringe. As a consequence, there has been a growth in a variety of new build developments on the edges of cities with ready access to motorway links and shopping centres, as well as in self-contained developments around what once were free standing towns and villages (Wynne, 1998). All are built with the car in mind and to meet the needs of families, often with two working parents.

At the same time back in the city, there have been an increasing number of new build developments or change-of-use conversions, of which the most extensive, expensive and spectacular are those in London's Docklands. A number of major cities have encouraged such developments, usually extolling the virtues of living in or near the 24/7 vibrancy of the city centre entertainment districts of major regional cities. Birmingham, Leeds and Manchester are all examples of this, and in the latter two cases the developments were fuelled, in part at least, by large student villages which have helped to sustain a burgeoning central city, night time economy. In Manchester, the so-called 'pink pound' has been a theme in the marketing strategies for such developments, which was no doubt helped by the success of the television series *Queer as Folk* in the case of Manchester, where Canal Street is now known internationally as the centre of the city's gay quarter. In the case of Leeds, considerable publicity was given to the sale of the city's first half-million pound city centre apartment.

Nevertheless, these often spectacular developments notwithstanding, there is a qualitative difference between the scale of gentrification in London and the developments taking place elsewhere in British cities. It is only in Edinburgh, albeit on a much smaller scale, that there has been the same colonization of the inner areas of the city by the middle classes. What London and Edinburgh have in common is a concentration of financial service industries (with all their supporting panoply of expertise) and being a capital city. However, not even Edinburgh with its financial services, governmental offices and international festivals can compete with the 'pull' of London as a global, metropolitan centre. Thus although we can identify areas in other cities which are gentrifying – Didsbury or Chorlton in Manchester, Kingsbury in Bristol – they are not of the same order as what has been taking place in Barnsbury, Battersea or Brixton.

The gentrification of London

The term 'gentrification' was first coined, as we have already noted, by the urban sociologist Ruth Glass 40 years ago in her observations about what was taking place in parts of north London:

One by one, many of the working class quarters of London have been invaded by the middle-class – upper and lower – shabby modest mews and cottages . . . have been taken over when their leases expired, and have become elegant, expensive residences. Larger Victorian houses, downgraded in an earlier or recent period – which were used as lodging houses or were otherwise in multiple occupation – have been upgraded once again . . . Once this process of 'gentrification' starts in a district it goes on rapidly until all or most of the working class occupiers are displaced and the whole social character of the district is changed. (Glass, 1964, p. xviii)

This description of gentrification is almost chilling in its prescience about how London has been transformed in the years which have elapsed since these initial observations. Her focus on working-class displacement and the changing 'social character' have also proved remarkably accurate in relation to what has happened and what have been the main themes in the study of gentrification. This displacement of working-class residents was, we now know, part of a larger picture in which industrial employment was to suffer massively particularly in large metropolitan centres such as London which was to lose upwards of half a million manufacturing jobs over the period (Buck *et al.* 1986). We have witnessed a generational change take place in which 'working-class' jobs have largely been replaced by middle-class jobs and insecure marginal employment; a process of occupational upgrading (Hamnett, 1994a) and 'sedimentation and bump-ing down' (Buck and Gordon, 2000) have taken place at more or less the same time. In housing market terms, owner occupation has spread out of the reach of not only the emasculated working class but many of the middle class, and social housing has become the new social stigmata. In such a situation it is not surprising that much of the academic study of gentrifica-tion has been on the displaced working class (Atkinson, 2000), but it is also perhaps not surprising that many were not reluctant displacees. They were able to translate a move out of inner London rented accommodation to a move into owner occupation, and often into white-collar or managerial employment outside London (white flight is a largely unexplored concept in Britain but was clearly at work during much of this period; see Butler, 1997; Hamnett and Randolph, 1988).

The other side of this process has been the remaking of much of inner London by a new middle class whose 'others' are less the traditional white working class but those who have themselves been displaced by the forces of economic globalization into becoming 'economic migrants'. The fact that both of these groups are there through 'choice', albeit variously constrained, gives their study an added dimension to that traditionally assumed in sociology. This is particularly the case for the middle classes who have driven the gentrification process. However, as we have already noted, the exercise of choice may operate in complex ways which have to do with the ways in which they express their social, and specifically class, identity through place. Unlike the previous generation of the middle class, who diligently patrolled the class boundaries below them whilst watching those above them with equal anxiety, the contemporary middle classes appear to be less concerned to create class identities in relation to other groups than to manufacture forms of distinction in relation to other parts of the middle class. So, as Savage *et al.* (2001) show, although they are highly aware of the language of class and utilize its narratives to understand their personal trajectories, they do not express their own position in class terms but in terms of 'ordinariness'. However, as Savage also notes, this is perhaps largely explained by the extent to which they are in fact over-whelmed by the power of class. To a greater or lesser extent, this is marked out by complex choices about who they are, which then become repre-sented by broad choices about the kinds of neighbourhoods in which they live.

Gentrification and globalization

Gentrification in the 1990s took on the frenetic pace of the financial services economy and colonized whole new areas of the inner city (e.g. Clerkenwell in London and Brooklyn Heights in New York). Lees (2000) identifies some of the linkages between this and the restructuring of the global economy. She notes that it is the 'financifiers' – the super-rich thrown up by the financial industries of London and New York – who are now 're-gentrifying' areas which were originally gentrified 24 years previ-ously. She also notes issues of immigration, 'race' and liveability in contemporary accounts of gentrification (Lees, 2000, p. 402). These are crucial issues but ones which are all functions of contemporary globaliza-tion and, as such, have broader consequences both for cities and city living. What is happening in London (and New York) is not simply an onward and upward phenomenon of renewed gentrification. The globalization which is driving the London economy is affecting all of those living in its orbit, whether they are, to use the contemporary language, 'winners' or 'losers'.

Many of the former live very much on the edge: traditional rulebooks have been torn up, space and time have become compressed and distorted: work is meeting the next deadline and your reputation is as good as your last presentation. Whilst many may welcome the rewards and excitement of working in such an environment, they are often, at the same time, keen to lay down some markers in their personal lives. This is particularly so where there are children and both parents are working. The dilemmas faced by these people are most eloquently described by Richard Sennett in *The Corrosion of Character* (1998), in which he suggests that many of the most devoted functionaries of the new economy have become uneasy about the consequent loss of structure and stability in their lives. In many cases both partners are working in stressful and demanding jobs where long hours and travel are part of the culture. Lack of security is what distinguishes this new economy from the one in which they grew up and, for many, it is this that creates the frisson which drives them on. However, they begin to recognize the strengths in the old household forms and employment relations in which their parents put up with the present in the expectation that their children would lead a very different future, as indeed they have. In particular, they fear for the effects their lives are having on their children – one of Sennett's respondents described them as having become 'mall rats' – who, naturally enough, take their parents' privileged status as a given.

Sennett's respondents may come from the glamorous end of the middle class but the changes to which he refers have had an impact on most middle-class families, whether or not they are working within the interstices of the new global economy and whether or not both parents are at work. On the one hand, they are escaping from the remembered boredom of their parents' ordered lives: dad at work, mum at home, often in single class suburbs. On the other, they are often frantic about the lack of structure in their lives and fear for the effects of this on their children. The current gentrification of London is in part an attempt to reconcile this present with a somewhat nostalgic view of the past. This is manifested by a desire to build a local community within the global city that maps on to their particular set of values, backgrounds, aspirations and resources.

What has emerged from recent research is that there are quite distinctive processes of gentrification taking place in inner London. All are concerned with establishing neighbourhoods in which the reference points of globalization are crucial to this process but manifest themselves in different ways. In this section we sketch how this has played out in the areas in which we carried out fieldwork. All represent different responses to the encroaching globalization of urban space and the reconstitution of social divisions in London.

We selected six areas in which to undertake our fieldwork which were intended to encompass the diversity of the middle classes in London (the details of the research are more fully described in Butler, 2004; Butler with Robson, 2003). We drew on one key distinction made by Warde (1991) between gentrification by 'collective action' and by 'capital'. Most of what has taken place in London can be described as the former: individual households or occasionally small developers doing up old, usually Victorian, houses. Once the pioneers have done their stuff, then the areas take off into self-sustained growth, often trading on the reputation of the early pioneers (five of our areas represented different stages of this process). In London, gentrification by capital has been largely confined to Docklands, where we did fieldwork in the three sub-areas – the Isle of Dogs, Surrey Quays and the Royal Docks – in which large and medium sized firms took advantage of the possibilities offered by devalued land to make large profits. In terms of the literature on gentrification, the former process was driven largely by the supply of gentrifiers who, as a result of changes in the socio-economic structure, were seeking out gentrified properties in the inner city (Ley, 1996). In the case of the latter, this was a process driven by the workings of the land market, and the supply of gentrified property, which has been best theorized by Neil Smith (1979, 1996) in terms of an emerging 'rent gap'.

Taken as a whole, our respondents were attracted to living in areas with 'people like us'; broadly, although Docklands was a notably exception, each of the areas tended to have common characteristics in terms of social background and contemporary outlook and lifestyles of respondents. Respondents identified with these and found them to be amongst the main attractions for living in their particular area. Respondents tended to make friends with people like themselves and their social networks were often based around friendships that went back to university, and sometimes to school and family, or with people who had themselves moved into the same broad geographical area of inner London. Children often formed the basis for the parents' social networks, particularly in Telegraph Hill. All areas had in common a general disengagement from non-middle-class social groups and a lack of involvement in both formal and informal aspects of urban governance. The main dimension of involvement for those with children predictably concerns education, although this manifested itself in individualized and instrumental ways. There was little evidence of what Hirschmann (1970) has termed 'voice' or 'loyalty', but neither was there much evidence of 'exit'; the only consistent reference to this came, ironically and intriguingly from the most urbanized respondents in Brixton, many of whom were considering leaving London altogether in the face of what they saw as impossible dilemmas over finding suitable schools for their children.

Patterns of gentrification in inner London

All respondents shared a commitment to urban living, partly out of a wish to distance themselves from their own upbringing and partly out of a wish not to spend long hours travelling to and from work, but mainly because they wanted the excitement and culture that they saw only a cosmopolitan city like London being able to provide. The suburbs and small towns and villages from which many came were 'boring'. University provided an escape from this and London enabled them to continue that way of life. This of course also matched the transformation that had taken place in the economy, where middle-class jobs are to be found less in managing Fordist enterprises and more in the emerging service sectors of the 'new economy'.

The nature of the commitment to urban living varied considerably, however. At some level, respondents in Battersea hankered after the country life, but it simply was not a practical proposition at this time in their lives when at least one member of the household needed to work long hours in the City. The ready property market and relatively good rail and road communications, however, kept the idea alive of eventually making it to Wiltshire or somewhere else commutable. Respondents in Docklands were not anti-urban but felt that where they lived was largely a relationship born of convenience rather than commitment; the attraction of Docklands was its lack of commitment. Perhaps this was symbolized by the fact that, unlike the other areas, this was 'new build' gentrification, so there was no possibility of any community 'in the mind' or sense of history with which one might form an identification.

It is this notion of a community 'in the mind' which both unites and separates our respondents. In each of our areas there were different narratives which tied them to where they lived. In nearly every case this could be seen as an abstracted and idealized version of community. Again, this was probably weakest in Battersea where, as we have argued elsewhere (Butler, 2004; Butler with Robson, 2003), respondents tended to 'motor along' on their stock of economic capital, whereas elsewhere the gentrification process depended, at least nominally, on the deployment of varying amounts of social and cultural capital. Even in Battersea, however, it was apparent that respondents were able to draw on considerable stocks of social capital if needed, although normally this was regarded as a latent resource and relations were conducted through the market (what we have characterized as 'eating out as opposed to joining in'). The well-developed local consumption infrastructure, as it were, mediated relationships through spending. Given the relatively long-standing nature of gentrification in Battersea (Munt, 1987), it might even be argued that gentrification itself has become the idealized narrative: elsewhere respondents would go to some lengths to distance themselves from the term. This gives Battersea a peculiar cognitive map: the middle-class community is highly bounded and inward looking, and only opens outwards to equivalent areas such as Clapham and Fulham. There is no sense here of the middle classes being embedded in a more 'authentic', volatile or rounded London. This is a case of isolation based not upon the bringing up of the metaphorical drawbridge but on the extensive colonization of a whole swathe of the city, the very fabric of which has been transformed in the image of a private/managerial/hedonistic group. This is the creation of a new urban space, in which Battersea has been lifted out of the local, and into the global, economy. Of all the areas we studied, it conformed most closely to Neil Smith's notion of a 'revanchist' middle-class gentrification re-taking the city.

Barnsbury has much in common with Battersea. Upper Street in Islington and Northcote Road in Wandsworth are both places to go for a night out in which restaurants, themed bars, kitchen/bathroom shops and estate agents have edged out the retailers of a past era. Both have become global spaces, servicing the international service class diaspora in a safe environment that acknowledges the cultural capital of the customer, even if it involves a rather repetitious narrative about the life cycle of seared tuna. Whilst Barnsbury surfs the wave of globalization with Battersea, it does so in discernibly different ways. Its population is equally solidly middle class but, whereas those who make up Battersea's population might be corporate financiers drawn from 'the home counties', those in Barnsbury tend to be legal and other professionals largely drawn via Oxbridge from a national, if predominantly middle-class, background.

Unlike Battersea, where gentrification has been enabled by a sympathetic and right-wing local council, in Islington the process of re-gentrification that is taking place is largely based on the idea of buying into a social capital rich environment by a group who do not have the same time or commitment to make to the area. A once coherent narrative of a mixed community settlement (white working-class natives, liberal middle-class incomers) is now being fractured by the presence of incomers who neither belong to nor understand this history. The newcomers are finding the script difficult to 'read', even if it is in their interests to do so. The values of inner urban community experience are being displaced by values revolving around money and market-based solutions to inner London life, *à la* Battersea. This has disrupted the continuity of the established community – although this would still appear to be very strong – and raised the level of unease between the 'haves' and Islington born and bred 'have-nots'. Whereas the initial gentrifiers educated their children in the local schools at all levels, we did not find a single respondent who had a child at a secondary school in Islington. Upper Street has, almost literally, moved into another world. It has been lifted out of the local economy into the global one, as a central part of the new metropolis. This has generated the development of a peculiar virtual and privatized landscape in which, despite its apparent 'buzz', social interactions are limited, with very little possibility of accidental meetings (there being no more 'local' pubs or shops, for example).

Brixton, like Barnsbury and Battersea, has become a global space but a very different one. Long the centre for London's Afro-Caribbean community, what middle-class Brixton demonstrates is an identification and/or accommodation with other (non-middle-class) groups. We have described its social structure as 'tectonic' (Robson and Butler, 2001). This describes the ways in which the various social groups behave towards each other; they move across each other in ways that do not apparently involve much interaction but there is still a high degree of awareness of each other's presence. The experience of rubbing along with others of different cultural, social and ethnic background is a very important element of the frisson of living in a somewhat uncomfortable and 'edgy' area. We have described this group as being in some senses in flight from the obligations of social capital (Butler with Robson, 2003); they are seeking out difference and not attempting to huddle around with 'people like us', so characteristic of inner London gentrification elsewhere (Butler, 1997). Brixton is moving on from being a site for London's Afro-Caribbean population to being a focus for many of the manifestations of current globalisms of people, culture and entertainment. Multicultural globalism *is* Brixton, and it is this atmosphere that is attractive to our respondents here. The social and cognitive maps of the area which emerge out of this dialectical 'Brixton of the mind' make it possible for the middle classes – and particular this ascetic fraction – to include themselves in a model of urban living which is 'vibrant', heterogeneous, informally segregated and paradoxical but 'real': it is also almost entirely white.

In contrast to the celebration of different aspects of contemporary globalization in Barnsbury, Battersea and Brixton, elsewhere we discovered a withdrawal from aspects of the global city and particularly its structures of consumption. In both Telegraph Hill and London Fields there was a conscious effort to build enclaves, part of whose attraction was the absence of such infrastructures and links to the rest of the world. In their place we found social capital rich networks of personal relationships which gave the areas their particular structure of meaning. One of the things respondents like about Telegraph Hill is the sense of permanence of its residents that gives them a sense of 'belonging'; most had no intention of moving. The belonging is nonetheless real and is rooted in 'sameness'. This is celebrated as being open-minded towards others but, in reality, it is about different groups of liberal/welfare professionals getting on with each other as opposed to people from different ethnic or social groups (see G. Robson and Butler, 2001, for a further discussion of this point). Networking amongst residents begins at the gate of the local primary school, which has been systematically adopted and transformed by the 'Hill'. Parents then create sub-narratives for exploiting the 'local circuit of education', whether in the extensive provision of high quality private schooling in the south of neighbouring Southwark or state selective schools, one of which is located in the research area. Telegraph Hill becomes an enclave, a 'village in the mind', from which forays are then made out into the wider city.

London Fields, whilst sharing some of these quasi-localist tendencies, is rather more humble both in its physical disposition and its narrative construction. This is the least formed 'group' in the study, and therefore the most difficult to typify. Of all our areas, this is the one in which some kind of 'pioneer spirit' is still easily discernible. Although it is, perhaps, both ontologically and socially fragile, it has generated a coherent narrative based on the non-normative and multicultural and, to some extent, risk or 'edge living'. Two things emerge as particularly interesting. First there is a 'residue of community' narrative, in which a 'Hackney of the mind' has as its characteristics an (oppositionally inflected) attachment to communal life, of which the residual working-class population is the guarantor, and a sense of loyalty to what is seen as one of the last unique and 'authentic' places in the capital. Hackney has a strong association with traditional working-class/London values which is attractive to many gentifiers (Butler, 1997). Second, there is the area's connection to the new 'artistic East End', in which a novel cognitive/cultural map connects it to Clerkenwell, Shoreditch, Old Street and Hoxton (Foord, 2000; Zukin, 1988).

Over the last two decades, Docklands, despite a number of hiccups and false starts, has been successfully transformed. Almost all the respondents were living in Docklands because they wanted to be somewhere which was near to work and involved minimum social and maintenance commitments. Very few had children living with them and quite a number were what are described as 'empty nesters'; often there was a second property outside London to which they went at weekends and where the family had been brought up or in some cases lived full time. This group was most likely to go out at night both to eat and for cultural or other leisure pursuits. They were not attracted to the 24/7 lifestyle which is often promoted in the new city centre developments in Manchester, Leeds and Birmingham. Many were tied to extended work hours in the City which often meant compulsory after-hours entertaining. They did not wish to become involved in their neighbourhoods or with their neighbours, and simply wanted 'efficient' living arrangements with minimal commitments. They worked long hours and their lives were perhaps more dominated by work than those in other areas. It was more difficult to characterize them as coming from any particular social or regional background, and perhaps they perceived fewer of the social contradictions of globalization than those in other areas, neither wishing to surf it as one might characterize respondents in Barnsbury, Battersea or Brixton, nor ostentatiously retreat from it and its attendant consumption infrastructure, as did those in Telegraph Hill and London Fields. Their patterns of association were much less local than respondents in other areas and they were more likely to have made their friendships through work.

Conclusions

Urban – and in some areas rural – gentrification has become increasingly widespread not just in the UK, Australia and North America but also recently Europe and South America. However, the nature of that gentrification is very different between those cities that can be characterized as 'global centres' and the rest. This chapter has concentrated on London largely because the process of gentrification is more advanced here than elsewhere. In some ways, the gentrification of cities outside London can be likened to the early gentrification of inner London: a slightly oddball choice in a situation where the vast majority still lived in the suburbs. Whilst Edinburgh is already largely gentrified, the gentrification of cities such as Manchester is gathering pace. Nevertheless there still remains both a quantitative and qualitative difference with London, which as Savage (personal correspondence) has argued remains the benchmark for urban living. I have argued that in London, different areas have different 'structures of meaning'. The gentrification of different areas is distinguished by the deployment of cultural, social and economic capital in differing proportions. This is the mechanism through which they are able to create neighbourhoods which meet the needs not only of their often dysfunctional work lives but also their desires to create a harmonious and well-ordered domestic environment.

In this there is often a sharp juxtaposition of work lives which are at the cutting edge of contemporary globalization (or threatened with restructuring as a consequence) and a wish to replicate the managed domestic environments of the era in which they grew up. The means by which this is managed vary. For some, this is managed by the deployment of social and cultural capital into person-based social networks which to a degree cut them off from some aspects of the global city. In other cases, considerable amounts of economic and cultural capital are deployed in buying into the social capital heritage of an area gentrified in a different era. For yet others, diversity and multiculturalism are embraced – at least in principle – as a way of managing the tensions of economic and cultural globalization. It may simply be about buying community through the deployment of economic resources in the elaborate infrastructure of consumption ('eating out rather than joining in'). What is being argued is that it is by these strategies that the London middle class are able make sense of their individual lives in a situation where class and place cultures provide little guidance about how to negotiate contemporary work/life boundaries.

Chapter 11

Governance, Social Cohesion and Neighbourhood Participation

ROBINA GOODLAD and RICHARD MEEGAN

Introduction

This chapter explores the complex relationships between citizen involvement in urban governance, social cohesion and economic competitiveness. Democratic governance plays a mediating role in what Fainstein (2001a) describes as either a virtuous circle of competitiveness and social cohesion or a vicious cycle of economic decline and social exclusion. In the mutually reinforcing web of relationships characterizing a virtuous circle, a cohesive society encourages people to be productive and companies to invest in human capital. The increased productivity promotes economic growth, which mitigates social conflict and promotes further cohesion, thus providing trust in the institutions that further enhance competitiveness, whether directly through business linkages (such as in recruitment and collaboration) or indirectly through the quality of governance. The role for governance is therefore to secure a combination of competitive advantage and social cohesion. According to this argument, effective governance requires democracy and, post-1968, this means participation beyond the ballot box.

At neighbourhood and urban level, coming together with neighbours and officials has, according to the NCW, a vital effect in ways that reflect two of Nick Buck's three dimensions of social cohesion (see Chapter 3 above). First, it fosters social *connectedness*, demonstrated in social capital and enhanced trust in government and fellow citizens, and improved government performance, measured by responsiveness to citizens' aspirations. Second, it enhances the prospects for social *equality* (or inclusion), directly by improving living conditions and life chances and indirectly by the personal development and increased confidence that participation can bring.

In contrast, a vicious circle is driven by the economic impacts of rising global competition, which forces governments to reduce welfare expenditures and firms to depress wages and substitute capital for labour. The resultant unemployment and low wages raise social tensions that are compounded by increasing socio-spatial segregation. When domestic product stagnates or falls, metropolitan areas experience a flight of investment and population that can result in the abandonment of neighbourhoods. These forces operate on those at the lowest income levels to constrain access to housing, education, employment and health services *and to encourage political disengagement*. The uneven distribution of the benefits of economic and social development are likely to reinforce the advantages of middle-class neighbourhoods, while in poor neighbourhoods the disadvantages of economic and social exclusion are likely to be compounded by exclusion from governance. A vicious circle emerges, where high concentrations of deprivation co-exist with exclusion from governance and other aspects of social and economic life, compounding poverty and the waste of economic capacity.

The rest of this chapter examines how far this conventional wisdom is reflected in the literature on urban governance and in research intended to explore the role of citizens in neighbourhood governance in central Scotland and on Merseyside. In the former, two Glasgow and two Edinburgh neighbourhoods were the main focus for fieldwork. One neighbourhood in each city was relatively deprived, and was the focus of a regeneration policy called social inclusion partnerships (SIPs). The other neighbourhoods had mixed socio-economic profiles. The fieldwork consisted of a household survey; interviews at city and neighbourhood level with officials, activists and elected representatives; and focus groups of residents. The study on Merseyside focused on a regeneration initiative – known as 'Pathways to Integration' – funded under Objective One of the European Union's Structural Funds. This tackled social exclusion, with spatial targeting and citizen involvement in 38 deprived areas, containing almost 500,000 people. The research used mainly qualitative methods in 11 case study 'Pathways for Integration Area Partnerships' (PIAPs). This involved semi-structured interviews; participant observation in various types of meetings of PIAPs; and focus groups with community representatives, trainees on PIAP courses, and professionals running PIAPs or PIAP projects. In both locations, fieldwork was undertaken in 1999 and 2000.

Our overall purpose, then, is to discuss the extent to which participation in regeneration initiatives at neighbourhood level in central Scotland and Merseyside was contributing to two dimensions of social cohesion: social connectedness (or social capital) and social inclusion (or social equality). But first we introduce the concept of citizen participation in contemporary cities.

Participation and citizenship

Changing attitudes to governance and citizenship, introduced here, provide a context for the discussion of citizen participation that follows. Alan Harding, in Chapter 4, outlined the forces driving the shift from urban government to urban governance and its expression in inter-organizational linkages, bargaining and coalition-building. Within this, place is accorded importance in a new participatory rhetoric (Healey *et al.*, 2002a, p. 10), and reformers of local government in many countries search for 'the best combination of complementary procedures of representative and participatory democracy (including direct democracy)' (Buĉek and Smith, 2000, p. 3; see also Hoggart and Clark, 2000). Citizen participation is seen as a response to questions about local electoral mandates, traditional local government practices and the alleged lack of accountability of non-elected local institutions. It is fed by a loss of faith in the state as mediator of interests, and the redefinition of the meaning of professionalism to encompass participation.

The recent ascendancy of neighbourhood citizen participation has its origins not only in the changing governance of cities, but also in the changing nature of citizenship practice. Two key features of this new citizenship are, first, that political participation is not evenly distributed across space or social groups. Factors that predispose people to participation are related to economic status, and high educational attainment is the best single predictor (Parry *et al.*, 1992). Socio-spatial segregation means that the most socially and economically disadvantaged wards exhibit the lowest electoral turnouts and, arguably, non-electoral political activity. Second, we need to emphasize the connection between political participation and social inclusion. 'Exclusion' has economic, social and *political* dimensions (Lister, 1997, pp. 105–6). Political exclusion is seen by many commentators increasingly to demonstrate a distinctive socio-spatial segregation, with exclusion concentrated in 'inner cities, on peripheral housing estates, or in poor rural communities' (Geddes, 1995, p. 8; quoted in Percy-Smith, 2000, p. 148).

Policy rhetoric is matched by evidence of a growth of 'community participation' arrangements in Britain (Lowndes *et al.*, 1998), particularly in some services such as housing (Goodlad, 2001) and in area regeneration (Goodlad, 2002). The strengthening under the Labour government elected in 1997 of the 'turn to the community' detected by Duffy and Hutchinson (1997) is illustrated by the National Neighbourhood Renewal Strategy, which stresses the value of community participation in planning and service delivery (Wallace, 2001). Initiatives target resources and attention on to neighbourhoods, sometimes with sanctions for non-delivery of citizen involvement. In the words of one civil servant: 'Whilst we've said for years that the community must be involved, this time we really do mean it' (Foley and Martin, 2000, p. 482). At European level, too, the Commission's regional policy has had a growing impact on the development of local and, increasingly, neighbourhood participation in area partnerships that steer local development and employment initiatives. The neighbourhood has therefore provided an arena for experiments with local participatory democracy as well as for concerted assaults against urban decline and degeneration.

Participation has been used without qualification or definition but, like citizenship, it is a complex and slippery concept that can have a range of competing motivations and different guises (Jones, 1999). A wide definition would cover participation in community and voluntary organizations or in neighbourly behaviour that is not primarily focused on public policy although it may provide a base for that. Our approach here is more narrowly to see citizen participation as any action by a citizen that is intended to influence public policy. This chapter therefore focuses not only on participation arising from initiatives by public bodies but also on forms activated by citizens. Following Nelson and Wright (1995) and Cooke and Kothari (2001), participation should not be a focus that ignores the complexity of power or obscures broader inequalities and injustices. Participation needs to be applied in a way which recognizes that the 'interests' and participatory structures involved should be critically interrogated (Jones, 1999; White, 1996). Political intervention offers spaces for engagement, which communities can or may not exploit to their advantage. The outcome of participation is contingent. Cairncross *et al.* (1997) further usefully distinguish structures (and methods) of participation from processes (i.e. what actually takes place within structures for participation).

Social connectedness and citizen participation

This section considers the relationship between social connectedness and citizen participation, initially in relation to the ways in which citizen participation was creating new networks and structures, and then in relation to the role that citizen participation might play in fostering trust and social capital.

Participation structures and methods

In common with many cities, formal mechanisms for citizen participation at neighbourhood level exist in Glasgow, Edinburgh and the five local authority districts that make up Merseyside. They include area committees with councillor and community representation (Glasgow and Liverpool), community councils (Glasgow and Edinburgh), tenant management co-operatives (Glasgow), community-based housing associations and co-operatives (Glasgow, Edinburgh, Knowsley and Liverpool) and local economic development agencies with voluntary sector involvement (Glasgow and Merseyside), for example. However, these structures do not always fulfil their promise at neighbourhood level. Some cover large areas not recognized as 'communities' by residents and may therefore barely touch the consciousness of citizens, while others achieve patchy coverage.

The extent and maturity of the infrastructure for citizen participation varies considerably between the cities and neighbourhoods. The two Scottish SIP areas have relatively well-developed structures and a long history of attempts to involve citizens in renewal. Most attention appears to have been given to increasing resident involvement in three ways: through tenants' associations and housing associations and co-operatives; supporting the voluntary sector which in turn provides many social services; and inviting representatives of the community to join partnerships of agencies working to co-ordinate strategies for renewal, employment or social development, as in SIPs. These have followed the government's agenda in promoting citizens' panel surveys, focus groups and citizens' juries. The situation is somewhat different on Merseyside where citizen participation has had a chequered history with local political attitudes towards it ranging from indifference to outright hostility. The 1990s, however, have seen a gradual introduction of participatory structures, reflecting not least the requirements of European funding and changing central government priorities. The election in Liverpool in 1998 of a Liberal Democrat administration with a particular enthusiasm for 'Modernising Local Government' has produced a complicated geography of participation with area committees, a community consultation framework for the Local Strategic Partnership's 'community plan' and a Neighbourhood Renewal Strategy for neighbourhoods that includes the PIAPs. Community groups in the latter did receive funding to support their activities from the Objective One programme. In addition, as in Scotland, the partnerships spent money on surveys, public meetings and newsletters and other media.

These participation policies and structures have had two immediate effects. First, they have made connections between people who would otherwise not have communicated. The SIPs and PIAPs were multi-agency partnerships involving central (two tiers in Scotland) and local government, public agencies, the voluntary and private sectors and, for Merseyside at the level of the overall Objective One funding programme, the European Commission. The PIAPs and the SIPs were illustrative of the 'micro-politics of neighbourhood governance' (Allen and Cars, 2002) and brought together the informal networks of the local residents of the areas (in the form of representatives of community organizations, tenants' and housing associations and other local interest-based activities) with formal networks of professional officers and agencies and, where it existed and representation was forthcoming, local business. The central difficulty of governance was, as Allen and Cars (2002) argue, creating webs between different sets of networks. The mixed neighbourhoods in Scotland that were not SIPs had no such difficulty, but equally they had no apparent structures to link the tiers and sectors of governance, as residents and activists in the Glasgow mixed neighbourhood (aware of their SIP neighbour) complained.

Second, social cohesion effects of participation were seen in the development of a range of additional services, activities and structures arising from participation. These varied from training schemes, after-school playschemes and arts activities, for example, to new structures for participation itself. The latter included the development of new community groups or fora to assist existing groups to play the roles envisaged for them in regeneration. For example, on Merseyside the Objective One programme prompted the development of a network of local community activists and representatives of community organizations which was called the Merseyside Pathways Network, and this, in turn, opened a space for formal involvement in the overall governance of the programme. The genesis of this Network can be traced to a perception by a group of community activists that their voice was not being sufficiently heard whereas the public agencies and voluntary and private sector organizations already had their own influential networks. The Network secured formal representation on the programme's Monitoring Committee and Technical Panels. It went on to assess the first programme and, importantly, to participate in the informal group set up to lead the preparation of the plan for the second round of Objective One and, especially, its 'Pathways' Mark II component. The Network is formally represented on the Monitoring Committee and three sub-committees for this second round of funding. In summary, participation had involved the creation of new structures and relationships.

We should note that there was considerable variation in the operation of community participation in the partnerships and neighbourhoods, not only between local authorities but also within them. To an extent this reflected the prior history of community development. In Scotland, the Glasgow SIP was working to overcome a history of poor relationships with and between community groups. Some of the PIAPs (which varied in size of population from a few hundred to over 40,000) had long-established tenants' associations and other community bodies, while others had very few (Meegan and Mitchell, 2001).

Trust

Discussion of the effects of participation soon turns from structures to relationships and then to the role of social capital. The concept is important for the way in which it foregrounds trust. However, there is a danger in using the concept here, concerning the direction of causality. Much research has attempted to derive measures of 'generalized social trust' as a proxy for 'social capital' that can then be related to levels of political participation and economic performance (Pennington and Rydin, 2000). The direction of causality is assumed to run from the networks and norms associated with social capital to generalized trust to particular socio-economic outcomes and good government. Following this approach would lead us to conclude that poorer neighbourhoods will show lower levels of trust from evidence which shows that higher levels of associational involvement are found amongst middle-class compared with working-class people. They 'are likely to know twice as many of their neighbours fairly well' (Hall, 1999, p. 438). Lower social trust is associated with dislocating experiences such as divorce, poverty or unemployment. Overall, the two groups 'increasingly marginalized' from civic society are the working class and the young (p. 455).

However, an alternative account sees the state as promoting the conditions in which social capital can be created (Maloney *et al.*, 2000). Expressions of trust appear to reflect the particular social and economic positions of those involved and are the product (not the cause) of the socio-economic context in which they operate. High levels of trust in one context may not operate in another, even in the same place. For example, trust in neighbours, friends and relatives within deprived neighbourhoods can simultaneously exist with low levels of trust in outside agencies (Forrest and Kearns, 1999). Trust, therefore, needs to be understood in specific social, political and geographical contexts and only constitutes social capital where individuals in specific settings draw upon trust and networks to act (Pennington and Rydin, 2000).

The partnerships and neighbourhoods discussed in this chapter provide such contexts. We were interested in two aspects of trust: trust in the institutions of governance and trust in fellow citizens, community groups in particular. Recognizing that the *association* between class and social capital may not demonstrate that poorer people are predisposed to be less trusting when it comes to neighbourhood governance, we looked for other factors associated with the neighbourhoods as places that might influence trust. These include the opportunities for participation and the responses residents receive when raising problems and issues they see.

Surveys, focus groups and direct observation produced some evidence of a supportive local context in 'Pathways' and SIPs. In Scotland, we might have expected residents of the more middle-class mixed neighbourhoods to be more trusting, but there was virtually no difference between the four neighbourhoods in relation to the trust felt by residents in the council 'to do what is right'. A second measure of trust – willingness to work together with others to improve their neighbourhood – showed marginally more of the Glasgow and Edinburgh SIP residents than residents of the mixed areas to be trusting, but the differences were small. In other words, there may be factors at work building higher than anticipated levels of trust in the poorest areas. Indeed, in these areas, citizens generally welcome opportunities for citizen participation and take comfort from the knowledge that efforts are being made to involve them even though they do not take part themselves. In the SIP areas, more residents were aware of efforts by the council to keep them informed than residents of the mixed neighbourhoods. However, in the Glasgow SIP views were polarized: a higher number also felt that the council did not keep them informed than in the mixed area (Docherty *et al.*, 2001).

The second aspect of trust is that between citizens, in particular between citizens and community groups. Trust in councils and other official bodies is not sufficient for participation in the new urban governance. Also required is trust in community groups. Implicit in many models of citizen participation is a reliance on community groups to represent the interests of the residents of an area to public officials, and this role is acknowledged in the funding and other support provided for groups in renewal areas and elsewhere. If groups are to play their part, they too require to be trusted by citizens who may otherwise feel as excluded by activists as they feel excluded by the formal political process.

Residents of the two poorer neighbourhoods in Glasgow and Edinburgh were more likely to feel that activists are 'out for themselves' than residents in the mixed areas (Docherty *et al.*, 2001). Residents of the mixed areas also had the highest levels of associational memberships. It seems that the socio-economic composition of the neighbourhoods, and perhaps the problems of disorder it brings, was overriding the local efforts to support the representation role of community groups. Also, on Merseyside, there were instances where distrust between neighbourhood groups and individuals within them had negative effects on partnership working. In one case, complaints made about groups allegedly dominating partnership activities were made formally to the local MP. This incident underscored the extent to which 'neighbourhoods' are socially constructed and that neighbourhood-based community organizations with their own histories and politics can come into conflict when brought into partnership working. Levels of distrust are carried into the partnership. Breaking down that distrust is heavily reliant on communication and the transparency of the partnership process.

If residents of poor areas generally distrust community activists, the activists themselves had a more complicated attitude to trusting officials. Community representatives and local 'key informants' underlined the pronounced degree of distrust that historically existed between residents and 'outside' agencies, including local councils. Yet, with some exceptions, they also provided evidence of a transformation of some relationships as networks of trust and channels of communication between community activists and agencies developed. Although some cases of individual activists withdrawing from partnership structures were reported, public policy was making a difference in that activists generally felt fairly positive about the value of their role. Almost unanimously activists talk about how it could be improved rather than arguing against participation. Many feel they make a difference to service delivery, planning or community life.

Two examples of transformed relationships illustrate the factors at work. In the first, on Merseyside, the decision to grant to PIAPs (and their appraisal panels that contained local residents) part of the scoring of project bids served to change the attitudes of some of the large agencies towards the partnerships (having their project bids 'scored down' came as something of a shock to some of them), and also helped to build the trust of the residents involved. Particularly valued was the quality of the relationships developed between community representatives and the 'pathways co-ordinators' and local authority link persons (Hibbitt, Jones and Meegan, 2001). In Scotland, evidence from residents in the Edinburgh SIP suggested that the neighbourhood's stock of active community groups had encouraged the council to adopt a more active stance towards citizen participation. These groups arose not necessarily spontaneously but partly as a result of the support provided by the council. More generally, community-based housing associations and co-operatives had already provided a mechanism for building more trusting working relationships with public agencies before the SIPs were established. Their staff and committee members were able to adapt to the opportunity offered by the SIPs with relative ease, compared with many other groups, especially in Glasgow. In addition, the housing association staff and committee members were trusted more by their tenants than was the city council by anyone. Community-based housing associations offer the sort of service responsiveness and participation that other opportunities often fail to fulfil, especially in Glasgow.

Developing trust

The development of trust appears to depend heavily on a number of factors, of which we stress two here. First, the new modes of governance such as those represented by the partnerships require highly flexible structures (Healey *et al.*, 2002b). The research suggests that these flexible structures need an element of informality to negotiate the 'micropolitics' of neighbourhood governance. An example was provided in Liverpool by the 'Driver 5' group (named after the spending priority in the Single Programming Document), which was formally constituted as a sub-committee of the Liverpool Partnership Group. It comprised a representative from each of the city's eleven PIAPs and eight from agencies interested in accessing funding. It played an important role in mediating conflicts of interest between PIAPs and funding agencies and, towards the end of the first programme, its meetings also provided a forum for virement of funding. It had been agreed early in the programme that each PIAP would be given an allocation of funding based on 'need' (using a combined population/unemployment proxy). In the event, however, some partnerships had been unable to come up with projects by the deadline. The Driver 5 group provided a means of breaking this logjam. Project bids were compared and prioritized and, crucially, because the informal rules of its meeting were such that decisions were never taken when there was a minority of community representatives present, this prioritization was achieved without damaging trust. While community activists were not happy to see the needs-based allocation principle breached, they recognized that they had been involved in the discussions and that priorities over spending have to be settled.

The acceptance of virement was a demonstration of what Abers (1998) describes as the 'negotiated solidarity' that participation can produce: individuals and groups being prepared to put aside self-interest as a result of participation in decision-making. Perhaps what was crucial here was that activists could see that they were taking part in a process that made a difference. This brings us to the second factor implicated in building trust. People who felt that their participation was having or would have a worthwhile effect on material conditions in the neighbourhood(s) were far more positive about it than those who felt it was pointless. In central Scotland, ordered logistical regression showed that high 'trust' scores were associated with those individuals who rated their neighbourhood as a very good place to live, those who thought their neighbourhood had improved over the last two years and people with a degree or academic school qualifications. This was strikingly consistent with qualitative evidence such as the views of council tenants in the Glasgow SIP who were frustrated with a poor repairs service and uncertain about a proposal to transfer housing to alternative landlords (Docherty *et al.*, 2001).

Social equality and citizen participation

We have discussed social cohesion as 'connectedness' in general and trust in particular. Now we consider the possibilities of participation in securing greater social equality. It can be argued that participation enhances the prospects for social equality (or inclusion) in three ways. First, it enables the outcome of political processes to reflect the needs and aspirations of participants. However, the political process will compound social inequalities by privileging the participation of dominant groups unless steps are taken to avoid this. As a consequence, a call for appropriate means of political participation has characterized new social movements (Lister, 1997; Young, 1990), as well as the recent policy focus on poor neighbourhoods. It is, though, unrealistic to expect citizen participation in neighbourhood governance alone to bring about radical social and economic change, given the obstinacy and multidimensional character of social exclusion.

Second, participation fosters personal development. The increased knowledge and confidence that participation brings can have implications for quality of life (and government performance) beyond the initial focus. Third, participation can be valued in the sense that exclusion from this right of citizenship can denote social inequality or low status, compounding other forms of exclusion. This relatively neglected aspect of participation can be hard to distinguish from the second – if participation is felt to be status-enhancing, it is also likely to be seen as enhancing personal development. The key theoretical distinction is that participation can be seen as both valuable in its own right – a right of citizenship irrespective of outcome – *and* as a means to personal development.

Taking the three social equality possibilities of participation in turn, we start with whether material circumstances may be improved through the participation of a relatively small number of citizens in influencing public policy and service provision at neighbourhood level. That community representatives want to see practical benefits from their participation with others is seen in central Scotland and on Merseyside. Community activists gave a wide range of reasons for wanting to participate, varying from a concern with housing conditions, unemployment and associated social problems (especially as these impact on the future prospects of children) and general environmental and quality of life concerns. They saw participation as a way of tackling these. Generally activists seemed to feel that the ultimate test of participation was the difference it made to their material conditions. This suggests that the scale of participation is affected by the feelings of citizens about how worthwhile their action will be or has been, although wishing to bring about change is not the same thing as achieving it.

We found mixed perceptions of what had been achieved through participation. While there was evidence of improved – more responsive and sensitive – government performance occurring (e.g., in the work of community-based housing organizations), there was also a significant degree of frustration with the outcomes of neighbourhood governance. One factor in creating dismay was the time it took for citizen participation to make an impact. For example, the Pathways Network of community organizations was involved in applying the scoring system developed for project funding which meant bids had to meet 'quality threshold' criteria that included community participation in the design of the project. As the programme progressed, it was possible to see that projects approved had more 'community' flavour than they had had at the beginning, especially in relation to projects funded by ERDF (Hibbitt, Jones and Meegan, 1999). In interviews, there were numerous references to the fact that the early outputs of the programme, especially in the form of training (using the European Social Fund), were not 'visible' but there was also recognition that this 'invisibility' was being addressed as the ERDF-funded capital projects started to come on-stream towards the end of the spending period in the shape, for example, of multipurpose community centres and neighbourhood-based Jobs, Education and Training (JET) Centres.

In Scotland, there was evidence of a virtuous cycle of participation appearing to lead to improved conditions. The Edinburgh SIP area had by far the highest proportion of residents who felt that the neighbourhood had improved and fewer than half of the residents felt that conditions had stayed the same or got worse: far fewer than in the three other areas (Docherty *et al.*, 2001). In all four neighbourhoods, residents who thought conditions had stayed the same or got worse, along with those in social classes D and E, were significantly more likely to feel excluded. Differences in housing tenure also influenced residents' sense of inclusion; in particular, residents living in housing association housing were alone among those who rented property in feeling included.

These results supported the view that instrumental gains from participation will engender more participation as well as other, wider benefits that together contribute to social equality. In the Edinburgh SIP neighbourhood residents reported relatively high rates of political action, compared with the other neighbourhoods. They also had the highest score in a 'neighbourhood inclusion index'. The rating of the neighbourhood as a place to stay correlated strongly: the lower the rating the less the sense of inclusion. Residents of the SIP neighbourhoods have noticed that efforts are being made to improve their area but this does not result necessarily in a sense of inclusion if people feel, as in Glasgow, that their area is not improving. Residents in the two Glasgow neighbourhoods were more likely to draw on negative personal experiences of council decisions, and council tenants in particular feel more hopelessness and futility about the idea of taking action, especially over housing, and this attitude percolated more generally into attitudes towards the council.

Second, participants benefiting from the increased knowledge and self-confidence that participation brings were reported, and observed, in the partnerships and neighbourhoods researched. This had individual benefits such as a broadening of activism, an enhanced in quality of life and even a return to the labour market. However, as we have seen, trust in the community activists from the wider community did not always result and the increased self-confidence of activists may have paradoxically compounded the distrust felt towards them by others. Officials also found the role of activists hard to understand: on the one hand they relied on them to transmit community opinion, and on the other they often regretted that 'the usual suspects' appeared on many committees.

Third, a boost to self-esteem and status was apparent in many activists' accounts of participation and also, more graphically, in accounts of the indignity resulting from lack of participation, disrespect and the unresponsiveness of public services. Lack of or poorly conducted participation was deplored, yet attitudes demonstrated ambivalence: on the one hand, participation for its own sake was valued, but if activists felt their contribution was ignored, they thought the effort not to have been worthwhile.

Whatever the benefits or disappointments in terms of social equality, we need to note that the number of activists relative to the population in the neighbourhood forms of participation discussed here can never be very large. At the end of the first Merseyside PIAP programme there were some 260 residents/representatives of community organizations sitting on the boards of the 38 PIAPs. This might be thought a small number from a population of half a million, but it is 260 more than would have taken part only a few years ago. However, the PIAPs and SIPs have also held public meetings which, from observation, have had attendances numbered in tens or, on occasion with controversial issues, hundreds. It is therefore extremely difficult to measure levels of participation. On Merseyside, electoral turnouts in wards containing PIAPs are consistently below those of other wards and one PIAP ward recently set a national record for low turnout in local elections (6 per cent). In Scotland self-reported turnouts for recent national elections had been around 10 per cent lower in the SIP neighbourhoods than in the two mixed areas. In these latter areas, participation structures were not as well developed in comparison with the SIP areas, so the partnerships can be seen to be compensating for the lower rates of political participation demonstrated by residents of deprived areas.

Another characteristic of the community participation reported here has important implications for political inclusion. While individuals and groups experiencing the most extreme social exclusion are rarely engaged in elected government, the active citizenship of some of the participants in PIAPs and SIPs arguably more closely reflects these normally excluded citizens than does formal representative politics. The high proportion of registered unemployed residents shows that exclusion from the labour market does not necessarily signify exclusion from active citizenship. The organizations represented by those we interviewed also cut across a range of community organizations, including residents' and tenants' associations, community groups and projects (including credit unions), community, disability and health fora and one Local Agenda 21 group: people with experience of some forms of social exclusion and usually with a high degree of contact and empathy with the individuals, groups and places at which regeneration is targeted.

Conclusions

This chapter has explored the relationships between citizen participation and two aspects of social cohesion: connectedness and inclusion/equality. The relationships between citizen participation in urban governance, social cohesion and competitiveness are complex. The relationship between social cohesion and competitiveness is particularly indeterminate and can take either virtuous or vicious circular form, albeit heavily weighted towards the latter as competition in the global market economy intensifies. Likewise governance can operate in ways that can either reinforce or miti-gate the operation of the virtuous or vicious relationships between social cohesion and competitiveness. What we have argued here is that citizen participation in governance can be a crucial element in this mix, as it has the ability to build trust and cohesion and encourage greater equality of political engagement with positive governance outcomes; alternatively, low participation can engender distrust and reflect as well as contribute to poor governance outcomes. The two aspects of social cohesion operate in a mutually reinforcing manner: participation that involves normally excluded people and achieves better conditions (as perceived by residents) also builds support for further participation.

While the lack of social cohesion may not impede urban competitive-ness and evidence on the impacts of competitiveness on social cohesion and social exclusion remains limited, the polarization of economic and social circumstances within British cities not only persists but, in some respects, appears to be becoming more pronounced. Boddy (2002) argues that this trend demands active policy measures to link all sections of the community and neighbourhoods within cities to the benefits of economic growth and competitiveness. Given that these measures are explicitly about achieving social and economic connectedness and equality, we would argue that they are more likely to be effective if they are built around adequately supported citizen participation.

We finish with some suggestions for public policy. First, it needs to be more fully appreciated that encouraging community involvement is seeking a radical transformation of civic behaviour, especially in poor cities and neighbourhoods. Overall, although not amounting to mass participation, there has been citizen participation in urban programmes on Merseyside and in central Scotland at unexpected levels for some areas in which the political climate in the past had veered between hostility and lukewarm encouragement. What is perhaps significant is that participation was achieved at all and, as one Merseyside local government officer put it, has persisted despite all the frustrations and setbacks. Citizen participation in governance is hard to achieve anywhere, because it involves a transformation of civic behaviour and relationships between neighbours on one hand, and between residents and public agencies on the other. It is particularly hard in many regeneration areas because of the socio-economic circumstances that are least propitious for community participation. There may also be impediments such as short timescales for consultation. However, 'top-down' efforts by public bodies can have a crucial impact on the creation of mechanisms and structures for participation, especially where conditions for achieving such connections are not propitious. The experience of the Merseyside 'Pathways' initiative and the Scottish SIPs suggests that local policies and structures can be developed which achieve inclusion and power sharing for residents' representatives, even in adverse circumstances. In other policy fields, the skewed nature of participation patterns may not be so apparent, requiring attention to the question of who participates and how those who tend to self-exclude can be included.

Second, activists need support to take part and the large-scale public funding of voluntary organizations in many spheres of public policy shows that this is recognized. The resources required include *sustained* support for voluntary and community groups, as well as other resources for training, information and surveys of public opinion to supplement activists' inputs, for example. The corollary of this argument is that public policy which ignores the differences in people's ability to take advantage of participatory arrangements and opportunities is likely to reinforce existing social, political and economic inequality. Further, professionals and politicians also need support to develop participation.

Third, citizen participation in urban governance necessarily brings representative and participatory democracy up against each other in often difficult and conflictual circumstances. While the former claims political representativeness, the latter claims 'reflectiveness' with political legitimacy rooted in the democratic structures of the community organizations represented. But by encouraging participation in the first place, representative democracy has

given it political validation and only through joint working can a new relationship be achieved. This requires the development of constructive working relationships between activists, community groups, local politicians
and officers involved in the partnerships in which citizens participate.
Again the emphasis is on co-working and co-learning, for only in these
circumstances can the trust that underpins the virtuous circle of governance
and cohesion be built.

Fourth, the debates on trust and social capital remain contested but we
would argue that the concept of social capital is useful analytically
provided that it is grounded in concrete political and institutional contexts.
Several examples from Merseyside and central Scotland demonstrate how
participation in governance can build networks, or social capital. This
social capital, embodied in new learning and institutional capacity, is the
direct product of engagement in the governance process. Participation is a
process in which both trust and mistrust can be generated between partners,
and the outcome is heavily dependent on (formal and informal) partnership
structures and operational procedures, including language and information
exchange and transparency. Given the deep-seated mistrust that exists
between citizens and public policy-makers in some areas, the process of
transforming mistrust into trust will almost inevitably involve some degree
of conflict and a lot of time. While such conflict might be a positive sign
that the partnership process is genuinely under way, there need to be effective systems for conflict resolution for trust to emerge. The building of
trusting relationships needs to be a core element of the regeneration
process. It is about building social capital through the 'scaling-up' of
community networks to the wider power structures of local authorities and
beyond to the various statutory and non-statutory agencies and institutions
involved at several levels of government. The connections that citizen
participation can bring are valued for themselves and also, crucially, for the
results they achieve in improved neighbourhoods and life chances.

Chapter 12

Synchronization, Salesmanship and Service Delivery: Governance and Urban Competitiveness

IAIN DEAS

Background

The search for effective mechanisms through which to govern urban areas, and thereby promote social cohesion and bolster city competitiveness, has remained an enduring concern for policy-makers. This, in part, explains why British cities have been bombarded with a variety of institutional entities and policy initiatives, all designed, in various ways, to help resolve the intractable array of social and economic difficulties widely held to afflict them. In the mid-1970s, it was clear that responsibility for inducing urban social and economic revival was the exclusive province of a partnership of central and local government, the latter being, in the oft-quoted words of the 1977 White Paper *Policy for the Inner Cities*, the 'natural agencies to tackle inner area problems' (Department of the Environment, Scottish Office, Welsh Office, 1977). But by the publication of the successor urban White Paper (DETR, 2000c) the delivery of urban policy had undergone fundamental change, as the governance of cities (formerly almost the sole preserve of local government) became fragmented across a complex assortment of non-departmental public bodies – quangos – in harness with a variety of private and voluntary sector bodies.

As Chapter 4 indicated, the British experience of changing urban governance is in tune with a general international one that has seen a decline in monolithic local government and the parallel arrogation of responsibility by looser networks of institutional actors within cities. Paralleling this has been the emerging policy orthodoxy that economic development in cities and regions is best pursued on a 'partnership' basis. Such a perception partly reflects the straightforwardly pragmatic view that there has to be some attempt to redress the fragmentation of power, responsibility and resource across the complex and disparate network of policy and institutional actors that materialized during the 1980s and 1990s. But it also reflects the emergence in the 1990s of a consensual view that saw cross-sector, inclusive partnership working as itself inherently preferable to the narrower, outmoded styles characteristically pursued by local government. In essence, what might be characterized as the governance thesis, put simply, has it that 'local governance' is not only a description of the dynamics of institutional and political change, but a prescriptive programme encapsulating what is held by its proponents to be the ideal process through which policy coherence can be constructed and resources marshalled in the context of highly fragmented institutional environments characterized by an absence of the sort of primacy previously enjoyed by elected local authorities.

Alongside this fundamental shift in the structures through which cities are governed and policies delivered, there has also been an equally far-reaching transformation in the substantive content of urban policy efforts. Although the focus on area-based intervention remained in place in the period between the urban White Papers of 1977 and 2000, policy also began to acquire broader horizons, moving beyond a preoccupation with restoring the fortunes of particular 'problem' urban areas and towards a concern with revitalizing cities more generally. Three factors were of particular import in prompting this shift. First, there was the emergence of the voguish view that urban economic vitality was an essential ingredient of broader national competitiveness. Second, and more prosaically, it reflected a view that the major British provincial cities were underperforming relative to their international counterparts (Robson, 2000). And third – again reflecting wider international experience – part of the broadening of the scope of urban policy also related to the emerging discourse of global urban economic competition and urban entrepreneurialism, and the contested view that the way in which urban, regional and other subnational territories are governed has become more important in the context of the globalization of economic activity and what is asserted to be the diminishing importance of the nation-state in exercising economic management functions (see, e.g., Brenner, 1999; Jessop, 2000; Scott, 2001b).

As a consequence of these three stimuli, the conclusion drawn was that urban policy in its broadest sense ought to focus more directly on stimulating urban economic competitiveness, and this was wedded to a corresponding view that more effective governance was a critical and necessary element in the broader effort to revivify the economies of the major British cities. However, this general commitment to modernize urban governance conceals dimensions of competitiveness that are conceptually quite different (Harding *et al.*, 2000). The first relates to the proclivity for urban policy-makers to perceive their cities as competing with each other, and to frame policy in that light. Local coalitions of elite actors, for example, compete amongst themselves, directly and indirectly, for resources from central government, most obviously in the context of competition between city-based organizations for the award of discretionary regeneration resources, but also through lobbying for nominally non-discretionary formula-driven resource allocations from the centre. Inward investment promotion also remains a prominent feature on the policy agenda, and provides another example of this first type of competitiveness (though largely at the scale of regions rather than individual cities).

The second way in which urban governance impinges upon competitiveness relates to the notion that a city's competitive standing is conditioned by the extent and nature of its mix of assets, and the degree to which these can assist business start-ups and relocations and enhance the competitive performance of individual firms. The actions of local and non-local policy-makers are of key importance in determining whether the precise mix of assets can help provide firms with competitive advantages of different sorts. Under this reading, the competitiveness of an area is perceived not just as the simple aggregate of the performance of constituent firms, but also as something that has a geographical component in that the contextual characteristics of places help condition firm performance. It is in helping create these conditions that institutional configurations and policy emphases are seen as important. A varied and disparate range of factors have been identified as influences upon competitiveness, including the collective benefit that can arise from clustered trading networks of small firms, the significance of quality of life in urban areas for the attraction and retention of skilled workers, the importance of physical assets such as communications infrastructures and stocks of sites and premises, the significance of skills levels amongst the work force, and the form and extent of state regulation and intervention (see, for example, Boddy, 1999; Kresl, 1995; Porter, 1990). It is this that explains the enduring emphasis on cultivating supply-side assets through policies delivered at the urban and regional level, and sometimes channelled through institutions that derive functions and resources through deconcentration and devolution from the central state.

These two conceptions of urban competitiveness do not map on to each other in a straightforward way. It is perfectly plausible to conceive of instances in which cities are competitive in the first sense, but not the second. A city could accommodate individual firms which, in aggregate, are sufficiently competitive to contribute to overall urban economic well-being, but also one that is uncompetitive in terms of efforts to attract discretionary grant resource, lure inward investors, attract high profile development and so on. Indeed, there are logical grounds for arguing that the correlation between the two dimensions of urban competitiveness could be a negative one: the less propitious the collective health of firms and the aggregate economy of a city, the greater the pressure to compensate by competing for government resources, tourists, affluent economic migrants, inward investment, flagship events and so on.

In light of this brief summary of the contours of the various ideas that underlie conceptions of urban governance and its role in cultivating competitiveness, the chapter now moves on to provide a synoptic overview of current forms of governance in cities. It draws in particular on the results of different strands of the *Cities* programme in order to map urban governance arrangements and provide a synthesis of the evidence on its impact upon competitiveness, particularly with regard to the nature and composition of strategic-level partnerships, their policy focus and effectiveness, and the limitations that network styles of governance entail in respect of fermenting economic development. On the basis of this evidence, the chapter concludes by offering some pointers on the ways in which the form and nature of governance can potentially condition city competitiveness in an effective way.

Mapping urban governance arrangements

The most obvious and immediate, and perhaps rather glib, conclusion to be drawn about the nature of urban governance is that it is complex, multifaceted and diverse. Nonetheless, it is helpful, drawing on research across the *Cities* programme, to propose a coarse threefold taxonomy – the three Ss – around which to structure an initial exploration of forms of urban governance and the way in which they relate to competitiveness. Broadly, interventions are of three different (though overlapping) types: those relating to attempts to co-ordinate institutions and policy-making (*synchronization*); those which seek to promote and cultivate local attributes in order to develop competitive advantage (*salesmanship*); and those which aim to provide a range of services in an effective and efficient way (*service delivery*).

Synchronization

Attempts to co-ordinate the range of interventions in cities have long been a prominent objective of urban policy. Interest has centred as much on the ways in which urban policy is managed, in an institutional-administrative sense, as with its efficacy or impact. At national level, the preoccupation with policy co-ordination was reflected, in the late 1980s, in the inception of the Action for Cities programme as a means of harmonizing area-based interventions emanating from a range of central government departments, and of encouraging mainstream departmental spending to work in complementary ways. More recent policy innovations also reflect continuing concern at central government level with regularizing policy initiatives. The tendency for periodic proliferation of area-based programmes to be followed by efforts to consolidate and rationalize is reflected in the Blair administration's predilection for 'joining-up' area-based initiatives (ABIs: DETR, 2000a). The former Performance and Innovation Unit of the Cabinet Office exhorted greater co-ordination across the multiplicity of ABIs, in part through the establishment of a Regional Co-ordination Unit (Cabinet Office, 2000). The initial report of the government's Social Exclusion Unit (1998) also resulted in further investigation of the scope for joining-up as part of the National Strategy for Neighbourhood Renewal (DETR, 2000b), while the urban White Paper addressed the need for better co-ordination by announcing the launch of a cabinet committee on urban affairs and an urban policy unit within DETR (2000c).

These national initiatives have spawned a variety of local bodies whose principal task is often one of retrospective strategy-building, so that different area-based initiatives adhere (or appear to adhere) to some wider, 'strategic' objectives. The establishment by the Blair government in England of initiatives such as Local Strategic Partnership (LSPs), in the 88 local authority districts eligible to receive Neighbourhood Renewal Fund resources, and the requirement that they produce Local Neighbourhood Renewal Strategies, provides one example. At the intra-urban scale, the inception of the New Deal for Communities (NDC) and the advent of Urban Regeneration Companies (URCs) have been posited partly on a view that there is a need to co-ordinate the work of geographically over-lapping ABIs, as well as to ensure that mainstream local authority and public agency expenditure and private sector activities adhere to common sets of objectives.

Despite the enduring rhetorical preoccupation with effecting better co-ordination, however, the evidence across much of the *Cities* research suggests that urban policy continues to be compartmentalized in an artificial and unhelpful way. This applies both sectorally, as separate policy domains continue to operate with less interaction than might be expected, and geographically, as individual ABIs operate insularly and as different tiers of governance fail to work in harmony. Even in the context, for example, of somewhere like East Manchester, held by some to represent an exemplar of innovation and good practice in relation to neighbourhood revitalization, progress has been hampered by the need to marry the work of in excess of a dozen area-based funding streams, many with differing remits, objectives and geographical coverage (Robson *et al.*, 2003).

Yet in spite of such practical difficulties, energies continue to be devoted to co-ordinating policy and, in particular, developing the 'strategic capacity' felt to be essential in the context of international inter-city competition, but seen as having diminished as power has dissipated across elaborate networks of institutions. One of the most significant of the early attempts to address this, and to develop a city-wide strategy benefiting from consensual cross-sector multi-agency support, was the City Pride initiative, launched in 1994 in Birmingham, London and Manchester, and later extended, less successfully, to seven additional cities. Prompted at one level by a desire to co-ordinate the multiplicity of regeneration initiatives in each city, the real significance of City Pride lay in its reflection of a perception on the part of both central government and local urban policy actors that urban economic revitalization (or, in the case of London, further growth) required strategic policy-making capacity. The argument was that only by thinking strategically, ambitiously and imaginatively, viewing each city in terms of its de facto city-region and creating a series of related initiatives and institutions, could competitiveness be sustained in the global context.

Ten years on from its inception, City Pride can be viewed to a large extent as another short-lived imposed entity, its viability substantially undermined once central government support evaporated. But this conceals differing experiences amongst some of the City Pride initiatives, and these shed light on the extent to which the local peculiarities of individual cities – their institutional and personal chemistry, their jurisdictional ambit, the particular emphases given to policy – impact on the degree to which 'governance' can successfully underpin competitiveness. Whereas in some of the designated cities – notably Birmingham – the City Pride model survived and retained a degree of salience for a decade after its inception, the Manchester equivalent, while remaining formally in existence and receiving formal support from city elites, saw its real influence and significance wane. For Liverpool, by way of further contrast, the launch of the initiative, following the announcement of a second wave of City Pride designations in 1997, was stymied at the outset by inter-district wrangling and, it might be inferred, by the absence of the minimum degree of institutional cohesion which underpinned the coalitions that formed in Birmingham and Manchester. The message here may be that local distinctiveness is an important element in building strategic capacity, and that – as the experience of Glasgow and Edinburgh further suggests (Turok *et al.*, 2003) – developing locally tailored institutional configurations, as well as policy interventions, is markedly more effective than top-down, one-size-fits-all approaches of the sort arguably exemplified by City Pride.

The uneven effectiveness of these early institutional innovations perhaps explains why extensive efforts continue to be devoted to effecting better co-ordination and developing strategic capacity: 'steering', in the words of Kleinman (2001), as opposed to the formerly dominant local government role of 'rowing', or straightforward service delivery. Attempts to marshal funds and broker agreement amongst stakeholders about strategy – creating what Robson, Peck and Holden (2000) call 'partnerships of partnerships' – remain significant challenges in a context of only partly reduced fiscal pressure on local government and continuing institutional proliferation and diffusion. The *Cities* research found clear evidence that the latter continues to present no little difficulty: creating coherence out of the plethora of institutions within cities remains a significant challenge. In Bristol, for example, the nature of network governance is said by one *Cities* study to exemplify 'a situation of loose governance where multi-organisational partnerships co-exist in a fragmented system, and where no single organisation or person offers clear direction' (Sweeting *et al.*, 2003, p. 11), and by another to comprise a 'complex proliferation of partnerships and networks [which] is weakly integrated and . . . lacking in collaborative capacity and strategic direction' (Boddy, 2003, p. 11).

At the same time, the underbounding that constrained Manchester in relation to City Pride continues to represent a significant barrier for many of the major British cities. Following local government reorganization and its resultant Balkanization in the early 1990s, Glasgow stands out as one of the cities confronted with the greatest difficulties in this respect. Its city-region is fragmented across numerous local authority jurisdictions, reinforcing the need to ensure, as the Glasgow–Edinburgh *Cities* study concludes, 'that there are suitable forums for strategic thinking and other opportunities for cross-boundary cooperation and joint working' (Turok *et al.*, 2003, p. 27). This is a challenge to which Glasgow, perhaps reflecting the daunting scale of difficulty involved, has responded with significant, if still preliminary, efforts to create new collaborative structures. This has involved, for example, voluntaristic joint arrangements for structure planning, replacing the formal mechanism formerly in place via the upper tier of Scottish regions. However, such efforts face the difficulty of arriving at consensual solutions that are acceptable across a fragmented array of actors, and the experience in Bristol, for example, is that development of such strategy across the city-region inevitably results in unsatisfactory compromise and 'strategically sub-optimal outcomes' (Boddy, 2003, p. 13).

Similar efforts to develop strategy at the city-region scale are evident across many of Britain's principal cities. They relate to many of the arguments proffered by the Core Cities Group, a lobbying body established in the mid-1990s to articulate the case of eight of England's principal provincial cities. At the heart of the case posited by the Core Cities Group (and echoing the NCW: see Chapter 1 above) is the two-pronged argument that economic underperformance in the major cities outwith London is detrimental to national competitiveness, and that government should acknowledge the need to empower these cities in order to help create the sort of dynamic, innovative provincial cities and regions evident in much of the rest of Europe. Part of this empowerment, runs the argument, should involve the creation of new institutional formations which relate more closely to functional city-regional boundaries. This would involve rectifying the fragmentation of city-regions across neighbouring local government jurisdictions, and correcting their current underbounding through the creation of new inter-district alliances. New city-regional partnerships (probably on a loose voluntary basis, rather than what is held to be an old-fashioned statutory one) of local authorities and other institutional actors, rather than a return to some variant of formal metropolitan government, they contend, would be a solution which would work harmoniously alongside existing regional level bodies such as the English RDAs. In this way, they argue, it would be possible to ' "add more cylinders to the UK's economic engine" . . . [without] redistributing the wealth already created in London and the south east' (Core Cities Group, 2002, p. 6).

Alongside efforts to develop more coherent inter-institutional alliances at the scale of the city-region, a parallel (but more recent and less well-developed) axis of institution-building is evident in the form of incipient links between cities. Much of this, echoing the developments at the level of individual cities in the early-mid-1990s, has been driven by top-down efforts, though this time emanating from the EU Commission rather than central government. The desirability of promoting polycentric linkages between groups of cities, as Richardson and Jensen (2000) note, has underpinned the European Spatial Development Perspective, and such notions have begun to infuse policy-making at the urban and regional scale. For example, the Spatial Vision for North West Europe, produced as part of the European Interreg II programme to explore the means by which transborder spatial planning and economic development could best be promoted, championed the idea that policy should support the long-term development of polycentric areas – including Manchester–Liverpool–Sheffield–Leeds – as 'counter-weights' to correct the overheating claimed to characterize the European core around London, the South East of England and the Paris Basin (NWMA, 2000). Similar concerns – focusing on the need to foster collaboration and to pool individual city strengths in order to compete more effectively in the global economy – underlay the decision by the North West (regional) Development Agency to commission a Liverpool–Manchester Vision study (SURF Centre, 2001). The resultant concordat between the two cities, pitched in the vague terms of a commitment to collaborate rather than compete 'when outside the [North West] region' (NWDA, 2001), was a predictable product of compromise, its real value the symbolic one of appearing to subscribe to a common regional agenda. However, the fact that it initially stalled when the leaders of the two cities failed to agree on the location of the venue at which it would be launched provided a telling illustration of the limited extent to which meaningful collaboration is feasible in a context of consistent inter-city rivalry and in the absence of any real or direct financial incentive from central government.

The emphasis on cultivating polycentric linkages is relatively recent, and confined largely to the realms of rhetoric rather than real policy-making. What few inter-urban links already exist relate in large measure (as in the idea of 'global gateways' propounded in the Spatial Vision) to often abstract notions around the potential for bolstering the international standing of cities by developing synergies and capitalizing on supposed niche specialisms. The reality is often more prosaic. Bailey and Turok (2001), in relation to the scope for developing Glasgow and Edinburgh as a polycentric entity, identify limited evidence of existing functional link-ages. As the Glasgow–Edinburgh *Cities* study argues, however, such a conclusion ought not to preclude the scope for joint working between the two, so long as the emphasis can be on practical co-operation rather than improbable aspirations to develop globally significant 'synergies' (in line with what Hay, 2000, and others call 'globaloney'). Overheating in Edinburgh, for example, could be eased by developing strategy and policy within an overarching framework extending across both cities, and which might focus on intensifying the reuse of the surfeit of degraded and under-utilized brownfield sites in Glasgow (Turok *et al.*, 2003, p. 35). The diffi-culty, though, is in developing genuinely complementary approaches along such lines in a context of institutional and policy fragmentation both within and across cities, and in the absence of any significant financial stimulus to collaborate.

Salesmanship

It is clear that the focus of many of these efforts to synchronize institutional actions and agendas, and to co-ordinate policy, has been on image and appearance as much as practical issues around service delivery. At the heart of these efforts has been a concern amongst urban policy-makers to send out the right signals, whether in terms of the message that a city's institu-tions are sufficiently adept to warrant the award of additional central government or EU resources, or that a city has the right mix of assets to lure inward investors, flagship events or visitors. Such concerns have been central to the agendas of many or most of the examples documented, rein-forcing the importance of the second broad dimension of urban gover-nance: the policy-maker preoccupation with what might be summarized as salesmanship.

The most obvious context in which salesmanship applies is in bidding by coalitions of urban actors for policy resources allocated competitively by central government on a discretionary basis, as was the case in much of the 1990s in respect of area-based regeneration monies through, for instance, the Single Regeneration Budget Challenge Fund (in England) and Programme for Partnership (in Scotland). Here, there is evidence of variable aptitudes across cities to attract resources in this way. Some cities have received regular injections of funding which can be attributed to an adeptness on the part of urban elites in forming apparently cohesive 'grant coalitions', in interpreting entitlement rules and identifying funding opportunities in effective ways, and in articulating a saleable case for funds and garnering resources accordingly (even if, as Jones and Ward, 1998, note, this is not automatically correlated with judicious use of such monies). Other cities – as evidenced by the experiences of Bristol and Salford under the City Challenge initiative in the early 1990s, for example (Malpass, 1994) – have been markedly less successful in attracting discretionary grant funding, sometimes in spite of strong 'objective' cases based on indices of deprivation. In the case of Bristol, this reflected concern from central government about inter-institutional friction at the local level, a history (in the 1980s) of overt local authority hostility to central government, the supposed marginalization of the private sector and a continued weddedness to what were seen as outmoded distributional concerns viewed as conflicting with the centre's more entrepreneurial outlook (Boddy, 2003; Deas *et al.*, 2000).

Despite the declining emphasis of this form of 'challenge funding' under the Blair government of 1997, and renewed efforts to allocate area-based regeneration resources on the basis of quantitative measures of deprivation, inter-city competition remains a prominent concern for policy-makers in respect of flagship cultural and sporting events. For example, the competition to be awarded European Capital of Culture status for 2008 involved bids, *inter alia*, from Birmingham, Bristol and Newcastle, as well as Liverpool, the eventual winner. That the competition attracted media interest on a scale entirely disproportionate to the modest funding on offer to the successful city was partly reflective of the significance policy-makers attached to the initiative. This, in turn, reflected the policy-maker consensus, following the experience of Glasgow in 1990 as European City of Culture, that substantial spin-off benefits could be generated directly as a result of the award of Capital of Culture status and the resultant growth in tourist and visitor numbers, and indirectly as a result of the fillip to the winning city's international status and visibility (Boyle, 1997; Turok *et al.*, 2003).

A number of examples from the *Cities* programme illustrate the striking degree to which salesmanship has become a central goal of urban policy-making, and in doing so has supplanted the predominant emphasis of urban governance on ensuring effective and efficient service delivery. One centres on strategy-building efforts in London, which betray the profound extent to which the substantive focus of urban policy-making in Britain shifted over the period roughly from 1980 to 2000. As Kleinman (2001) demonstrates, the London Industrial Strategy produced by the former Greater London Council (GLC) in 1985 is markedly different from the Economic Development Strategy developed by the London Development Agency (LDA) fifteen years later. Whereas the former produced an elaborate interventionist strategy across industrial sectors and viewed London exclusively within a UK context, the latter, in tune with its time, adopted a predictably international, market-oriented, pro-growth outlook, aspiring to reinforce London's putative global economic significance. Significantly, the various means by which this goal could be facilitated revolve to a large extent around salesmanship: 'promoting London as a place for people and business' is one of the key policy objectives (Kleinman, 2001, p. 9). Similarly, as Gordon (2003a) notes, the draft London Plan published in 2002 pitched its 'vision' not in the workaday language of the spatial planning efforts it was intended to guide, but in terms of the altogether more ambitious desire 'to develop London as an exemplary sustainable world city' (Gordon, 2003, p. 7).

These examples are illustrative of the more general way in which local policy actors have bought, often unquestioningly, into the rhetoric of global urban competition. But such conviction, as Lovering (1999, 2001) has argued forcefully, conceals limited understanding amongst urban and regional policy-makers of the ways in which they can capitalize upon the ostensible opportunities said to have been opened up by globalization, and is based on a lack of any clear evidence that cities and regions are as dependent upon, or integrated with, the global economy as contemporary policy orthodoxy implies. Indeed, there is evidence from the *Cities* programme to the contrary, suggesting that the extent to which firms have international functional linkages is dramatically overstated. In Glasgow and Edinburgh, for example, a survey of firms found that only 7–10 per cent of businesses operating in externally-traded sectors were geared predominantly to overseas exports, and the bulk of economic linkages were clearly related to the two cities' roles as regional service centres (Turok *et al.*, 2003). And even in the more internationalized context of London, where one would expect domestic trade to be of relatively limited import, amongst firms which trade principally outside London and the South East, 71 per cent of employment is in firms operating largely or exclusively within the UK (Gordon, 2003, p. 5).

There is a convincing case, in light of this, that policy-makers are overly preoccupied with bolstering cities' international standing, seduced by fanciful talk of global competitiveness at the expense (as the Glasgow–Edinburgh study notes) of more mundane but underappreciated issues, for example ensuring an adequate supply of developable land, providing infrastructure, or maintaining and enhancing consumption services. Yet, as the chapter now goes on to explore, these roles have long presented urban policy-makers with considerable challenges, and there are now signs of the beginnings of an increased awareness of the role of effective governance in ensuring that service provision makes a positive contribution to broader competitiveness.

Service delivery

Delivery of services (or facilitation of service delivery) remains, in practical terms, the most important element of urban governance. In a UK context one would expect it to have increasing salience in the light of the second Blair administration's professed focus on delivery rather than strategy or policy-making. But the evidence from across the *Cities* programme suggests that it remains marginal to the discourse of urban governance, if not to the reality of day-to-day activity. Yet there are some signs of the growing, if still modest, awareness of the role (or potential role) that service provision can have in underpinning competitiveness, and of an appreciation that the effectiveness of governance arrangements is likely to be a critical factor in conditioning the extent to which this materializes.

Such a perspective informs part of the 'mainstreaming' agenda with which some urban policy-makers (particularly in the context of neighbourhood regeneration) are currently grappling. At the heart of the mainstreaming agenda is a desire to encourage public agencies to utilize mainstream service budgets in ways that are in tune with (and which supplement) resources directed through area-based initiatives, with the long-term aspiration that the latter can be phased out as mainstream programmes begin to take on the role in respect of disadvantaged areas currently filled by targeted central government regeneration policy. This is a philosophy that is central to many of the policies that comprise the National Strategy for Neighbourhood Renewal (NSNR) in England. The Blair government's flagship urban initiative, the New Deal for Communities (NDC), for example, emphasizes the need to align potentially complementary mainstream resources with those channelled directly through the NDC Partnerships themselves.

However, there is limited evidence to imply this has occurred to any significant extent during the early years of the initiative, and much more in the way of evidence to suggest that effecting mainstreaming is proving extremely problematic (see, for example, Robson, Castree and Rees, 2003, in relation to the NDC programme in East Manchester, or Russell, 2003, in respect of Liverpool). There is, as a critical House of Commons select committee report notes, confusion amongst policy-makers about what mainstreaming entails. There is also, the report contends, limited scope for employing mainstream resources as a longer-term alternative to direct area-based resourcing on the grounds that the former is subject to an array of countervailing central government targets, some of them inimical to regeneration goals (HofC HPLGRC, 2003). Indeed the reality, in the context of strained local authority budgets, continues to be that mainstream local resources are sometimes withdrawn from areas benefiting from the injection of central government regeneration resource (see Deas *et al.*, 2003, on Oldham NDC in Greater Manchester).

Despite these difficulties, there is at least an increasing awareness that services impact upon the fortunes of neighbourhoods, though rather less in the way of acknowledgement that the way in which, and the effectiveness with which, they are delivered is also likely to affect city-wide economic well-being. This reflects the tendency to view area-based initiatives in the largely social terms set out in the NSNR, and an absence of any concerted effort to link neighbourhood revitalization to city-wide or regional economic fortunes. The City Growth Fund in Scotland, while bringing resources (£90 million over three years) of modest scale in relation to the economic issues they are intended to address, represents one of a surprisingly small number of current initiatives intended to revitalize urban economies (Turok *et al.*, 2003). In England, by contrast, in spite of policy-maker rhetoric about cultivating city competitiveness, spatial policy efforts to bolster economic performance under the Blair governments have come largely at the scale of the region rather than the city (or the city-region), and principally through RDAs. Although there have been some efforts at the intra-urban scale to support local economic rejuvenation – for example, via the 14 Urban Regeneration Companies established between 1999 and 2003 – area-based initiatives under the NSNR, in spite of acknowledgement of the importance of inter-linkages between social cohesion and economic advancement, have tended in the main to prioritize social and community issues. As the Core Cities Group and others have argued, there have been few if any concerted attempts to view competitiveness in terms of functional city-regions and to frame policy interventions in that light. Although RDAs have increasingly begun to develop sub-regional strategies geared partly towards a recognition of functional urban areas, the focus of policy has remained on regions as a whole, and on intra-urban neighbourhoods, reflecting what Harding (2002) has called the 'missing middle' in English governance: the absence of any formal institutional layer based at the city-region scale.

Recent urban institutional innovation, it appears, has done little to help promote the linkage between service delivery and broader economic advancement. Here, London provides a telling illustration. The advent of the GLA (and the London Development Agency and Transport for London, which it oversees) marks out the city as better equipped in institutional or 'governance' terms, if not in terms of powers or resourcing, to develop interventions to address city-wide economic issues. It has already prompted some discernible changes in the emphases embodied in strategy and policy. One change has been to raise the sights of policy, with policy-makers apparently 'thinking big' and viewing London as a single, powerful economic entity in a global context. This is evidenced by the stream of ambitious interventions planned and in train: the decision to urge central government to support a bid for the 2012 Olympic Games, or to press government to develop the Thames Gateway, provide two such instances. These, and other high-profile activities pursued by Mayor Ken Livingstone, are intended to reinforce London's primacy in national terms and its standing as a global city. Lobbying for the completion of strategically significant infrastructure projects, such as the Crossrail project, with city-wide economic implications represents another aspect of this.

The key point here is that London, if viewed in narrow institutional terms, is clearly better endowed than other major British cities (even if city-regional governance is weak relative to its major international comparators: see, for example, Jouve and Lefevre, 2002). Its policy-makers have already begun to develop policy and build strategy, and its political leaders to articulate the supporting case, with a view to enhancing its competitive standing. But even in what, to other British cities, would appear to be this enviable context, there are still arguments that London is poorly equipped, in governance terms, in relation to the scale of the economic challenge it faces. London institutions could be given a broader and more meaningful geographical remit that embraces part or all of the administrative regions that encircle it, and with which it has a high level of functional integration.

Even though London – with the introduction of a Mayor in 2000, inspired by the US model – has a central figure to champion its cause, and a powerful figure to oversee the development of strategy within London itself, the GLA itself is poorly resourced and the Mayor, in this sense, is in a weak position (Sweeting *et al.*, 2003). For example, the GLA lacks responsibility for the majority of the significant areas of service delivery, such as education (which remains the responsibility of the lower tier of 32 London boroughs) or major infrastructure projects (which is the province largely of central government, its executive agencies and the private sector). Both examples limit the extent to which city-regional institutions can help nurture competitiveness and, more specifically, constrain the degree to which service provision can be consciously managed so as to complement city-wide economic development objectives. Equally, resourcing, alongside the absence of responsibility for particular services, also presents incipient metropolitan government with a problem. The LDA has benefited from significant increases in funding from central government to English RDAs, but remains, in per capita terms, poorly resourced in comparison to its counterparts in the North and Midlands, and simultaneously hamstrung by its need to devote the bulk of its finance to the delivery of national programmes (Gordon, 2003a; Kleinman and Hall, 2002).

While these undoubtedly represent constraints, however, they are of smaller magnitude than in most provincial cities. The London city-region has a formal institutional layer with guaranteed resources and statutory powers, unlike the situation in English provincial cities. London's governance may continue to be fragmented across a network of actors, but it is a network that converges upon a body with the legitimacy (and at least part of the capacity) to co-ordinate it. This puts it in marked contrast to cities such as Liverpool, Bristol and Manchester, where – partly because of underbounding of the core district authority, and partly because no single champion akin to the GLA has emerged – city-regional governance is much less well developed (see, e.g., Deas, 2005, in respect of Manchester, or Boddy, 2003, on Bristol). And partly because of that, most cities are constrained or prevented from making the link between service provision and city-wide competitiveness.

Conclusion: does governance matter to city competitiveness?

In light of the NCW (Chapter 1) that the precise form of urban governance can have important impacts on competitiveness, in both the senses outlined, it is worth exploring in more detail the ways in which institutional structures and policy initiatives have affected (and can affect) urban economic fortunes. It is useful to reiterate that the relationship between urban governance and city competitiveness is a complex, multifaceted one which defies straightforward précis. But it is possible, nonetheless, to highlight four broad conclusions which synthesize findings across the *Cities* programme and which augment the broad typology of aspects of urban governance outlined above.

Flexibility and inclusivity

The first conclusion is that cities need to be governed in ways that are flexible and respond to local circumstances. This is not the facile truism, redolent of 'mission statements', that it might at first seem. As the *Cities* research on London shows, there is considerable uncertainty in relation to demographic and economic trends: uncertainty that has been accentuated, it is argued, by internationalization (especially in relation to labour migration) and flexibilization (in relation to labour markets). The implication, it is contended, of this increased capriciousness in urban economic trends is that there is a 'volatility to [London's] economy, which makes quite different outcomes possible and mean[s] that . . . [s]trategies for the city have to be flexible enough to cope' (Buck *et al.*, 2002, p. 363).

Similar conclusions can be drawn from experiences chronicled elsewhere in the *Cities* programme. Part of the explanation for the effectiveness of policy-making in Manchester relative to Liverpool centred on the ability of key actors in the former to operate opportunistically: what Alan Harding *et al.* (2003) term 'the ability to adopt and realise a horses-for-courses approach to inter-governmental and public–private sector partnership'. It was this that enabled Manchester to pursue high profile projects such as the Olympic/Commonwealth Games, tapping into networks of supporters in central government and the private sector.

Ambition, imagination and strategy

The second conclusion relates to the variable capacity across cities to act and think strategically. Manchester's emblematic transformation from a city in the 1980s in which, in the words of the then slogan of the City Council, the goal of policy was 'defending jobs and improving services', to one in the 1990s in which the emphasis was the apparently more entrepreneurial one of 'making it happen' (Williams, 1998) is clearly one with broader rhetorical resonance. It is clear that local authorities and urban policy-makers more generally have bought into notions around city competition and the policy prescriptions implied by the NCW. But the Manchester slogan is also one that dramatically overstates the real extent of the practical transition undergone in urban policy-making, at least insofar as it applies to local government. Local authorities, despite rhetorical and symbolic commitment to promoting competitiveness through the establishment of and involvement in a variety of new agencies espousing conventional contemporary formulae for economic revitalization, continue in practice to devote most time and effort to their core functions of delivering services. Nonetheless, while the core business of urban governance (and especially local government) continues to be the not insignificant one of ensuring effective service provision, either directly or through a co-ordinating or enabling role, the development of strategy and high-profile policy continues to receive ever increasing prominence.

There is also an argument that while strategy building is important in view of the dearth of such activity, especially at the city-region scale, as monolithic institutions have been dismantled or have declined, and as network governance has grown, the emphasis is too squarely on grandiose issues of global urban competition, rather than the more important issues of service delivery – land, infrastructure, training, consumption services – which can more realistically benefit city competitiveness. The conclusion to be drawn from much of the *Cities* research is that there is surprisingly little alertness amongst policy-makers to the notion that it is these areas of activity which impact (indirectly but in a significant way) on competitiveness.

The recent concern by central government to encourage an appreciation of the need to conceive service delivery and other aspects of their 'core business' not just in terms of direct consequences for consumers, but also in relation to the knock-on consequences for economic performance, is an important first step in dislodging this kind of narrow, partial view of the role of governance in encouraging competitiveness. Exhortations by the centre to employ mainstream service resources for more broadly conceived regeneration objectives are an important part of this. Underlying current neighbourhood regeneration policy in England, as we have seen, is the longer-term aspiration that mainstream local resources should ultimately replace centrally allocated regeneration funds (directed largely on an area basis), giving local policy-makers more autonomy over outgoings but also encouraging them to view service expenditure in more expansive and ambitious (but also realistic) terms. Here, the early evidence is not wholly encouraging. The centre's promptings, it appears, have generated little more than platitudinous commitments to mainstreaming, while the reality is sometimes one of substitution or 'reverse mainstreaming'. Nevertheless, there is at the very least a commitment from the centre that service delivery should be viewed as an important part of the local government role in cultivating urban economic well-being.

The need for meaningful institutional geographies

The third conclusion centres on the critical issue of the demarcation of urban administrative areas. Arguments that administrative or political territories, and policy-making efforts, need to be aligned to functional economic space are not, of course, new. Nevertheless, the *Cities* research reinforces long-standing arguments that policy-making ought to be organized around more expansively delimited city-regions, in contrast to the predominantly narrow, artificial territories that comprise most urban districts in Britain. Drawing on US experiences, Hill and Nowak (2002) argue the case that effective urban governance relies on drawing institutional geometries which reflect the functional extent of housing, labour and business market areas. This can help prevent the sorts of fiscal stress associated with politico-geographical incongruities whereby the maintenance of important assets (as well as the costs of social liabilities) are borne disproportionately by underbounded municipalities. Though premised on the rather different context of often extreme underbounding in US cities, such arguments, while familiar, continue to have relevance in a British context. But while this contention is a long-established one, what is of especial interest is the apparently growing realization that narrowly bounded city authorities contain not just disproportionate fractions of low income households, but also some significant assets which ought to be of real benefit to satellite towns and suburban hinterlands. This could be critical in gainsaying the established view that more expansive city delimitation would bring with it unambiguous costs for the outlying suburban districts.

Encouraging more meaningful institutional geographies would also help resolve the many 'scalar' conflicts that have arisen between agencies organized around different geographical territories. The precise form of institutional restructuring in Britain has resulted in local authorities sitting alongside a welter of regional and sub-regional bodies that include as part of their remit contributing to the sub-national competitiveness agenda. There is certainly an argument that, in order to alleviate such conflict, central government ought to devote more effort to ensuring 'elite cohesion' across institutional and sectoral boundaries, not least by reigning in the continuing upsurge in new economic development bodies. Adopting a top-down rationalization of initiatives and institutions is already happening, for example, through the Regional Co-ordination Unit (RCU) in England (RCU, 2002, 2003), but retaining such an approach could plausibly enhance the capacity of cities and regions to promote competitiveness, rather than immerse themselves in maintaining good stakeholder relations.

Linking the urban, the regional and the national

The issue of scalar conflict reinforces the importance of the fourth conclusion: that there needs to be greater effort to ensure that governance and policy-making at different levels are complementary. This is particularly important because, even if its aggregate impact is significant, the potential for effective urban governance and policy-making is significantly constrained by the national policy context. London's economic fortunes in the late 1980s and early 1990s, for example, were dictated in large measure not by formal urban governance and policy-making, but by the altogether more profound forces of national economic restructuring and the tendency towards periodic recession. Likewise, part of the nature of its contemporary labour market position is conditioned not just by what city or even national institutions do, but by exogenous factors such as the happenstance of patterns of international labour migration (Buck *et al.*, 2002).

The message here is that while there is now widespread recognition, if only partial understanding, of the important role played by urban economies in contributing to national competitiveness, there needs to be greater sensitivity at the centre to the consequences of national policy for cities. Such a perspective would not be new: for example, the advent of

Action for Cities in England in the late 1980s was premised partly on a desire to encourage government departments to anticipate the urban consequences of apparently unrelated policy. Yet it is clear that 'urban proofing' along these lines has yet to materialize and that alertness to the urban consequences of national (English) policy does not extend to any significant degree beyond the Office of the Deputy Prime Minister. Were co-ordination of policy in this way to continue beyond the traditional 'spatial' areas of activity – area-based regeneration, land-use planning and so on – and embrace other areas of policy-making, city-based institutions would be faced with a less daunting task in developing policy and strategy to promote competitiveness and maintain or enhance social cohesion.

Yet, at the same time, there is clearly a tension between, on one hand, arguments that urban authorities and their local partners ought to be given much more autonomy over the nature and form of urban policy interventions (see HofC HPLGRC, 2003) and, on the other, that central government should devote more energy to ensuring that different area-based initiatives complement each other. For example, a narrow reading of the Sustainable Communities plan for England (ODPM, 2003b) might imply that resources are being channelled towards the resurrection of sluggish housing markets in the northern cities, and that growth pressures in the South East are being accommodated by diverting development to less buoyant or pressurized sub-areas such as the Thames Gateway. But while both strands appear, individually, to be logical and justifiable responses to particular sets of local circumstances, they ignore the uneven consequences across regions. The issues confronting London – overheating, social polarization, maintaining its international standing – should not induce policy responses that are divorced from their national consequences. The two-pronged view, which is central to the NCW, that cities are important engines of national economic growth and also need to be accorded greater policy-making autonomy, is one that risks exacerbating inter-regional inequality. Although it is possible to argue that bodies such as the GLA ought to be accorded increased power and resourcing, there is a danger, if it is not married to robust central government oversight, that this could lead to the sort of insularity that might inadvertently undermine economic development efforts elsewhere.

This is an argument that appears not to have been taken on board by central government in England, where the enduring preoccupation is with joining up ABIs at the local and regional scale without necessarily considering the implications of urban interventions for inter-regional disparity. But if urban governance is ultimately to prove effective in advancing city competitiveness, the onus is as much on national as local policy.

Chapter 13

Urban Properties: Spaces, Places and the Property Business

SIMON GUY, JOHN HENNEBERRY and GLEN BRAMLEY

Introduction

Internationalization, globalization and the shift to more flexible, specialized production present major challenges to cities. To remain globally competitive cities must manipulate and re-present their assets to an international audience. One key asset is property. Processes of production, socialization and consumption all take shape through the transformation of built form, 'grounding' economic, political and social relations in physical property. Yet there is a startling gap between the consideration and characterization of property by urban researchers (whether geographers, sociologists, political analysts or economists) and that of property analysts (applied economists, financial analysts and valuers). The former have given surprisingly little attention to the property business, while the latter have attended only to property and have not connected with wider urban debates. The result is a limited appreciation of inter-relations between property development and investment, on the one hand, and the wider processes of urban change, policy and governance, on the other. In this chapter we hope to demonstrate how even a modest attempt to bridge this divide can enhance understanding and inform policy in both domains.

The chapter is in four sections. First, we examine the relations of production and governance framing development in two sectors, that of offices and housing. In doing so we highlight the diverse development trajectories of these sectors, and in particular the contrasting relations of governance shaping the development of each sector. We then turn our attention to the urban level and to the spatial patterns of development characterizing each sector in a number of British cities, exploring both historical and contemporary patterns of urban development. We then examine emerging inter-linkages between housing and offices through an analysis of recent strategies of city centre, mixed-use developments. Finally, we argue that development and developers are in the business not simply of constructing homes and offices, but rather are integral to the making of urban places. To understand the urban implications of this process in social, spatial, economic and environmental terms entails looking beyond standard textbook accounts of the development process or conventional policy images of development activity, to explore the competing logics and pathways of contemporary development in situated urban localities.

Structural change

Changes in the office market

Post-Fordist changes in the wider economy have been echoed in the property sector. They have altered fundamentally the structure and behaviour of the commercial property market and its role in urban development. The relations between building owners, occupiers and producers have been significantly re-cast.

Over the last 20 years the private sector has assumed the role of the predominant supplier of buildings in Britain. In 1977 roughly half (49 per cent) of new construction orders were made by the private sector; by 1998 the private sector accounted for more than three-quarters (79 per cent) of all new construction orders. '[S]uch a significant shift in the composition of fixed capital investment has important consequences for the property sector' (Ellison, 1998, p. i). The reduction in the public sector's relative and absolute contribution to building production has diminished its stabilizing effect on overall development trends. At the same time, construction projects have become larger and construction periods have become significantly shorter, increasing the elasticity of supply of new buildings. Development has, consequently, become a much more volatile activity with a basic dynamic set by the private sector, making it much less tractable by public policy.

Within this general context, the growth of flexible specialization has made new demands of property. Property suppliers have responded by offering flexibility through the terms both of occupation of accommodation and of its built form. Leases are increasingly preferred over freehold interests and are getting shorter, so firms are not tied to buildings for long periods. Buildings are designed to accommodate a range of occupiers and to cope with expansion or retrenchment. This flexibility has been achieved through a fundamental change in the organization and means of production of buildings: the substantial growth in the rented sector of the property market.

This can be viewed from two perspectives. For tenant companies it represents a classic response to competitive pressure: out-sourcing. It frees their capital to be applied to core business and leaves what for them is the occasional, specialized and costly process of property development to others better equipped to undertake it. For these others – property developers and investors – property supply is an opportunity to profit from the application of expertise and capital and the acceptance of risk. But this means that buildings produced by developers must satisfy the requirements of occupiers and investors: requirements for functional efficiency and financial performance, which are in tension. The way in which developers interpret and respond to these competing requirements, the balance which they strike between occupiers' and investors' needs (while still ensuring that they make a profit), determines what gets built.

The ability of developers to exploit the opportunity for profit presented by urban property markets is contingent upon their access to external capital, because development is a capital-intensive process and because developers' asset base is inadequate to meet such demands for capital. Two types of capital are needed: short-term debt finance to cover the development period and long-term investment finance to cover the life of the building. The former is generally provided by banks and the latter by investors, dominant among which are the institutions. Callender and Key (1996) estimate that around 45 per cent by value of the UK commercial and industrial property stock may be held by investors, of which about half (24 per cent of the stock) is held by UK institutions.

Globalization, deregulation and the development of new financial instruments have increased the availability of capital, but control over its supply has become more concentrated. This is particularly so in the UK. The City of London is a major, global financial centre and it exerts a predominant influence over lending and investment patterns at national level. Banks' credit decisions are highly centralized (Mackay and Molyneux, 1996). The bulk of the decisions relating to property investment are taken by a small number of portfolio managers based in London (Martin and Minns, 1995). These actors have debt and investment portfolios of which the property element is only a relatively small part. Consequently, the supply of capital to real estate depends upon the latter's attractiveness as a loan or investment opportunity, relative to other such financial media. This leaves the balance of power firmly with the suppliers of capital. If property does not meet lenders' or investors' requirements, they can always put their money elsewhere.

Property investment finance is provided on the suppliers' terms. Institutions like large buildings, built to superior design and specification parameters, occupied by major international companies and let on 'clean' leases: that is, prime property. Such property has low management costs and low risk covenants but is attuned to a global market in both occupier and ownership terms. The pursuit of such development and investment opportunities has had profound effects on the property market. One relates to the pattern of development.

Developers develop if they can make profits; and profits are value-driven. There are two components of urban development values. The first is rents, which are determined by the demand for accommodation of locally active industrial and commercial occupiers in the face of local building supply. The second is yields (property jargon for rates of return), which are determined by the views on the performance and risk of investment properties in that locale held by investors. The rent of a property divided by the yield gives its capital value. It follows that the capital value of two similar buildings currently producing the same rent but in different cities will vary according to the investors' judgement of their future performance and risk. Cities such as Manchester or Birmingham have few 'institutional standard' buildings compared with London, reducing liquidity and increasing risk. Consequently, investors pay higher prices for property investments in London and the South East than elsewhere. Higher prices result in greater potential development profitability and more development. The reverse is the case in peripheral regions and cities. As a consequence, the 'South' is relatively well provided with new buildings compared with the 'North' (see Figure 13.1).

Policy related to property development has had very little influence on the broad patterns of change outlined above. Planning regulation with respect to offices became markedly less restrictive with the introduction of the revised Use Classes Order of 1987. A surge in the development of out-of town business parks resulted (Wootton Jeffreys Consultants and Bernard

Figure 13.1 *The relative distribution of institutional investment and of development activity, 1984–98*

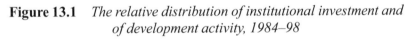

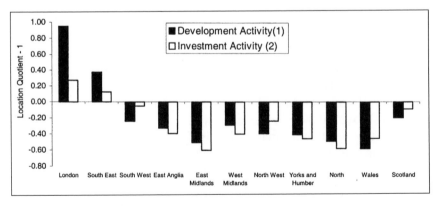

(1) Location Quotient describing the relative distribution of new orders (DETR Regional Distribution of New Orders data 1966–1998) using BFIBS GDP as location benchmark.
(2) Location Quotient describing the relative distribution of IPD recorded investment expenditure using BFIBS GDP as the location benchmark.

Thorpe, 1991). Planning policies are generally very supportive of business development because they provide job opportunities for local people (Bramley and Lambert, 2002). This is to be expected in areas with high unemployment but the trend can be seen even in very prosperous areas. Vodafone Airtouch plc obtained planning permission for a major head-quarters development on an unallocated green field site in Newbury, Berkshire, at a time when the local unemployment rate was less than 1 per cent (Campbell *et al.*, 2001).

Other policies have the effect of extending institutional investors' influence in urban property markets. The levering-in of private finance is a central component of urban regeneration policy. To achieve this, measures are pursued which improve financial performance of property investment (e.g. rent support and/or supply subsidies) and reduce its risk (e.g. the provision of market information and the development of new liquidity vehicles). We question later whether this conversion of a greater proportion of urban property into a form which better meets institutional investment criteria is the most effective way to promote urban development.

Structural features of the housing market

The structure of the housing market has moved in quite a different direction from that characterizing commercial property. Instead of renting, housing has moved decisively towards owner occupation as the dominant tenure. Whilst in some other Western countries private renting remains significant, in Britain it is a niche tenure attracting only small-scale capital (Freeman *et al.*, 1996). Large institutional landlordism is the preserve of a residualized social rented sector. New housing supply is the preserve of specialized housebuilder-developers, who may be likened to the specialist developers of commercial property (Bramley *et al.*, 1995). But large-scale capital does not involve itself in the long-term ownership and management of housing as an investment, except very indirectly through lending to social land-lords. Consequently it is arguably not that interested in the image or fate of residential areas in cities.

It is the atomized mass of individual owner occupiers who must concern themselves with housing decisions (Ford *et al.*, 2001). This entails consideration simultaneously of income prospects and affordability, the consumption benefits of housing and location and the future investment value of housing property. This has profound implications both for their individual behaviour in the market and also for their engagement with local political processes which bear on housing property values. As an example of the first kind, there is significant evidence from migration studies of apparently perverse patterns of behaviour, with people moving towards areas of high and rising prices rather than the opposite, which a simple economic model of demand would suggest (Fotheringham *et al.*, 2002). The second kind of effect is seen when owner occupiers participate in local political processes relating to planning for new development or redevelopment, with impacts which turn out to be important for the whole supply side of the market.

Mass owner occupation gives greatly enhanced importance to the behaviour of housing markets over time and space. Britain has exhibited considerable instability in this respect, with successive booms followed by prolonged slumps in the housing market, and with increasingly wide disparities in market performance between regions and localities (Bramely, Pawson and Third, 2000; Maclennan *et al.*, 1997; Meen, 1998). As owner occupation has become a mass tenure with few barriers to entry, a growing proportion of owners is drawn from lower income sections of the population exposed to increased risk in both the labour and housing markets (Burrows and Wilcox, 2001). Booms in their early phases can promote mobility, but as they peak more new buyers or inter-regional migrants are priced out, while in the slumps negative equity and disconnected chains frustrate mobility. In the peak areas of the housing market, buyers may be forced to look further afield and commit themselves to long commuting journeys. These problems frustrate the flexible supply of labour sought by the new economy.

Commentators such as Maclennan berate the British system for its lack of a large middle market of rented housing to promote mobility and flexibility. The majority of rented housing is in the social sector, which plays only a peripheral role in the economy. In the decades before 1980, when social renting housed many working households it was criticized for frustrating geographical labour mobility (Hughes and McCormick, 2000). Now, the profile of social tenants is overwhelmingly skewed towards the economically inactive. Although social tenants are becoming more mobile (Pawson and Bramley, 2000), this is seen as more of a problem in terms of community stability and cohesion, and less as an opportunity to facilitate labour mobility. Much of the existing social rented stock is perceived as a problem part of the urban system, housing large concentrations of the poor and socially excluded in unattractive, stigmatized estates.

Instability in the housing market can be induced by fluctuations in the macro-economy and monetary conditions. While the structure and operation of the housebuilding industry is partly to blame here, the most important factor is land supply and this is governed by planning controls, bringing governance into the picture in a significant way.

Planning treats new housing development in a much more restrictive way than most business property development. Evidence for this can be cited from various studies, including work within the central Scotland ICS on land availability and take-up (Bramley *et al.*, 2001). The restrictive treatment of housing arguably reflects the local political economy of housing (Evans, 1991; Industrial Systems Research, 1999). Planning regulation is exercised primarily at local level through elected local government, which is bound to reflect the sentiment of local residents towards new development proposals. With most residents (and even more of those who vote) being owner occupiers, there is a general preoccupation with protecting residential amenity and local property values. In many instances this will lead to a preference to restrict or prevent new housing development, particularly in more attractive suburban and edge-of-city locations (Bramley, Bartlett and Lambert, 1995). The interests of the potential occupiers of such new housing are not represented in local decision-making. Bramley (1998) shows that planning restrictions on new housing are systematically stronger in more affluent and attractive localities with strong economies, such as those characteristic of much of southern England.

Recent shifts in national policy in England have reinforced these tendencies. The preoccupation with urban regeneration has led to a strong focus on the recycling of brownfield land, and this has given licence to an even more restrictive stance towards greenfield development in the recent national guidance (DETR, 2000d). While consistent with the current urban policy agenda (DETR, 1999a), these shifts could also be seen to reflect national electoral dependence of government upon marginal voters in the rural and small town constituencies of 'middle England'. But the pattern is long established, with even the deregulationist Thatcher government of the 1980s forced to retreat quickly from attempts to loosen up planning control in these areas (Bramley and Lambert, 1998).

At the same time, it is precisely these areas which display the greatest economic resilience and provide the locations for some of the most dynamic knowledge-based clusters of industry (Begg, 2002b; Simmie, 2002, and Chapter 7). Planning's permissiveness towards economic development, the end of traditional regional economic policy, and the competitive developmentalist stance of both local authorities and Regional Development Agencies facilitates the continued growth of economies in these areas. But such growth is running into increasing constraints on labour supply relating to the availability and affordability of housing. Arguably this is a significant threat to Britain's overall competitiveness, and (along with transport) is the most important problem which planning is failing to address.

Housing supply and affordability problems are also impinging on other aspects of government policy. In London and the South East there is a growing crisis of recruitment and retention of staff in key public services, such as teaching, health services, police and public transport. This poses a major threat to government commitments to targets for improved service delivery. Such services are vital to the 'liveability' agenda for cities and to the cohesion of urban communities. In the case of education this is a key to increasing human capital, which plays an essential role in many models of urban economic growth (Black and Henderson, 1999).

Diverse developments

A number of contrasts between modes of production, governance and habitation in the office and housing sectors become immediately apparent even through our brief analysis. Perhaps most obvious is the contrasting emphasis on owner occupation in the housing sector and renting in the office sector, which in turn reveals the divergent attitudes to risk, security and identity in British approaches to living and working.

From a policy perspective, we can also quickly note some major contrasts between these sectors. Of particular interest is the minor influence of policy on the broad patterns of office development compared with complex inter-relationships between housing development, land availability and planning control. These regulatory dynamics of liberation and restriction have played a major part in shaping the form, volume and spatial mix of office and housing developments. They also highlight the tension that often emerges between economic and environmental policy across each sector for, while out of town office parks have flourished, the flow of housing to support them has not often followed to any matching degree. This also points to a rather confused policy attitude to the relationship between development as the engine of prosperity (e.g. property-led urban regeneration) and a notion, particularly noticeable in 'middle' and southeast England, of housing development as burden. This difficulty in reconciling economic growth with urban vitality and environmental sustainability is one of the core challenges of contemporary urban policy.

A further difficulty facing urban policy in these sectors is the focus of policy engagement and image of the regulated underpinning policy development. In the housing sector it appears as if the developer/investor is often viewed as a threat, someone to be contained and managed. Consequently, policy takes on a restrictive image aimed at curbing the worst instincts of development activity. Again, by contrast, in the office sector the policy focus is reversed. Here the developer/investor is viewed as something of a saviour in need of support and persuasion, with policy-makers focusing their efforts on helping to extend and to reinforce institutional investors' influence on city developments, and hence the levering-in of private finance is a central component of urban regeneration policy. To achieve this, measures are pursued which improve financial performance of property investment, including rent support and/or supply subsidies, and reduce its risk (e.g. the provision of market information and the development of new liquidity vehicles).

In turning our attention now to the urban level and to localized development activity, we begin to question these restrictive and liberatory logics of urban policy and ask whether or not this conversion of a greater proportion of urban property into a form which better meets institutional investment criteria, while restricting other forms of development activity, is necessarily the most effective way to promote urban development? In fact we might ask how far does it actually ignore the 'local' part of the local–global relationship?

Local heterogeneity in urban office markets

It is a tenet of 'glocal' analysis that cities are sites of interaction between the homogenizing forces of globalization and the particularities of places. Local circumstances interact with wider financial and development trends to produce unique outcomes. However, a highly integrated and mature finance capital sector is exerting a growing influence over the property market. This leads Leitner (1994) to suggest that locality-specific factors, while remaining the major influence on the character of urban office markets, have decreasing scope within which to play themselves out.

Institutions concentrate on investing in specific types of property satisfying pre-determined investment criteria within markets which possess certain specific investment characteristics. The exercise of this strategy, and the response of developers in offering buildings which meet its objectives, have produced the prime business districts in the centres of our cities: the 'Square Mile' in the City of London; the 'Square Half Mile' in Manchester; the area around Colmore Row in Birmingham and around St Vincent Street in Glasgow; and so on. The character of these office cores is so well defined that several can be separately mapped in a number of cities (e.g. Leeds). Some have retained more local character than others (as in Edinburgh), although this is often only skin- (or, more accurately, façade-) deep. However, these established office cores have been subject to increasing pressures to accommodate more and larger, high-specification buildings for large corporate occupiers. This produces three broad responses.

The first is the ad hoc redevelopment of sites in the existing prime office areas. However, where historic, aesthetic or physical constraints are such as to threaten the supply of appropriate buildings, more substantive action is required. This offers the opportunity for local planning authorities to influence development patterns. Major additions to cities' prime office areas result. Some adjoin or are near to the original cores, such as the area around Victoria Street in Bristol, Lothian Road/Morrison Street in Edinburgh, or south of Wellington Street/Boar Lane in Leeds. Others take the form of major business parks or larger, edge-city business areas, such as South Gyle, Edinburgh, Frenchay, Bristol or Salford Quays, Manchester.

Such developments incorporate and reflect a particular investment view and a particular way of seeing cities. This view clearly makes cognitive and strategic sense to institutional development actors. It also makes cultural sense in that it corresponds to a set of pre-conceived values and assumptions about the locations and building types that, on the basis of previous experience, are likely to generate surplus value. Given the highly risk-averse nature of institutional investors, it is perhaps not surprising that they tend to confine their activities to cities and sectors with which they are familiar, leaving their urban 'foot-prints'. Innovation within these organizational confines is very difficult, as new investment proposals will be evaluated with reference to established guidelines and to previous practice and experience.

This inherent conservatism poses problems. The consumption of international business districts is not always as depicted in the glossy development brochures. Celebrated international business centres sometimes struggle to deliver an urban experience that meets occupier demand. In Paris, many French companies left La Defense for what was often less flexible, poorly specified space to benefit from the cultural ambience of the historic centre. The more recent Potsdamer Platz development in Berlin provides a home for international giants such Sony and Daimler Benz, but you are more likely to find the dynamic 'dot.com' companies that are attempting to kick-start the Berlin economy in the outlying districts of the former east. These localized property markets form alternative islands of development driven by a very different sense of place and correspondingly shaped by different location, infrastructure and design parameters. With institutional developers and investors preferring to focus their activities on property 'hot-spots' that conform to international standards, other locally-based developers are quietly and effectively filling the development vacuum with an alternative development agenda.

We can begin to delineate the approach of these 'independent' developers by noting a preference for fringe locations that tend to be ignored by institutions. Hall notes in his review of world cities how 'innovative places . . . were not at the centre but neither were they off the edge of the world altogether' (Hall, 1999b, p. 41). Echoing this, independents tend to work in the shadows of mainstream developers, counter-balancing low rental values with a close proximity to the city core as in the Northern Quarter of Manchester. Working in such peripheral zones often necessitates dealing with smaller lot sizes, multiple tenancies and mixed uses. While such property characteristics are anathema to institutional investors, independents appear to recognize the links between such social complexity and the urban vitality which is central to regeneration processes and ultimately to rising rental values. Engaging closely with a locality is the key to negotiating the relationship between cultural and economic capital (O'Connor, 1999b, p. 85), and is central to the approach of independent developers.

Independents also strive to add value through an emphasis on distinctive design, often with a preference for conservation of local vernacular styles through the re-use of former warehouses or department stores. As an independent local developer said, 'I believed that good design doesn't cost more money as it actually generates value.' This aestheticization of property contrasts with the overt ambitions of many institutional investors to distance themselves from the visual impact of buildings, the better to value them 'objectively'. Attitudes to development risk also appear to differ. While institutions broker trust and mediate risk through national and international networks of advisers and researchers, independents are linked to more community-based networks of other cultural intermediaries who share investment and offset development risks through collaborative projects and initiatives (Banks *et al.*, 2000).

Most starkly, what is at stake here is a very different vision of prospective urban development. While institutions tend to base estimates of future investment performance on an extension of past trends when evaluating likely profiles of risk and return, independents strive to develop a different urban future. In Manchester, which is committed to a 'post-industrial script' around cultural entrepreneurship (Quilley, 2000, p. 613), the service economy and city living, areas such as the Northern Quarter have been symbolically as well as physically reconstructed. In this way, older buildings have been successfully adapted to new uses which blend with a distinctive local image and ambience, thereby highlighting 'the potential for urban economies to avoid serial subjection to the "universal force of capital circulation" ' (Banks *et al.*, 2000, p. 463).

As the examples of institutional and independent actors illustrate, cities are home to a diverse and dynamic set of approaches to property development and investment. Competing development pathways result in the construction of a range of development 'islands' in each city. These 'islands' have evolved in specific ways as a result of the sometimes resonant, and sometimes dissonant, actions of local property actors, national and international investors, and local and national government policy. No single blueprint, vision, or investment strategy can explain their character. Each island is differently envisioned by competing development actors, embodies different histories and cultures, and has its boundaries maintained, threatened or extended by different assemblages of social, physical and organizational processes.

Urban housing developments: local contrasts

The critical importance of these diverse development pathways is immediately apparent when considering the contemporary policy agenda in Britain, expressed most eloquently in Lord Rogers' Urban Task Force report (DETR, 1999a), but reflected in official policy documents such as the Urban White Paper (DETR, 2000c; Robson *et al.*, 2000) and planning policy guidance (DETR, 2000d). In different ways, each document is aimed at securing an urban renaissance. This entails people choosing to live in towns and cities, and new housing development being built to meet this demand in a way which promotes an appropriate and sustainable 'urban way of life' (Barton, 2000; Jenks *et al.*, 1996). There are a number of specific manifestations of this 'new urbanist' agenda in terms of the forms of housing development and associated planning policies: compactness of urban form; re-use of brownfield land; higher densities, especially at central and nodal locations; mixed use; socio-economic and tenure mix. However, such outcomes would represent a significant change in established trends involving substantial decentralization and out-migration of population (Champion *et al.*, 1998).

In many ways this agenda parallels the emerging US debate about 'sprawl' versus 'smart urban growth' (Danielsen *et al.*, 1999; Knaap, 2002; SCSC, 2001). Although the US situation is more extreme, in terms of the extent of decentralization and the relative lack of policy intervention, the debate provides a refreshing exposure of some of the fundamental issues.

While the recent British experience provides many examples of 'success' in terms of the urban housing agenda, it is actually a mixed picture, with major differences between different sectors of each city, between cities in a different overall economic and market situation, and between different forms of development.

The big success story is central city housing. Most larger cities can point to successful high density housing being profitably developed in the central business district and adjacent locations. In cases such as Liverpool and Manchester the total population now living in areas which were previously seen as non-residential is substantial, of the order of 10,000 in each case, and this adds significantly to the vitality of central city life and services. This demand can spill out into adjacent inner areas, particularly where there are favourable contextual features – for example, waterfronts or higher education institutions – as in Salford, Greater Manchester, or Leith, Edinburgh. Many of these developments involve the refurbishment of redundant commercial buildings such as multistorey warehouses, so contributing to architectural conservation and the reinforcement of a distinctive urban heritage and environment. Some developers, notably Urban Splash in the north west of England (discussed below), have made their name by promoting such developments, sometimes in the face of scepticism about the possibilities of turning round formerly derelict quarters. Some developments have involved the re-orientation of former social rented high rise accommodation, with the provision of security-controlled access, leisure facilities, and sale or letting to working non-family households (examples are to be found in Manchester, Salford, Gateshead; see Bramley, Paws and Third, 2000, case studies). In London, such is the demand that a considerable amount of post-war office building has been converted into residential accommodation (Barlow and Gann, 1993).

A number of factors underpin this success story. Most of the growth in household numbers is currently in the form of single person households, particularly in the age range 25–60, and some of this group may be more willing to entertain living in higher density flats in urban settings (DOE, 1996; but see Hooper *et al.*, 1998, for a contrary view and some evidence). Students are a particular demand group whose orientation is usually strongly central, and numbers in higher education in Britain's cities have doubled over the last decade or so. The growth of city centres as major zones for entertainment, recreation and tourism reinforces their attraction to some of these groups as a place of residence, by facilitating particular lifestyles and interactions (e.g. 'loft living', *Friends*). The deregulation and development of mortgage finance has removed past restrictions on credit availability for home purchase in more urban locations or for less conventional dwellings, as well as for purposes other than straight owner occupancy. Private renting has been deregulated since 1988 and has experienced something of a revival, and a significant part of the new central city housing will have ended up privately rented, whether that was originally intended by the developers or not.

In high demand city-regions, notably London but also in cases such as Edinburgh and Bristol, the central city success of urban housing investment spreads out and is replicated, to some degree, through the inner areas and older suburbs. In Edinburgh, for example, almost any site which can command planning permission will be developed, so there is little vacant or derelict land, and housing is being built at densities well above the Rogers recommended levels of 50–70 dwellings per hectare. An already 'compact city' is reproducing its existing 4/5-storey tenemental form, and this is even encroaching on the suburbs. For such cities, the issue is how to achieve affordable housing, particularly for family households which are likely to seek a house with a garden of some sort.

The picture is very different in the non-central inner areas of low demand cities, particularly cities in the north of England such as Newcastle, Liverpool and Manchester/Salford, as well as Glasgow in the case of Scotland. In some parts of these cities the market has collapsed. Traditional forms of housing (off-street two-storey terraces) are seen as obsolete and are bypassed by first-time buyers, who can afford more modern and better products, and property is either unsaleable or only saleable at derisory prices (e.g. £5,000 for a house). Existing owners are trapped, properties fall vacant or are taken up by poor transient tenants of speculative landlords. The cumulative decline of neighbourhoods is reinforced by the vandalism of abandoned properties, the spread of crime and anti-social behaviour, and the decline of local shops, schools and other services (Bramley, Pawson and Third, 2000; Nevin *et al*., 2001; Power and Mumford, 1999).

Attempts at 'housing-led regeneration' of such areas are extremely risky and have in some cases either failed, or succeeded at the expense of displacing demand from neighbouring areas on the margins of decline. Where oversupply is mainly concentrated in the public sector, as in Glasgow or Sheffield, for example, it may be possible to reduce the surplus stock cheaply while still encouraging some private development to balance up the tenure profile, but this option is not open to areas such as those named above which have generic low demand and market failure in the private sector. Pawson and Bramley (2002) and Nevin *et al*. (2001) argue that there is an inadequate policy framework or funding level to deal with this. Cities such as Glasgow and Liverpool are toying with creating 'new neighbourhoods' within the urban area, possibly on cleared sites, which will attempt to capture a more middle-class family market by offering a more overtly suburban environment. Such initiatives can run into both local political difficulties ('gentrification', 'ethnic cleansing') and credibility problems, given the need to substantially improve the performance of neighbourhoods in terms of school quality and crime risk (see, for example, Glasgow's Market Information Team, 1997).

Part of the background to these intractable-seeming problems is residential segregation. The urban policy agenda embraces 'mixed and balanced communities' as a key expression of social cohesion, although this is based on faith as much as evidence (Atkinson and Kintrea, 2000; Jupp, 1999). In Scotland, there has been considerable success in bringing owner occupation into former public housing estates and, to some degree, changing their image. However, rather less has been achieved at the other end of the scale, in bringing more affordable and rented housing into mono-tenure owner occupier suburbs (perhaps reflecting the general local resistance alluded to earlier). In the south of England, however, increasing use has been made over the 1990s of planning policies and agreements to introduce a proportion of affordable housing into what would otherwise have been private market developments (Monk and Whitehead, 2000). Some versions of the urban policy agenda, such as that associated with the idea of 'urban villages', links ideas about cohesion, interaction and social mix with actual mixing of land uses (Aldous, 1992; Urban Villages Forum,

1995). This idea, discussed further below, has been achieved in some central city refurbishment/redevelopment contexts, but is rarely applied in new developments (Colin Buchanan and Partners, 2001).

Mixing up development

As we have seen, many inner-city areas display similar characteristics which inhibit development and investment: fragile markets with weak and volatile demand, poor tenants' covenants, few large investment opportunities, complex patterns of land ownership and a very limited market. For institutional investors, this means relatively high risks and low returns. Given the highly risk-averse nature of institutional investors, it is perhaps not surprising that they tend to confine their activities to cities, sectors and uses with which they are familiar. Innovation within these organizational confines is very difficult as new investment proposals will be evaluated with reference to established guidelines and to previous practice and experience. Only in locations such as the City of London and Reading is it possible to talk in terms of a coherent, consistent and commonly legible property market. Here, the continued dominance of the institutional sector of the market results in a familiar uniformity in approach and style of development. Elsewhere a more diverse and dynamic set of approaches to property development and investment is apparent. In Manchester, for example, a number of independent developers, as identified above, have begun to develop a new way forward. Critically, these developers have strayed far from the traditional institutional core. Working in the shadows of the institutions, they have trodden where institutions fear to tread, in the marginal development zones of empty buildings where rents fall below £10 per square metre.

Typical are Tom Bloxham and Jon Falkingham who established Urban Splash in 1993. Based in the north-western, post-industrial cities of Manchester and Liverpool, Urban Splash has developed, over the past five years, into one of the leading property developers in the country. The company now boasts a staff of 300 employees and a series of ongoing projects worth in excess of £100 million, representing the creation of nearly 600 homes and 2500 jobs in the North West. Now widely recognized through numerous design and development awards as the region's most established developers of loft apartments, rivalled only by the Manhattan Loft Corporation, the company started off with the conversion of a large old industrial building formerly used as a chemical laboratory. Encouraged by 'great windows and exposed brickwork', it was transformed into what is now known as Sally's Yard in Manchester, offering a range of apartments based on the concept of loft living. Urban Splash has expanded its operation considerably in the 'niche' market for high quality, affordable and accessible work and living space produced by restoring and converting disused buildings in city centre and fringe locations. More recently, they have diversified into office and leisure development. For Bloxham, the 'missing ingredient for renewal in the urban core is developers with "bottle", developers who have the vision and confidence to propose, finance, develop and market buildings to niche markets' (1995, p. 2).

For instance, in the summer of 1995, Urban Splash approached the established architects of Stephenson Bell with the brief, 'We've bought this building. Excite me!' The building they had just bought was actually a city block comprised of nine individual buildings in an area known as the Northern Quarter. Once a thriving commercial centre, with famous high-street names including British Home Stores, Woolworth's, C&A, Marks and Spencer's, Freeman Hardy Willis and Affleck & Brown, the construction of the Arndale Shopping Centre in the mid-1970s changed both the future and the economic status of the Northern Quarter. The Northern Quarter represents a typical blind spot for institutions. However, Urban Splash hoped that they could capitalize on a growing cultural vitality in the area that had developed due to the attraction of cheap rents for local artists, musicians and independent retailers: 'What is happening around Oldham St is much more where the cultural heart of the city is at the moment, where the underground cultural scene is taking place' (local developer). Their target was the former home of Affleck & Brown, a department store that won much acclaim as the 'Harrods of the North' and was situated on one of the central thoroughfares that bisects the Northern Quarter, Oldham Street.

The building lay destitute and in need of renovation and repair, a monument to the demise and dereliction of the once prosperous area surrounding it. With the backing of Manchester City Council and of the local community association, now known as the Northern Quarter Association, Urban Splash obtained a grant from English Partnerships to help purchase and develop the property, the main premise being that the revitalization of what eventually became known as Smithfield Buildings would create a new mix of activities in the area that would encourage more people to want to live and work in this district. The brief settled on a mixed target audience that included young married couples to retired pensioners, requiring accommodation and services within a range of prices. Now successfully sold or let, and with associated retail spaces accommodating the independent retailers that inspired its development, many see it as a model of urban regeneration. Critically, the challenge of combining an ill assortment of nine buildings (each with its own individual architectural style, structure and floor-to-ceiling heights) into a coherent entity did not dissuade the developers from proceeding as it would an institution. Rather, the development of a design that kept the city block's overall character and richness was the prime factor in Urban Splash's decision to invest in this property. According to Urban Splash's own figures, they invested £12 million in Smithfield in buildings of 144,500 square feet gross, bringing a 0.62 acre site into use, creating 245 jobs and releasing 81 apartments (http://www.urbansplash.co.uk).

Reviewing similar examples of urban development such as Salt's Mill in Bradford and Camden Lock in North London, Charles Landry points out that such 'organic' regeneration projects tend to 'rely less on strategy than on intuition', and that 'this approach is rare in mainstream development.' (Landry *et al.*, 1996, p. 36) Similarly, Peter Hall's analysis of innovative cities notes 'the continuing importance of bottom-up, individualistic innovation' (Hall, 1999b, p. 40), arguing that a creative city 'needs such outsiders' whose autonomy from the mainstream 'presupposes a certain fundamental schism in ideas and values' (p. 39). Drawing on the work of Sharon Zukin (1988), Justin O'Connor (1999b) describes such independent developers as 'cultural intermediaries' (p. 77), who make up the 'critical infrastructure' of urban renewal (p. 82). However, while Zukin suggests that these cultural intermediaries merely translate culture to the service of capital, O'Connor identifies a more complex relationship in which: 'a specific localisation involves a series of negotiations around the new emergent landscape which can be laden with meanings very different to the standardised 'postmodernity' of the development models' (O'Connor, 1999, p. 83).

Conclusions: Towards heterogeneous urban spaces

Much of the debate on the globalization of cities assumes a growing homogenization of urban space. In real estate terms this means cities are reshaped to meet the perceived demands of global institutions for prime location, highly serviced and increasingly fortressed property islands, whether commercial or domestic. A process of physical purification often results in space 'prepared' and packaged to match the tastes of corporate consumers. Cities scramble to attract mobile capital through the creation of commercial enclaves instantly familiar and therefore reassuring to incoming occupiers. Moving between Tokyo, Paris, Berlin and then on to Manchester, Leeds and Newcastle should not provide any shock or disjunction for the business traveller. Likewise, a combination of NIMBY regulatory power and economic and technological fortressing of housing zones has encouraged notable segmentation in the housing sector. In this way, by strongly shaping choices about design, location, infrastructure and uses, the property business is central to the making of places and to the wider urban debate. This is, of course, a well-established debate. The 'evil developer' is a familiar character in much urban research, but the process of investment and development is not as prescribed as many of the text-books would suggest. Forms of socio-economic contestation that are the staple of many urban studies are also played out in the property business.

In the Urban Splash example explored above, we can see how the ability to re-think and redevelop an inner-city zone deemed too risky by insti-tutional developers can go a long way to regenerating city space. In particular, we can note how independents such as Urban Splash ignore the conventions of the institutions, such as the need to separate uses and the avoidance of multiple tenants and flexible leases, by championing quality design and actively seeking to mix uses to create urban ambience. Independents see themselves as participants in a strategy of place-making rather than simply as individual project developers. Open to the criticism that they are merely creating new exclusive enclaves that serve to push low-income groups further to the margins of the city, Urban Splash are now working on a 'Millennium village' development around the Cardroom estate in Ancoats. Again, the idea (promoted by English Partnerships) is to demonstrate the value of mixed-use development in creating community spaces. Located between the city centre and East Manchester, the scheme will transform a 204-home estate, a disused hospital, primary school and industrial site into a mix of social housing, private housing and some commercial development, including live-work spaces. Wider urban plan-ning will include a canal link connecting Rochdale and Ashton canals and an emphasis on innovative and sustainable construction and design. Critically, if successful, this may point the way to linking up some of the more successful city-centre living and working schemes to more peripheral urban areas and so start to ease some of the urban polarization and blight highlighted earlier in the chapter.

Of course it is vital to avoid too quickly polarizing 'institutional' and 'independent' development, or demonizing the one while elevating the other. Instead, the research opportunity is to employ the development process as a 'window' on wider urban restructuring, and to integrate social and economic analyses in studying this contested process. In doing so we can explore how debates about living and working, innovation and heritage, diversity and tradition, and critically, the local and the global, are all played out in cities through the language of rents, yields, capital values, uses, tenancy, location and specification. Seen this way, investment and development choices are far from value-free and are certainly not deter-mined solely by global economic forces. Critically, this means that policy debates about the role of institutional investors in urban regeneration, the nature, construction and utilization of investors' strategic rationality, and the ways in which these intersect with local development needs must be urgently addressed. Policy-makers need to conceptualize the physical reproduction of cities in a way which recognizes both a multiplicity of development pathways and the strength of local diversity. Connecting property studies to urban studies immediately highlights both the economics of culture and the culture of economics, and rightly sets urban development in a 'glocal' context.

Chapter 14

How Urban Labour Markets Matter

IAN GORDON and IVAN TUROK

Introduction

Labour markets play a pivotal role in relation to urban competitiveness and cohesion, just as the employment relation is a crucial link between the economic and social domains. Historically, urban unemployment resulting from economic weakness and deficient demand for labour was an important cause of poverty, hardship, homelessness, disease, crime and other social problems (see, for example, Stedman Jones, 1971, on nineteenth-century London, and Checkland, 1981, on twentieth-century Glasgow). And is argued that rising worklessness in many British, European and US cities over the last two decades as a result of deindustrialization and decentralization has had many similar consequences (see, for example, Wilson, 1996, on contemporary Chicago, and Gallie *et al*. 1994, Lawless *et al*. 1998, or Webster, 2000, on various British cities and towns).

In the meantime, labour appears to have become a more prominent factor in business location decisions as the need for proximity to material inputs and product markets has diminished. This is partly because labour markets are relatively place-bound, while firms are more footloose. More particularly, recent ideas suggest that the economic potential of large cities has improved because of their attractiveness to highly skilled labour and creative talent, and the flexibility of their 'thick' labour markets. Their capacity to spread knowledge through worker mobility between firms and informal networks ('knowledge spillovers') is also thought to have become more important, as discussed in Chapter 2.

Both sets of arguments are currently deployed about most major cities in the UK and elsewhere (see, for example, OECD, 2001b; ODPM, 2003a). They are perceived to have serious labour market problems still, but also positive possibilities. This suggests that urban labour markets are multidimensional and function in uneven ways, which underlines their importance for the achievement of competitiveness and cohesion.

This variability also complicates the formulation of appropriate labour market policies for cities. There are different interpretations of urban employment changes and challenges, some of which we explore in this chapter.

It is helpful initially to distinguish between labour market *outcomes*, underlying *processes* and the influence of urban *contexts* on each of these. It is obvious from casual observation that labour market outcomes vary between places in relation to their economic 'competitiveness', in the terms discussed in previous chapters. Residents of more successful cities enjoy the benefits through lower unemployment, better jobs and higher earnings, while those in 'uncompetitive' places tend to be worse off. This could be interpreted as reflecting some kind of labour market 'failure' or even two, in failing both to bring individual local labour markets into full employment equilibrium, *and* to balance out remaining disparities between areas. Textbook models of how markets are supposed to behave would explain this with some combination of: wages being insufficiently flexible, workers not being mobile enough, and some people effectively choosing not to work. This is obviously one-sided and devoid of any urban context. If urban labour markets really matter for competitiveness and cohesion it is because markets for human labour do not operate like other markets defined simply in terms of price, supply and demand. Moreover, they may function differently in different places, producing distinctive economic and social outcomes.

We are concerned with several kinds of labour market *outcomes*, including unemployment, earnings, job security and progression. Our interest is in how they vary between and within cities, and what these variations mean for competitiveness and cohesion. There has been some discussion of this in earlier chapters, including the impacts of concentrated unemployment on aspects of cohesion (such as inequality and social order) in distressed neighbourhoods, and of human capital resources on city competitiveness. The focus here is on how these outcomes may link competitiveness with cohesion, as postulated by the NCW.

We are also interested in how different labour market *processes* influence these outcomes, whether by mediating the effects of economic growth and the demand for labour, or by actually affecting economic performance. The processes include schooling and skills development, geographical and occupational mobility, and employers' recruitment/ training strategies. The central issue addressed is how labour market institutions and processes shape the outcomes experienced by different social groups in different places. A specific interest is in how urban *contexts* (i.e. places) affect the ways in which these processes operate. This may stem from the spatial structure or physical form of cities, local housing systems and property markets, local customs and cultures, or established industrial, institutional and governance structures and networks.

The empirical focus is on the performance of British cities over the last two decades or so, the period to which the NCW is supposed to relate. It would be quite wrong, however, to assume that the major labour market developments in these cities during this time directly reflect the operation of a new economic regime, since some traditional factors have operated with great force during this period. These include, first, a continuance of long-term shifts in labour demand which have been generally unfavourable for the cities in relation to changes in their labour supply, resulting in a shortfall in employment opportunities or 'jobs gap' (Begg, Moore and Altunbas, 2002; Breheny, 1999; Turok and Edge, 1999). Second, there have been major shifts in the national macro-economic context, with two deep recessions involving years of very high unemployment interrupted by a short boom. A period of more steady growth has followed (bringing a reduction in ILO unemployment rates from 11 per cent in 1993 to around 5 per cent nationally). But accumulated effects of these bad years remain evident within many cities, in terms of low rates of work force participation and occupational progression.

Alongside these, the major new factor is expected to have been some qualitative change in the functioning of labour markets, associated with deregulation and increased emphasis on flexibility. Such changes could have benefited the larger cities by boosting the locational advantages of thick labour markets that are better able to absorb shocks, support specialized skill pools and facilitate upward mobility for the ambitious. Against this, greater 'turbulence' in such urban labour markets might have discouraged investment in work force development and presented new risks to unqualified workers in places where secure manual jobs were disappearing (Buck and Gordon, 2000). A related factor has been the shift in government policy during this period towards the supply side of the labour market, with both national programmes (such as the New Deal) and targeted local Employment Zones emphasizing skills, employability and work incentives. These policies at least (though not all neighbourhood renewal initiatives) reflect a view that by the late 1990s unemployment had been reduced to a matter of localized 'pockets' within commuting reach of plentiful economic opportunities (HM Treasury, 1997, 2000, 2001a). Both the realism of this assumption, and the ability to separate supply and demand side factors, are among the key issues to be considered in this chapter.

We start by examining the context in terms of demand shifts and macro-economic factors. We then discuss the connection between urban labour markets and competitiveness. This is followed by consideration of what has been learned about the effectiveness of urban labour market adjustment to shifting patterns of labour demand. Finally, we discuss the role of urban labour markets in relation to social exclusion.

The context: demand shifts and macro-economic fluctuations

Nationally and internationally, the 1980s and 1990s witnessed major changes in patterns of labour demand and supply. Sectorally in the UK there was a continuation of the *deindustrialization* that had been under-way since the early 1960s, in the form of shrinking employment in goods-related sectors of the economy (including the energy industries, freight transport and distribution). Overall manufacturing employment fell by a third between 1981 and 2001, representing two million fewer jobs. Losses were exacerbated in the early 1980s by large-scale shake-outs and rational-izations in many manufacturing sectors, including Fordist industries of the inter-war period (such as motor cars) as well as the older heavy industries. This had severe consequences for cities in the Midlands, as well as in the industrial regions of northern Britain. Combined with a continuing process of employment *decentralization* from all core urban areas into their surrounding regions (especially in space-extensive manufacturing activi-ties), this produced particularly high rates of industrial employment contraction. The core areas were thus faced both with large net job losses and rapid structural change. On the positive side, there was some growth in service jobs, although this was concentrated in office-based business and financial services of various kinds, with narrower skill requirements.

These sectoral shifts varied in their effects on total employment between city-regions, according to their inherited industrial structure. They yielded overall negative outcomes where (declining) manufacturing industries predominated over (growing) producer service sectors, and positive outcomes where the reverse applied. With the larger British cities, apart from London, being concentrated in the more industrial regions of the Midlands and North, most were negatively affected by this shift.

The consequence was a very substantial reduction in the number of manual job opportunities (especially skilled and semi-skilled manual jobs) and an increase in the proportion of professional, managerial and technical jobs. This was compounded by occupational changes *within* many indus-tries, reducing the proportion of blue-collar workers and expanding senior white-collar opportunities, which increasingly were held by university graduates. Britain's 20 largest cities lost manual jobs at a rate roughly three times higher than the rest of the country between 1981 and 1991 (Turok and Edge, 1999). The long-term impact of these structural shifts on the match-ing of labour demands and supplies was attenuated to some extent by a continuing upward trend in the level of educational qualifications attained by each new cohort entering the labour market. However, in some major cities the rate of structural change in demand clearly exceeded the increase in educational attainment among the native population. This was particularly the case in London, where the proportion of managers, professionals and semi-professionals rose from 28 per cent to 48 per cent between 1979 and 2000 (Buck *et al.*, 2002). The corresponding national shift was from 24 to 38 per cent, an increase of 14 per cent, compared with 20 per cent in London. These large-scale shifts reflected technological change, an unfavourable macro-economic environment for manufacturing in the UK and the cities' pattern of comparative advantage, nationally and internationally.

Overall, the major structural and spatial shifts affecting UK cities during the 1980s and 1990s represented more of a continuation and intensification of trends established in the 1960s and 1970s than a radical break with the previous era. The changes and challenges facing urban labour markets were no less significant for that. Over the last 50 years the overall share of national employment in Britain's cities has fallen substantially, mostly to the benefit of towns and rural areas, which grew rapidly from a small base. The seven conurbations performed worst, with absolute job losses in every decade between 1951 and 1991 (Moore and Begg, 2004, Table 6.2). They did particularly badly in terms of full-time jobs, especially for men (Turok and Edge, 1999). There was some improvement during the 1990s, principally because of the scale of the upturn in London, though there is also evidence of some recovery in most other conurbations. Overall, during the period from 1981 to 2001 total employment in the conurbations, the free-standing cities and the smaller northern cities all increased by about 10 per cent, while in both the smaller southern cities and in small towns and rural areas the increase was around 25 per cent. The urban–rural shift peaked in the 1970s and then slowed somewhat in the next two decades. Manufacturing employment fell by half in the conurbations between 1981 and 2001, around one-third in the other city types, both North and South, but only by about one-seventh in the towns and rural areas (Moore and Begg, 2004, Table 6.4). Between 1981 and 1991 falls in city employment implied clear 'job gaps' in all cities insofar as their working age populations were still showing natural increases (Turok and Edge, 1999). Trends over the following decade are harder to assess, since 2001 was closer to a cyclical peak than 1991 had been, and because the growth of refugees and other international migrants (particularly in London) presented another element of employment need.

The scale of macro-economic fluctuations after the late 1970s was more novel than these spatial shifts, and an additional source of insecurity and stress. Between 1979 and 1983 UK employment fell by 8 per cent, then rose by 16 per cent to 1989, fell again by 9 per cent to 1994, and rose once more by 9 per cent to 2002. This volatility was particularly apparent in the London region, reflecting speculative aspects of the new urbanism (Buck *et al.*, 2002; Fainstein, 2002). Although the underlying trend in national employment was upwards, at least in the second half of this period, it did not match the growth in labour supply. Consequently, there were many years of high unemployment, peaking well above anything since the 1930s. The claimant count rate of unemployment was above 5 per cent continuously between 1981 and 1997, and above 7.5 per cent for 13 of those years. Unemployment was substantially worse in the north and west of the country, especially in the major cities. Over the past decade national unemployment rates (on the now conventional ILO definition) have fallen substantially in all regions; but this has not been true of economic inactivity rates, reflecting some continuing shifts of people from unemployed to inactive status (for reasons discussed below). The upturn has not been sufficiently broad-based or sustained as yet to benefit many in Britain's northern conurbations, where there remains considerable slack in the local labour market. For instance, the employment rate for men with low qualifications was broadly unchanged between 1993 and 2002 at about 52 per cent in Merseyside, Clydeside and Tyneside, whereas the rate for the equivalent group increased from 74 per cent to 80 per cent in the tighter labour market of the South East (Gregg and Wadsworth, 2003).

The experience of unemployment and economic inactivity has had debilitating effects on household incomes, levels of debt and stress, health conditions, drug and alcohol addictions, family breakdown, educational attainment, training and career prospects for many workers and their dependents (Alcock *et al.*, 2003; Bailey *et al.*, 1999; CCBI, 1997; Shaw *et al.*, 1999). The disruption and suffering have been especially marked among working-class communities in the inner cities and peripheral council estates, as well as in many coal, steel and shipbuilding towns whose economic base was decimated during the 1980s.

Urban labour markets and competitiveness

One of the most important reasons for the NCW's optimism about the competitive potential of cities relates to the role of agglomeration in labour markets. Thick urban labour markets may offer valuable advantages for the accumulation and deployment of skills in a more 'flexible' era when employers are less self-reliant in these functions (HM Treasury, 2001b; Scott, 2002; Storper, 1997). A shift in emphasis from internal to external labour markets benefits those places with a larger pool of workers with relevant skills, especially where there is reasonable mobility in this pool and it is refreshed with a stream of suitable inward migrants. Agglomeration economies, in the matching of skills to positions, have been argued to produce both higher productivity and higher returns to skill acquisition in the larger urban labour markets (Wheeler, 2001). There may be a downside, in that the choice of alternatives could make workers less committed to particular posts than employers would like, and both groups may underinvest in skills and expertise with longer-term pay-offs. There may be a tension here between characteristics that attract firms and workers to a city and those that make it generally more productive. The main point is that in a more flexible economy the balance of advantage is likely to swing towards relatively dynamic local labour markets and those with the deepest skill-sets, particularly in expanding occupations. This should be particularly relevant to smaller firms serving competitive or volatile product markets, including innovative activities and industries. Key advantages of clustering for them may include access to a pool of specialized skills, and diffusion of tacit knowledge and best-practice technology, through worker mobility between firms and other knowledge spillovers. Some evidence for this was indicated in Chapters 6 and 8 (and by Turok, 2003).

The mobilization of advanced skills in particular labour markets may reflect a city's effectiveness in developing the capacities of local people and/or its success in attracting talent from elsewhere. As far as formal schooling is concerned, the reputation of Britain's larger cities is not strong (DETR, 2000c), underlined by government publication of national league tables of school examination results. For the GCSE exam taken in the last year of compulsory education, the 2002 league table for English Local Education Authorities (LEAs) shows two-thirds of those from core cities (defined as the inner London boroughs plus Liverpool/Knowsley, Manchester/Salford, Birmingham, Newcastle, Sheffield and Leeds/Bradford) in the bottom quartile of results and none in the top quartile. This is heavily influenced by social segregation within the major conurbations, with the core areas containing many more children from disadvantaged backgrounds, whether defined in terms of income, social class, race or family circumstances. The relevant basis of comparison is the functional urban region, at which scale very little association is evident between educational achievement and city size, although higher unemployment in bigger city-regions seems to boost the number of complete failures there (Gordon and Monastiriotis, 2003). Even in London the pattern seems to be highly variable, rather than generally higher or lower, standards of attainment (Buck *et al.*, 2002). Recent value-added measures based on individual progression between exams, controlling for some social influences, actually suggest the performance of London secondary schools is quite good (Gordon *et al.*, 2003), though other conurbation education authorities remain below average.

The extent to which cities have concentrations of highly qualified workers depends on their economic functions and pressure of labour demand as well as their size or status. There is no tendency for the largest British cities (defined in terms of functional region) to have a higher share of degree holders, despite their strong representation of universities. This is partly because many of them still have a higher than average share of industrial jobs. It also reflects a continuing propensity among professionals, managers and technical workers for net out-migration from the conurbations, although London is something of an exception (Champion and Fisher, 2004). In the American literature there has been recent interest in what attracts well-qualified migrants to particular cities. Glaeser has argued that opportunities for career progression, rather than higher initial earnings, attract migrants who are not too risk-averse and can benefit from opportunities for advancement (Glaeser, 1999; Glaeser and Marc, 2001). Cities also offer agglomeration economies in the sphere of consumption and lifestyle (Glaeser *et al.*, 2001; HM Treasury, 2001b), and hence they hold particular attractions for those with a choice about where they take their skills. Data from the BHPS suggest that the rising population of university graduates has a stronger taste for 'urban' types of recreation compared with other members of the middle classes. Florida (2002b) suggests that a broader range of social preferences may be involved, with 'talent' being particularly attracted to cities offering an open, tolerant environment (the so-called BoHo factor), rather than places simply with better facilities. The direction of casuality is not entirely clear, however, and Florida seems to underestimate the importance of the scale and range of job opportunities in attracting skilled workers to cities. We return to the issue of upward mobility shortly, but it is important to note that these arguments clearly fit some cities better than others, particularly those with a specialization in advanced producer and consumer services.

Glaeser's argument hinges *both* on the availability of jobs that provide opportunities for building up scarce skills *and* on the potential for workers to capitalize on these by moving on elsewhere. This combination is something that employers might be expected to resist for obvious reasons, and there is evidence of British employers providing less training in centres with a higher business density (Brunello and Gambarotto, 2004). However, for specialized jobs in service activities it may be impossible to prevent workers from acquiring such assets if they are to perform effectively. In addition, firms choosing to stay in high turnover agglomerations will hope to gain as much as (or more than) they lose from such mobility. This is consistent with Fielding's (1991, 1995) observation that south-east England served as an 'escalator region' in the 1970s and 1980s by attracting young migrants, promoting upward social mobility and then exporting some of them to other regions. Using longitudinal data from the BHPS the

London project confirmed that this escalator phenomenon continued to operate among well-qualified young people, although after controlling for selective factors (including level of career ambition) the margin of advantage was relatively modest and the effect had not increased since the 1970s (Buck *et al.*, 2002). There is less sign of similar advantages operating in other conurbations, although local universities play an important role in attracting young people. The strong presence of universities in the major cities is a magnet for school leavers from the surrounding regions and beyond, though the proportion staying on after graduating seems to depend primarily on local career prospects associated with the quality and range of employment opportunities available (Turok and Bailey, 2004b). In relation to mobility between jobs, higher rates of turnover were found in the London region, notably among young people and in professional/managerial jobs, but not in the other conurbations, where a lower pressure of demand for labour seems to cancel out any expected effects of density on mobility. Consequently, Glaeser's argument does not seem to hold strongly outside London. Overall, the analyses found no evidence that these processes had become more important since 1980. Contrary to general belief, overall job turnover rates had not increased in London or elsewhere.

The effectiveness of adjustment processes

Three kinds of adjustment may occur in response to shifts in labour demand or supply. If the change alters the overall balance between job opportunities and available labour supply, orthodox economic theory suggests that workers would modify their wage expectations. This should rebalance the numbers of jobs offered by employers and the numbers of people who find it worthwhile to participate in the labour market. If the change affects one locality more than others, the same logic suggests that a difference should emerge in the real wage rate (for similar jobs) between the areas, leading to a rebalance through the movement of jobs, people and/or commuting patterns. If the change affects one occupation more than others, their relative wages should change (at least temporarily), prompting some restructuring of the employment mix and a shift of workers between occupations, and/or encourage young people to alter the kinds of human capital that they choose to invest in acquiring.

This is very much a textbook picture and in real labour markets other mechanisms and constraints come into play. Nevertheless, some adjustment along all three dimensions is to be expected when an urban economy experiences significant contractions or expansions in particular industries. How strongly or rapidly these occur in practice may have significant consequences for local competitiveness, in terms of employers' ability to fill their vacancies. It is also very important for urban cohesion, in terms of the level of involuntary unemployment, which remains a key determinant of poverty and social exclusion.

In fact, wages are a lot less flexible than prices in other kinds of market, partly because employers value a more stable (social) relation with their work force. Yet versions of all three processes can operate without wage flexibility. At the aggregate level people may enter or withdraw from the labour market according to the prospects of getting a suitable job, or employers may alter their business plans depending on the recruitment possibilities. Between areas, shifts in the distribution of vacancies or in the chances of gaining employment may be sufficient to alter commuting and migration patterns. The same may hold for shifts between occupations, except that it may be more difficult to transfer human capital between jobs with greater, lesser or simply different demands. This form of adjustment may be eased by employers modifying their expectations of what is required for a job if they have too many or too few applicants. Yet the general expectation is that a shift in demand away from one specialization towards another will leave workers in lower status jobs. Some of them will also be left unemployed, depending on the general strength of labour demand. There is evidence that the loss of skilled manual jobs over the last two decades has resulted in downward movement for men into less-skilled, lower-paid jobs and casual work, especially for those with few qualifications (Elias and Bynner, 1997).

In both spatial and occupational contexts, it has been argued that adjustments occur through 'waves' of local adjustments, rippling through the labour market towards the areas and occupations of relatively strong demand, rather than through large amounts of long distance movement. This is easier where there are overlapping sub-markets, as in and around metropolitan regions, where it contributes to the flexibility of their labour markets. 'Ripples' of this kind can also operate up and down the hierarchy of occupations in response to shifts in the relative pressure of demand between job types. In the context of a generally deficient demand for labour, this takes the form of 'bumping down' (Reder, 1964), whereby skilled workers 'price themselves back into a job' by winning one at a (slightly) lower level against less qualified competitors, even though wages in particular jobs stay fixed. Unless wages at the bottom of the labour market are extremely flexible, the consequence is to concentrate unemployment among the least qualified groups, even if demand is not especially weak in the kind of jobs they would normally occupy. As a second best, this adjustment process is relatively efficient, wasting less human capital than otherwise. However, it has very unequal social effects, which will accumulate until such time as full employment is achieved and upward movement is re-established.

An important point emerging from this is that adjustment may occur in response to spatial and occupational shifts in demand, even in situations with persistent concentrations of unemployment and economic inactivity. The strength and speed of adjustment in the context of particular labour market customs and institutions is an empirical question, which several studies by researchers from the ESRC *Cities* programme investigated. Focusing on Britain's 20 largest core cities over the decade 1981–91, Bailey and Turok (2000) used regression analysis to assess how shifts in employment were reflected in migration, commuting, participation rates and unemployment. For men, the results suggested that for every 1,000 male jobs lost, net out-commuting rose by about 480, while about 380 economically active men migrated elsewhere, leaving about 170 men still unemployed or inactive at the end of the decade (i.e., on average 5 years after the time of job loss). For women, the picture was rather different with much weaker spatial adjustment, and a much stronger effect on local participation rates. For every 1,000 jobs lost in the cities, net out-commuting by women was estimated to rise by just 200, with about 280 women migrating elsewhere, leaving about 450 extra women economically inactive at the end of the decade (Bailey and Turok, 2000). This contrast reflects the greater constraints on women's mobility associated with lower incomes, part-time working and domestic responsibilities. For both men and women there were also clear differences between occupational groups, with much stronger spatial adjustment to changes in professional/managerial employment than to changes in manual jobs, again reflecting differences in constraints on (or assistance with) mobility. For women in less-skilled jobs, commuting responses seemed quite insignificant and the estimated effect on participation was consequently much greater.

Rather similar results were obtained in a study using data for British travel to work areas for men and women together (Gordon, 1999c). Even at this broader level some 80 per cent of the changes in employment for professionals/managers and 40 per cent for other groups were absorbed through spatial adjustments. Two-thirds of this came through shifts in commuting patterns. In analysing the remaining impact on worklessness at the end of the decade, a distinction was made between change in manual and non-manual sectors. In the former case, the impact of a change of 1,000 in numbers of full-time jobs on the total of unemployment and inactivity was estimated at 150, as compared with just 80 in the case of the non-manual jobs. Interestingly, in areas experiencing sharp manual job losses the estimated impacts on worklessness were almost twice as great (Gordon, 2003b). (A complementary result is that when a non-linear term is introduced into the Bailey/Turok regression model, the commuting response is found to be much weaker in those cities with the highest rates of job loss: see Gordon, 2003b.) This is consistent with theoretical expectations (and

US evidence) that spatial adjustments are much stronger and more effective in the context of growth than decline (Gordon, 1995).

Another aspect of adjustment is highlighted in a third study, using data for functional regions across three European nations (France, Italy and the UK). It looked at the impact of employment decline in one city on other centres in its hinterland (Cheshire *et al.*, 2004). Changes in commuting flows across the boundaries responded strongly to differences in growth performance, with an apparent lag before the strongest effect of about three years. Time separation between centres, rather than simply distances, attenuated this response. Nevertheless, some effects were evident between regions with centres up to 100 minutes apart. Commuting flows did not simply restore equilibrium: there was evidence that the presence of nearby centres experiencing relative decline assisted growth in the more successful city-regions by increasing their labour supply. Productivity was enhanced as well as employment, perhaps reflecting selective attraction of more skilled in-commuters, or the achievement of dynamic agglomeration economies (Cheshire and Magrini, 1999).

Despite examples of adjustment processes operating over quite long distances, especially where there are efficient transport links and the context is one of growth, the relative ease of commuting means that these processes must be much more effective *within* particular functional regions than between them. This was underlined in work for the London integrative study, which found that population and employment changes within London did not have a more significant impact on local unemployment levels than such changes in the wider South East region, which appears to behave as one very extended labour market (Buck *et al.*, 2002).

The results of these studies have a number of implications for policy, some of which are clear while others are still contested. First, they confirm that at the scale of whole cities – and still more at the city-region scale – spatial adjustment processes cannot be counted on to resolve the consequences of large-scale loss of manual jobs, even over a long period of 5–10 years. With commuting being the dominant form of adjustment, one of the obvious reasons for this is that (apart from London) cities with the worst record of job losses tend to be in regions with weak overall performance. Shifts in commuting patterns are a solution only to the extent that there are areas within commuting range experiencing more favourable trends. The fact that spatial adjustment mechanisms are quite strong, however, means (second) that the scale of additional employment required to resolve such problems cannot be simply judged from the residual level of involuntary worklessness in an area. Indeed, it is likely to be much greater (at least equal to the scale of the original job loss, and probably more) since job growth stimulates more mobility than do job losses. A third implication following from this is that effective action to limit job losses would have a greater impact on levels of worklessness in a city than attracting replacement jobs. This goes against the ethos of government industrial policy since the late 1970s. Fourth, where such jobs can be created, the local impact will be greatest if they are targeted at the least mobile groups of workers: notably those in manual occupations and women. And finally, the extent to which local job creation can be expected to make a difference depends on the openness of the target area in commuting terms, being reasonably strong at the level of functional regions and lower at the level of urban neighbourhoods. Disparities in unemployment observed at this scale involve additional factors that we discuss in the following section.

Labour market processes and social exclusion

Involuntary exclusion from employment is probably the principal determinant of social exclusion in advanced capitalist societies, where paid jobs are the main source of income, social status and identity, social interaction outside the family, daily time-structure and meaningful activity (Castells, 1998; Gallie *et al.*, 1994; Jahoda, 1982; Turok *et al.*, 1999). Unsurprisingly, access to employment opportunities is one of the two key pillars of the EU's model of social cohesion (European Commission, 1996). Traditional labour economics suggested that absence from the labour market was a matter of choice. However, effective exclusion from employment is quite possible in the face of weak or falling demand for labour, if wages in more stable parts of the labour market are inflexible downwards, and the wage required in its more flexible lower segments in order to clear the market as a whole falls below benefit levels and/or what is socially acceptable. The incidence of such exclusion may be exacerbated by discrimination against groups of workers with characteristics undesired by large numbers of employers.

Involuntary unemployment was high across large parts of the UK for much of the 1980s and early 1990s and it still is in some cities and regions even after a sustained period of national economic growth. In principle, commuting adjustment should reduce unemployment disparities at the urban and neighbourhood scales, especially in the long-term, yet there is considerable evidence of very persistent areas of high unemployment. Our analysis of 2001 Census data shows that two-thirds of the variation in unemployment rates between wards (a neighbourhood-scale unit) is actually *within* functional urban regions, despite these being defined on the basis of strong internal commuting links. The ILO unemployment rate was an average of 5.0 per cent across England and Wales, compared with an average of 11.2 per cent in the worst 10 per cent of wards, and just 1.9 per cent in the best 10 per cent. In former industrial and mining areas of the country involuntary unemployment has increasingly taken the form of long-term sickness among workers discouraged by the poor employment prospects (Alcock *et al.*, 2003; Beatty *et al.*, 2002). In Glasgow, Liverpool and Manchester almost one in five of the working age population (19.4 per cent, 18.5 per cent and 16.5 per cent respectively) claim sickness or disability benefits (as of February 2003). This is between three and four times their rates of registered unemployment. By contrast, in 1981 no British cities had a rate of working age sickness above 4.2 per cent. The status of unemployment relative to sickness has also worsened through reductions in the level and duration of unemployment benefits and increased pressure on people to find a job. Adding all those aged 16–74 declaring themselves inactive on sickness grounds (rather than retired, studying or engaged in domestic duties) to the Census unemployment figure yields a 'real' unemployment rate in 2001 of 12.3 per cent for England and Wales. The spatial disparities were even greater when this real rate is considered: it was an average of 26.2 per cent in the worst 10 per cent of wards against 4.5 per cent in the best 10 per cent.

Clearly spatial adjustment has not rebalanced these local labour markets. Indeed, the disparities seem to have worsened in two respects over the last two decades. During the 1980s unemployment became more concentrated in inner-city neighbourhoods (identified by their residential densities), with an additional tendency in London for greater concentration in areas that already had high unemployment (Buck *et al.*, 2002). During the 1990s recorded unemployment fell everywhere with the economic upturn, but more people moved on to sickness benefits, especially where unemployment was relatively high, so the 'real' rate of unemployment fell less in these areas than elsewhere (Beatty *et al.*, 2002; Gregg and Wadsworth, 2003; Webster, 2004).

The extent to which particular city-regions contain localities with very high rates of unemployment reflects both the overall pressure of demand prevailing in the functional region (as reflected in the ratio of vacancies to unemployment) and sources of inequality in the incidence of unemployment as between groups and areas within the region. Many of the highest unemployment wards in Britain are concentrated in a fairly limited number of major cities, notably within inner areas of Merseyside, Glasgow, Manchester, Tyneside and London. In the first four of these, this is associated with a relatively weak pressure of demand for labour, reflecting a long-term process of erosion of the sub-regional employment base, which has also left a layer of structural unemployment. This does not, however, account for the London case, where long-term employment decline in the core was more or less matched by population decentralization, and where declining areas are connected to ones with substantial expansion. The main point here is that unemployment tends to be highly spatially concentrated, with a group of localities experiencing rates of unemployment 5–10 times the average for the functional region.

These concentrations of high unemployment are not simply the outcome of *localized* job losses; rather (as has been argued in a series of studies since the 1970s, starting with Metcalf and Richardson, 1976) they reflect a combination of the uneven incidence of unemployment across different population groups, with the operation of local housing systems (both public and private) in sorting people with different social, economic and demographic characteristics into different parts of the city. People who are most at risk of joblessness tend to be concentrated in inner-city neighbour-hoods and peripheral council estates because this is where the lowest qual-ity, least desirable housing is. Unemployment is relatively high in these areas because the people who live there are more vulnerable to being out of work. They have a higher risk of worklessness because they have relatively few skills and qualifications, or because of other undesired personal char-acteristics (as discussed below). Those who manage to increase their human capital and obtain jobs often move away to better housing in less stigmatized areas. The sale of higher quality former public housing in 'better' neighbourhoods over the last two decades has contributed to a process of residualization within the social housing sector and increased polarization across cities. Gregg and Wadsworth (2003) present the strik-ing statistic that only 25 per cent of men with low qualifications living in social housing in Merseyside, Clydeside and Tyneside were in work in 2002, compared with 65 per cent for the same group in the South East and moreover, the employment rate of the former actually fell between 1993 and 2002 despite strong national growth. Similar kinds of process operate in settlements of all sizes, but the results are much more conspicuous – and perhaps of more real importance – in the larger urban and metropolitan labour markets, where relatively segregated areas are more extensive and more populous (as one of the *Cities* projects has demonstrated: Buck and Gordon, 2004; Gordon and Monastiriotis, 2003).

Whether unemployment is actually any worse because it is spatially concentrated in this way depends on whether there are significant spillover effects in areas of concentrated poverty. It is possible that the life-chances of residents in deprived neighbourhoods are further disadvantaged by where they live. One study in the *Cities* programme (discussed in chapter 9) found tentative evidence that people in poor areas have more localized social networks that may limit their knowledge of and links into wider job opportunities (Atkinson and Kintrea, 2001). Residents of such areas certainly feel disadvantaged by the stigma affecting their neighbourhoods. Both factors may reduce their chances of gaining employment or increase their vulnerability to unemployment. Nevertheless, one of the study's main conclusions was that conditions within the wider urban labour market were much more influential. This finding is consistent with Jargowsky's (1997) US research which showed that metropolitan-wide changes in employment explained 80 per cent of the higher poverty in deprived areas, compared with only 20 per cent identified with neighbourhood effects. The symptoms of a supposed 'culture of poverty' actually disappeared as labour market opportunities improved and the long-term unemployed were absorbed into employment.

The evidence that a combination of disadvantaging individual characteristics and selective housing processes are very largely responsible for local concentrations of unemployment in particular parts of the city begs two important questions about the underlying causal processes shaping the incidence of worklessness:

(a)   why people with certain characteristics are more vulnerable;
(b)   what lies behind those characteristics which are not fixed at birth.

Answers to these questions may also play a part in explaining why spatial concentration has increased over the last two decades. There are likely to be different kinds of characteristics that affect the risks of intermittent spells of unemployment and of longer-term exclusion from work. These attributes (and specific groups most vulnerable to unemployment) include: age (the youngest or oldest groups); ethnicity (members of black or other minority groups); marital status (lone parents); health (people with physical or mental disabilities or chronically ill); education and skills (people with low or no formal qualifications or recent relevant experience); and housing tenure (those in social housing). All of these may exert an independent influence on people's employability through employers' decisions about recruitment, training, promotion and retention, as well as decisions by workers themselves.

Personal characteristics may enter into employers' decisions in various ways. At one extreme, there may be pure prejudice without foundation or evidence of differences in productivity, reliability or other aspects of performance. At the other, there may be objective assessment of work force attributes linked directly to performance. These extremes are epitomized by characteristics related to race and 'skills', which we discuss in turn.

Ethnicity and discrimination

Race and ethnicity provide the clearest examples of discrimination in the labour market. A series of studies based on matched pairs of job applicants has uncovered systematic contrasts in people's experiences depending on their ethnic backgrounds. The *Cities* programme did not attempt to replicate any of these well-documented findings. Instead, projects focused on identifying how factors related to ethnicity affect key transitions, especially young people's entry into the labour market (Bowlby *et al.*, 2004; Husband, 2001) and the perceptions of employers and workers about their labour market experiences (Buck *et al.*, 2002). Most of this research focused on areas within the London region and confirmed that ethnicity remains important in labour market practices, even where the pressure of demand for labour is strong. Moreover, it has particular salience in service industries where personal and cultural attributes are perceived to be much more directly relevant to performance than in traditional factory work (Duster, 1995). The 'skills' agenda of employers emphasized communication/interpersonal skills, adaptability and willingness to learn, reliability, enthusiasm and motivation. These 'soft' attributes are hard to define operationally and are seen to be beyond the scope of training. Ethnicity was intertwined with class and gender in employers' stereotypes. For example, Bowlby *et al.* (2004) observe that: 'comments by employers on women's possession of communication skills, suggest that the image of the "good" young employee is not only white English and "middle class" but also "feminine" ' (p. 339).

Some interview evidence suggested that locality might be a fourth dimension, with a number of East London employers being very explicit about perceived shortcomings of the local labour force (Buck *et al.*, 2002). In the Thames Valley a young interviewee said that 'Pakistani boys in Slough' had a particular 'reputation for being trouble' (Bowlby *et al.*, 2004, p. 335). The point may just be that these areas have high proportions of working-class and South Asian residents respectively. However, it may also be that already disadvantaged young people in these communities are less willing to assume ('act out') the image wanted by (white) service employers if this conflicts with their own strategies for securing 'respect' (Duster, 1995) or cultural identities.

Direct recognition or acknowledgement of discrimination was limited on either side. Minority ethnic interviewees tended to deny having experienced it, even when reporting apparently clear examples. Employers claimed to be operating equal opportunities policies even when employing few members of local minority groups relative to other similar firms or the reported balance of job applicants (Buck *et al.*, 2002). Most employers had little to say about the issues involved, except occasionally in relation to the religious requirements of South Asian groups (Bowlby *et al.*, 2004). Hardly anything was said about hiring or employing black workers, or about schooling, where Afro-Caribbean males also experience some of the worst problems (Buck *et al.*, 2002).

Consistent statistical evidence of discrimination damaging people's employment prospects is very significant for cities, partly because minority ethnic groups are heavily represented in most large cities, especially their inner areas. They are also the fastest growing section of the popula-tion, through natural change and immigration. Systematic economic inequalities in these places are also highly relevant to social cohesion concerns, including community stability, social interaction, civic participa-tion and cultural tolerance (see also Amin, 2002). Evidence of discrimina-tion in the labour market based on race means there may also be discrimination on the basis of other characteristics, such as social class. In a service economy various aspects of working-class culture may be regarded by employers as relevant indicators of productivity. Indeed, part of the significance of ethnicity seems to lie in the way in which different class identities have come to be associated with particular groups. The fact that social housing tenure also appears to be associated with higher risks of unemployment, even when factors such as qualifications and occupation are controlled for, lends support to the view that class-based discrimination is significant in the labour market, in addition to age, gender and ethnicity. This substantially increases the proportion of core urban residents whose labour market position may depend on some combination of discrimina-tion and the way people present themselves.

Skills mismatch, competition and sedimentation

Skill seems to lie at the other extreme from race in terms of an objective economic connection with employability. It is obviously relevant to shifts in the occupational mix of urban jobs and the overrepresentation of people with low qualifications among the unemployed. On this basis, skills mismatch is commonly invoked as an explanation of high unemployment, in the sense that there is a permanent excess supply of labour in sub-labour markets characterized by low or obsolete skills (e.g. Cabinet Office, 2001; HM Treasury, 2001a, 2001b). One qualification of this argument has already been noted: namely, that skills and qualifications have been increasing on the supply side between successive cohorts of workers. Another is that the rate of worklessness for groups with particular levels of skill and qualification varies greatly in different parts of the country depending on the pressure of demand for labour (Erdem and Glyn, 2001). There are further reasons for challenging traditional notions of skills mismatch. In summary, these are that:

(a) occupational sub-labour markets overlap, with 'rippling' tending to shift labour across boundaries in response to shifts in demand;
(b) 'skill' requirements involve issues of character or trust as much as hard technical capacities, making the issue always one of competition for better vacancies or workers rather simple success or failure in fitting 'pegs' into 'holes';

(c)   'bumping down' in situations of generally deficient-demand means
that unemployment gets concentrated among those who last worked
in less skilled positions, without the pressure of demand for them
necessarily being particularly weak (Gordon, 2003b).

From this perspective it would be too simple to say that growing urban
concentrations of unemployment merely reflect an accelerated shift in the
nature of labour demand as a result of deindustrialization. They may also
represent the residues of prolonged experience of generally deficient
demand in the wider regions concerned: that is, the outcome of 'sedimentation' processes (Buck and Gordon, 2000). These include bumping down
as well as factors pushing some of the unemployed towards the margins of
the labour market through discouragement, demoralization, stereotyping,
family breakdown, ill-health, loss of informal networks and decay of work
habits. Over longer timescales, educational underachievement by children
of poor lone parents and other deprived households in areas of high male
unemployment (Buck and Gordon, 2004) may also contribute to the reproduction of structural unemployment in situations initially involving a
simple failure of demand. The significance of sedimentation processes has
been contested by research showing a strong relationship historically and
spatially between long-term unemployment (and/or sickness) and the
general state of the labour market (Turok and Webster, 1998; Webster,
1997, 2004). Indeed, persistence of unemployment is fundamentally a
consequence of a weak pressure of demand for labour in particular city-
regional labour markets, and should be largely reversible through sustained
employment growth. It is not our view that marginalization makes many
people permanently unemployable, but rather that it substantially reduces
the competitive prospects of those affected, while at the same time congest-
ing the lower rungs of the labour market where they would otherwise have
realistic chances of gaining employment. In these two respects it becomes
a structural problem, with a local geography reflecting the residential
distribution of the marginalized groups.

The London integrative study explored some of these links, particularly
in relation to bumping down among people experiencing spells of unemployment during the 1990s (Buck *et al.*, 2002). It sought to explain the
intensification of unemployment in a crescent-shaped set of areas around
the eastern side of the central business district during a period of strong
economic growth in the city. A substantial gap in unemployment rates
consequently emerged between Greater London and the surrounding outer
metropolitan area. Changes in population and the composition of jobs
explained only a small part of this. The preferred interpretation was that
this reflected processes of cumulative marginalization during periods of
labour market slackness within the past 25 years, which pushed people in

the weakest competitive position out of employment. Clear evidence was found both of bumping down the occupational ladder by those who had experienced some unemployment, and that concentration occurred cumulatively during years of deficient demand. That this occurred particularly in the eastern crescent area was because it happened to house many of those most vulnerable to marginalization. In other cities where demand deficiency has been a chronic rather than cyclical feature, the links may be less obvious, but the cumulative impact will have been even more important in generating localized concentration of deep unemployment and economic disadvantage. The most visible manifestation of this may be the high incidence of sickness and disability claimants (Turok and Bailey, 2005).

Such developments during the 1980s and 1990s were distinctly 'urban' in their location and consequences, and may well have been intensified by neighbourhood level processes such as the attrition of job information networks. They were more severe than anything like this experienced for decades. They also became more conspicuous alongside signs of growing urban prosperity and visible affluence. However, they do not appear to have much to do with the new 'urban era' of the NCW. Instead, they seem to reflect the combination of traditional processes of competition and discrimination in urban labour markets with exceptionally deep recessions in the macro-economy. If there is something new, it may be the impacts on socially disadvantaged groups of employers' increasing emphasis on personal attributes associated with 'soft' skills.

Conclusions

Britain's major urban labour markets have experienced profound changes over the last two decades, most of which have little to do with the new economy or the processes highlighted in the NCW. The most basic of these are caused by a combination of macro-economic factors, especially two deep recessions which affected all parts of the country, and continuing structural change including large-scale manufacturing job losses in all the major cities, with a particular impact in the North. The economic upturn experienced by many cities since the mid-1990s has not been sufficiently broad-based or sustained as yet to undo the effects of this experience.

An important element in the new sense of optimism about the economic prospects of cities has been a view that labour market processes gain from agglomeration, which provides both for greater flexibility and upward mobility. A large and dynamic pool of specialized skills potentially offers important externalities to small, lean and innovative enterprises and industries. Similar externalities should be available to workers in terms of the choice of employers and enhanced career opportunities. For London at least there is clear evidence of these processes operating, but there are questions as to their salience in smaller, less diversified cities with more limited capacity to attract or retain qualified young workers.

However, labour market flexibility is no more the answer to all of the employment problems of the cities than employment rigidity was their cause. Discrimination of various kinds continues to exacerbate inequality of access to good, secure jobs with opportunities for advancement, especially in the context of weak demand for labour. Adjustment processes tend over time to disperse the effects of employment change, although more effectively in the context of growth than of decline. In slack labour markets they contribute to both the concentration of open unemployment and the diversion of potential workers into marginalized positions in various forms of hidden unemployment. In the process, they create forms of structural unemployment that respond little to marginal increases in employment opportunities or the pressure of demand for labour, but rather show very considerable persistence.

This analysis has important implications for policy, which in the UK has recently concentrated on a combination of: labour market deregulation; national supply-side programmes (the various New Deals) targeted at different marginalized groups, notably long-term unemployed youth and lone parents; and neighbourhood regeneration initiatives, one of whose aims is to get people into jobs by increasing their employability. For reasons that we have just noted, increasing labour market flexibility has very little relevance to the problem of concentrated urban unemployment. Job creation is much more salient, at least in the northern city-regions suffering a general weakness of demand. However, the appropriate scale for this goes beyond the immediate neighbourhoods concerned, since the effects get dispersed across the wider urban area (Gordon, 2000). Much larger-scale (and sustained) employment growth is needed in order to counter the effects of decades of decline. Some of this may be targeted at available vacant and derelict sites within commuting range of deprived estates, but economic development efforts should not be restricted to these possibilities and other opportunities should also be exploited.

In relation to concentrated unemployment in the most disadvantaged communities, supply-side initiatives seem to be important, since – despite roots in demand deficiency – the immediate barriers to employment of a high proportion of those in such areas are personal characteristics which weaken their position in competing for jobs. In some instances the appropriate response should be to direct vigorous equal opportunities policies at employers. In other respects it seems appropriate to ameliorate individuals' competitive position, as the New Deal programmes have sought to do, albeit in a limited way. Nationally these seem to have assisted substantial numbers of people to obtain jobs, though it is not easy to separate their impact from the improved macro-economic context (HofC EESC, 2001). A study that sought to do so by taking job duration, substitution and recycling effects into account suggested that the net effects of the New Deal have been quite modest (Riley and Young, 2001). In terms of the programmes' own criteria there have been sharp spatial variations in success, with lower levels of achievement in many of the areas where the problems are most severe (Martin *et al.*, 2003). This is partly a problem of deficient demand, especially as there is evidence that recycling through the programme is more common in regions with weak employment growth. On the key criterion of gaining sustained employment, the much lower success rate achieved in core urban areas is really striking, not only in regions of weak demand but especially in inner London. Here candidates for the programme are much more likely to display a series of personally disadvantaging characteristics than in areas where youth unemployment directly reflects a lack of opportunities. From this perspective, one might simply conclude that such programmes need more intensive resourcing in core urban areas to deal with multiple barriers facing the most socially disadvantaged groups. However, in all the areas where success seems limited, another constraint is the 'crowding' of job-seekers in the entry-level segment of the labour market as a result of 'bumping down', which means that improvement of the competitive position of some of the 'excluded' will often involve the displacement of others whose realistic employment aspirations are also limited to such jobs. Resolving this entry-level congestion requires some combination of a sustained strong pressure of demand in the regional economies concerned and efforts to develop human capital and promote upward mobility amongst a much broader cross-section of the local labour force (Gordon, 1999b). As in the spatial case, targeting the 'margins' of urban labour markets – the areas and groups experiencing the worst problems – both misses the fact that problems have some of their roots in more central parts of the labour market, and encourages unrealistic expectations about what can be achieved with modest, one-off initiatives in the face of chronic long-term problems (Buck *et al.*, 2002). Taking a broader, more realistic view, the requirements of competitiveness and cohesion actually converge, but strong governance is necessary to sustain action on the scale required beyond normal political and local horizons.

Urban labour markets matter because the processes operating in them produce rather complicated sets of outcomes, involving combinations of supply and demand factors (whose relative significance will vary over time and space), which need to be better understood by urban policy-makers if either competitiveness or cohesion are to be secured. Fundamental to much of what has been observed in British cities during recent times has been the long-term effect of chronic shortages of demand, rather than anything especially novel. The NCW holds out long-term hopes for many cities, though not for all of those with problems left over from the last urban era. However, it should not distract attention from a series of continuing issues associated with the malign effects of both deindustrialization and discrimination in urban labour markets.

Chapter 15

Conclusion: Moving Beyond the Conventional Wisdom

NICK BUCK, IAN GORDON, ALAN HARDING and IVAN TUROK

Introduction

Cities *are* changing, but not all in the same way, nor all in ways that are so different from the past. In relation to the largest US core cities, Beauregard (2004) has shown that while about one-quarter turned around from a decline in population to (modest) growth between the 1980s and the 1990s, about twice as many did not, and another quarter experienced consistent growth. The last group were concentrated in the sunbelt, while those with continuing decline were all in the rustbelt. Regional location – and inherited industrial structure – still makes a big difference. The characteristics that seem (on his analysis) to distinguish the 'resurgent' cities are more subtle, including inheritance of a well-educated professional population, the capacity to attract foreign immigrants, stability in racial mix (which may indicate the absence of 'white flight') and a degree of loyalty to the area on the part of its middle classes, favouring good governance. This sketch is preliminary, and some of these attributes may reflect success as much as contribute to it, but it makes the point that a new optimism about the prospects for cities does not imply that all will start doing much better.

Among major British cities – the focus of our research programme – only Greater London qualifies as resurgent on Beauregard's definition, which involves changes observed over whole decades, although Leeds-Bradford appears to have experienced continuous slow growth (Moore and Begg, 2004). On other criteria (such as trends in GDP) or in relation to a broader area (extended metropolitan regions), London may never actually have been in decline, but it *has* clearly improved its relative position over the last 20 years. In terms of Beauregard's distinguishing characteristics, it is definitely the number one destination for immigrants of all kinds. It also has the highest levels of work force qualification (many drawn in from elsewhere), although during the years of its turnaround it clearly lacked local leadership, or indeed a city government. (Trends in ethnic or racial

265

balance are probably irrelevant to London's position, since no British city seems to have experienced significant 'white flight'.) As in the USA, however, regional location and industrial structure also matter, and most of the other British conurbations have experienced continuing disadvantage owing to their greater dependence (and that of their regions) on manufacturing activities that are in general decline in the UK. Nevertheless, some of the larger northern conurbations have displayed signs of recovery since the mid-1990s.

It is important to emphasize that the NCW argues for a revaluation of certain kinds of 'urban asset' associated with density, flexibility and diversity, which not all cities possess to the same degree. The new emphasis on 'quality' attributes also implies that places (including big cities) that are below par will fall further behind. It would not be fair therefore to judge the NCW by whether all cities (or even most) show evidence of resurgence, though some should be doing so by now if it is to carry credibility. At least as important is the question of how far it provides an intelligible, coherent and verifiable framework for analysis and policy formulation in particular kinds of place. At the outset we adopted a rather sceptical position in this regard, since many of the NCW ideas seemed designedly fuzzy, and better suited to consensus building than empirical testing.

We return now to consider how far this view has been borne out by the research reported in the preceding chapters, and whether this points towards some sharper (less 'conventional') ideas, be they new, old or a mixture of both. The balance between novelty and familiarity may actually not be too significant, since both can serve conservative functions. The real question is whether the ideas are adequate to identify and explain key features of contemporary urban development relevant to the opportunities and quality of life available to various population groups. These ideas should also shed light on the key policy choices (whether easy or difficult) that bear upon these outcomes.

This is an ambitious agenda on which we can honestly only hope to partly deliver. In pursuing it, we shall follow the logic of Part I of this book, discussing in turn issues associated with each of the three main concepts of the NCW – competitiveness, cohesion and governance – and then their interaction. This might seem a bit odd given our criticism of the scientific adequacy (and political implications) of these 'legs' of the NCW stool. One reason is that each has its roots in one discipline of the traditional division of labour in the social sciences, between the economic, the social and the political. This retains substantial power, despite ultimately being arbitrary. The other is that the way in which the NCW refocuses each of these concepts is far from arbitrary, in relation to real changes in the world, as well as in relation to political agendas for coping with these.

Competitiveness

Competitiveness is an elusive idea relating to the drivers of prosperity in a more open economy, where success depends largely on qualititative factors. The NCW suggests that this new environment offers distinctive competitive advantages for cities, which are reinforced by a vertical disintegration of production, and a growing knowledge economy. By re-establishing the value of face-to-face contact and encouraging collaboration, these changes should make firms more sensitive to the kinds of externalities, spillovers or synergies only available in substantial cities. Proximity to specialized services, technical institutions, social networks, sophisticated labour markets and international connections are all believed to have become more important. In a more flexible economy, access to a bigger choice of employers, customers and collaborators should benefit both skilled labour and suppliers of advanced services. Furthermore, talent is more likely to be attracted by the diverse amenities, cultural facilities and tolerant social environment of major cities, or at least some kinds of them.

This is a persuasive argument about a widely discussed set of emergent tendencies, but how far does the research evidence on change in British cities actually support these propositions? And how much of the change, in terms of economic success and failure, which they have experienced over this period can be accounted for in these terms, as compared with the influence of other factors that are older and/or less specifically 'urban'? A simple answer is that, over the entire period of the last two decades (when these processes are supposed to have come to the fore), there is rather little evidence that most cities in Britain have benefited to any significant extent from the enhanced competitiveness suggested by the NCW. Until the mid-1990s at least, continuity with previous patterns was more important than change, and almost every major British core city continued to experience declines in employment and population. Things do seem to have improved since then (with the suggestion of a turnaround in both Manchester and Glasgow). But it is not yet clear how far this is a purely cyclical phenomenon, reflecting short-term national growth in demand for quite traditional urban services (private and public), rather than anything less prosaic and more likely to be sustained. At the city-region scale, much clearer evidence has emerged of the link between urban mass and productivity levels – in Britain (Rice and Venables, 2004) as well as internationally (Rosenthal and Strange, 2004) – but not as to whether this link has become more significant. The exception is for London, the largest city, which has substantially extended its lead over the rest in earnings terms, although this may have more to do with a general shift in the UK labour market toward less equal rewards than enhanced performance by London businesses (Buck *et al.*, 2002).

As we have seen, two major elements in persistent weak performance by most of Britain's core cities have been a continuation of deindustrialization and spatial deconcentration, combined with a relative failure of the northern regions as a whole (which include all the provincial conurbations) in capturing expanding service and high technology activities. Overall, these old factors seem to swamp any benefits that may be accruing from the processes foregrounded by the NCW. In terms of relative performance, clear evidence of change in the factors associated with growth in British urban areas is limited to a couple of attributes, with both levels of human capital and sectoral diversity becoming significant (favourable) influences for the first time during recent decades. (Unpublished regression results from Moore and Begg's (2004) analyses of city employment growth between 1951 and 2000 show that levels of educational qualification only *became* a significant positive influence in the 1990s; sectoral diversity became a positive influence on aggregate growth from the 1970s onwards, while from the 1990s it showed a significant positive effect on growth in four of their eight sectors.) There has been a continuing tendency for particular sectors to show more positive changes away from their areas of main concentration, suggesting that any industrial clustering effects were weak and outweighed by the benefits gained from dispersal (Moore and Begg, 2004). And it is the more diversified of the provincial cities (notably Manchester) which have shown signs of a turnaround over recent years. Generally, however, the places growing fastest of all have been the former New Towns, which benefited from sustained public investment in physical business infrastructure, housing supply and good transport systems. This supports a wider point about the continuing significance of traditional 'hard' assets in supporting urban growth and revitalization, including a supply of serviced land and property for economic and residential uses, and efficient internal and external transport connections.

Assessing what empirical support there is so far for NCW-based expectations of a turnaround in the competitive position of cities requires a view to be taken about what kind of spatial units appropriately represent these 'cities'. Both theoretical expectations and empirical claims tend to wander between a focus on central business/residential areas, the core cities (defined in terms of continuously built-up areas), and the much broader 'functional urban regions' that have inherited various functions of the traditional cores. The focus of policy interest in urban revival is also ambiguous, though normally somewhere between the first two of these levels, with only limited recognition of (or interest in) what is happening to wider city-regions, at least until very recently. In terms of actual change, the most conspicuous evidence in the UK has been for central city areas, many of which have been clearly revitalized through a combination of growth in marketed urban services and the rediscovery of city centre living among middle and upper-income groups.

We should be cautious about taking this as confirmation of the fundamental change in cities' competitiveness predicted by the NCW (despite the optimism of British policy-makers; e.g. ODPM, 2003a), since the changes are generally localized and not entirely new. Two major elements are the continued growth of office-based business services and population gentrification, each of which can be traced back to the early 1960s, when they first came to prominence in central London. They have steadily grown in importance since then, both across London and in the central areas of many provincial cities. Both may be seen as expressions of a knowledge society, in the centrality of information processing to office services, and the stronger taste for urban living evident among the graduate population. However, their recent development does not provide clear evidence of a radical break so much as the working through of established trends to a point where they are having major impacts, at least in those cities with some base of attractions for these activities and groups. In cities such as Manchester, Glasgow, Newcastle and Leeds, the sheer scale and up-market character of recent city centre residential property development and rehabilitation does appear to be quite distinctive from trends in the 1970s and 1980s.

At the second level, in relation to the continuous built-up area the evidence of change is less clear-cut, as we have already noted. London is the one clear example, though a case can be made that it should be taken as a *harbinger*: always liable to respond most rapidly, strongly and visibly to a revaluation of urban assets, because it starts off with the strongest stock of all these; but not unique in the kind of advantages that it possesses and hence likely to be followed by others. Against this optimistic view, there are two main kinds of objection: one emphasizing the extent to which its (truly unique) 'global' role has been the key to resurgence since the 1980s; and the other suggesting that its success (rooted in historic advantages) undermines the potential of otherwise competitive British cities, particularly through sucking in highly qualified young workers from the provinces to fill a qualitative gap in its own labour supply. Research in the programme rejected the first of these arguments – the strong 'global city' thesis – on the basis that the global sector was responsible only for a minority of London's growth, reflecting rather than causing its competitive advantage in advanced services (Buck *et al.*, 2002). In relation to the second of the arguments, escalating living costs might discourage migration to London, but there is no evidence yet that other British cities offer anything like the 'escalator effect' on career advancement that draws ambitious young people to London.

There are some other 'straws in the wind' in relation to urban performance since the late 1990s, with new sub-national capitals such as

Edinburgh and Cardiff seemingly prospering. But extrapolating from London's recent success to the prospects for other central cities remains a matter of faith, theory and casual observation, rather than well-grounded fact; and we should also note that London's enhanced performance has gone with both greater instability and greater inequality.

At the broader, functional region level, the key empirical issue is less that of turnaround, since actual decline has been rarer at the city-region scale, but rather of how much of the anticipated new growth in 'urban' activities might actually occur away from the central city, and how far this matters for the welfare of its residents. Some of the revalued urban assets (density, diversity and flexibility) do relate most clearly to core cities, and especially to central areas at the hub of the regional transport system, but a good deal of evidence has been found of agglomeration economies and face-to-face based economic relationships operating across broader city-regions. This was most clearly – and perhaps most unexpectedly – demonstrated in relation to the studies of innovation, where in the 'London' case the whole Greater South East region emerged as a relevant scale of agglomeration, with much of the greatest dynamism well away from the centre. Translating this to the situation of Manchester, for instance, the favoured area under the NCW could turn out not to be the city itself but the polycentric urban region of north-west England. More complex spatial patterns seem to be emerging than in the past, with particular kinds of activities favouring dispersed, high amenity locations around major agglomerations and operating within a broader geography of economic interactions than traditional central city functions.

A general point is that among activities benefiting from spatial externalities, not all want or need the same combination of proximities and location factors, and this turns out to be true even amongst innovative, high-tech activities and their creative work forces. In the USA, Florida (2002b) has pointed out that these have been attracted not only to established cities with a lot of cultural capital, but also to 'nerdistans' in Silicon Valley and to 'latte towns' with good access to outdoor amenities. Equivalent distinctions may be made *within* city-regions, with quite different kinds of locale (some central, others peripheral) emerging as successful. For example, software writers and new media professionals may well have different work and residential preferences from research scientists, design engineers and management consultants. Greater sensitivity on the part of planners and policy-makers to different locational rationales is important, alongside pursuing practicable actions to relieve some of the mundane environmental factors contributing to decentralization. Although increasing numbers of young professionals are living within core urban areas, there is no evidence of a slowing of the outward movement of middle-class families beyond city boundaries to the outer rings. The long-established desire of families for homes with gardens and space for expansion in lower density suburbs is an enduring challenge to the 'urban renaissance' agenda. In relation to the 'jobs gap' of the core areas, continuance of population decentralization ought to be a good thing; but actually the effect is rather modest, since most of these flows remain within the functional region, where labour markets tend to be rather tightly integrated. Increasingly this is a spatial scale demanding joined-up planning and economic management of the complex and dynamic spatial mosaic of inter-related residential and business locations of which modern urban agglomerations are constituted.

In terms of the specific processes which the NCW suggests to be underpinning the rebuilding of urban competitive advantage, our research found little evidence to support the significance which has been attached to local industrial clusters fostered by social networks and personal relationships and linked to the distinctive cultural traditions and identities of places. The external economies of scale and scope associated with urban size and diversity generally seem more significant to business performance than inter-firm co-operation and cohesive institutions. The sheer scale and diversity of the London metropolitan region, in particular, was found to support a flexible mix-and-match approach to commercial and informational linkages. Access to excellent air connections from leading city-regions also facilitated interaction with world-class suppliers and customers, helping businesses to access leading edge technology and sustain their competitive position through ongoing learning. Time proximity thus enabled firms from these regions to maintain certain kinds of face-to-face contact without geographic proximity.

In relation to urban competitiveness, the NCW risks exaggerating the significance of both novel activities and new urban attributes in ways that are potentially very misleading for policy-makers. Established business service activities still contribute much more growth than do biotechnology or the creative sectors. Business collaboration, institutional networks and other soft assets do not diminish the significance of an effective supply of land and property, good transport connections, a skilled labour supply and access to a range of business suppliers and services. And the opportunities provided by the sheer size and diversity of successful leading cities cannot realistically be matched simply through encouragement of networking, trust and collaboration in smaller and less well endowed specialist centres. Many old industrial cities lacking relevant historic strengths that can be recuperated are in a weak position to compete, while those – including particularly Glasgow and Manchester in the UK – which do have some of these assets (and are showing encouraging trends at present) are disadvantaged by the weakness of surrounding regional economies. These are major challenges for public policy at all levels, at a time when the tendency is to decentralize economic responsibilities. It may require more consistent support from central government for urban and regional economic development, with more concerted use of available levers such as investment in infrastructure, science policy and higher education (Parkinson *et al.*, 2004; Simmie *et al.*, 2004).

Social cohesion

The limitations of social cohesion as an analytical construct for research on cities are rather more fundamental. The term itself is not widely used in mainstream social research, and even when it is disaggregated into its main dimensions – connectedness, order and equality – its coverage is partial. This is especially clear when the intention is to understand the drivers of social structure and social processes in the 'new urban era'. While the NCW apparently provides a more significant place for the social dimension in understanding cities, its conception is driven by what is important for economic success. This is not a new problem, since a persistent issue for urban social analysis has been to provide an account of social structure or social change that is not driven by economic determinism.

In considering how the NCW agenda might contribute to the development of urban social research, it is useful to make the following distinction. First, there are studies *in* cities; studies of particular, more or less narrow issues, but with a clear recognition of the urban context within which processes are taking place, and interested in how this context might affect the processes. Second, there are studies *of* cities, concerned with explaining urban change from a more holistic perspective. The NCW embodies an account of the processes and inter-relationships that are supposed to lead to the success or failure of cities, and so it provides an agenda for the latter approach. However, because it also prioritizes certain issues it may also shape the agenda for a wider range of social research in cities. We suggest that the NCW framework does not particularly help to understand the contribution of social change to urban change. It has certainly influenced some aspects of social research in cities, but significant areas of research could have proceeded without the framework, at no great loss.

It is conventional to equate cohesion and competitiveness with the social and the economic, which is what has been done earlier in the book. In practice this has limitations, because the overall social structure of cities and the processes that cause it to change may contribute both to competitiveness (since it determines the stock of human capital), and to cohesion (since different social structures lead to different levels of inequality and connectedness). Change in the social structure lies at heart of any social research agenda for cities, but this is disguised by its separate contribution to competitiveness and cohesion issues. This separation may be exacerbated by the fact that cohesion-orientated social research focuses on the bottom end of the social structure, whilst competitiveness-oriented research tends to focus on the top end.

Looking at competitiveness and cohesion together ought to allow links to be made across these divides. At a basic level it raises questions about how far urban social problems are a consequence of competitive failure, or whether the pursuit of competitive success can be damaging for local social cohesion (in one or more of its senses). Research within our programme in the more economically successful British cities provides a lot of relevant evidence but suggests no simple answers. Persistent concentrations of poverty and deprivation are found in these places (as well as in the less successful cities), notably in London but also, though on a far smaller scale, in Bristol and Edinburgh. This suggests that there are limits on the extent to which the benefits of growth trickle down, especially when the sectoral or occupational composition of that growth is narrow or imbalanced. However, there is little evidence of increasing problems of disorder or disconnectedness associated with growth in these cities. While income inequality has risen, this is mostly because incomes at the top end of the spectrum have been rising fast, rather than because incomes at the bottom have been falling. Moreover, the numbers in absolute poverty in these cities have been falling since around the mid-1990s, although there is some evidence of increasing spatial concentration through processes of residualization within the housing market (Dorling and Rees, 2003; Lupton, 2003).

More generally, there are important issues associated with the spatial scale of social processes. They may be critical for all three components of social cohesion: inequality, connectedness and order. Research has considered both the city-wide scale, where the basic causes of difference are associated with the relative success or failure of the city as a whole, and the neighbourhood scale, where concentrations of deprivation arising from residential segregation may damage life chances. Overall, the evidence suggests that neighbourhood effects are real, but not particularly large when compared with other influences on individual life chances (Buck and Gordon, 2004; Turok and Bailey, 2004b). There is clearly more research to be done in establishing how far residential segregation has general and demonstrable effects on the components of social cohesion. One of the limitations of UK research has been the lack of direct focus on situations where there is an ethnic dimension to segregation. Nevertheless, one can be fairly confident that there are no effects comparable in scale to those found by Wilson (1987) in the USA.

Aspects of social change are important for the competitiveness agenda as well as for cohesion, with Beauregard (2004) and Florida (2002b) each suggesting significant social dimensions to urban success. More generally, the social structure provides the basis for determining what skills, knowledge and human capital are available. From the point of view of urban social research, it is important to link changes in the social structure with their consequences for cohesion and competitiveness. This should lead to a greater focus on the sources and nature of change in social structures over time. These may follow from economic change, but they may also be partially independent of that change. This is partly because they are the result of complex individual adjustment processes, operating within limiting institutional structures and built forms, and where places can have significant symbolic value and meaning for different social groups. One of the consequences is that the formation of the urban social structure involves conflicts over urban resources. This phenomenon tends to be seriously neglected in the NCW.

One also needs to consider rather more broadly the drivers of social structure and social processes in the 'new urban era'. In the introduction we referred to a number of propositions about social change that underpinned the NCW. These questioned whether some of the old expectations about the social order could continue to be met in the new circumstances. Some of the changes implied by the NCW, such as increased turbulence in individual lives and the decline of institutions offering security (which may force people to be more self-reliant) are not necessarily urban in origin. Urban research has not yet pursued these issues sufficiently to explore how far there are specific urban effects. To put it another way, research has tended to focus on established themes, such as poverty and deprivation, which affect limited parts of the population. There has been far less work on changes which may have shaped the lives and life chances of broader groups, including issues of insecurity arising from more precarious forms of employment, increasing levels of family fission, and changing levels of tolerance towards minority communities stemming from threats to livelihoods.

Taking forward the urban social research agenda also requires better linkage with more general approaches to the sociology of the development of modern societies. The move towards a focus on individualization leaves no clear place for the structural regularities that lead to inequalities in life chances. Recent urban research has shown that these inequalities have persisted and deepened, in spite of the alleged end of class society. Traditional class analysis is in something of a crisis, unable fully to respond to the profound changes which are evidently occurring to social structure, although Savage (2000) suggests some ways forward. Drawing on this and on findings from the London integrative study (Buck *et al.*, 2002) we suggest four promising lines for future urban sociological research.

First, while there may have been increasing instability in work careers, and a decline in the role of institutions and organizations which structure those careers, this has happened in a complex and spatially differentiated manner. The breakdown of organizational affiliation in favour of entrepreneurial careers has gone furthest in some of the largest agglomerations. However, these also contain many individuals in central organizational niches. The most successful social groups in these places contain a mixture of people who have exploited their human capital through careers of considerable mobility, and those who can extract a rent from organizational centrality. Other social groups manage this volatile environment with more difficulty. Understanding the consequence of an urban social structure such as this is a key issue for social research.

Second, we should look at how the cultural distinctiveness of particular cities affects the ways in which class divisions are articulated. For example, the relatively tolerant environment, as well as the economic dynamism of some metropolitan areas (such as London), tends to weaken traditional class identities and facilitate the emergence of new identities, which may diverge from mainstream values. But that does not make them less class-divided, and some cultural forms play precisely the roles of exclusion and distinction that Bourdieu (1985) posited.

Third, we need to take account of other actual and potential lines of social division, especially ethnicity, gender and household structure, and their consequences for life chances and social reproduction. Issues include the question of how far processes related to ethnic identity (e.g. residential segregation) serve to consolidate social divisions, or the extent to which inequalities related to household structures have impacts on future life chances, and potentially on inter-generational transmission of resources and values.

Finally, while it can be argued that property assets do not form a major independent line of social cleavage since they depend largely on labour market careers, in a spatial context property assets do take on an additional force. Neighbourhoods constitute resources which may have positive or negative consequences for life chances, and which residents will seek to protect and enhance. The protection and enhancement of neighbourhoods is clearly a basis for urban conflict, either between residents and state institutions or between different groups of residents.

Urban governance

The NCW suggests both that new, more complex and more responsive forms of urban governance are critical to securing competitiveness and cohesion, and that these concerns should actually be displacing more traditional forms of central urban policy and local government activity. How far these arguments hold in the UK over the last couple of decades is not easy to judge, because of the complexity and variability both in patterns of urban change and in the way in which policy priorities, expenditure choices and processes of institutional reform unfold. Clear patterns and trends are hard to find and there is little evidence either that a balancing of competitiveness and cohesion has been achieved or that promoting it – with more than 'warm words' – has been the primary goal of any of the range of organizations involved in 'urban' policy in its broadest sense.

The revival of the traditional role of selected cities as centres for exchange, consumption, connectivity, higher education and social as well as economic creativity has been supported in many ways by a broad array of institutions concerned with urban governance, in its widest sense. They are only partially addressed by urban (for which read 'local') governments, and are barely influenced by the focused initiatives that fall under the label of urban policy. Decades of experimentation with urban policy initiatives, partnerships and networks to deliver them, and a recent emphasis upon integrating traditional services in order to improve life chances in the poorest neighbourhoods, seem unable to generate equitable economic and social change. The incidence of absolute poverty has fallen at a time when the national economy has been relatively buoyant for an unusually long period, but the gap between the poorest sections of society and the richest continues to widen, partly because of the changing structure of the labour market and the growth in earnings for professionals, managers and skilled technical workers.

Evidence of the radical changes suggested in the regulation accounts of the shift from welfare to competitiveness objectives, and of decentralization of economic policy, is mixed. Whilst the UK is often seen, within continental Europe, as the EU member that has moved furthest towards a regressive, quasi-American approach to social policy and greater reliance upon markets, this does not appear to have influenced national attitudes to cities. Indeed, it remained all but invisible in the period during which most of the research for this book was completed. Within the UK, the fact is that cities are simply not relevant units of analysis or action for most national government departments. One department – the Office of the Deputy Prime Minister (ODPM) – has dominated formal urban policy, whilst others lack any obvious 'urban mission' or interest in their differential urban effects, even though their policies and spending patterns have significant implications for cities. The idea that globalizing processes limit freedom for political manoeuvre and policy choices, that (selective) urban economies can be identified as critical to national economic well-being, and that their development would thus be pursued by a broad government coalition, is inconsistent with the evidence that UK urban policy has generally been defined by ODPM efforts to pursue localized economic solutions to urban social problems.

Only very recently (in 2003) have the key UK central government departments and the major city authorities been brought together, in a Working Group on Cities, Regions and Competitiveness. Their analysis and arguments about the contribution of cities to regional and national economies are potentially transformative. They suggest, for example, that because city-regions are increasingly central to regional wealth and productivity, because London is the focus of the UK's most dominant city-region, and because the efficiency of the UK economy can only be maximized by encouraging it to 'fire on all cylinders', the governance of city-regions may become a key political issue in years to come. At the time of writing, however, it is fair to observe that, whilst this may be the harbinger of more fundamental long-term change, experience suggests that other outcomes may be just as likely.

The final reason why it has proved so hard to come up with clear 'rules' about the relationship between competitiveness, cohesion and governance at the urban scale is very simple. It is in the very nature of governance that there should be relatively unpredictable and variable outcomes. Governance is about political choices, and the mobilization of a variety of economic and social forces in support of those choices. It is not about the predictability of 'successes', measured against any particular yardstick, flowing from these choices. The difficulty with overarching conceptual literatures that predict certain broad and invariant patterns of change but then identify changes in urban governance as critical to them is that they tend to assume that structural, institutional changes – where these can be found, in practice – determine the way institutions are used. Yet it is central to the study of governance that the behaviour of a range of actors (within and between institutions) affects outcomes in ways that, cumulatively, can be important.

This is not to argue that institutional structures are unimportant. In the UK case, for example, it is clear that the relative absence of mechanisms for integrating the efforts of different levels of government in pursuit of an 'urban agenda' that values cities and recognizes their differential contributions to the pursuit of competitiveness and cohesion has meant that 'urban policy' has lacked weight, direction and consistency. It has also meant that the search for a broader conception of urban governance, which begins to link together the variety of actions attributable to the public sector that shape urban competitiveness and cohesion, has depended upon relatively heroic efforts of local politicians and executives to 'co-ordinate from below'.

What an institutional perspective misses is the importance of governance and leadership to the process of widening and deepening 'urban policy', as it is practised in particular places, and making it more effective, whether that be in pursuit of competitiveness, cohesion or a more equitable trade-off between the two. If the richness and diversity of the case study research in this volume demonstrates anything amidst the complexity of its findings, it is that effective governance is needed more in some places than in others, but that whether or not cities get the governance they need or deserve is difficult to predict with any accuracy. The 'game' that urban authorities have had to engage in when trying to pursue competitiveness and cohesion has changed markedly over the last 20 years in the face of globalizing pressures, a shift towards a more complex and often more centralized system of multilevel governance, and a redefinition of the public–private division of labour. A variation of an old adage continues to apply, however, that cities – or rather those agencies and interests that act within them or on their behalf – can shape their own futures, but not in circumstances of their own choosing.

If we are to make further progress in understanding the role of urban governance in promoting and linking competitiveness and cohesion, we need to stop expecting to be able to find simple explanations and changes that hold good, cross-nationally, and put some investment into assessing the way in which cross-national variation does or does not continue to matter. In other words, the idea that there is cross-national convergence in the forms, functions and purposes of the different institutions of urban governance needs to be seen as an interesting hypothesis, not a 'truth' that underpins research strategies. In developing a more open, comparative approach, it would be useful to recognize some broad categories of potential distinctiveness, one of which is clearly the difference, already noted, between institutional forms and the way in which the platforms afforded by institutions are 'used', politically.

There are at least four other key analytical issues that have emerged from the research contained within this volume that would repay greater conceptual and empirical attention. The first is the need to have a broad conception of 'urban governance' as something that is multilevel and malleable rather than a product of fixed and predictable relationships between central and local authorities. The second is the need to have an equally broad view of 'urban policy', and the way in which the competitiveness and cohesion of urban areas are affected by policy choices, which refuses to be constrained by conventional labels and attempts to make visible the many hidden ways in which public sector programmes and investments, often inadvertently, produce differential and potentially profound spatial effects. The third is the need to focus upon city-regions, rather than what are often arbitrarily defined core urban administrative areas. As noted above in the British context, a restrictive administrative/geographical focus can be seriously misleading for our understanding of urban competitiveness and cohesion in a way that analyses of broader metropolitan areas are less prone to. Finally, there is the issue of elite versus popular mobilization within the processes of urban governance, where some analysis of the relationship between the fragmentation, depoliticization and delocalization of local government (and its effect on the accountabilty of policy elites) could usefully be explored in relation to the evident decline in trust in politicians and the political process.

Integrating these concepts

One of the aspects of the NCW which we strongly applaud is the emphasis on 'joining up', both at the level of thought and of action. Our main reservation about this (as about the individual terms which are now to be joined up) is whether in practice the pursuit of this aim is grounded in hard analysis and empirical investigation, or just stems from wishful (short-circuited) thinking and platitudes. A useful rule of thumb might be that, if problems seem easier (rather than harder) to resolve when viewed in a 'joined up' way, it is more probably a case of wishful thinking.

There are several distinct dimensions to the integration that is advocated, paralleling those conventional boundaries that the new 'governance' is supposed to transcend: notably, the social/economic, local/global and public/private. At its most radical, this suggests a need to cut across (or at least challenge) all the old divisions of labour, in practical, intellectual and ideological terms. Common sense suggests, however, that there are limits both to the feasibility and the utility of this integrative programme. In practice a selective approach is clearly required: focusing on some particularly important channels of interaction; redrawing some of the lines of division of labour; and providing for periodic strategic reviews to readjust these judgements in the light of experience and identified changes in the environment. Everything *is* connected to everything else, as becomes obvious at the urban scale, together with the fact that every*where* is connected with everywhere else. But these connections can only be attended to selectively, and a key function of research is to indicate which of the links are both substantively important and problematic, in terms of the ways in which they are normally managed.

One particular theme in the NCW is the need, in a changing world, to recognize, understand and respond to connections between social cohesion, economic competitiveness and responsive governance, especially at the urban level. As we have seen throughout this book, there are problems with this (rather plausible) idea, since: none of these concepts is as simple as it sounds; each one involves multiple elements that are uncertainly linked with each other; and all are ideologically freighted. Placing the contentious words on one side, and stripping the proposition down to one asserting the importance of links between the economic, social and political aspects of urban systems, seems to leave little more than a platitude, though one often disregarded in practice (i.e., a piece of *old* conventional wisdom). The new element really is not the belief that there are connections, but that in the 'new economy' these have been re-shaped in ways that *require* us to pay attention to them, since the old intellectual and practical ways for dealing with these relationships are no longer adequate or appropriate – justifying special efforts at 'joining up', until suitable new institutions and routines have been developed. Of course, what is 'suitable' and 'appropriate' is a political matter – varying according to the different interests and agendas of those offering judgements – as we have already seen in discussing the choice of competitiveness, cohesion and (responsive) governance as the new terms to characterize the economic, social and political dimensions. But research has a critical role to play in examining which of the putative connections do really seem to matter, how and for whom.

So, what have we learned about these issues from this research programme? Well, to start at a rather elementary level, we have observed that in the less competitively successful cities – notably Liverpool, Glasgow and Manchester among those referred to in this book – substantially larger numbers of people have lives which are deeply affected by poverty, insecurity and poor living conditions, principally their own and their family's, but to some extent also that of others in their local community. This is not really new, but in some key respects problems did intensify in the last 20 years or so (the period on which our studies have focused as representing the possible emergence of 'a new urban era'). Earnings inequalities grew, both within and between cities, though it is not at all clear how far the relative competitive success of London and other parts of the South was a contributory cause *or* a consequence of the much broader societal shift towards differentiating individual rewards in relation to performance and market power. Concentrations of unemployment (and increasingly of actual withdrawal from the labour market) among particular groups and areas within the cities also intensified, with the worst effects in those city-regions experiencing continued long-term losses of manual jobs, but also with a conspicuous deepening of concentrations within more successful cities, notably in inner east London.

At an equally elementary level, it should be said that we have not found simple evidence of the impact of better governance on urban economic performance across British cities. It is notable that the turnaround from numerical decline to growth in London seems to have occurred during the years when Greater London lacked any formal governmental structure (and a nascent network mode of governance lacked either power or strategy). Yet Liverpool, with the most disorganized and least pro-active governance structure during the 1980s, had the worst performance of all cities in terms of competitiveness and cohesion. These two instances really stand out because of their peculiarity, and across the great bulk of British cities we cannot claim to have found strong evidence of the impact of either local governance structures or particular local strategies on economic or social success. The London and Liverpool cases might suggest several things:

(a)   that governance matters much less when a city is in a naturally strong position than when the economic tide is running against it;

(b)   that there are vicious circles in the relation between performance and governance (if not necessarily virtuous ones);

(c)   that, at the city-wide scale, 'no government' may be better than bad government, with the proviso that someone has to provide basic services (it was boroughs in the London case).

In the (highly centralized) British context, the last point might better be expressed in relation to the perceptions of central government, as the key resource holder for all urban development. London conspicuously prospered in terms of public investment during the period between abolition of one politically difficult city administration and creation of another, while Liverpool really suffered in the 1980s from its inability to co-operate in delivery of centrally defined urban policies. These are, however, both clearly extraordinary cases, and wider European evidence does suggest that the existence of broader governmental structures across large parts of the functional urban region is positive for economic growth (Cheshire and Magrini, 2002).

At a rather more sophisticated level, an orginal feature of our research was an attempt to examine a range of potential paths of linkage from aspects of social cohesion to stronger economic competitiveness. The main results (summarized in Chapter 5) suggested that, in the situations we examined, most of these links (including some of the fashionable ideas about social bases for trust relations between local businesses) were substantively rather weak. The main exception involved the impact of deprivation on the stock of local people with middling levels of educational qualification. The qualification that had to be made to these sceptical findings was that there were quite likely to be threshold levels of inequality, disorder and disconnectedness beyond which economic competitiveness was seriously affected, although these did not seem to have been reached in major British cities. The problem, of course, is knowing how close to a threshold particular cities might be. This is an issue that deserves substantial further work, focused on cities that actually seem to have crossed that edge. But the broad implication of our findings is that on a local scale it would be more appropriate to revert to considering the (very real) social and personal impacts of inequality, disconnection and disorder rather than being diverted by NCW arguments into focusing on hypothetical economic effects.

A number of these findings about the apparent strength or absence of relations between versions of competitiveness and some aspects of cohesion actually relate to a second important dimension of joining up: namely, the spatial one. In discussions contributing to the NCW, it is fashionable to refer to this as the global/local issue, although this notion is an extremely ambiguous one. In particular, there is a tendency to contrast a version of the 'global', involving universal, spaceless, competitive pressures, costless communication and convergent cultural tendencies, with a 'local' which represents difference, social embeddedness and face-to-face connections. At best, this is a caricature, with an unfortunate tendency to obscure the continuing unevenness of integrative processes, the continuing centrality of national units for many purposes, and the spatially complex structuring of city/metropolitan regions and their districts and neighbourhoods. It is because of these complications that there are increasingly significant issues of 'joining up' or co-ordination across spatial scales, rather than simply a matter of 'glocalization': that is, of developing 'the local' in ways that maximize the chances of success/survival in a competitive 'global arena'.

One reason why local connections between the social and the economic seem rather weak – whether this is in terms of the impact of local competitive success on levels of poverty, or of local social networks on business success – is that in economic and housing market terms, localities and administratively defined core 'cities' are often very 'open' entities. This openness actually helps to explain how they can be so sharply differentiated structurally, functionally and in terms of aggregate indicators of social/economic outcomes from other adjacent areas. For many purposes it is the functional region (or some combination of these) which is the relevant entity, while in a number of important respects it is still actually national factors and conditions that matter. And certainly the intensified concentrations of deprivation emerging in all of the cities we studied within the last 20 years cannot be understood outside the context of two deep and extended national recessions, and (for most of the major cities) the fact that these were more severe across the northern, traditionally industrial half of the country. Economically, as well as politically, nations do still matter for their cities, even in an era when their cities are becoming increasingly important – economically and perhaps socially – for nations.

References

Abers, R. (1998) 'Learning Democratic Practice: Distributing Government Resources through Popular Participation in Porto Alegre, Brazil', in Douglass, M. and Friedmann, J. (eds), *Cities for Citizens: Planning and the Rise of Civil Society in a Global Age*, Chichester: John Wiley, 39–66.

Adorno, T. W. (1991) *The Culture Industry: Selected Essays on Mass Culture*. London: Routledge.

Aglietta, M. (1979) *A Theory of Capitalist Regulation: The US Experience*. London and New York: New Left Books.

Alcock, P., Beatty, C., Fothergill, S., Macmillan, R. and Yeandle, S. (2003) *Work to Welfare: How Men Become Detached from the Labour Market*. Cambridge: Cambridge University Press.

Aldous, T. (1992) *Urban Villages: A Concept for Creating Mixed-use Urban Developments on a Sustainable Scale*. London: Urban Villages Group.

Allen, J. and Cars, G. (2002) 'The Tangled Web – Neighbourhood Governance in a Post-Fordist Era', in Cars, G., Healey, P., Madanipour, A. and De Maghalhães, C. (eds), *Urban Governance, Institutional Capacity and Social Milieux*. Aldershot: Ashgate, 90–105.

American Assembly (1993) 'Final Report', in Cisneros, H.G. (ed.), *Interwoven Destinies: Cities and the Nation*. New York: Norton.

Amin, A. (ed.) (1994) *Post-Fordism: A Reader*. Oxford: Basil Blackwell.

Amin, A. (1999) 'An institutionalist perspective on regional economic development', *International Journal of Urban and Regional Research*, 23: 9, 365–78.

Amin, A. (2000) 'The Economic Base of Contemporary Cities', in Bridge, G. and Watson, S. (eds), *Companion to the City*. Oxford: Basil Blackwell, ch. 11.

Amin, A. (2002) 'Ethnicity and the Multicultural City', *Environment and Planning* A, 34: 6, 959–81.

Amin, A. and Thrift, N. (1992) 'Neo-Marshallian nodes in global networks', *International Journal of Urban and Regional Research*, 16, 571–87.

Amin, A. and Thrift, N. (2002) *Cities: Reimagining the Urban*. Cambridge: Polity Press.

Amin, A., Massey, D. and Thrift, N. (2003) 'Decentring the Nation: A Radical Approach to Regional Inequality', *Catalyst Paper 8*, London: Catalyst.

Anyadike-Danes, M. *et al.* (2001) *Labour's New Regional Policy: An Assessment*. Seaford: Regional Studies Association.

Arts Council, (1999) *Addressing Social Exclusion: A Framework for Action*. London: Arts Council of England.

Association of London Government (1997) *The London Study: The Future of the City*. London: ALG.

Atkinson, A. (1998) 'Social Exclusion, Poverty and Unemployment', in Atkinson, A. and Hills, J. (eds), *Exclusion, Employment and Opportunity*. London: CASE paper 4, LSE.

283

Atkinson, A. (2000) 'The Hidden Costs of Gentrification: Displacement in Central London', *Journal of Housing and the Built Environment*, 15, 307–26.

Atkinson, R. and Kintrea, K. (2000) 'Owner-occupation, Social Mix and Neighbourhood Impacts', *Policy and Politics*, 28: 1, 93–108.

Atkinson, R. and Kintrea, K. (2001) 'Disentangling Area Effects: Evidence from Deprived and Non-Deprived Neighbourhoods', *Urban Studies*, 38: 12, 2,277–98.

Atkinson, R. and Kintrea, K. (2002) 'A Consideration of the Implications of Area Effects for British Housing and Regeneration Policy', *European Journal of Housing Policy*, 2: 2, 1–20.

Atkinson, R. and Kintrea, K. (2004) 'Opportunities and Despair, It's All in There: Practitioner Experiences and Explanations of Area Effects and Life Chance', *Sociology*, 38: 3, 437–56.

Audretsch, D. (2001) 'R&D Spillovers and the Geography of Innovation and Production', paper given to International Workshop on '*Innovation Clusters and Interregional Competition*', Kiel Institute of World Economics, 12–13 November.

Audretsch, D. B. and Feldman, M. P. (1996) 'R&D Spillovers and the Geography of Innovation and Production', *The American Economic Review*, 86, 630–40.

Aydalot, P. (ed.) (1986) *Milieux Innovateurs en Europe*, Paris: Presses Universitaires de France.

BAAA (1989) *Arts and the Changing City: An Agenda for Urban Regeneration*. London: BAAA.

Bailey, N. and Turok, I. (2000) 'Adjustment to Job Loss in Britain's Major Cities', *Regional Studies*, 34, 631–53.

Bailey, N. and Turok, I. (2001) 'Central Scotland as a Polycentric Urban Region: Useful Planning Concept or Chimera?', *Urban Studies*, 38: 4, 697–715.

Bailey, N., Docherty, I. and Turok, I. (2002) 'Dimensions of City Competitiveness: Edinburgh and Glasgow in a UK Context', in Begg, I. (ed.), *Urban Competitiveness*. Bristol: Policy Press, 135–59.

Bailey, N., Turok, I. and Docherty, I. (1999) *Edinburgh and Glasgow: Contrasts in Competitiveness and Cohesion*, Glasgow: University of Glasgow.

The Banker (2002) 'Top 1000 World Banks', *The Banker*, July issue.

Banks, M. (2002) 'Wearing it Out: Going Global in Small Fashion Firms', in Janssen, S., Halbertsma, M., Ijdens, T. and Ernst, K. (eds), *Trends and Strategies in the Arts and Cultural Industries*, Rotterdam: Barjesteh, 25–38.

Banks, M., Lovatt, A., O'Connor, J. and Raffo, C. (2000) 'Risk and Trust in the Cultural Industries', *Geoforum*, 31, 453–64.

Barlow, J. and Gann, D. (1993) *Offices into Flats*, York: Joseph Rowntree Foundation.

Barton, H. (ed.) (2000) *Sustainable Communities: The Potential for Eco-Neighbourhoods*, London: Earthscan.

Bassett, K., Griffiths, R. and Smith, I. (2002a) 'Cultural Industries, Cultural Clusters and the City: The Example of Natural History Film-making in Bristol', *Geoforum*, 33: 2, 165–77.

Bassett, K., Griffiths, R. and Smith, I. (2002b) 'Testing Governance: Partnerships, Planning and Conflict in Waterfront Regeneration', *Urban Studies*, 39, 1,757–75.

Beath, J. (2002) 'UK Industrial Policy: Old Tunes on New Instruments?', *Oxford Review of Economic Policy*, 18: 2, 221–39.

Beatty, C., Fothergill, S., Gore, T. and Green, A. (2002) *The Real Level of Unemployment 2002*, Sheffield: Centre for Regional Economic and Social Research, Sheffield Hallam University.

Beauregard, R. A. (2004) ' The Resilience of U.S. Cities: Decline and Resurgence in the 20th Century', paper presented to Leverhulme International Symposium on *The Resurgent City*, London School of Economics. Available from: http://www.lse.ac.uk/collections/resurgentCity/Papers/Opening plenary/robertabeauregard.pdf.

Beazley, M., Loftman, P. and Nevin, B. (1997) 'Downtown Redevelopment and Community Resistence: An International Perspective', in Jewson, N. and Macgregor, S. (eds), *Transforming Cities*, London: Routledge, 181–92.

Beccatini, G. (ed.) (1987) *Mercato e Forze Locali: il distretto industriale*, Bologna: Il Mulino.

Beck, U. (1992) *Risk Society: Towards a New Modernity*, London: Sage.

Begg, I. (2002a) ' "Investability": The Key to Competitive Cities and Regions?', *Regional Studies*, 36: 2, 187–93.

Begg, I. (ed.) (2002b) *Urban Competitiveness: Policies for Dynamic Cities*, Bristol: Policy Press.

Begg, I. and Moore, B. (2001) 'Economic Change in Cities: Influences on Urban Competitive Advantage and Prospects for the British Urban System', *Cities Summary 10*. Liverpool: ESRC Cities Programme, Liverpool John Moores University.

Begg, I., Moore, B. and Altunbas, Y. (2002) 'Long-run Trends in the Competitiveness of British Cities', in Begg, I. (ed.), *Urban Competitiveness*, Bristol: Policy Press, 101–33.

Bennett, T. (1998) *Culture: A Reformer's Science*, London: Sage.

Bernard, N. (2002) *Multilevel Governance in the European Union*, Dordrecht: Kluwer European Monographs.

Bianchini, F. (1999) 'Cultural Planning for Urban Sustainability', in Nystrom, L. (ed.), *City and Culture*. Karlskrona: Swedish Urban Environment Council, 34–51.

Bianchini, F. and Parkinson, M. (1993) *Cultural Policy and Urban Regeneration*, Manchester: Manchester University Press.

Black, D. and Henderson, V. (1999) 'A Theory of Urban Growth', *Journal of Political Economy*, 107: 2, 252–84.

Blokland, T. and Savage, M. (2001) 'Network, Class and Space', *International Journal of Urban and Regional Research*, 25: 2, 221–6.

Bloxham, T. (1995) 'Regenerating the Urban Core', *Urban Design International*, 53 (Jan.), 1–3.

Boddy, M. (1999) 'Geographical Economics and Urban Competitiveness: A Critique', *Urban Studies*, 36: 5–6, 811–42.

Boddy, M. (2002) 'Linking Competitiveness and Cohesion', in Begg, I. (ed.), *Urban Competitiveness*, Bristol: Policy Press, 33–54.

Boddy, M. (2003) 'Competitiveness and Cohesion in a Prosperous City-region: The Case of Bristol', in Boddy, M. and Parkinson, M. (eds), *Changing Cities*, Bristol: Policy Press.

Boddy, M. and Parkinson, M. (eds) (2004) *City Matters: Competitiveness, Cohesion and Urban Governance*, Bristol: Policy Press.

Bondi, L. (1999) 'Gender, Class, and Gentrification: Enriching the Debate', *Environment and Planning D: Society and Space*, 17, 261–82.

Bourdieu, P. (1984) *Distinction: A Social Critique of the Judgement of Taste*. London: Routledge.

Bourdieu, P. (1985) 'The Forms of Capital', in Richardson, J. (ed.), *Handbook of Theory and Research for the Sociology of Education*. New York: Greenwood.

Bourgois, L. (1995) *In Search of Respect: Selling Crack in El Barrio*, Cambridge: Cambridge University Press.

Bowlby, S., Lloyd-Evans, S. and Roche C. (2004) 'Youth Employment, Racialised Gendering and School-Work Transitions', in Boddy, M. and Parkinson, M. (eds), *City Matters*, Bristol: Policy Press.

Boyle, M. (1997) 'Civic Boosterism in the Politics of Local Economic Development: "Institutional Positions" and "Strategic Orientations" in the Consumption of Hallmark Events', *Environment and Planning A*, 29, 1,975–97.

Boyle, M. and Hughes, G. (1991) 'The Politics of Representation of the "Real": Discourses from the Left on Glasgow's Role as European City of Culture', *Area*, 2, 21–8.

Bramley, G. (1998) 'Measuring Planning: Indicators of Planning Restraint and its Impact on the Housing Market', *Environment and Planning B: Planning and Design*, 25, 31–57.

Bramley, G. and Lambert C. (1998) 'Regulation Entrenched: Planning for Housing', in Allmendinger, P. and Thomas, H. (eds), *Urban Planning and the British New Right*, London: Routledge.

Bramley, G. and Lambert, C. (2002) 'Managing Urban Growth', in Begg, I. (ed.), *Urban Competitiveness*, Bristol: Policy Press.

Bramley, G., Bartlett, W. and Lambert, C. (1995) *Planning, the Market and Private Housebuilding*. London: UCL Press.

Bramley, G., Kirk, K., Morgan, J. and Russell, J. (2001) 'Planning Central Scotland: The Role of Infrastructure, Urban Form and New Development in Promoting Competitiveness and Cohesion', *Policy Paper 2*, Scottish Executive. Glasgow: Department of Urban Studies, University of Glasgow.

Bramley, G., Pawson, H. and Third, H. (2000) *Low Demand Housing and Unpopular Neighbourhoods*, Housing Research Report. London: DETR.

Breheny, M. (ed.) (1999) *The People: Where Will They Work?*, London: Town and Country Planning Association.

Brenner, N. (1999) 'Globalisation as Reterritorialisation: The Re-scaling of Urban Governance in the European Union', *Urban Studies*, 36: 3, 431–51.

Breughel, I. (1996) 'Gendering the Polarisation Debate, a Comment On Hamnett's: "Social Polarisation, Economic Restructuring and Welfare State Regimes" ', *Urban Studies*, 33, 469–90.

Brighton, A. (2000) 'Towards a Command Culture: New Labour's Cultural Policy and Soviet Socialist Realism', in Wallinger, M. and Warnock, M. (eds) *Art for All? Their Policies and Our Culture*, London: PEER, 40.

Brint, S. (1984) ' "New Class" and Cumulative Trend Explanations of the Liberal Political Attitudes of Professionals', *American Journal of Sociology*, 90, 30–71.

Bristow, G., Munday, M. and Gripaios, P. (2000) 'Call Centre Growth and Location: Corporate Strategy and the Spatial Division of Labour', *Environment and Planning A*, 32, 519–38.

British Chambers of Commerce (2004) *Setting Business Free from Crime: 2004 Crime against Business Survey*, London: BCC.

British Invisibles (2000) *Fund Management: City Business Series 2000 Statistical Update*. London: BI.

Brooks-Gunn, J., Duncan, G., Klebanov, P. and Sealane, N. (1993) 'Do Neighbourhoods Influence Child and Adolescent Development?', *American Journal of Sociology*, 99, 353–95.

Brunello, G. and Gambarotto, F. (2004) 'Agglomeration Effects on Employer-Provided Training: Evidence from the UK', *CESifo Working Paper Series No. 1150*, Munich.

Buĉek, J. and Smith, B. (2000) 'New Approaches to Local Democracy: Direct Democracy, Participation and the "Third Sector" ', *Environment and Planning C: Government and Policy*, 18, 3–16.

Buck, N. (2001) 'Identifying Neighbourhood Effects on Social Exclusion', *Urban Studies*, 38: 12, 2,251–75.

Buck, N., and Gordon, I. R. (2000) 'Turbulence and Sedimentation in the Labour Markets of Late Twentieth Century Metropoles', in Bridge, G. and Watson, S. (eds), *Companion to the City*, Oxford: Blackwells, chapter 16.

Buck, N. and Gordon, I. R. (2004) 'Does Spatial Concentration of Disadvantage Contribute to Social Exclusion?', in Boddy, M. and Parkinson, M. (eds), *City Matters*, Bristol: Policy Press.

Buck, N., Gordon, I. and Young, K. (1986) *The London Employment Problem*, Oxford: Clarendon Press.

Buck, N., Gordon, I. R., Hall, P., Harloe, M. and Kleinman, M. (2002) *Working Capital: Life and Labour in Contemporary London*, London: Routledge.

Buckingham, D. and Jones, K. (2001) 'New Labour's Cultural Turn: Some Tensions in Contemporary Educational and Cultural Policy', *Journal of Education Policy*, 16: 1, 1–14.

Burgess. P., Hall. S., Mawson, J. and Pearce, G. (2001) *Devolved Approaches to Local Governance: Policy and Practice in Neighbourhood Management*. York: Joseph Rowntree Foundation.

Burrows, R. and Wilcox, S. (2001) *Half the Poor: Home-Owners with Low Incomes*. London: Council of Mortgage Lenders.

Butler, T. (1997) *Gentrification and the Middle Classes*. Aldershot: Ashgate.

Butler, T. (2004) 'The Middle Class and the Future of London', in Boddy, M. and Parkinson, M. (eds), *City Matters*, Bristol: Policy Press.

Butler, T. with Robson, G. (2003) *London Calling: The Middle Classes and the Future of Inner London*, Oxford: Berg.

Cabinet Office (2000) *Reaching Out: Action Plan*, London: Cabinet Office.

Cabinet Office (2001) *A New Commitment to Neighbourhood Renewal: National Strategy Action Plan*, London: Social Exclusion Unit, Cabinet Office.

Cairncross, L., Clapham, and Goodlad, R. (1997) *Housing Management, Consumers and Citizens*, London: Routledge.

Callender, M. and Key, T. (1996) 'The Total Value of Commercial Property in the UK', paper presented at the 'Cutting Edge' Property Research Conference of the RICS, Bristol, September, http://www.rics-foundation.org/research.

Campbell, H., Ellis, H., Gladwell, C., Henneberry, J., Poxon, J. and Rowley, S. (2001) 'Planning Obligations and the Mediation of Development', *RICS Foundation Research Papers*, 4: 3, 1–40.

Carlin, W., Haskel, J. and Seabright, P. (2001) 'Understanding the Essential Fact about Capitalism', *National Institute Economic Review*, 175, 67–84.

Castel, R. (1998) *Les métamorphoses de la question sociale*. Paris: Fayard.

Castel, R. and Laé, J.F. (1992) *Le revenu minimum d'insertion – une dette sociale*, Paris: éditions l'Harmattan.

Castells, M. (1977) *The Urban Question*, London: Edward Arnold.

Castells, M. (1983) *The City and The Grassroots*. London: Edward Arnold.

Castells, M. (1996) *The Rise of the Network Society*, Oxford: Basil Blackwell.

Castells, M. (1998) *End of Millennium*, Oxford: Basil Blackwell.

Champion, T., Atkins, D., Coombes, M. and Fotheringham, S. (1998) *The Determinants of Migration Flows in England*. London: Council for the Protection of Rural England.

Champion, T. and Fisher, T. (2004) 'Migration, Residential Preferences and the Changing Environment of Cities' in Boddy, M. and Parkinson, M. (eds.) *City Matters*, Bristol: Policy Press, pp. 111–28.

Chatterton, P. and Holland, R. (2001) *Changing our 'Toon': Youth, Nightlife and Urban Change in Newcastle*, Newcastle: CURDS/Dept of Sociology and Social Policy, University of Newcastle.

Checkland, S. (1981) *The Upas Tree: Glasgow 1875–1980*, Glasgow: Glasgow University Press.

Cheshire, P. (1995) 'A New Phase of Urban Development in Western Europe? The Evidence from the 1980s', *Urban Studies*, 32, 1045–64.

Cheshire, P. and Gordon, I. R. (1996) 'Territorial Competition and the Predictability of Collective (in)action', *International Journal of Urban and Regional Research,* 20, 383–99.

Cheshire, P. and Gordon, I. R. (1998) 'Territorial Competition: Some Lessons for Policy', *Annals of Regional Science*, 32, 321–46.

Cheshire, P. and Magrini, S. (1999) 'Investigating the Causes and Effects of Localised Income Divergences in the EU', 39th European Regional Science Association Congress, Dublin.

Cheshire, P. and Magrini, S. (2002) 'Counteracting the Counterfactual: New Evidence on the Impact of Local Policy from the Residuals', in Johansson, B., Karlsson, C. and Stough, R. R. (eds), *Regional Policy and Comparative Advantage*. Cheltenham: Edward Elgar, 209–39.

Cheshire, P. and Monastiriotis, V. (2003) 'Income Inequality and Residential Segregation: Labour Market Sorting and the Demand for Positional Goods', in Martin, R. and Morrison, P. (eds), *The Geography of Labour Market Inequality*, London: Routledge, pp. 83–109.

Cheshire, P., Magrini, S., Medda, F. and Monastiriotis, V. (2004) 'Cities are not Isolated States', in Boddy, M. and Parkinson, M. (eds), *City Matters*, Bristol: Policy Press.

Cheshire, P. C., Monastiriotis, V. and Shepherd, S. (2001) 'Income Inequality and Residential Segregation: Labour Market Sorting and the Demand for Positional Goods', in Martin, R. and Morrison, P. (eds), *Geographies of Labour Market Inequality*, London: Routledge.

Coalter, F. (2001) *Realising the Potential of Cultural Services: The Case for the Arts*, London: Local Government Association.

Coe, N. M. and Townsend, A. R. (1998) 'Debunking the Myth of Localised Agglomerations: The Development of a Regionalised Service Economy in South-East England', *Transactions of the Institute of British Geographers, NS*, 23, 385–404.

Coleman, J. (1988) 'Social Capital in the Creation of Human Capital', *American Journal of Sociology*, 94, S95–S120.

Coleman, J. (1990) *Foundations of Social Theory*. Cambridge, MA: Belknap Press.

Colin Buchanan and Partners (2001) *Key Sites Appraisal*, Edinburgh: Scottish Executive Central Research Unit.

Comedia (2002) *Releasing the Cultural Rotential of our Core Cities*, Birmingham Core Cities Group.

Cooke, B. and Kothari, U. (eds) (2001) *Participation: The New Tyranny?* London and New York: Zed Books.

Cooke, P. (2002) *Knowledge Economies*, London: Routledge.

Cooke, P. and Morgan, K. (1998) *The Associational Economy: Firms, Regions and Innovation*, Oxford: Oxford University Press.

Cooke, P. and Wills, D. (1999) 'Small Firms, Social Capital and the Enhancement of Business Performance through Innovation Programmes', *Small Business Economics*, 13, 219–34.

Cooke, P., Clifton, N. and Huggins, R. (2001) 'Competitiveness and the Knowledge Economy', *Regional Industrial Research Report No. 30*, Cardiff: Centre for Advanced Studies, Cardiff University.

Cooke, P., Davies, C. and Wilson, R. (2002a) 'Innovation Advantage of Cities: From Knowledge to Equity in Five Basic Steps', *European Planning Studies*, 10, 233–50.

Cooke, P., Davies, C. and Wilson, R. (2002b) 'Urban Networks and the New Economy: The Impact of Clusters on Planning for Growth', in Begg, I. (ed.), *Urban Competitiveness*, Bristol: The Policy Press, 233–56.

Core Cities (2002) *Core Cities Website*. (http://www.corecities.com).

Core Cities Group (2002) *Cities, Regions and Competitiveness*. Interim report, Birmingham: Birmingham City Council.

Cosh, A., Hughes, A. and Wood, E. (1999) 'Innovation in UK SMEs: Causes and Consequences for Firm Failure and Acquisition', in Acs, Z., Carlsson, B. and Karlsson, C. (eds), *Entrepreneurship, Small and Medium-Sized Enterprises and the Macroeconomy*, Cambridge: Cambridge University Press.

Council for Churches of Britain and Ireland (1997) *Unemployment and the Future of Work*, London: CCBI.

Crafts, N. (1996) 'Post-Neoclassical Endogenous Growth Theory: What are its Policy Implications?', *Oxford Review of Economic Policy*, 12: 2, 30–47.

Crewe, L. and Beaverstock, J. (1998) 'Fashioning the City: Cultures of Consumption in Contemporary Urban Spaces', *Geoforum*, 29, 287–308.

Dabinett, G., Lawless, P., Rhodes, J. and Tyler, P. (2001) *A Review of the Evidence for Regeneration Policy and Practice*, London: DETR.

Danielsen, K., Lang, R. and Fulton, W. (1999) 'Retracting Suburbia: Smart Growth and the Future of Housing', *Housing Policy Debate*, 10: 3, 513–40.

Deas, I. (2005) 'Reinventing the Metropolitan Region: Experiences of Scalar Conflict in Manchester', in Harding, A. (ed.), *Rescaling the State in Europe and North America*, Oxford: Basil Blackwell.

Deas, I., Baker, M. and Rees, J. (2003) *New Deal For Communities: National Evaluation Main Phase: Report on the Hathershaw and Fitton Hill Partnership, Oldham*, Manchester: Centre for Urban Policy Studies, University of Manchester.

Deas, I., Robson, B. and Bradford, M. (2000) 'Re-thinking the Urban Development Corporation "Experiment": The Case of Central Manchester, Leeds and Bristol', *Progress in Planning*, 54: 1, 1–72.

DCMS (1998), *Creative Industries Mapping Document*, London: DCMS.

DCMS (1999), *Policy Action Team 10: Report on Social Exclusion*, London: DCMS.

DCMS (2001a) *Building on PAT 10: Progress Report on Social Exclusion*. London: DCMS.

DCMS (2001b) *Guidance to District Councils on the Development of Local Cultural Strategies*, London: DCMS.

Department of the Environment (1996) *Household Growth: Where Shall We Live?* Cm. 3471. London: HMSO.

Department of the Environment, Scottish Office and Welsh Office (1977) *Policy for the Inner Cities*, Cmnd 6845, London: HMSO.

Department of the Environment (1988) *Action for Cities*, London: Cabinet Office.

DETR (1999a) *Towards an Urban Renaissance*, Final Report of the Urban Task Force chaired by Lord Rogers of Riverside. London: The Stationery Office.

DETR (1999b) *Unpopular Housing: National Strategy for Neighbourhood Renewal*; Report of Policy Action Team 7, London: DETR.

DETR (2000a) *Collaboration and Co-ordination in Area-Based Regeneration Initiatives*, London: DETR.

DETR (2000b) *Joining it up Locally;* Report of Policy Action Team 17, London: DETR.

DETR (2000c) *Our Towns and Cities: the Future. Delivering an urban Renaissance*, Urban White Paper, Cm. 4911. London: The Stationery Office.

DETR (2000d) *Planning Policy Guidance Note 3: Housing* (PPG3). London: DETR.

Dixon, R. J. and Thirwall, A. P. (1975) 'A Model of Regional Growth Rate Differentials along Kaldorian Lines', *Oxford Economic Papers*, 27, 201–14.

Docherty, I., Goodlad, R., and Paddison, R. (2001) 'Civic Culture, Community and Citizen Participation in Contrasting Neighbourhoods', *Urban Studies*, 38: 12, 2,225–50.

Dorling, D. and Rees, P. (2003) 'A Nation Still Dividing: The British Census and Social Polarisation 1971–2001', *Environment and Planning A*, 35, 1,287–313.

Draper, P., Smith, I., Stewart, W. and Hood, N. (1988) *The Scottish Financial Sector.* Edinburgh: Edinburgh University Press.

DTI (2001) *Business Clusters in the UK – A First Assessment*, London: DTI.

du Gay, P. and Pryke, M. (eds) (2002) *Cultural Economy: Cultural Analysis and Commercial Life: Culture, Representation and Identities*, London: Sage.

Duffy, K. and Hutchinson, J. (1997) 'Urban Policy and the Turn to Community', *Town Planning Review*, 68: 3, 347–62.

Duncan, G., Clark-Kauffman, E. and Snell, E. (2004) 'Residential Mobility Interventions as Treatments for the Sequelae of Neighborhood Violence', paper presented at the Analysing Neighbourhoods and their Impact Conference, June 2004, University of Bristol.

Dunleavy, P. (1980) *Urban Political Analysis*, London: Macmillan.

Duranton, G. (1999) 'Distance, Land, and Proximity: Economic Analysis and the Evolution of Cities', *Environment and Planning A*, 31: 2, 169–88.

Duster, T. (1995) 'Post Industrialization and Youth Unemployment: African Americans as Harbingers', in McFate, K., Lawson, R. and Wilson, W.J. (eds), *Poverty, Inequality and the Future of Social Policy*, New York: Russell Sage Foundation.

Dwelly, T. (2001) *Creative Regeneration: Lessons from Ten Community Arts Projects*, York: Joseph Rowntree Foundation.

The Economist (2002) 'Birmingham: The Doughnut Effect', 19 January.

Ehrenreich, B.(1989) *Fear of Falling: The Inner Life of the Middle Class*, New York: Pantheon.

Elias, P. and Bynner, J. (1997) 'Intermediate Skills and Occupational Mobility', *Policy Studies*, 18, 101–24.

Elkin, S. L. (1987) *City and Regime in the American Republic*, Chicago, IL: University of Chicago Press.

Ellen, I. and Turner, M. (1997) 'Does Neighbourhood Matter? Assessing Recent Evidence', *Housing Policy Debate*, 8: 1, 833–66.

Ellison, L. (1998) *Examining the Implications for Property Development of the Increased Role of the Private Sector in Domestic Fixed Capital Formation*', Paper presented at the 'Cutting Edge' Property Research Conference of the RICS, Leicester, September; http://www.rics-foundation.org/research.

Engels, F. (1892) *The Condition of the Working Class in England in 1844*, London: Allen & Unwin.

Erdem, E. and Glyn, A. (2001) 'Job Deficits in UK Regions', *Oxford Bulletin of Economics and Statistics*, 63, 737–52.

Erikson, R. and Goldthorpe, J. (1993) *The Constant Flux: A Study of Class Mobility in Industrial Societies*. Oxford: Clarendon Press.

European Commission (1996) *First Report on Economic and Social Cohesion*, Luxembourg: Office for Official Publications of the European Communities.

Evans, A. (1991) 'Rabbit Hutches on Postage Stamps: Planning, Development and Political Economy', *Urban Studies*, 28: 6, 853–70.

Evans, G. (2001) *Cultural Planning: An Urban Renaissance?* London: Routledge.

Fainstein, S. S. (2001a) 'Competitiveness, Cohesion and Governance: A Review of the Literature', ESRC *Cities* initiative, http://cwis.livjm.ac.uk/cities/fs_news.htm.

Fainstein, S. S. (2001b) 'Competitiveness, Cohesion, and Governance: Their Implications for Social Justice', *International Journal of Urban and Regional Research*, 25, 884–8.

Fainstein, S. S. (2002) *The City Builders*, 2nd edn. Lawrence, KS: University Press of Kansas.

Featherstone, M. (1991) *Consumer Culture and Postmodernism*, London: Sage.

Feist, A. (2001) 'The Relationship between the Subsidised and the Wider Cultural sector', in Selwood, S. (ed.), *The UK Cultural Sector: Profile and Policy Issues*, London: Policy Studies Institute, 189–200.

Fielding, A. J. (1991) 'Migration and Social Mobility: South East England as an Escalator Region', *Regional Studies*, 26, 1–15.

Fielding, A. J. (1995) 'Migration and Middle Class Formation in England and Wales 1981–91', in Butler, T. and Savage. M. (eds), *Social Change and the Middle Classes*, London: UCL Press.

Fleming, T. (ed.) (1999) *The Role of the Creative Industries in Local and Regional Development*. Manchester Forum of the Creative Industries/Government Office for Yorkshire and Humber.

Florida, R. (2002a) 'Bohemia and Economic Geography', *Journal of Economic Geography*, 2, 55–71.

Florida, R. (2002b) *The Rise of the Creative Class, and how it's Transforming Work, Leisure, Community and Everyday Life*, New York: Basic Books.

Foley, M. and Edwards, B. (1999) 'Time to Disinvest in Social Capital?', *Journal of Public Policy*, 19, 141–73.

Foley, P. and Martin, S. (2000) 'A New Deal for the Community? Public Participation in Regeneration and Local Service Delivery', *Policy and Politics*, 28: 4, 479–91.

Foord, J. (2000) 'Creative Hackney: Reflections on "Hidden Art" ', *Rising East: The Journal of East London Studies*, 3: 2, 38–66.

Foord, J. and Ginsburgh, N. (2004) 'Whose Hidden Assets? Inner City Potential for Social Cohesion and Economic Competitiveness', in Boddy, M. and Parkinson, M. (eds), *City Matters*, Bristol: Policy Press.

Ford, J., Burrows, R. and Nettleton, S. (2001) *Home Ownership in the Risk Society: A Social Analysis of Mortgage Arrears and Possessions*, Bristol: Policy Press.

Ford, T. and Champion, A. (2000) 'Who Moves into, Out of and Within London? An Analysis Based on the 1991 Census 2% Sample of Anonymised Records', *Area,* 32, 259–70.

Forrest, R. and Kearns, A. (1999) *Joined-Up Places? Social Cohesion and Neighbourhood Regeneration*, York: York Publishing Services.

Forrest, R. and Kearns, A. (2001) 'Social Cohesion, Social Capital and the Neighbourhood', *Urban Studies*, 38: 12.

Fotheringham, S., Bramley, G., Champion, A., Eyre, H., Hollis, J., Kalogirou, S., McGill, J., Rees, P. Stilwell, J. and Wilson, T. (2002) *Development of a Migration Model*, London: Office of the Deputy Prime Minister.

Freeman, A., Holmans, A. and Whitehead, C. (1996) *Is the UK Different? International Comparisons of Tenure Differences*. London: Council of Mortgage Lenders.

French, S. (2000) 'Rescaling the Economic Geography of Knowledge and Information: Constructing Life Assurance Markets', *Geoforum*, 31, 101–19.

French, S. (2002) 'Gamekeepers and Gamekeeping: Assuring Bristol's Place within Life Underwriting', *Environment and Planning A*, 34, 513–41.

French, S. and Leyshon, A. (2003) 'City of Money?', in Boddy, M. (ed.), *Urban Transformation and Urban Governance: Shaping the City Region of the Future*, Bristol: Policy Press, 32–51.

Fromhold-Eisebith, M. (1999) 'Bangalore: A Network Model for Iinnovation-oriented Regional Development in NICs?', in Malecki, E. and Oinas, P. (eds), *Making Connections*, Aldershot: Ashgate.

Galbraith, J. K. (1958) 'The Concept of the Conventional Wisdom', in *The Affluent Society*, London: Hamish Hamilton.

Gallie, D., Marsh, C. and Vogler, C. (eds) (1994) *Social Change and the Experience of Unemployment*, Oxford: Oxford University Press.

Geddes, M. (1995) 'Poverty, Excluded Communities and Local Democracy', *CLD Research Report 9*, London: Commission for Local Democracy.

Gentle, C. (1993) *The Financial Services Industry: The Impact of Corporate Reorganisation on Regional Economic Development*. Aldershot: Avebury.

Geroski, P. (1999) 'The Growth of Firms in Theory and Practice', *Centre for Economic Policy Research Discussion Paper 2092*.

Gillespie, A., Richardson, R. and Cornford, J. (2001) 'Regional Development and the New Economy', *EIB Papers*, 6: 1, 109–31.

Glaeser, E. (1999) 'Learning in Cities', *Journal of Urban Economics*, 46, 254–77.

Glaeser, E. and Marc, D. (2001) 'Cities and Skills', *Journal of Labor Economics*, 19, 316–42.

Glaeser, E. L., Kolko, J. and Saiz, A. (2001) 'Consumer City', *Journal of Economic Geography*, 1, 27–50.

Glass, R. (1964) 'Introduction' in Centre for Urban Studies (ed.), *London: Aspects of Change*. London: McGibbon & Kee.

Goodlad, R. (2001) 'Developments in Tenant Participation: Accounting for Growth', in Cowan, D. and Marsh, A. (eds), *Two Steps Forward: Housing Policy into the New Millennium*. Bristol: The Policy Press, 179–97.

Goodlad, R. (2002) 'Neighbourhood Regeneration Policy: Rebuilding Community?', in Nash, V. (ed.), *Reclaiming Community*. London: Institute for Public Policy Research, 65–84.

Gordon, I. R. (1995) 'Accounting for Inter-State Unemployment Disparities in the USA', *Discussion Paper 26*, Reading: Geography Department, Reading University.

Gordon, I. R. (1997) 'Densities, Urban Form and Travel Behaviour', *Town and Country Planning*, 66, 239–41.

Gordon, I. R. (1999a) 'Internationalisation and Urban Competition', *Urban Studies*, 36, 1001–16.

Gordon, I. R. (1999b) ' "Move on up the Car": Dealing with Structural Unemployment in London', *Local Economy*, 14, 87–95.

Gordon, I. R. (1999c) 'Vacancy Chains and the Openness of Spatial Labour Markets', 39th European Regional Science Association Congress, Dublin.

Gordon, I. R. (2000) 'Targeting a Leaky Bucket: The Case against Localised Employment Creation', *New Economy*, 6: 4, 199–203.

Gordon, I. R. (2003a) 'Capital Needs, Capital Growth and Global City Rhetoric in Mayor Livingstone's London Plan', paper to the Association of American Geographers annual meeting, New Orleans, 7th March.

Gordon, I. R. (2003b) 'Unemployment and Spatial Labour markets: Strong Adjustment and Persistent Concentration', in Martin, R. and Morrison, P. (eds), *Geographies of Labour Market Inequality*, London: Routledge.

Gordon, I. R. and McCann, P. (2000) 'Industrial Clusters: Complexes, Agglomeration and/or Social Networks?', *Urban Studies*, 37: 3, 513–32.

Gordon, I. R. and McCann, P. (2005) 'Innovation, Agglomeration and Regional Development', forthcoming in *Journal of Economic Geography*.

Gordon, I. R. and Monastiriotis, V. (2003) 'Urban size, segregation and educational outcomes', *Research Papers in Environmental and Spatial Analysis*, 87, London: London School of Economics.

Gordon, I. R. and Monastiriotis, V. (2005) 'Criminal Behaviour and Social Context: The Role of Spatial Effects', Research Paper in Environmental and Spatial Analysis (forthcoming), London: London School of Economics.

Gordon, I. R., Travers, T. and Whitehead, C. M. E. (2003) *London's Place in the UK Economy 2003*, London: Corporation of London.

Gottlieb, P. D. (1995) 'Residential Amenities, Firm Location and Economic Development', *Urban Studies*, 32, 1,413–36.

Gough, I. (1999) 'Social Welfare and Competitiveness: Social versus System Integration?', in Gough, I. and Olofsson, G. (eds), *Capitalism and Social Cohesion*, London: Macmillan, pp. 85–106.

Gouldner, A. (1979) *The Future of Intellectuals and the Rise of the New Class: A Frame of Reference, Theses, Conjectures, Argumentation and an Historical Perspective*, London: Macmillan.

Gray, C. (2002) 'Local Government and the Arts', *Local Government Studies*, 28, 77–90.

Gray, M., Golob, E., Markusen, A. and Park, S. (1998) 'New Industrial Cities? The Four Faces of Silicon Valley', *Review of Radical Political Economy*, 30: 4, 1–28.

Green, A. and Owen, D. (2001) *Skills, Local Areas and Unemployment*, SKT39, Nottingham: Department of Education and Skills Publications.

Gregg, P. and Wadsworth, J. (2003) 'Labour Market Prospects of Less Skilled Workers over the Recovery', in Dickens, R., Gregg, P. and Wadsworth, J. (eds), *The Labour Market under New Labour*, Basingstoke: Palgrave Macmillan.

Griffiths, R., Bassett, K. and Smith, I. (1999) 'Cultural Policy and the Cultural Economy in Bristol', *Local Economy*, 14, 257–64.

Griffiths, R. (2001), 'Neighbourhood Renewal: The Contribution of Arts and Culture', paper presented at the European Urban Research Association conference, 'Area-based initiatives in contemporary urban policy', Copenhagen, 17–19 May.

Griliches, Z. (1979) 'Issues in Assessing the Contribution of R&D to Productivity Growth', *Bell Journal of Economics*, 10, 92–116.

Gripaios, P., Bristow, G. and Munday, M. (1999) 'Call Centre', in Cambridge Econometrics (ed.), *The South West Economy, Trends and Prospects* Cambridge: CE.

Halfpenny, P., Britton, N. J., Devine, F. and Mellor, R. (2004) 'The "Good" Suburb as an Urban Asset in Enhancing a City's Competitiveness', in Boddy, M. and Parkinson, M. (eds), *City Matters: Competitiveness, Cohesion and Urban Governance*, Bristol: Policy Press.

Hall, P. A. (1999) 'Social Capital in Britain', *British Journal of Political Science*, 29: 3, 417–61.

Hall, P. G. (1999a) *Cities in Civilisation*, London: Weidenfeld & Nicolson.

Hall, P. G. (1999b) 'The Creative City in the Third Millennium', in Verwijnen, J. and Lehtovuori, P. (eds), *Creative Cities: Cultural Industries, Urban Development and the Information Society*, Helsinki: UIAH Publications, 36–57.

Hall, P. G. (2000) 'Creative Cities and Economic Development', *Urban Studies*, 37, 639–49.

Hall, S. and Jacques, M. (eds) (1989) *New Times: The Changing Face of Politics in the 1990s*, London: Lawrence & Wishart.

Hamnett, C. (1994a) 'Socio-Economic Change in London: Professionalisation Not Polarisation', *Built Environment*, 20, 192–203.

Hamnett, C. (1994b) 'Social Polarisation in Global Cities: Theory and Evidence', *Urban Studies*, 31, 401–24.

Hamnett, C. and Randolph, W. (1988) 'Labour and Housing Market Changes in London: A Longitudinal Analysis', *Urban Studies*, 25, 380–98.

Hannigan, J. (1998) *Fantasy City: Pleasure and Profit in the Postmodern Metropolis*. London: Routledge.

Harding, A. (1990) 'Regulation Theories in Retrospect and Prospect', *Economy and Society* 19: 2, 153–216.

Harding, A. (1999) 'North American Urban Political Economy, Urban Theory, and British Research', *British Journal of Political Science*, 29: 3, 447–72.

Harding, A. (2002) *Is There a 'Missing Middle' in English Governance?*, London: New Local Government Network.

Harding, A., Deas, I. A. and Wilks-Heeg, S. (2003) 'Re-inventing Cities in a Restructuring Region? The Rhetoric and Reality of Renaissance in Liverpool and Manchester', in Boddy, M. and Parkinson, M. (eds), *Changing Cities*, Bristol: The Policy Press.

Harding, A., Deas, I. A., Evans, R. and Giordano, B. (2000) 'Does Local Governance Matter? Responding to Economic Change in Liverpool and Manchester', paper presented to the ESRC Cities Programme 'Governance' Theme Group Conference, 26–27 September, Bristol.

Harding, R. (2000) Venture Capital and Regional Development: Towards a Venture Capital "System" ', *Venture Capital*, 2, 287–312.

Harloe, M. (2001) 'Social Justice and the City: The New "Liberal Formulation" ', *International Journal of Urban and Regional Research*, 25, 889–97.

Hart, D. and Simmie, J. M. (1997) 'Innovation, Competition and the Structure of Local Production Networks: Initial Findings from the Hertfordshire Project', *Local Economy*, 12, 235–46.

Harvey, D. (1973) *Social Justice and the City*, London: Edward Arnold.

Harvey, D. (1997) 'New Urbanism and the Communitarian Trap', *Harvard Design Magazine*, 1, 68–9.

Harvey, D. (2002) 'The Art of Rent: Globalisation, Monopoly, and the Commodification of Culture', in Panitch, L. and Leys, C. (eds), *The Socialist Register: A World of Contradiction*, New York: Monthly Review Press, 94–110.

Hay, C. (2000) 'Globalization, Social Democracy and the Persistence of Partisan Politics: A Commentary on Garrett', *Review of International Political Economy*, 7: 1, 138–52.

Healey, M., Cars, G., Madanipour, A. and De Maghalhães (2002a) 'Transforming Governance, Institutional Analysis and Institutional Capacity', in Cars, G., Healey, P., Madanipour, A. and De Maghalhães, C. (eds), *Urban Governance, Institutional Capacity and Social Milieux*, Aldershot: Ashgate, 6–28.

Healey, M., Cars, G., Madanipour, A. and De Maghalhães, C. (2002b) 'Urban Governance Capacity in Complex Societies: Challenges of Institutional Adaptation', in Cars, G., Healey, P., Madanipour, A. and De Maghalhães, C. (eds), *Urban Governance, Institutional Capacity and Social Milieux*, Aldershot: Ashgate, 204–25.

Hendry, C., Brown, J. and Defillip, R. (2000) 'Regional Clustering of High Technology-based Firms: Opto-electronics in Three Countries', *Regional Studies*, 34, 129–44.

Hesmondhalgh, D. (2002) *The Cultural Industries*. London: Sage.

Hibbitt, K., Jones, P. and Meegan, R. (1999) 'Pathways to Integration: Tackling Social Exclusion on Merseyside: Selecting the Case-Study Pathways Areas', *ESRC Pathways Project Working Paper* 2, Liverpool: Department of Geography, University of Liverpool.

Hibbit, K., Jones, P. and Meegan, R. (2001) 'Tackling Social Exclusion: The Role of Social Capital in Urban Regeneration on Merseyside – from Mistrust to Trust', *European Planning Studies*, 9: 2, 141–61.

Higgins, J., Deakin, N., Edwards, J. and Wicks, M. (1983) *Government and Urban Poverty*, Oxford: Basil Blackwell.

Hill, E. W. and Nowak, J. (2002) 'Policies to Uncover the Competitive Advantages of America's Distressed Cities', in Begg, I. (ed.), *Urban Competitiveness: Policies for Dynamic Cities*, Bristol: Policy Press, 257–82.

Hilpert, U. (1992) *Archipelago Europe – Islands of Innovation*, Brussels: FAST programme, Commission of the European Community.

Hirschman, A. (1970) *Exit, Voice and Loyalty*, Cambridge, MA: Harvard University Press.

HM Treasury (1997) *The Modernisation of Britain's Tax and Benefit System: Employment Opportunity for All Throughout Britain*, London: HM Treasury.

HM Treasury (2000) *The Goal of Full Employment: Employment Opportunity in a Changing Labour Market*, London: HM Treasury.

HM Treasury (2001a) *The Changing Welfare State: Employment Opportunity for All*, London: HM Treasury.

HM Treasury (2001b) *Productivity in the UK: 3 – The Regional Dimension*, London: HM Treasury.

Hoggart, K. and Clark, T. N. (eds) (2000) *Citizen Responsive Government*, New York: Elsevier.

Holmans, A. and Simpson, M. (1999) *Low Demand: Separating Fact from Fiction*, Coventry: Chartered Institute of Housing.

Home Office (2001) *Community Cohesion*, London: HMSO.

Hooper, A., Dunmore, K. and Hughes, M. (1998) *Home Alone*, London: National House Building Council.

Hoover, E. M. (1937) *Location Theory and the Shoe and Leather Industries*. Cambridge, MA: Harvard University Press.

House of Commons Education and Employment Select Committee (2001) *New Deal: An Evaluation*, Fifth Report 2000/1, HC58, London.

House of Commons Housing, Planning, Local Government and the Regions Committee (2003) *The Effectiveness of Government Regeneration Initiatives*, Seventh Report of Session 2002/03, Volume 1, HC 76-I, London: The Stationery Office.

Hughes, G. and McCormick, B. (2000) *Housing Policy and Labour Market Performance*, London: Office of the Deputy Prime Minister.

Husband, C. (2001) 'Youth Entry into the Labour Market of a Multi-Ethnic City', *Cities Summary*, ESRC Cities programme. Liverpool: European Institute for Urban Affairs, Liverpool John Moores University.

Hutton, W. (1996) *The State We're In*. London: Vintage.

Industrial Systems Research (1999) *Political Barriers to Housebuilding in Britain: A Critical Case Study of Protectionism and its Industrial-Commercial Effects*, Manchester: Industrial Systems Research.

Jacobs, J. (1961) *The Death and Life of Great American Cities*, New York: Random House.

Jacobs, J. (1969) *The Economy of Cities*, Harmondsworth: Penguin.

Jacobs, J. (1984) *Cities and the Wealth of Nations*, New York: Random House.

Jager, M. (1986) 'Class Definition and the Aesthetics of Gentrification: Victoriana in Melbourne', in Smith, N. and Williams, P. (eds), *Gentrification of the City*, London: Allen & Unwin, ch. 5.

Jahoda, M. (1982) *Employment and Unemployment: A Social-Psychological Analysis*. Cambridge: Cambridge University Press.

Jargowsky, P. (1997) *Poverty and Place: Ghettos, Barrios, and the American City*, New York: Russell Sage Foundation.

Jauhiainen, J. (1995) 'Waterfront Urban Development and Urban Policy: The Case of Barcelona, Cardiff, and Genoa', *European Planning Studies*, 3, 3–18.

Jencks, C. and Mayer, S. (1990) 'The Social Consequences of Growing Up in a Poor Neighbourhood', in Lynn, L. and McGeary, M. (eds), *Inner City Poverty in the United States*, Washington, DC: National Academic Press, 111–86.

Jenks, M., Burton, E. and Williams, K. (eds) (1996) *The Compact City: A Sustainable Urban Form?* London: E & F Spon.

Jermyn, H. (2001) *The Arts and Social Exclusion: A Review Prepared for the Arts Council of England*, London: Arts Council of England.

Jessop, B. (1990) 'Regulation Theories in Retrospect and Prospect', *Economy and Society*, 19, 153–216.

Jessop, B. (2000) 'The Crisis of the National Spatio-Temporal Fix and the Tendential Ecological Dominance of Globalizing Capitalism', *International Journal of Urban and Regional Research*, 24: 2, 323–48.

Jessop, B. (2001) 'Good Governance and the Urban Question: On Managing the Contradictions of Neo-Liberalism', published by the Department of Sociology, Lancaster University at http://www.comp.lancs.ac.uk/sociology/soc075rj.html.

Jessop, B., Peck, J. and Tickell, A. (1996) 'Retooling the Machine: Economic Crisis, State Restructuring and Urban Politics', Paper given to the Association of American Geographers meeting, Charlotte, North Carolina.

Johnson, E. W. (1999) *Chicago Metropolis 2020*, Chicago, IL: Commercial Club of Chicago and American Academy of Arts and Sciences.

Johnson, P. S. and Thomas, R. B. (2001) 'Assessing the Economic Impacts of the Arts', in Selwood, S. (ed.), *The UK Cultural Sector*, London: Policy Studies Institute, 202–15.

Jones, A. (1998) 'Issues in Waterfront Regeneration: More Sobering Thoughts – a UK Perspective', *Planning Practice and Research*, 13, 433–42.

Jones, M. and Ward, K. (1998) 'Grabbing Grants? The Role of Coalitions in Urban Economic Development', *Local Economy*, 13, 28–39.

Jones, P. (1999) 'Researching "Participation": Methodological Issues for the Pathways Project', *Pathways to Integration Project Working Paper* 3. Liverpool: Department of Geography, University of Liverpool.

Jouve, B. and Lefevre, C. (eds) (2002) *Local Power, Territory and Institutions in European Metropolitan Regions*, London: Frank Cass.

Jupp, B. (1999) *Living Together: Community Life on Mixed Tenure Estates*. London: Demos.

Kaldor, N. (1970) 'The Case for Regional Policies', *Scottish Journal of Political Economy*, 17, 337–48.

Kanter, R. M. (1995) *World Class: Thriving Locally in the Global Economy*, New York: Simon & Schuster.

Kearns, A. and Turok, I. (2000) 'Power, Responsibility and Governance in Britain's New Urban Policy', *Journal of Urban Affairs*, 22: 2, 175–91.

Kearns, G. and Philo, C. (eds) (1993) *Selling Places: the City as Cultural Capital, Past and Present*, Oxford: Pergamon Press.

Kelly, A. and Kelly, M. (2000) *Impact and Values – Assessing the Arts and Creative Industries in the South West,* Bristol: Bristol Cultural Development Partnership.

Kimberlee, R., Hoggett, P. and Stewart, M. (2000) *The Bristol Regeneration Partnership's SRB4 Scheme: First Interim Evaluation*, Bristol: University of the West of England.

Kelly, M. (2000) 'Inequality and crime', *Review of Economics and Statistics*, 82, 530–9.

Kesteloot, C. (1998) 'The Geography of Deprivation in Brussels and Local Development Strategies', in Musterd, S. and Ostendorf, W. (eds), *Urban Segregation and the Welfare State*. London: Routledge.

Kleinman, M. (2001) 'Government and Governance: Does it Matter?', paper presented to the IPD conference 'What Next for British Cities: Who Wins, Who Loses, What Matters?', 22 October.

Kleinman, M. and Hall, P. (2002) *The Greater London Authority and network governance: initial impacts*, end of award report to the ESRC, available from http://www.regard.ac.uk.

Knaap, G. (2002) *Land Market Monitoring for Smart Urban Growth*. Cambridge, MA: Lincoln Institute of Land Policy.

Kresl, P. (1995) 'The Determinants of Urban Competitiveness', in Kresl, P. and Gappert, G. (eds), *North American Cities and the Global Economy*, London: Sage, 45–68.

Krugman, P. (1991) 'Increasing Returns and Economic Geography', *Journal of Political Economy*, 99, 483–99.

Krugman, P. (1996a) 'Making Sense of the Competitiveness Debate', *Oxford Review of Economic Policy*, 12: 3, 17–25.

Krugman, P. (1996b) *Pop Internationalism*, Cambridge, MA: MIT Press.

Landry, C. (2000) *The Creative City*, Stroud: Comedia.

Landry, C. and Bianchini, F. (1995) *The Creative City*, London: Demos.

Landry, C., Greene, L., Matarasso, F. and Bianchini, F. (1996) *The Art of Regeneration: Urban Renewal through Cultural Activity*, London: Comedia.

Lash, S. and Urry, J. (1994) *Economies of Signs and Space*, London: Sage.

Lawless, P., Martin, R. and Hardy, S. (eds) (1998) *Unemployment and Social Exclusion*, London: Jessica Kingsley.

Leadbeater, C. and Oakley, K. (1999) *The Independents: Britain's New Cultural Entrepreneurs*, London: Demos.

Leccese, M. and McCormick, K. (eds) (2000) *Charter of the New Urbanism*, New York: McGraw-Hill.

Lee, P. and Murie, A. (1997) *Poverty, Housing Tenure and Social Exclusion*, Bristol: Policy Press.

Lees, L. (2000) 'A Reappraisal of Gentrification: Towards a "Geography of Gentrification" ', *Progress in Human Geography*, 24, 389–408.

Leitner, H. (1994) 'Capital Markets, the Development Industry, and Urban Office Market Dynamics: Rethinking Building Cycles', *Environment and Planning A*, 26, 779–802.

Levitas, R. (1998) *The Inclusive Society? Social Exclusion and New Labour*, London: Macmillan.

Ley, D. (1996) *The New Middle Class and the Remaking of the Central City*. Oxford: Oxford University Press.

Leyshon, A. and Thrift, N. (1995) 'Geographies of Financial Exclusion: Financial Abandonment in Britain and the United States', *Transactions of the Institute of British Geographers, New Series*, 20, 312–41.

Leyshon, A., Thrift, N. and Tommey, C. (1989) 'The Rise of the British Provincial Financial Centre', *Progress in Planning*, 31: 3, 155–229.

Lipietz, A. (1987) *Mirages and Miracles: The Crises of Global Fordism*, London: Verso.

Lister, R. (1997) *Citizenship: Feminist Perspectives*, London: Macmillan.

Llewelyn-Davies (1997) *Review of Urban Capacity Studies: Report for the UK Round Table on Sustainable Development*. London: Department of the Environment.

Llewelyn-Davies (1994) *Providing More Homes in Urban Areas*, Report to Joseph Rowntree Foundation, Bristol: SAUS Publications.

Loftman, P. and Nevin, B. (1996) 'Prestige Projects and Urban Regeneration in the 1980s and 1990s: A Review of Benefits and Limitations', *Planning Practice and Research*, 10, 299–315.

Logan, J. R. and Molotch, H. (1987) *Urban Fortunes: The Political Economy of Place,* London: University of California Press.

Lovatt, A. (1996) 'The ecstasy of urban regeneration: regulation of the night-time economy in the transition to a post-Fordist city', in O'Connor, J. and Wynne, D. (eds), *From the Margins to the Centre: Cultural Production and Consumption in the Post-Industrial City*, Aldershot: Arena, 141–61.

Lovering, J. (1999) 'Theory Led by Policy? The Inadequacies of the New Regionalism in Economic Geography Illustrated from the Case of Wales', *International Journal of Urban and Regional Research*, 23, 379–95.

Lovering, J. (2001) 'The Coming Regional Crisis (and how to avoid it)', *Regional Studies*, 35: 4, 349–54.

Lowndes, V., Stoker, G., Pratchett, L., Leach, S., and Wingfield, M. (1998) *Enhancing Public Participation in Local Government*. London: DETR.

Lupton, R. (2003) *Poverty Street: The Dynamics of Neighbourhood Decline and Renewal*, Bristol: Policy Press.

Mackay, R. and Molyneux, P. (1996) 'Bank Credit and the Regions: A Comparison within Europe', *Regional Studies*, 30, 757–63.

Maclennan, D., Meen, G., Gibb, K. and Stephens, M. (1997) *Fixed Commitments, Uncertain Incomes*, York: Joseph Rowntree Foundation.

MacLeod, G. (2001) 'New Regionalism Reconsidered: Globalisation and the Remaking of Political Economic Space', *International Journal of Urban and Regional Research*, 25: 4, 804–29.

Madanipour, A., Cars, G. and Allen, J. (eds) (1998) *Social Exclusion in European Cities*. London: Jessica Kingsley.

Maillat, D. (1991) 'The Innovation Process and the Role of the Milieu', in Bergman, E., Maier, G. and Tödtling, F. (eds), *Regions Reconsidered: Economic Networks, Innovation and Local Development in Industrialized Countries*. London: Mansell, 103–17.

Maloney, W. A., Smith, G. and Stoker, G. (2000) 'Social Capital and Associational Life', in Baron, S., Field, F. and Schuller, T. (eds), *Social Capital: Critical Perspectives*, Oxford: Oxford University Press, 212–25.

Malpass, P. (1994) 'Policy Making and Local Governance: How Bristol Failed to Secure City Challenge Funding (Twice)', *Policy and Politics*, 22: 4, 301–12.

Market Information Team (1997) *Greater Glasgow Housing Choice Survey: Results of the Postal Survey*, Glasgow: Glasgow Regeneration Alliance.

Markusen, A. (1999) 'Fuzzy Concepts, Scanty Evidence, Policy Distance', *Regional Studies*, 33: 9, 869–84.

Marshall, J. N. and Richardson, R. (1996) 'The Impact of "Telemediated" Services on Corporate Structures: The Example of "Branchless" Retail Banking in Britain', *Environment and Planning A*, 28: 1, 843–58.

Marshall, R. (ed.) (2001) *Waterfronts in Post-Industrial Cities*, London: E&F Spon.

Martin, R. (ed.) (1999) *Money and the Space Economy*. Chichester: John Wiley.

Martin, R. and Minns, R. (1995) 'Undermining the Financial Basis of Regions: The Spatial Structure and Implications of the UK Pension Fund System', *Regional Studies*, 29, 125–44.

Martin, R. and Sunley, P. (1998) 'Slow Convergence? The New Endogenous Growth Theory and Regional Development', *Economic Geography*, 74, 201–27.

Martin, R. and Sunley, P. (2003) 'Deconstructing Clusters: Chaotic Concept or Policy Panacea?', *Journal of Economic Geography*, 3, 5–35.

Martin, R., Nativel, C. and Sunley, P. (2003) 'The Local Impact of the New Deal: Does Geography Make a Difference?' in Martin, R. and Morrison, P. (eds), *Geographies of Labour Market Inequality*, London: Routledge, 175–207.

Massey, D. (1984) *Spatial Divisions of Labour: Social Structures and the Geography of Production*, London: Macmillan.

Massey, D., Allen, J. and Pile, S. (eds) (1999) *City Worlds*, London: Routledge.

Matarasso, F. (1997) *Use of Ornament? The Social Impact of Participation in the Arts*, Stroud: Comedia.

McCann, P. and Sheppard, S. (2001) 'Public Investment and Regional Labour Markets: The Role of UK Higher Education,' in Felsenstein, D., McQuaid, D., McCann, P. and Shefer, D. (eds), *Public Investment and Regional Economic Development*. Cheltenham: Edward Elgar, 135–53.

McCulloch, A. (2001) 'Ward Level Deprivation and Individual Social and Economic Outcomes in the British Household Panel Survey', *Environment and Planning A*, 33, 667–84.

McGuigan, J. (2001) 'Three Discourses of Cultural Policy', in Stevenson, N., *Culture and Citizenship*, London: Sage, 124–37.

Meegan, R. and Mitchell, A. (2001) 'It's Not Community Around Here, It's Neighbourhood', *Urban Studies*, 38: 12, 2167–94.

Meen, G. (1998) 'Modelling Sustainable Home-Ownership: Demographics or Economics?', *Urban Studies*, 35, 1,919–34.

Meen, G. and Andrew, M. (2004) 'The Role of Housing in City Economic Performance', in Boddy, M. and Parkinson, M. (eds), *City Matters: Competitiveness, Cohesion and Urban Governance*, Bristol: Policy Press.

Metcalf, D. and Richardson, R. (1976) 'Unemployment in London', in Worswick, G.D.N. (ed.), *The Concept and Measurement of Involuntary Unemployment*, London: Allen & Unwin.

Mingione, E. (ed.) (1996) *Urban Poverty and the Underclass*. Oxford and Cambridge, MA: Basil Blackwell.

Mitchell, D. (2000) *Cultural Geography*, Oxford: Basil Blackwell.

Molotch, H. (1996) 'LA as Design Product: How Art Works in a Regional Economy', in Scott, A. and Soja, E. (eds), *The City: Los Angeles and Urban Theory at the End of the Twentieth Century*, Berkeley, CA: University of California Press, 225–75.

Monk, S. and Whitehead, C. (2000) *Restructuring Housing Systems*. York: Joseph Rowntree Foundation.

Montgomery, J. (1996) 'Developing the Media Industries', *Local Economy*, 11, 158–68.

Moore, B. and Begg, I. (2004) 'Urban Growth and Competitiveness in Britain: A Long Run Perspective', in Boddy, M. and Parkinson, M. (eds), *City Matters: Competitiveness, Cohesion and Urban Governance*, Bristol: Policy Press, 93–109.

Munt, I. (1987) 'Economic Restructuring, Culture and Gentrification: A Case Study of Battersea, London', *Environment and Planning A: Government and Planning*, 19, 1,175–97.

Murray, C. (1996) 'The Emerging British Underclass', in Lister, R. (ed.), *Charles Murray and the Underclass: The Developing Debate*, London: Institute for Economic Affairs, 23–52.

Myerscough, J. (1988) *The Economic Importance of the Arts in Britain*, London: Policy Studies Institute.

Nelson, N. and Wright, S. (1995) *Power and Participatory Development*, London: Intermediate Technology Group.

Nevin, B., Lee, P., Goodson, R., Groves, R., Hall, S. Murie, A. and Phillimore, J. (2001) *Liverpool's Housing Market Research Programme 1999/2001: A Review of the Main Findings and Policy Recommendations*. Research Report by the Centre for Urban and Regional Studies, University of Birmingham. Liverpool: Regeneration Portfolio.

Newman, P. and Smith, I. (2000) 'Cultural Production, Place and Politics on the South Bank of the Thames', *International Journal of Urban and Regional Research*, 24, 9–24.

North West Metropolitan Area (2000) *Draft Spatial Vision for North West Europe*. Lille: NWMA Secretariat.

Northwest Development Agency (2001) *Liverpool and Manchester Joint Concordat*, Warrington: NWDA. Available: http://www.nwda-cms.net/DocumentUploads/LivManJointConcordat.doc.

Norton, R. (2000) *Creating the New Economy: The Entrepreneur and the US resurgence*, Cheltenham: Edward Elgar.

O'Connor, J. (1999a) *The Cultural Production Sector in Manchester*, Manchester City Council/Manchester Institute for Popular Culture, MMU. Available: http://www.mmu.ac.uk/h-ss/mipc.

O'Connor, J. (1999b) 'Popular Culture, Reflexivity and Urban Change', in Verwijnen, J. and Lehtovuori, P. (eds), *Creative Cities: Cultural Industries, Urban Development and the Information Society*, Helsinki: UIAH Publications, 76–100.

O'Connor, J. R. (1973) *The Fiscal Crisis of the State*, New York: St Martin's Press.

O'Malley, E. and O'Gorman, C. (2001) 'Competitive Advantage in the Irish Indigenous Software Industry and the Role of Inward Foreign Investment', *European Planning Studies*, 9, 303–22.

Oakey, R., Kipling, M. and Wildgust, S. (2001) 'Clustering Among Firms in the Non-Broadcast Visual Communications (NBVC) Sector', *Regional Studies*, 35, 401–14.

Oatley, N. (1996) 'Sheffield's Cultural Industries Quarter', *Local Economy*, 11, 172–9.

Oatley, N. (ed.) (1998) *Cities, Economic Competition and Urban Policy*, London: Paul Chapman.

Office of National Statistics (2001) *Gross Domestic Expenditure on R&D 2000*, London: ONS.

Office of the Deputy Prime Minister (2003a) *Cities, Regions and Competitiveness*, Second Report from the Working Group of Government Departments, the Core Cities and the Regional Development Agencies, London: Office of the Deputy Prime Minister.

Office of the Deputy Prime Minister (2003b) *Sustainable Communities: Building for the Future*, London: The Stationery Office.

OECD (2001a) *Cities for Citizens: The Role of Metropolitan Governance*, Paris: OECD.

OECD (2001b) *Devolution and Globalisation: Implications for Local Decision-Makers*, Paris: OECD.

OMIS research (2003) *Britain's Best Cities 2003–4: executive summary*. Available at: http://www.omis.co.uk/Pdfs/BBC03.pdf.

Orton, B. (1996) 'Community Arts: Reconnecting with the Radical Tradition', in Cook, I. and Shaw, M. (eds), *Radical Community Work*, Edinburgh, Moray House, 172–85.

Ostendorf, W., Musterd, S. and de Vos, S. (2001) 'Social Mix and Neighbourhood Effect: Policy Ambitions and Empirical Evidence', *Housing Studies*, 16, 371–80.

Pahl, R. (1975) *Whose City?* Harmondsworth: Penguin.

Parkinson, M., Hutchins, M., Simmie, J., Clark, G. and Verdonk, H. (2004) *Competitive European Cities: Where do the Core Cities Stand?* London: Office of the Deputy Prime Minister.

Parr, J. B. (2002) 'Agglomeration Economies: Ambiguities and Confusions', *Environment and Planning A*, 34, 717–31.

Parr, J. B. and Budd, L. (2000) 'Financial Services and the Urban System: An Exploration', *Urban Studies*, 37: 3, 593–610.

Parry, G., Moyser, G., and Day, N. (1992) *Political Participation and Democracy in Britain*, Cambridge: Cambridge University Press.

Pawson, H. and Bramley, G. (2000) 'Understanding Recent Trends in Residential Mobility in Council Housing in England', *Urban Studies*, 37, 1231–59.

Pawson, H. and Bramley, G. (2002) 'Low Demand for Housing: Incidence, Causes and National Policy Implications', *Urban Studies*, 39, 393–422.

Peck, J. (2001) 'Neoliberalising States: Thin Policies/Hard Outcomes', *Progress in Human Geography*, 25, 426–47.

Peck, J. and Tickell, A. (2002) 'Neoliberalising Space', *Antipode*, 34: 3, 380–404.

Pennington, M. and Rydin, Y. (2000) 'Researching Social Capital in Local Environmental Contexts', *Policy and Politics*, 28: 2, 233–49.

Percy-Smith, J. (2000) 'Political Exclusion', in Percy-Smith, J. (ed.), *Policy Responses to Social Exclusion. Towards Inclusion?* Buckingham: Open University Press.

Piore, M. J. and Sabel, C. F. (1984) *The Second Industrial Divide*, New York: Basic Books.

Polanyi, K. (1944) *The Great Transformation*. New York: Rinehart.

Porteous, D. (1995) *The Geography of Finance: Spatial Dimensions of Intermediary Behaviour*. Aldershot: Avebury.

Porteous, D. (1999) The Development of Financial Centres: Location, Information Externalities and Path Dependence', in Martin, R. (ed.), *Money and the Space Economy*. Chichester: John Wiley.

Porter, M. E. (1990) *The Competitive Advantage of Nations*, New York: The Free Press.

Porter, M. E. (1995) 'The Competitive Advantage of the Inner City', *Harvard Business Review*, 73, 55–71.

Porter, M. E. (1998a) 'Clusters and the New Economics of Competitiveness', *Harvard Business Review*, December, 77–90.

Porter, M. E. (1998b) *On Competition*, Boston, MA: Harvard Business School Press.

Porter, M. E. (2000) 'Location, Competition, and Economic Development: Local Clusters in a Global Economy', *Economic Development Quarterly. The Journal of American Economic Revitalization*, 14,15–34.

Porter, M. E. (2001) 'Regions and the New Economics of Competition', in Scott, A. J. (ed.), *Global City Regions: Trends, Theory, Policy*, Oxford: Oxford University Press, 139–57.

Portes, A. (1998) 'Social Capital: Its Origins and Applications in Modern Sociology', *Annual Review of Sociology*, 24, 1–24.

Potts, G. (2002) 'Competitiveness and the Social Fabric: Links and Tensions in Cities', in Begg, I. (ed.), *Urban Competitiveness*, Bristol: Policy Press.

Power, A. and Mumford, K. (1999) *The Slow Death of Great Cities? Urban Abandonment or Urban Renaissance*, York: York Publishing Services.

Power, A. and Tunstall, R. (1997) *Dangerous Disorder: Riots and Violent Disturbances in Thirteen Areas of Britain, 1991–1992*, York: York Publishing/Joseph Rowntree Foundation.

Pratt, A. (1997) 'Production Values: From Cultural Industries to Governance of Culture', *Environment and Planning A*, 29, 1,911–17.

Putnam, R. D. (1993) *Making Democracy Work: Civic Traditions in Modern Italy*, Princeton, NJ: Princeton University Press.

Putnam, R.D. (2000) *Bowling Alone: The Collapse and Revival of American Community*, New York: Simon & Schuster.

Quilley, S. (2000) 'Manchester First: From Municipal Socialism to the Entepreneurial City', *International Journal of Urban and Regional Research*, 24, 601–15.

Reder, M. W. (1964) 'Wage Structure and Structural Unemployment', *Review of Economic Studies*, 31, 309–22.

Regional Coordination Unit (2002) Review of Area-based Initiatives: *Action Plan*, London: ODPM. Available at http://www.government-offices.gov.uk/abi/whatsnew/abireview.pdf (accessed 4 December 2002).

Regional Coordination Unit (2003) *Review of Area-Based Initiatives: Impacts and Outcomes*, London: Office of the Deputy Prime Minister. Available: http://www.government-offices.gov.uk/abi/impactsandoutcomes.pdf (accessed 5 June 2003).

Rex, J. and Moore, R. (1967) *Race, Class and Conflict*. Oxford: Oxford University Press.

Rice, P. and Venables, A. J. (2004) 'Spatial Determinants of Productivity: Analysis for the UK Regions', research paper, Economics Department, London School of Economics. Available at http://econ.lse.ac.uk/staff/ajv/rvregtxt14.pdf.

Richards, G. (2000) 'The European Cultural Capital Event: Strategic Weapon in the Cultural Arms Race?', *Cultural Policy*, 6, 159–81.

Richardson, R. and Marshall, N. (1999) 'Teleservices, Call Centres and Urban and Regional Development', *Service Industries Journal*, 19: 1, 96–116.

Richardson, R., Belt, V. and Marshall, N. (2000) 'Taking Calls to Newcastle: The Regional Implications of the Growth in Call Centres', *Regional Studies*, 34: 4, 357–69.

Richardson, T. and Jensen, B. (2000) 'Discourses of Mobility and Polycentric Development: A Contested View of European Spatial Planning', *European Planning Studies*, 8, 503–20.

Riley, R. and Young, G. (2001) *Does Welfare-to-Work Increase Employment? Evidence from the UK New Deal for Young People*, London: National Institute for Economic and Social Research.

Robson, B. (2000) 'Slim Pickings for the Cities of the North', *Town and Country Planning*, 70, 126–8.

Robson, B., Castree, N. and Rees, J. (2003) *New Deal For Communities: National Evaluation Main Phase: Report on the East Manchester NDC Partnership*, Manchester: Centre for Urban Policy Studies, University of Manchester.

Robson, B., Parkinson, M., Boddy, M., and Maclennan, D. (2000) *The State of English Cities*. London: DETR.

Robson, B., Peck, J. and Holden, A. (2000) *Regional Development Agencies and Area-Based Regeneration*, Bristol: The Policy Press.

Robson, G. and Butler, T. (2001) 'Coming to Terms with London: Middle-class Communities in a Global City', *International Journal of Urban and Regional Research*, 25, 70–86.

Rogers, R. and Power, A. (2000) *Cities for a Small Country*, London: Faber.

Rosenthal, S. S. and Strange, W. C. (2004) 'Evidence on the Nature and Sources of Agglomeration Economies', forthcoming in Henderson, V. and Thisse, J. (eds), *Handbook of Urban and Regional Economics*, Vol. 4.

Russell, H. (2003) *New Deal for Communities: National Evaluation Main Phase: Report on the Kensington Partnership, Liverpool*, Liverpool: European Institute for Urban Affairs, Liverpool John Moores University.

Sassen, S. (1994) *Cities in a World Economy*, London: Pine Forge Press.

Sassen, S. (1991) *The Global City: New York, London, Tokyo*, Princeton: Princeton University Press.

Saunders, P. (1986) *Social Theory and the Urban Question*, 2nd edn, London: Routledge.

Savage, M. (2000) *Class Analysis and Social Transformation*. Buckingham: Open University Press.

Savage, M., Bagnall, G. and Longhurst, B. (2001) 'Ordinary, Ambivalent and Defensive: Class Identities in the Northwest of England', *Sociology*, 35: 4, 875–92.

Savage, M., Barlow, J., Dickens, P. and Fielding, A. (1992) *Property, Bureaucracy and Culture: Middle Class Formations in Contemporary Britain*, London: Routledge.

Savage, M., Bagnall, G. and Longhurst, B. (2004) *Globalization and Belonging*, London: Sage.

Saxenian, A. (1994) *Regional Advantage,* Cambridge, MA: Harvard University Press.

Sayer, A. (1997) 'The Dialectic of Culture and Economy', in Lee, R. and Wills, J. (eds), *Geographies of Economies*, London: Edward Arnold.

Schumpeter, J. (1939) *Business Cycles: A Theoretical, Historical and Statistical Analysis of the Capitalist Process,* New York: McGraw-Hill.

Schumpeter, J. (1975) *Capitalism, Socialism and Democracy*, New York: Harper.

Scott, A. J. (1988) *New Industrial Spaces: Flexible Production Organisation and Regional Development in North America and Western Europe*, London: Pion.

Scott, A. J. (1996) 'The Craft, Fashion and Cultural Products Industries of Los Angeles: Competitive Dynamics and Policy Dilemmas', *Annals of the Association of American Geographers*, 86, 306–23.

Scott, A. J. (1997) 'The Cultural Economy of Cities', *International Journal of Urban and Regional Research*, 21: 2, 323–39.

Scott, A. J. (2000) *The Cultural Economy of Cities*, London: Sage.

Scott, A. J. (2001a) 'Capitalism, Cities, and the Production of Symbolic Forms', *Transactions Institute of British Geographers*, 26, 11–23.

Scott, A. J. (2001b) 'Globalization and the Rise of City Regions', *European Planning Studies*, 9: 7, 813–26.

Scott, A. J. (2002) 'Competitive Dynamics of Southern California's Clothing Industry', *Urban Studies*, 39: 8, 1287–306.

Sennett, R. (1998) *The Corrosion of Character*. London: Norton.

SFE (2002) *Building on Success: Planning for the Future of Edinburgh. A Discussion Paper from Scottish Financial Enterprise*. Edinburgh: SFE.

Shaw, M., Dorling, D., Gordon, D. and Smith, G. D. (1999) *The Widening Gap: Health Inequalities and Policy in Britain*, Bristol: The Policy Press.

Simmie, J. M. (ed.) (2001) *Innovative Cities*, London: E & F Spon.

Simmie, J. M. (2002) 'Trading Places: Competitive Cities in the Global Economy', *European Planning Studies*, 10, 201–15.

Simmie, J. M. (2003) 'Innovation Clusters and Competitive Cities in the UK and Europe', in Boddy, M. and Parkinson, M. (eds), *City Matters: Competitiveness, Cohesion and Urban Governance*, Bristol: Policy Press.

Simmie, J. M. (2004a) 'Innovation and Clustering in the Globalised International Economy', *Urban Studies*, 41, 1095–112.

Simmie, J. M. (2004b) 'Innovation Clusters and Competitive Cities in the UK and Europe', in Boddy, M. and Parkinson, M. (eds), *City Matters: Competitiveness, Cohesion and Urban Governance*, Bristol: Policy Press.

Simmie, J. M. *et al.* (2004) *Realising the Full Economic Potential of London and the Core Cities*, Oxford: Oxford Brookes University.

Simmie, J. M., Sennett, J., Wood, P. and Hart, D. A. (2002) 'Innovation in Europe: A Tale of Networks, Knowledge and Trade in Five Cities', *Regional Studies*, 36, 47–64.

Sjoholt, P. (1999) 'Culture as a Strategic Development Device: The Role of "European Cities of Culture", with particular reference to Bergen', *European Urban and Regional Studies*, 6, 339–47.

Smith, C. (1998) *Creative Britain*. London: Faber & Faber.

Smith, G. (1999) 'Area Based Initiatives: The Rationale and Options for Area Targeting', *CASE paper* 25, London: Centre for Analysis of Social Exclusion, London School of Economics.

Smith, N. (1979) 'Towards a Theory of Gentrification: A Back to the City Movement by Capital, not People', *Journal of the American Planning Association*, 45, 538–48.

Smith, N. (1996) *The New Urban Frontier: Gentrification and the Revanchist City*. London: Routledge.

Social Exclusion Unit (1998) *Bringing Britain Together: A National Strategy for Neighbourhood Renewal*, Cm. 4045, London: The Stationery Office.

Social Exclusion Unit (2001) *A New Commitment to Neighbourhood Renewal: National Strategy Action Plan*, London: Cabinet Office.

Soja, E. W. (1989) *Postmodern Geographies: The Reassertion of Space in Critical Social Theory*, New York: Verso.

Soja, E. W. (2000) *Postmetropolis: Critical Studies of Cities and Regions*. Oxford: Basil Blackwell.

Somerville, P. (1998) 'Explanations for Social Exclusion: Where Does Housing Fit In?', *Housing Studies*, 13: 6, 761–80.

Southern California Studies Center, University of Southern California (2001) *Sprawl Hits the Wall: Confronting the Realities of Metropolitan Los Angeles*, Los Angeles: SCSC, University of Southern California.

Stedman Jones, G. (1971) *Outcast London: A Study in the Relations between Classes in Victorian Society*, Oxford: Clarendon Press.

Stoker, G. (ed.) (2000) *The New Politics of British Local Governance*, London: Macmillan.

Stone, C. L. (1989) *Regime Politics: Governing Atlanta 1946–1988*, Lawrence, KS: University Press of Kansas.

Storper, M. (1993) 'Regional "Worlds" of Production: Learning and Innovation in the Technology Districts of France, Italy and the USA', *Regional Studies*, 27: 5, 433–55.

Storper, M. (1995) 'The Resurgence of Regional Economies, Ten Years Later', *European Urban and Regional Studies*, 2: 3, 191–221.

Storper, M. (1997) *The Regional World: Territorial Development in a Global Economy*, New York: Guildford Press.

Strategy Unit (2003) *London Analytical Report*, London: Strategy Unit.

Sustainable Urban and Regional Futures Centre (2002) *Liverpool–Manchester Vision Study*, Manchester: SURF Centre.

Sweeting, D., Hambleton, R., Huxham, C., Stewart, M. and Vangen, S. (2003) 'Leadership and Partnership in Urban Governance: Evidence from London, Bristol and Glasgow', in Boddy, M. and Parkinson, M. (eds), *Changing Cities*, Bristol: The Policy Press.

Swingewood, A. (1998) *Cultural Theory and the Problem of Modernity*, London: Palgrave.

Symon, P. and Williams, A. (2001) 'Urban Regeneration Programmes', in Selwood, S. (ed.), *The UK Cultural Sector: Profile and Policy Issues*. London: Policy Studies Institute, 54–65.

Talen, E. (2002) 'The Social Goals of New Urbanism', *Housing Policy Debate*, 13, 165–88.

Teubal, M. (2001) 'The Systems Perspective to Innovation and Technology Policy: Theory and Application to Developing and Newly Industrialised Countries', *World Industrial Development Report* draft, Vienna: United Nations Industrial Development Organization.

Thrift, N. (1994) 'On the Social and Cultural Determinants of International Financial Centers', in S. Corbridge, R. Martin and N. Thrift (eds) *Money Power and Space*, Oxford: Basil Blackwell, 327–55.

Turok, I. (2003) 'Cities, Clusters and Creative Industries: The Case of Film and Television in Scotland', *European Planning Studies*, 11: 5, 549–65.

Turok, I. and Bailey, N. (2004) 'The Theory of Polycentric Urban Regions and its Application to Central Scotland', *European Planning Studies*. 12: 3, 371–89.

Turok, I. and Bailey, N. (2005) 'Twin Track Cities: Competitiveness and Cohesion in Glasgow and Edinburgh', *Progress in Planning* (forthcoming).

Turok, I. and Edge, N. (1999) *The Jobs Gap in Britain's Cities*, Bristol: Policy Press.

Turok, I. and Hopkins, N. (1998) 'Competition and Area Selection in Scotland's New Urban Policy', *Urban Studies*, 35: 11. 2021–61.

Turok, I. and Webster, D. (1998) 'The New Deal: Jeopardised by the Geography of Unemployment?', *Local Economy*, 12: 4. 309–28.

Turok, I., Bailey, N., Atkinson, R., Bramley, G., Doherty, I., Gibb, K., Goodlad, R., Hastings, A., Kintrea, K., Kirk, K., Leibovitz, J., Lever, B., Morgan, J., Paddison, R. and Sterling, R. (2003) *Twin Track Cities: Linking Prosperity and Cohesion in Glasgow and Edinburgh*, Glasgow: Department of Urban Studies, University of Glasgow.

Turok, I., Kearns, A. and Goodlad, R. (1999) 'Social Exclusion: In What Sense a Planning Problem?' *Town Planning Review*, 70: 3, 363–84.

Urban Villages Forum (1995) *The Economics of Urban Villages*, London: Urban Villages Forum.

Veltz, P. (1996) *Mondialisation, villes et territoires, L'économie d'archipel* [Globalization, cities and territories: the archipelago economy] Paris: Presses Universitaires de France.

Verwijnen, J. and Lehtovuori, P. (1999) *Creative Cities: Cultural Industries, Urban Development and the Information Society*, Helsinki: UIAH Publications.

Wallace, M. (2001) 'A New Approach to Neighbourhood Renewal in England', *Urban Studies*, 38: 12, 2163–6.

Wallinger, M. and Warnock, M. (eds) (2000) *Art for All ? Their Policies and Our Culture*, London: PEER.

Warde, A. (1991). 'Gentrification as Consumption: Issues of Class and Gender', *Environment and Planning D: Society and Space*, 6, 75–95.

Warde, A. (2002) 'Production, Consumption and the "Cultural Economy" ', in du Gay, P. and Pryke, M. (eds), *Cultural Economy: Cultural Analysis and Commercial Life: Culture, Representation and Identities*, London: Sage, 185–200.

Webster, D. (1997) 'The L-U Curve: On the Non-existence of a Long-Term Claimant Unemployment Trap and its Implications for Employment and Area-Regeneration', *Occasional Paper* 36, Glasgow: University of Glasgow, Department of Urban Studies.

Webster, D. (2000) 'Scottish Social Inclusion Policy: A Critical Assessment', *Scottish Affairs*, 30, 30–50.

Webster, D. (2005) 'Long-term Unemployment, the Invention of "Hysteresis" and the Misdiagnosis of the UK's Problem of Structural Unemployment', *Cambridge Journal of Economics* (forthcoming).

Wheeler, C. H. (2001) 'Search, Sorting and Urban Agglomeration', *Journal of Labor Economics*, 19, 879–98.

White, S. C. (1996) 'Depoliticising Development: The Uses and Abuses of Participation', *Development in Practice*, 6: 1, 28–32.

Williams, G. (1998) 'City Vision and Strategic Regeneration – The Role of City Pride', in Oatley, N. (ed.) *Cities, Economic Competition and Urban Policy*, London: Paul Chapman, 163–80.

Williams, R. (1958) *Culture and Society*, London: Chatto & Windus.

Wilson, W. J. (1987) *The Truly Disadvantaged: The Inner City, the Underclass and Public Policy*, Chicago, IL: University of Chicago Press.

Wilson, W. J. (1996) *When Work Disappears: The World of the New Urban Poor*, New York: Knopf.

Win, P. (1995) 'The Location of Firms: An Analysis of Choice Processes', in Cheshire, P. and Gordon, I. (eds), *Territorial Competition in an Integrating Europe*, Aldershot: Avebury, 244–66.

Wootton Jeffreys Consultants and Bernard Thorpe (1991) *An Examination of the Effects of the Use Classes Order 1987 and the General Development Order 1988*. London: HMSO.

Wynne, D. (ed.) (1992) *The Culture Industry*, Aldershot: Avebury.

Wynne, D. (1998) *Leisure, Lifestyle and the New Middle Class, A Case Study*, London: Routledge.

Young, I. M. (1990) *Justice and the Politics of Difference*, Princeton, NJ: Princeton University Press.

Zook, M. (2000) 'Grounded Capital: Venture Capital's Role in the Clustering of Internet Firms in the US', paper given to the Association of Collegiate Schools of Planning 2000 Conference, Atlanta, November.

Zukin, S. (1988) *Loft Living: Culture and Capital in Urban Change*, London: Radius.

Zukin, S. (1991) *Landscapes of Power: From Detroit to Disney World*, Berkeley: University of California Press.

Zukin, S. (1995) *The Cultures of Cities*, Oxford: Basil Blackwell.

Index